Workshop on Computational Modeling of People's Opinions, Personality, and Emotions in Social Media (PEOPLES 2016)

Osaka, Japan
12 December 2016

ISBN: 978-1-5108-3323-4

Printed from e-media with permission by:

Curran Associates, Inc.
57 Morehouse Lane
Red Hook, NY 12571

Some format issues inherent in the e-media version may also appear in this print version.

Copyright© (2016) by the Association for Computational Linguistics
All rights reserved.

Printed by Curran Associates, Inc. (2016)

For permission requests, please contact the Association for Computational Linguistics
at the address below.

Association for Computational Linguistics
209 N. Eighth Street
Stroudsburg, Pennsylvania 18360

Phone: 1-570-476-8006
Fax: 1-570-476-0860

acl@aclweb.org

Additional copies of this publication are available from:

Curran Associates, Inc.
57 Morehouse Lane
Red Hook, NY 12571 USA
Phone: 845-758-0400
Fax: 845-758-2633
Email: curran@proceedings.com
Web: www.proceedings.com

Preface

Welcome to the first edition of PEOPLES (Workshop on Computational Modeling of People's Opinions, Personality and Emotions in Social Media), co-located with the 26th International Conference on Computational Linguistics (COLING 2016) in Osaka, Japan.

The idea of organizing PEOPLES stemmed from two related observations, namely the availability of large amounts of spontaneous data covering a range of personal aspects and the fact that such aspects are usually studied in isolation. Social media users nowadays freely express what is on their mind at any moment in time, at any location, and about virtually anything. These large amounts of spontaneously produced texts open up a unique opportunity to learn more about such users, e.g., predicting demographic variables (age, gender), but also personality types, as well as emotions and opinion expressions. This observation isn't new, of course, and this opportunity has largely been exploited in the recent years, with abundant works on sentiment analysis, emotion detection, and personality. However, such traits of human personality and behavior have indeed attracted a substantial amount of attention but have been mostly studied *in isolation*, often in different - but related - communities, such as NLP, CL, AI. Therefore, we thought that the time was ripe to bring these communities a step closer to study people's traits and expressions jointly and in their interplay on such large volumes of available data.

The communities' response with 33 received submissions coming from 22 countries and going well beyond typical NLP topics proved that there was a gap to be filled, and we are happy to be able to provide a context to start exchanging ideas.

In total, 20 papers were selected for inclusion in the proceedings. They cover a wide range of topics related to the three main PEOPLES themes (personality, emotion and opinion), their interaction and the impact of their modeling on social aspects like well-being, political preferences, humor and language use. We were pleased to see papers discussing different approaches to modeling, including active learning, distant supervision, multi-task learning, experimental studies with participants, and dealing with different data, including speech input and resources from multiple languages.

We hope that this might be the first in a series of workshops that brings together researchers in Computational Linguistics and Natural Language Processing who share an interest in personality, opinion and emotion detection, and especially in researching the intertwining of such traits and expressions.

We would like to thank our program committee consisting of 28 researchers from a variety of backgrounds for their insightful and constructive reviews. Without their support, this workshop would not have been possible. In addition, we thank all authors for submitting papers and making PEOPLES a big success. Also thanks to our invited speaker, Saif M. Mohammad (NRC, Canada), for having accepted to come to the workshop and share his expertise and ideas on PEOPLES' topics. We thank COLING for hosting us, and in particular the local organizers for their exceptional support, especially when having to deal, logistically, with an unexpectedly high number of submissions and participants to our workshop. Lastly, we are extremely grateful to our sponsors, CELI Language Technologies, and the Computational Linguistics group of the University of Groningen for their financial support, without which this workshop would not have gone through.

We look forward to welcoming you all at PEOPLES 2016 in Osaka, Japan!

Malvina, Viviana, Barbara

PEOPLES
https://peoples2016.github.io/

Organisers

Malvina Nissim, University of Groningen, The Netherlands

Viviana Patti, University of Turin, Italy

Barbara Plank, University of Groningen, The Netherlands

Programme Committee

Jason Baldridge, People Pattern, US

Pierpaolo Basile, University of Bari, Italy

Valerio Basile, INRIA Sophia Antipolis Méditerranée, France

Cristina Bosco, University of Turin, Italy

Gosse Bouma, University of Groningen, The Netherlands

Erik Cambria, Nanyang Technological University, Singapore

Fabio Celli, University of Trento, Italy

Chloé Clavel, LTCI-CNRS, Telecom-ParisTech, France

Walter Daelemans, University of Antwerp, Belgium

Morena Danieli, University of Trento, Italy

Dan Hardt, Copenhagen Business School, Denmark

Dirk Hovy, University of Copenhagen, Denmark

Richard Johansson, University of Gothenburg, Sweden

David Jurgens, Stanford University, US

Svetlana Kiritchenko, NRC-Canada, Canada

Florian Kuhnemann, Radboud Universiteit Nijmegen, The Netherlands

Bing Liu, University of Illinois at Chicago, US

Kim Luyckx, Biomina Research Group, Belgium

Saif Mohammad, NRC-Canada, Canada

Scott Nowson, Accenture Centre for Innovation, Dublin, Ireland

Dong Nguyen, University of Twente, The Netherlands

Martin Potthast, Bauhaus-Universität Weimar, Germany

Daniel Preotiuc-Pietro, University of Pennsylvania, US

Paolo Rosso, Technical University of Valencia, Spain

H. Andrew Schwartz, Stony Brook University, US

Carlo Strapparava, Fondazione Bruno Kessler Trento, Italy

Marko Tkalcic, Free University of Bolzano, Italy

Ben Verhoeven, University of Antwerp, Belgium

Sponsors

PEOPLES 2016 is organized with the support of CELI Language Technology (https://www.celi.it/en/) and the Computational Linguistics group of CLCG (http://www.rug.nl/research/clcg/), University of Groningen.

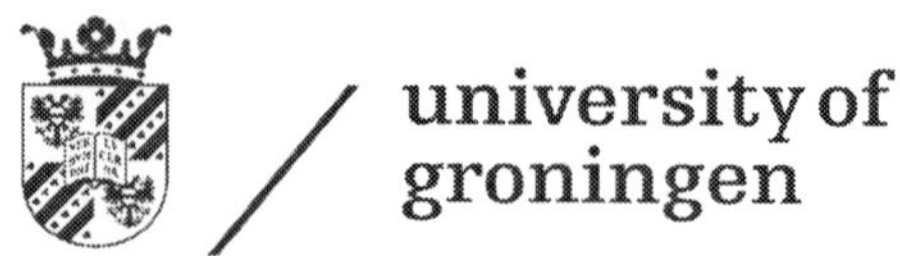

Keynote

Affect Associations in Creative Language
Saif M. Mohammad
NRC, Canada

Abstract: Beyond literal meaning, words have associations with sentiment, emotion, colour, and even music. Such affect associations are particularly salient in overtly creative instances of language, such as stories and poems. They are also found in implicitly creative day-to-day formulations such as metaphors, hashtags, and opposing polarity phrases (phrases made of one positive word and one negative word). I will first present methods that capture affect associations of words, phrases, and metaphoric expressions. Then I will show how these associations can be used for sentiment analysis of tweets, understanding semantic composition, determining the mechanisms underpinning metaphor, detecting personality traits, analyzing stories, and even generating music from novels.

Bio: Dr. Saif M. Mohammad is Senior Research Officer at the National Research Council Canada (NRC). He received his Ph.D. in Computer Science from the University of Toronto. His primary research interest is in Computational Linguistics, especially Lexical Semantics, Sentiment Analysis, Crowd Annotations, Computational Studies of Literature, and Information Visualization. His team developed a system that ranked first in recent SemEval shared tasks on the sentiment analysis of tweets and on aspect-based sentiment analysis. His word-emotion association resource, the NRC Emotion Lexicon, is widely used for text analysis and information visualization. His work on detecting emotions in social media and on generating music from text have garnered widespread media attention, including articles in Time, Slashdot, LiveScience, io9, The Physics arXiv Blog, PC World, and Popular Science. (Website: http://saifmohammad.com)

Table of Contents

Conference Program

December 12, 2016

12:30–12:35   Opening

12:35–13:35   Oral session 1: Gender, Emotion, Personality

Zooming in on Gender Differences in Social Media
Aparna Garimella and Rada Mihalcea

The Effect of Gender and Age Differences on the Recognition of Emotions from Facial Expressions
Daniela Schneevogt and Patrizia Paggio

A Recurrent and Compositional Model for Personality Trait Recognition from Short Texts
Fei Liu, Julien Perez and Scott Nowson

Distant supervision for emotion detection using Facebook reactions
Chris Pool and Malvina Nissim

13:35–13:55   Coffee break

13:55–14:45   Keynote

Affect Associations in Creative Language
Saif M. Mohammad

14:45–15:45   Posters and coffee

A graphical framework to detect and categorize diverse opinions from online news
Ankan Mullick, Pawan Goyal and Niloy Ganguly

Active learning for detection of stance components
Maria Skeppstedt, Magnus Sahlgren, Carita Paradis and Andreas Kerren

Detecting Opinion Polarities using Kernel Methods
Rasoul Kaljahi and Jennifer Foster

Effects of Semantic Relatedness between Setups and Punchlines in Twitter Hashtag Games
Andrew Cattle and Xiaojuan Ma

Generating Sentiment Lexicons for German Twitter
Uladzimir Sidarenka and Manfred Stede

Innovative Semi-Automatic Methodology to Annotate Emotional Corpora
Lea Canales, Carlo Strapparava, Ester Boldrini and Patricio Martinez-Barco

Personality Estimation from Japanese Text
Koichi Kamijo, Tetsuya Nasukawa and Hideya Kitamura

Predicting Brexit: Classifying Agreement is Better than Sentiment and Pollsters
Fabio Celli, Evgeny Stepanov, Massimo Poesio and Giuseppe Riccardi

Sarcasm Detection : Building a Contextual Hierarchy
Taradheesh Bali and Navjyoti Singh

Social and linguistic behavior and its correlation to trait empathy
Marina Litvak, Jahna Otterbacher, Chee Siang Ang and David Atkins

The Challenges of Multi-dimensional Sentiment Analysis Across Languages
Emily Öhman, Timo Honkela and Jörg Tiedemann

The Social Mood of News: Self-reported Annotations to Design Automatic Mood Detection Systems
Firoj Alam, Fabio Celli, Evgeny A. Stepanov, Arindam Ghosh and Giuseppe Riccardi

December 12, 2016 (continued)

15:45–16:45   Oral session 2: Affect in interaction, Speech, Well-being

Microblog Emotion Classification by Computing Similarity in Text, Time, and Space
Anja Summa, Bernd Resch and Michael Strube

A domain-agnostic approach for opinion prediction on speech
Pedro Bispo Santos, Lisa Beinborn and Iryna Gurevych

Can We Make Computers Laugh at Talks?
Chong Min Lee, Su-Youn Yoon and Lei Chen

Towards Automatically Classifying Depressive Symptoms from Twitter Data for Population Health
Danielle L Mowery, Albert Park, Craig Bryan and Mike Conway

16:45–17:00   Wrap-up

CELI (sponsor)
Andrea Bolioli

Zooming in on Gender Differences in Social Media

Aparna Garimella and **Rada Mihalcea**
University of Michigan
{gaparna,mihalcea}@umich.edu

Abstract

Men are from Mars and women are from Venus - or so the genre of relationship literature would have us believe. But there is some truth in this idea, and researchers in fields as diverse as psychology, sociology, and linguistics have explored ways to better understand the differences between genders. In this paper, we take another look at the problem of gender discrimination and attempt to move beyond the typical surface-level text classification approach, by (1) identifying semantic and psycholinguistic word classes that reflect systematic differences between men and women and (2) finding differences between genders in the ways they use the same words. We describe several experiments and report results on a large collection of blogs authored by men and women.

1 Introduction

Previous work on understanding gender differences has mainly focused on the authorship detection facet, trying to identify the gender of the author of a certain writing, be that a blog (Mukherjee and Liu, 2010), a tweet (Burger et al., 2011), or other works of fiction or non-fiction (Koppel et al., 2002). In this paper, we depart from this earlier research and attempt to move beyond the surface level of word occurrences and counts. We instead use semantic analysis to identify broad semantic classes that are specific to each gender, and also find differences that exist between genders in how they use certain concepts.

Specifically, the paper addresses the following two main questions. First, can we identify broad semantic and psycholinguistic classes that are predominantly used by men and women? We use linguistic ethnography in conjunction with three different resources and determine gender saliency scores associated with predefined word classes, which we can use to better understand the groups of words that differentiate men's and women's language use.

Second, can we distinguish between shades of word meanings, as used by the two genders? Do men and women use the word "car" in a similar way, or are there differences between the use of this word in their day-to-day life? We answer this question by using a word sense disambiguation framework, where each gender is regarded as a "sense," and we detect the gender corresponding to a given occurrence of a word. Using a large dataset of over 350 words, we show that gender-based word disambiguation is possible, and that there are indeed differences between the ways certain words are used by men and women.

2 Related Work

Field work in social and gender psychology has had much to say about the differences between men and women. The masculine is stereotyped as detached, rational, and aggressive, and the feminine as nurturing, gentle, and tactful (Doyle, 1985). While some stereotypes are unfounded, sociolinguists do affirm that some communication styles are gendered. It has been found for instance that men and women differ on private versus public speaking, on "report talk" versus "rapport talk"–these and other facets of relational dialectics are gendered and constitute so-called "GenderLens" (Tannen, 1991).

This work is licensed under a Creative Commons Attribution 4.0 International Licence. Licence details: http://creativecommons.org/licenses/by/4.0/

Proceedings of the Workshop on Computational Modeling of People's Opinions, Personality, and Emotions in Social Media,
pages 1–10, Osaka, Japan, December 12 2016.

One of the earliest studies concerned with the language differences between men and women is due to (Lakoff, 1972), who found several characteristics of women language, including words such as "lovely" and "adorable", or phrases such as "it seems to be" or "would you mind." There is also a large body of work on the connection between language and gender in the field of sociology (e.g., (Eckert and McConnell-Ginet, 2003)), which we do not address here due to the lack of space.

In computational linguistics, several studies addressed the role of gendered language and the "gender gap" in the blogosphere (Kennedy et al., 2005; Koppel et al., 2002; Schler et al., 2006; Mukherjee and Liu, 2010); the significance of gender differences in self-disclosure strategy in teenage blogs (Huffaker and Calvert, 2005); and the validity of author gender predictions based largely on function words (e.g. pronouns, determiners) (Herring and Paolillo, 2004). Several previous studies made use of LIWC (Pennebaker and Francis, 1999) categories to investigate gender differences in writing styles and content in blogs (Nowson and Oberlander, 2006; Schler et al., 2006). Work has also been done on Twitter data, where tweets are used to predict several profile features, including gender (Rao et al., 2010; Burger et al., 2011). In (Peersman et al., 2004), age and gender prediction is performed on short messages from social networking sites. The focus in these previous studies has been primarily on investigating the use of automatic classification to distinguish between men and women writings, and also on finding words that are specific to each gender by performing statistical analysis on large amounts of data.

Other related work includes recently published research by (Nguyen et al., 2014), who showed how a person's gender identity can be constructed by using various linguistic aspects of male and female speech in language. (Gianfortoni et al., 2011) used pattern-based feature creation approach in combination with word classes to classify author's gender from blog posts. Also of interest is the work by (Prabhakaran et al., 2014), who use topic segments to predict the behavioral patterns of political leaders in election campaigns. Our work is to some extent related to that research, as we also seek to understand and model behaviors from text, however we do this for men and women rather than political figures.

In speech, an analysis of the most frequently used words by males and females in telephone conversations was presented in (Boulis and Ostendorf, 2005), who found that swear words are more often used by males (bullshit, sucks, damn), whereas family-relation terms are more often used by females (children, marriage, boyfriend).

One exception from the general theme of previous work on surface-level gender classification is the work by (Sarawgi et al., 2011), where topic bias is explicitly avoided, with the goal of identifying stylistic differences between men and women writings. The authors use blogs addressing predefined topics (e.g., education, travel) and scientific publications, and show that differences can be found even when the data sources are controlled for topic. In our research, we zoom in even deeper, and try to identify semantic and psycholinguistic word classes that characterize gender differences, and also find the distinctive ways in which men and women use certain words.

2.1 Data

We use a large corpus of blogposts annotated for gender, which we collected from the *Blogspot* (http://www.blogspot.com) community (Liu and Mihalcea, 2007). We chose to use *Blogspot* as opposed to other blog communities such as *LiveJournal* because it has richer blogger profile annotations including gender, age, location, occupation, and others. The kind of writing found in a weblog is ideally suited to what we wish to discover, since weblogs often give an intimate account of personal everyday life, and personal viewpoint unto current events. More than just language and syntax, weblogs contain ample evidence of experiences and perceptions, which we attempt to uncover using corpus-based modeling and semantic analysis.

Starting with the names of approximately 300,000 blogs that were updated with a new entry during the time when the crawling was performed,[1] we collected the profile page of the blog owners (bloggers) and the corresponding profile features. We discarded all the blogs maintained by more than one blogger (collective blogs), and we also discarded the blogs corresponding to bloggers who chose not to include gender information in their profile. Finally, we parsed the entries from the remaining set of blogs, and

---

[1] The blogs were crawled in summer 2006.

retained only the blogposts written in English and having a length within a 200–4,000 character limit. Interestingly, although a large fraction of the blogs listed on *Blogspot* are spam, the constraints that a blogger have a profile and that the size of a blogpost be within certain limits removed almost all the spam – to the point that a random hand-check of 100 blogposts revealed clean spam-free data.

The post-processing and profile-based filters left us with a total of 160,000 blog entries annotated for gender, which after balancing between male and female authors, left us with the final set of 75,000 male blog entries and 75,000 female blog entries. It is to be noted that the blog data is not balanced across different genres, as we expect any existing genre-imbalance to convey some information about the interests of different genders. Table 1 shows two sample entries written by a male and a female writer. Table 2 shows three unigrams, bigrams, and trigrams with high probability in these blogs.

Male-authored blogpost
No word back from the Georges Island people on possible use of their power so I'm going to proceed with the QRP plans. Even though the QRP stuff is smaller than the 100 watt outfit, there will still be a significant amount of stuff I'll need to wrestle on to the island. I'll bring the Pelican 1510 case outfitted with the Elecraft K 2.
Female-authored blogpost
You could probably tell that I literally enjoy dressing up in costumes and crap. I just don't have the resources nor the skills to make a good costume. But I'm a resource for outlandish ideas. I remember shocking my host dad when I told him that I enjoy dressing up like that.

Table 1: Male and female authored blogposts

	Female	Male
Unigrams	knitting	microsoft
	hubby	democrats
	yarn	poker
Bigrams	my husband	my wife
	love him	of Israel
	so excited	prime minister
Trigrams	I love him	my wife and
	so much fun	of the United
	I miss my	the Bush administration

Table 2: Unigrams/bigrams/trigrams with high probability in men/women language

3 Gender Dominant Semantic and Psycholinguistic Word Classes

Can we move beyond the word-based discrimination of men and women writings, and find semantic patterns in word usage? Given a set of semantic and psycholinguistic word classes, we calculate a score associated with each word class, and consequently identify in a principled manner the word classes that are salient in each gender.

3.1 Calculating Word Class Saliency

We calculate the saliency of a word class using the distribution of occurrences for words belonging to the class inside the men and women writings. Given a class of words $C = \{W_1, W_2, ..., W_N\}$, we define the class coverage in the female corpus F as the percentage of words from F belonging to the class C:

$$Coverage_F(C) = \frac{\sum\limits_{W_i \in C} Frequency_F(W_i)}{Size_F}$$

where $Frequency_F(W_i)$ represents the total number of occurrences of word W_i inside the corpus F, and $Size_F$ represents the total size (in words) of the corpus F.

Similarly, we define the class C coverage for the male corpus M:

Resource	Class	Score	Sample words
			Female
LIWC	GROOM	1.74	cleaner, washer, perfume, shaved, shampoo, cleansing, soap, shower, toothpaste
LIWC	SLEEP	1.65	tiresome, sleeping, dazed, sleeps, insomnia, napping, siesta, nightmare, dreams
LIWC	I	1.52	me, myself, my, mine, I
LIWC	FAMILY	1.51	auntie, mommy, nephews, parents, daughter, motherhood, grandma, wives, cousin
LIWC	EATING	1.46	fat, dinner, tasting, drunken, fed, breakfast, cookie, eats, tasted, skinny, cookbook
WA	DISGUST	1.59	sickening, revolting, horror, sick, offensive, obscene, nauseous, wicked, offensive
WA	FEAR	1.23	suspense, creep, dismay, fright, terrible, terror, afraid, scare, alarmed, panicked
Roget	SEWING	3.46	mending, stitching, knitter, mend, tailor, suture, embroidery, seamstress, needle
Roget	PURPLENESS	1.87	purple, mauve, magenta, lilac, lavender, orchid, violet, mauve, mulberry, purply
Roget	SWEETNESS	1.80	syrup, honey, sugar, bakery, nectar, sweet, frost, sugary, dessert, glaze, nut
Roget	BROWNNESS	1.45	coffee, biscuit, walnut, rust, berry, brown, brunette, cinnamon, mahogany, caramel
Roget	CHASTITY	1.38	shame, elegant, decent, virtue, virgin, delicate, faithfulness, platonic, purity, spotless
			Male
LIWC	RELIG	1.47	bless, satanism, angel, communion, spirit, lord, faithful, immortal, theology, prayers
LIWC	METAPH	1.43	suicide, meditation, cemetary, temples, drained, immortalized, mercy, mourning
LIWC	SPORTS	1.41	running, jogged, pool, basketball, swimming, exercise, fitness, teams, aerobic
LIWC	TV	1.39	show, ad, comedies, tv, actors, drama, soaps, video, theaters, commercials, films
LIWC	JOB	1.30	credentials, department, financials, desktop, manage, employ, work, career
Roget	OPONENT	1.88	finalist, rival, enemy, competitor, foe, opposite, defendant, player, dissident
Roget	THEOLOGY	1.88	creed, scholastic, religious, secularism, theology, religion, divine, faith, dogma
Roget	UNIFORMITY	1.88	evenness, constancy, persistence, accordance, steadiness, firmness, stability
Roget	ENGINEERING	1.60	automotive, process, industrial, manufacture, measure, construction, technician
Roget	INFLUENCE	1.60	power, force, weak, weakness, inflexible, ineffective, charisma, charm, wimpy

Table 3: Sample dominant word classes in male and female blogs.

$$Coverage_M(C) = \frac{\sum_{W_i \in C} Frequency_M(W_i)}{Size_M}$$

The *dominance score* of the class C in the female corpus F is then defined as the ratio between the coverage of the class in the corpus F with respect to the coverage of the same class in the male corpus M:

$$Dominance_F(C) = \frac{Coverage_F(C)}{Coverage_M(C)} \tag{1}$$

A dominance score close to 1 indicates a similar distribution of the words in the class C in both the female and the male corpora. Instead, a score significantly higher than 1 indicates a class that is dominant in the female corpus, and thus likely to be a characteristic of the texts in this corpus. In a similar way, we define the $Dominance_M(C)$ score as the ratio between $Coverage_M(C)$ and $Coverage_F(C)$, where a score significantly higher than 1 indicates a class that is salient in the male corpus.

3.2 Word Classes

We use classes of words as defined in three large lexical resources: Roget's Thesaurus, Linguistic Inquiry and Word Count, and the six main emotions from WordNet Affect. For each lexical resource, we only keep the words and their corresponding class. Note that some resources include the lemmatised form of the words (e.g., Roget), while others include an inflected form (e.g., LIWC); we keep the words as they originally appear in each resource. Any other information such as morphological or semantic annotations is removed for consistency purposes, since not all the resources have such annotations available.

Roget. Roget is a thesaurus of the English language, with words and phrases grouped into hierarchical classes. A word class usually includes synonyms, as well as other words that are semantically related. Classes are typically divided into sections, subsections, heads and paragraphs, allowing for various granularities of the semantic relations used in a word class. We only use one of the broader groupings, namely the heads. The most recent version of Roget (1987) includes about 100,000 words grouped into nearly 1,000 head classes.

Linguistic Inquiry and Word Count (LIWC). LIWC was developed as a resource for psycholinguistic analysis (Pennebaker and Francis, 1999; Pennebaker and King, 1999). The 2001 version of LIWC includes about 2,200 words and word stems grouped into about 70 broad categories relevant to psychological processes (e.g., emotion, cognition). The LIWC lexicon has been validated by showing significant correlation between human ratings of a large number of written texts and the rating obtained through LIWC-based analyses of the same texts.

WordNet Affect (WA). WA (Strapparava and Valitutti, 2004) is a resource that was created starting with WordNet (Miller et al., 1993), by annotating synsets with several emotions. It uses several resources for affective information, including the emotion classification of Ortony (Ortony et al., 1987). We build an affective lexicon by extracting the words corresponding to the six basic emotions defined by (Ortony et al., 1987), namely anger, disgust, fear, joy, sadness, and surprise.

3.3   Gender Dominant Word Classes

Applying the word class saliency metric on the blog dataset using the three resources described before results in a score associated with each class. The following word classes were found to be dominant in either the female corpus or the male corpus, with a score that is away from the neutral score of 1 by a margin larger or equal to 0.20.

Roget. <u>Female</u>: SEWING (3.46), PURPLENESS (1.87), SWEETNESS (1.8), BROWNNESS (1.45), ORANGENESS (1.45), CHASTITY (1.38), TOUCH (1.38), ASCETICISM (1.37), FASTING (1.37), SPELL CHARM (1.37), SEMILIQUIDITY (1.35), PREDICTION (1.34), ENVY (1.34), BLUENESS (1.31), PULPINESS (1.31), SOURNESS (1.31), RAIN (1.29), GREENNESS (1.29), SENSATIONS OF TOUCH (1.29), ROUGHNESS (1.29), RECESSION (1.27), FORESIGHT (1.27), EVILDOER (1.26), TEXTURE (1.25), REFRIGERATION (1.24), REDNESS (1.23), SELFISHNESS (1.23), VIRTUE (1.23), INSOLENCE (1.22), RESINS GUMS (1.22), COURTESY (1.22), UNORTHODOXY (1.22), ONENESS (1.22), UNINTELLIGIBILITY (1.21), MATHEMATICS (1.2), CLOTHING MATERIALS (1.2), SECRETION (1.2), OVERESTIMATION (1.2) <u>Male</u>: THEOLOGY (1.88), OPPONENT (1.88), UNIFORMITY (1.88), UNSANCTITY (1.75), ENGINEERING (1.60), INFLUENCE (1.60), MISSILERY (1.60), PROHIBITION (1.58), QUADRUPLICATION (1.58), INSIPIDNESS (1.56), PHRASE (1.51), IDOLATRY (1.51), PRECEPT (1.49), ELECTRONICS (1.49), MISTEACHING (1.49), RELIGIONS CULTS SECTS (1.43), BODY OF LAND (1.43), PUBLIC SPIRIT (1.43), MECHANICS (1.43), ILLEGALITY (1.41), ETHICS (1.41), PREJUDGMENT (1.40), THIEF (1.39), LAND (1.34), UNITED NATIONS INTERNATIONAL ORGANIZATIONS (1.34), INORGANIC MATTER (1.34), PRECURSOR (1.34), FUEL (1.34), EARTH SCIENCE (1.33), WISE PERSON (1.33), AVIATOR (1.33), ARCHITECTURE DESIGN (1.31), MERCHANDISE (1.31), TRIBUNAL (1.30), DISCORD (1.30), TREATISE (1.28), ROCK (1.28), REVOLUTION (1.28), FOUR (1.28), REGION (1.26), TEACHER (1.26), NONRELIGIOUSNESS (1.26), FICTION (1.25), COUNTRY (1.25), LETTER (1.25)

LIWC. <u>Female</u>: GROOM (1.74), SLEEP (1.65), I (1.52), FAMILY (1.51), NONFL (1.48), EATING (1.46), SELF (1.44), POSFEEL (1.36), HOME (1.36), FEEL (1.34), FRIENDS (1.33), PHYSICAL (1.33), SEXUAL (1.31), PRONOUN (1.29), ASSENT (1.27), BODY (1.23), SIMILES (1.22) <u>Male</u>: RELIG (1.47), METAPH (1.43), SPORTS (1.41), TV (1.39), JOB (1.30).

WA: <u>Female</u>: DISGUST (1.25), FEAR (1.23)

Table 3 shows several salient word classes along with sample words belonging to these classes.

A few interesting observations can be made. First, there are indeed word classes, both semantic and psycholinguistic, which are dominant in one gender. While previous work has mainly focused on identifying individual words that have high frequencies in either men's or women's writings, our method allows us to identify patterns over these differences in the form of linguistically justified word classes.

Among the semantic word classes from Roget, many of the ones found to be dominant for women refer to sensorial concepts, e.g., PURPLENESS, GREENNESS, SWEETNESS, TOUCH, SOURNESS, TEXTURE, etc., which suggests that women have an increased sense of perception of the surrounding world. The ones that are predominant for men reflect a concern with religion, e.g., PUBLIC SPIRIT, THEOLOGY, RELIGIONS CULTS SECTS, or science and engineering, e.g., ARCHITECTURE DESIGN, AVIATOR, EARTH SCIENCE, INORGANIC MATTER, ENGINEERING.

In terms of psycholinguistic classes (LIWC), women appear to be more interested in family, e.g., FAMILY, HOME, FRIENDS and personal well being, e.g., GROOM, SLEEP, SELF, BODY, whereas men seem to be more interested in RELIGION, SPORTS, and JOB related topics.

Perhaps not surprisingly, among the WordNet Affect word classes, there are no emotions that are dominant for men. Instead, two emotions, DISGUST and FEAR, are salient for women.[2]

---

[2] All the other emotions had a $Dominance_F(C)$ score higher than 1 (even if below 1.20), which is probably justified by

4   Gender-based Word Disambiguation

We now turn to our second question, which is concerned with whether some words are used differently
by men and women, which can be regarded as a reflection of the differences in how they see the world
around them. To test our hypothesis, we use examples drawn from men's and women's writings for
a large number of words, and build disambiguation models centered on these target words. We are
therefore formulating our task as a word sense disambiguation problem, and attempt to automatically
identify the gender of the person using a certain target word.

4.1   Target Words

The choice of target words for our experiments is driven by the phenomena we aim to analyze. Because
we want to investigate the behavior of words in the language of the two genders, and verify whether the
difference in word behavior comes from changes in sense or changes in wording in the context, we choose
a mixture of polysemous words and monosemous words (according to WordNet 3.0 (Miller, 1995)), and
also words that are frequent in the writings of both genders, as well as words that are frequently used by
only one gender.

According to these criteria, for each open class (nouns, verbs, adjectives, adverbs) we select 100
words, 50 of which have multiple senses, and 50 with one sense only. Each of these two sets has a
30-10-10 distribution: 30 words that are frequent in both men and women writings, with a distribution in
the two genders falling in the [40%-60%] range, and 10 words per each gender such that these words are
only frequent in one gender (i.e., words that have a frequency for the dominant gender higher than 70%).

The initial set of target words consists of 400 open class words, uniformly distributed over the 4 parts
of speech, uniformly distributed over multiple-sense/unique sense words, and with the frequency based
sample as described above. From this initial set of words, we could not identify enough examples for
36,[3] which left us with a final set of 364 words.

4.2   Data Preprocessing

For each target word in our dataset, we collect 300 examples from each gender, for a maximum of 600
examples per target word. The average number of examples is 492 examples per target word.

All the extracted snippets are then processed: the text is tokenized and part-of-speech tagged using
the Stanford tagger (Toutanova et al., 2003), and contexts that do not include the target word with the
specified part-of-speech are removed. The position of the target word is also identified and recorded as
an offset along with the example.

4.3   Gender Disambiguation Algorithm

The classification algorithm we use is inspired by previous work on data-driven word sense disambiguation. Specifically, we use a system that integrates both local and topical features. The *local features*
include: the current word and its part-of-speech; a local context of three words to the left and right of
the ambiguous word; the parts-of-speech of the surrounding words; the first noun before and after the
target word; the first verb before and after the target word. The *topical features* are determined from the
global context and are implemented through class-specific keywords, which are determined as a list of
at most five words occurring at least three times in the contexts defining a certain word class (or epoch).
The features are then integrated in a Naive Bayes classifier. The final disambiguation system is similar
to several word sense disambiguation systems described in previous work (Dandala et al., 2013).

For evaluation, we calculate the average accuracy obtained through ten-fold cross-validations applied
on the data collected for each word. To place results in perspective, we also calculate a simple baseline,
which assigns the most frequent class by default.

---

the more emotional nature of women.

[3]A minimum of 100 total examples was required for a word to be considered in the dataset.

4.4 Results and Discussion

Table 6 summarizes the results obtained for the 364 words.[4] Overall, we find that there are indeed differences between the ways men and women use predefined target words, with an average error rate reduction of 7.64%. While improvements are obtained for all parts-of-speech, the nouns lead to the highest disambiguation results, with the largest improvement over the baseline, which interestingly aligns with previous observations from work on word sense disambiguation (Mihalcea and Edmonds, 2004; Agirre et al., 2007).

Among the words considered, there are words that experience very large improvements over the baseline, such as *husband* (with an absolute increase over the baseline of 15.50%), *read* (13.89%) or *here* (13.66%). There are also words that experience very small improvements, such as *laugh* (1.86%), *tonight* (1.62%) or awesome (1.56%), and even a few words which are dominant in one gender, and for which the disambiguation accuracy is below the baseline, such as *shop* (-18.82%), *largely* (-11.23%) and *pink* (-7.39%).

To understand to what extent the change in frequency has an impact on gender-based word disambiguation (GD), in Table 4 we report results for words that have high frequency in both genders, or in only one gender at a time. Somehow surprisingly, the words that are used more often by one gender are harder to disambiguate. While this may be an artifact of the higher baseline, it may also suggest that the words that "belong" to a gender are used in a similar way by both genders (e.g., *cozy*), unlike words that are frequent in both genders, which get loaded with gender-specific meaning (e.g., *helpful*).

POS	No. words	Avg. no. examples	Baseline	GD
High frequency in both genders				
Noun	56	594	50.00%	56.98%*
Verb	60	451	52.53%	57.98%*
Adjective	53	590	50.98%	57.08%*
Adverb	60	560	50.39%	56.96%*
OVERALL	234	533	50.99%	57.26%*
High frequency in one gender				
Noun	41	565	50.95%	57.38%*
Verb	30	350	61.11%	58.71%
Adjective	40	344	64.14%	57.85%
Adverb	19	367	65.13%	58.13%
OVERALL	130	419	59.42%	57.94%

Table 4: Results for words that have high frequency in both genders, or in one gender at a time

The second analysis that we perform is concerned with the accuracy of polysemous words as compared to monosemous words. Comparative results are reported in Table 5. Monosemous words do not have sense changes between men and women, so being able to classify them with respect to the gender of the speaker relies exclusively on variations in their context. The fact that we obtain similar improvements for both monosemous and polysemous words is an indication that the gender differences that we observe are not due to the use of different word meanings, but rather to men and women using a certain word in different ways.

To further understand the relation between word senses and gender, we select 12 words (adjectives: *young, strong, new*; adverbs: *together, later, fast*; nouns: *party, idea, couple*; verbs: *heat, cause, understand*), randomly choose 100 examples for each of these words with equal split between male and female, and manually annotate their senses using WordNet (Miller, 1995). From these annotations, we observe that the predominant senses used by each gender are largely the same for most words. For instance, the words *party* and *heat*, shown in Figure 1 have a similar distribution over word senses. There are also a few exceptions, as illustrated for instance for the adjective *strong* in Figure 1, where the sense

---

[4]Disambiguation results that are significantly better than the baseline are marked with $*$ (statistical significance measured using a t-test, $p < 0.05$).

POS	No. words	Avg. no. examples	Baseline	GD
Polysemous words				
Noun	51	581	50.48%	57.44%*
Verb	50	460	54.72%	57.78%*
Adjective	50	463	56.13%	57.23%
Adverb	43	509	54.76%	57.89%*
OVERALL	194	504	53.98%	57.57%*
Monosemous words				
Noun	46	582	50.30%	56.82%*
Verb	40	363	56.23%	58.78%*
Adjective	48	445	56.58%	57.57%
Adverb	36	518	52.94%	56.46%*
OVERALL	170	478	54.03%	57.42%*

Table 5: Results for words that are polysemous or monosemous.

POS	No. words	Avg. no. examples	Baseline	GD
Noun	97	582	50.39%	57.15%*
Verb	90	417	55.39%	58.22%*
Adjective	98	454	56.35%	57.40%
Adverb	79	513	53.93%	57.24%*
OVERALL	364	492	53.98%	57.50%*

Table 6: Results for different parts-of-speech.

of (*firm, strong and sure*) is more often used by females, while the sense of (*having strength or power greater than average or expected*) is more frequently used by males. An interesting example is the word *together*, where males use more often the sense of (*assembled in one place*), while females use it with the sense of (*in each other's company*). This is in line with the observation made before using semantic classes, that women focus more on family and friends, while men talk more about groups and work.

In general we find that the distribution of WordNet word senses for men and women for the 12 selected words is mostly similar. For an overall quantification, we use the Pearson and Spearman correlation metrics to calculate the correlation of word sense frequencies for the two genders, which resulted in a Pearson score of 0.94 and a Spearman score of 0.88, which reflect a high correlation. This suggests once again that the concept-centered differences that we observed between men and women are not due to distinct word meanings, but rather to different ways of using a certain word.

5 Conclusions

In this paper, we moved beyond the surface-level text classification approach to gender discrimination, and attempted to gain insights into the differences between men and women by using semantic methods that can point to salient word classes or differences in concept usage. We believe these distinctions at a deeper semantic level can be regarded as a reflection of the differences between the genders' perception of the world around them.

We first defined a metric for measuring the saliency of word classes, which we then used in conjunction with three semantic and psycholinguistic resources, resulting in a set of dominant word classes. With this metric, we were able to identify semantic and psycholinguistic word classes that are predominantly used by a gender, shading light on their interests and concerns.

We also introduced the task of "gender-based word disambiguation," and using examples drawn from a large collection of blogposts for over 350 words, we showed that we can identify the gender of the person using a word with an accuracy significantly higher than the most frequent baseline. Additional analyses suggested that changes in frequency and context contribute to these differences, while the distribution of word senses is mainly similar.

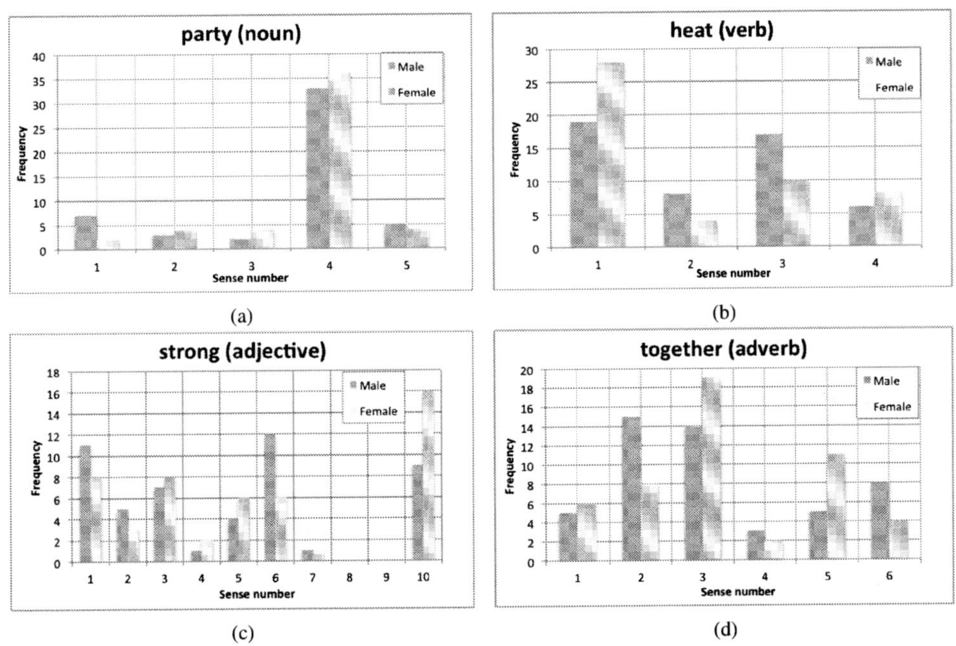

Figure 1: Distribution of WordNet senses for four words for male and female (100 examples)

In future work, we plan to extend the use of word classes to other resources, and also improve the disambiguation algorithm by including sociolinguistic and psycholinguistic features. We would also like to perform an in-depth analysis of the features that best characterize the differences in word usage between men and women.

Acknowledgments

This material is based in part upon work supported by the National Science Foundation (#1344257), the John Templeton Foundation (#48503), and the Michigan Institute for Data Science. Any opinions, findings, and conclusions or recommendations expressed in this material are those of the authors and do not necessarily reflect the views of the National Science Foundation, the John Templeton Foundation, or the Michigan Institute for Data Science.

References

E. Agirre, L. Marquez, and R. Wicentowski, editors. 2007. *Proceedings of the 4th International Workshop on Semantic Evaluations*, Prague, Czech Republic.

C. Boulis and M. Ostendorf. 2005. A quantitative analysis of lexical differences between genders in telephone conversations. In *Proceedings of the 43rd Annual Meeting of the Association for Computational Linguistics (ACL 2005)*, pages 435–442, Ann Arbor.

J. Burger, J. Henderson, G. Kim, and G. Zarrella. 2011. Discriminating gender on twitter. In *Proceedings of the Conference on Empirical Methods in Natural Language Processing*, pages 1301–1309.

B. Dandala, R. Mihalcea, and R. Bunescu, 2013. *Word Sense Disambiguation using Wikipedia*. Springer book series.

J.A. Doyle. 1985. *Sex and Gender: The Human Experience*. Wm. C. Brown Publishers.

P. Eckert and S. McConnell-Ginet. 2003. *Language and gender*. Cambridge University Press.

P. Gianfortoni, D. Adamson, and C. Rosé. 2011. Modeling of stylistic variation in social media with stretchy patterns. In *Proceedings of the First Workshop on Algorithms and Resources for Modelling of Dialects and Language Varieties*, pages 49–59. Association for Computational Linguistics.

S. Herring and J. Paolillo. 2004. Gender and genre variation in weblogs. *Journal of Sociolinguistics*.

D. Huffaker and S. L. Calvert. 2005. Gender, identity and language use in teenage blogs. *Journal of Computer-Mediated Communication*.

T. L. M. Kennedy, J. S. Robinson, and K. Trammell, 2005. *Does gender matter? Examining conversations in the blogosphere.*

M. Koppel, S. Argamon, and A. Shimoni. 2002. Automatically categorizing written texts by author gender. *Literary and Linguistic Computing*, 4(17):401–412.

R.T. Lakoff. 1972. *Language and woman's place.* Cambridge Univ Press.

H. Liu and R. Mihalcea. 2007. Of men, women, and computers: Data-driven gender modeling for improved user interfaces. In *International Conference on Weblogs and Social Media*.

R. Mihalcea and P. Edmonds, editors. 2004. *Proceedings of SENSEVAL-3, Association for Computational Linguistics Workshop*, Barcelona, Spain.

G. Miller, C. Leacock, T. Randee, and R. Bunker. 1993. A semantic concordance. In *Proceedings of the 3rd DARPA Workshop on Human Language Technology*, Plainsboro, New Jersey.

G. Miller. 1995. Wordnet: A lexical database. *Communication of the ACM*, 38(11).

A. Mukherjee and B. Liu. 2010. Improving gender classification of blog authors. In *Proceedings of the Conference on Empirical Methods in natural Language Processing*, pages 207–217.

D. Nguyen, D. Trieschnigg, A.S. Dogruöz, R. Gravel, M. Theune, T. Meder, and F. Jong. 2014. Why gender and age prediction from tweets is hard: Lessons from a crowdsourcing experiment. In *Proceedings of the 25th International Conference on Computational Linguistics*.

S. Nowson and J. Oberlander. 2006. The identity of bloggers: Openness and gender in personal weblogs. In *AAAI spring symposium: Computational approaches to analyzing weblogs*, pages 163–167.

A. Ortony, G. L. Clore, and M. A. Foss. 1987. The referential structure of the affective lexicon. *Cognitive Science*, (11).

C. Peersman, W. Daelemans, and L. Van Vaerenbergh. 2004. Predicting age and gender in online social networks. In *Proceedings of the 3rd Workshop on Search and Mining UserGenerated Contents*.

J. Pennebaker and M. Francis. 1999. Linguistic inquiry and word count: LIWC. Erlbaum Publishers.

J. Pennebaker and L. King. 1999. Linguistic styles: Language use as an individual difference. *Journal of Personality and Social Psychology*, (77).

V. Prabhakaran, A. Arora, and O. Rambow. 2014. Staying on topic: An indicator of power in political debates. In *Proceedings of the 2014 Conference on Empirical Methods in Natural Language Processing, Doha, Qatar, October. Association for Computational Linguistics*.

D. Rao, D. Yarowsky, A. Shreevats, and M. Gupta. 2010. Classifying latent user attributes in twitter. In *Proceedings of the Second international workshop on Search and mining user-generated contents*, pages 37–44.

R. Sarawgi, K. Gajulapalli, and Y. Choi. 2011. Gender attribution: tracing stylometric evidence beyond topic and genre. In *Proceedings of the Fifteenth Conference on Computational Natural Language Learning*, pages 78–86. Association for Computational Linguistics.

J. Schler, M. Koppel, S. Argamon, and J. Pennebaker. 2006. Effects of age and gender on blogging. In *Proceedings of 2006 AAAI Spring Symposium on Computational Approaches for Analyzing Weblogs*, pages 199–204, Stanford.

C. Strapparava and A. Valitutti. 2004. Wordnet-affect: an affective extension of wordnet. In *Proceedings of the 4th International Conference on Language Resources and Evaluation*, Lisbon.

D. Tannen. 1991. *You Just Don't Understand: Women and Men in Conversation.* London, Virago.

K. Toutanova, D. Klein, C. Manning, and Y. Singer. 2003. Feature-rich part-of-speech tagging with a cyclic dependency network. In *Proceedings of Human Language Technology Conference (HLT-NAACL 2003)*, Edmonton, Canada, May.

The Effect of Gender and Age Differences on the Recognition of Emotions from Facial Expressions

Daniela Schneevogt
University of Copenhagen
d.schneevogt@googlemail.com

Patrizia Paggio
University of Copenhagen
University of Malta
paggio@hum.ku.dk
patrizia.paggio@um.edu.mt

Abstract

Recent studies have demonstrated gender and cultural differences in the recognition of emotions in facial expressions. However, most studies were conducted on American subjects. In this paper, we explore the generalizability of several findings to a non-American culture in the form of Danish subjects. We conduct an emotion recognition task followed by two stereotype questionnaires with different genders and age groups. While recent findings (Krems et al., 2015) suggest that women are biased to see anger in neutral facial expressions posed by females, in our sample both genders assign higher ratings of anger to all emotions expressed by females. Furthermore, we demonstrate an effect of gender on the fear-surprise-confusion observed by Tomkins and McCarter (1964); females overpredict fear, while males overpredict surprise.

1 Introduction

Content in online social media is expressed not only in textual form, but also through pictures and videos. For example, YouTube has more than 1 billion users around the world, and it is estimated that 100 hours of video are uploaded every minute. Part of this content consists of video blogs where users express opinions about various topics. In order to mine the opinions that are expressed through images and videos, traditional text-based sentiment analysis must be complemented with similar techniques that are able to extract people's emotions and attitudes from the visual modality. Being able to extract emotions automatically, however, presupposes knowledge of how emotions are expressed and perceived. This paper focuses on two aspects of emotion understanding, i.e. whether gender and age play a role in the way people perceive emotions through facial expressions.

Several studies in the cognitive sciences have focused on studying people's perception and recognition of emotions in facial expression. The discussion about the relation between culture and emotions first started with Darwin in 1872 who argued that emotions and their expressions are universal (Darwin et al., 1998). Since then, an immense number of research studies on the universality of the basic emotions – anger, fear, disgust, happiness, sadness and surprise – has demonstrated that all healthy humans are able to recognize these emotions in images of human faces.

Recent studies also investigate possible differences in emotion recognition and find that subjects from different cultures indeed assign the same emotions, but show differences in perceived intensity and agreement level. Most recently, a study conducted with subjects from the American population shows an additional difference in emotion recognition based on gender (Krems et al., 2015). According to their research, women tend to see anger in other women's neutral facial expressions. Other studies indicate that these gender-specific differences decrease with advanced age (Calder et al., 2003; Mill et al., 2009).

Conducting a study only on an American sample raises the question of generalizability to other cultures. Therefore, our study was conducted to answer the following research questions: (1) For subjects with a different nationality than American, are there gender-specific differences in ratings of emotion expressions in human faces when offering a multiscalar rating scale? (2) Are these gender differences, if observed, comparable to the effects found by Krems et al. (2015)? (3) Do these differences change

This work is licenced under a Creative Commons Attribution 4.0 International License. License details: http://
creativecommons.org/licenses/by/4.0/

Proceedings of the Workshop on Computational Modeling of People's Opinions, Personality, and Emotions in Social Media,
pages 11–19, Osaka, Japan, December 12 2016.

with higher age? (4) Are the overall as well as the gender-specific ratings related to cultural and personal stereotypes? We chose to explore the first question by looking at Danish subjects, on the assumption that gender plays a different role in a Scandinavian culture.

We conduct an experiment including an emotion rating task with multiscalar rating scale and two questionnaires studying cultural stereotypes and personal beliefs. A selection of images from the NimStim Set of Facial Expressions (Tottenham et al., 2009) was used for the rating task. The questionnaires closely resemble the ones used by Plant et al. (2000) and are based on work by Fabes and Martin (1991). The experiment was conducted with 40 test subjects of two age groups.

2 Background

Over the years, a considerable number of studies have documented evidence for the existence of universal emotional expressions (e.g., Ekman (1994)). Various studies show that even across different cultures, humans are able to recognize the basic emotions of anger, fear, disgust, happiness, sadness and surprise in images of human faces. Recently, these studies expanded to investigate possible differences in emotion recognition across cultures and showed that subjects from different cultures indeed see the same emotions when presented with the same images, but show slight differences in the intensity ratings assigned to the respective emotion (Ekman et al., 1987; Matsumoto and Ekman, 1989; Biehl et al., 1997) and the precise level of agreement (Matsumoto et al., 2002; Russell, 1994; Biehl et al., 1997).

Biehl et al. (1997) and Martinez and Du (2012) also demonstrate the existence of different levels of agreement for emotion recognition, with happiness showing highest agreement, and disgust and fear the lowest. This confirms previous findings that showed fear to be the basic emotion most poorly recognized (Smith and Schyns, 2009; Biehl et al., 1997). A possible explanation is given by Tomkins and McCarter (1964) who suggest that emotions sharing similar expressive qualities – like fear and surprise – are most likely to be confused with each other. An alternative interpretation suggests that differences in the intensity assigned to an image could be based on low confidence (Biehl et al., 1997). Beaupré and Hess (2006) show that subjects are more confident when rating faces of in-group members and when rating expressions that are considered frequently expressed in their environment. Overall, subjects were found to be most confident in recognizing expressions of happiness (Beaupré and Hess, 2006), supporting the findings by Biehl et al. (1997).

Various research on cultural aspects of emotion recognition shows cultural differences in the level of agreement as well as the level of intensity assigned to the expressed emotions (Russell, 1994; Biehl et al., 1997; Elfenbein and Ambady, 2003). Further, Matsumoto (1991) found evidence for cultural display rules: While Japanese participants (collectivist culture) hide certain negative emotions when a person of higher status is present, American subjects (individualistic culture) openly show these emotions.

Several studies on gender differences in this field demonstrate a female advantage for decoding expressions of emotions. Hall and Matsumoto (2004) find that women are more accurate at identifying the correct pattern when rating emotions on a multiscalar rating scale, while this gender difference could not be observed for single choice tasks (Hall and Matsumoto, 2004). Moreover, women are believed to express sadness and fear more often than men, while men are believed to express anger more frequently (Fabes and Martin, 1991). Most recently, Krems et al. (2015) showed that women are biased to see anger in neutral female faces, whereas no such effect could be found for male faces or other emotions.

Plant et al. (2000) show that subjects behave in a stereotype-consistent manner when interpreting faces showing an ambiguous anger-sadness expression, rating women as more sad and less angry than men. Interestingly, even when shown unambiguous female anger expressions, participants rate these as a combination of anger and sadness, consistent with the subjects' stereotypes.

Studies on different age groups demonstrate that older subjects are less accurate at identifying emotions in facial expressions (Mill et al., 2009; Calder et al., 2003) and that this decline starts at 30 years of age for anger and sadness, and at 60 years of age for all other emotions (Mill et al., 2009). Calder et al. (2003) additionally show that performance on expressions of disgust improved for older participants.

3 Methodology

All data for our study was collected during May 2016. All experiments took place in a university laboratory and had the same protocol. Subjects were tested individually. First, subjects performed the emotion recognition task, and second, they filled in a Cultural Stereotype Questionnaire (CSQ) and a Personal Belief Questionnaire (PBQ). Afterwards, demographic data was collected. Two rounds of pilot experiments were run to eliminate technical and design-wise problems.

3.1 Stimuli selection

The data used in the emotion rating task was taken from the NimStim Set of Facial Expressions (Tottenham et al., 2009). The whole data set consists of 672 images of facial expressions posed by 43 actors. The emotions expressed are different versions of anger, disgust, fear, happiness, sadness and surprise, as well as neutral and calm expressions. From the total set of images, we first removed all images showing the calm facial expression as only the 6 basic emotions and neutral expressions were needed. Then, we selected a subset consisting of 112 images showing 7 distinct facial expressions by 16 actors – 8 males and 8 females. These actors were chosen such that for every actor all seven prototypical (Ekman and Friesen, 1978) expressions had an agreement score above 50 percent. In addition, 8 images were chosen for a practice phase in the beginning of each experiment session. The actors from the practice phase were not included in the final set of images.

3.2 Experimental setup and questionnaire design

The experiments were conducted using the open source software program OpenSesame (Mathôt et al., 2012) on an Apple MacBook Pro (13-inch) with OS X Yosemite (Version 10.10.3) installed. Each image (size: 506 x 650 pixels) appeared in the center of the screen for 5ms (the same duration as used in Beaupré and Hess (2005) and Beaupré and Hess (2006)). Each participant evaluated all 112 stimuli. The images were presented in a different random order for each of the 40 participants. After each image, a screen with a multiple rating scale for the 6 basic emotions (anger, disgust, fear, happiness, sadness, surprise) appeared. On screen, participants were instructed as follows: "Please indicate the extent to which you perceived each of the following emotions. 0=absent, 1=slight, 4=moderate, 8=strong". We based the design for the multiscalar rating in this task on the rating scale in Matsumoto (2005). Subjects then rated the intensity with which they perceived the 6 emotions in the previous image. Participants were allowed to either select one single emotion, several emotions, or to leave all emotions set to 0, indicating the absence of all 6 emotions and therefore a neutral expression.

After completing the rating task, participants were given two questionnaires studying subjects' stereotypes about the emotions of interest and additional questions on demographic details. Before starting the questionnaires, they were given oral instructions about the difference between them. Additional written instructions were given on screen for all parts of the experiment.

The two questionnaires we use in our study are short versions of stereotype endorsement questionnaires introduced by Fabes and Martin (1991) – a Cultural Stereotype Questionnaire (CSQ) and a Personal Beliefs Questionnaire (PBQ), and are based on the versions used by Plant et al. (2000). The CSQ studies cultural stereotypes about the frequency with which women and men experience and express emotions, while the PBQ investigates subjects' personal beliefs about this topic. Here, we study the same emotions examined in the emotion rating task – anger, disgust, fear, happiness, sadness and surprise.

For each emotion, subjects answered the following 4 questions on a scale from 1 (never) to 7 (very frequently) for the CSQ [1]:

(1) How often are men believed to experience ____?
(2) How often are men believed to express ____?
(3) How often are women believed to experience ____?
(4) How often are women believed to express ____?.

---

[1] We chose not to translate the questions into Danish since participants' proficiency in English was good enough to understand and answer the questions in English.

For each emotion in the PBQ, they were asked a slightly different version of each of the 4 questions, i.e.
for the first question:

> (1) How often do you believe men experience ____?

It was made clear both in the written and oral instructions that the first set of questions referred to
general beliefs, while the second referred to the subject's own opinions. As the order in which subjects
are presented the two questionnaires does not have an effect on the results (Plant et al., 2000), we present
the questionnaires in the same order for all participants.

3.3 Participants

A total of 40 individuals participated in this study – 20 in the younger age group (10 male, 10 female)
and 20 in the older age group (9 male, 11 female). All participants were Danish nationals born and
raised in Denmark. In the younger age group, the mean age of the participants was 24.75 years (SD =
2.83) ranging from 18 to 31 years. This age group consisted of 16 university students from a variety
of fields, as well as 2 high school students and 2 recent graduates. For the older age group, the mean
age of the participants was 57.60 years (SD = 5.14), ranging from 50 to 69 years. Twelve of the older
participants work at universities in a range of different positions (e.g. as professors, associate professors,
senior researchers or research associates).

Out of all 40 participants, 33 reported having a university degree (Bachelor, Master or Doctorate
degree) as the highest level of education. The remaining reported either a degree from primary school (3),
highschool (2) or university college (2) as the highest. 19 participants reported a very high proficiency
in English, 13 described their English as above average, 7 as average and only one person reported an
English proficiency below average.

3.4 Analysis

To measure the accuracy with which subjects rated certain types of images (gender of expressor, emotion), we developed 2 different correctness measures. Both are developed on the assumption that there
is always only one correct emotion, namely the emotion label given to each of the images in the data set
(either neutral or one of the 6 emotions).

The first *correctness measure (C1)* looks at whether the highest rating given to an image corresponds
to the correct emotion label. It was computed as follows for participant s rating an image i with a correct
emotion label y:

$$
C1(s,i,y) = \begin{cases} 100 & \text{if } y \neq neutral \wedge \arg\max_{e \in E} rating(s,i,e) = y \\ 100 & \text{if } y = neutral \wedge \sum_{e \in E} rating(s,i,e) = 0 \\ 0 & \text{otherwise} \end{cases}
$$

Here, E is the set containing the 6 basic emotions. If the highest rating for a given image-participant pair
is the rating for the correct emotion label, the value 100 is assigned, else the value 0. For neutral images,
the value 100 is assigned if no emotions are given positive rating, else 0. Then, we calculate the average
over all images per participant.

The second *correctness measure (C2)* considers the proportional rating of the correct emotion. It is
based on the percentage of the rating given to the correct emotion label for an image over the sum of all
ratings for that image. It is a real-valued variable (0%-100%) and was computed as follows: For every
image-participant pair, we calculate the percentage of the total rating points given to the correct emotion
label. Formally, $C2$ is calculated as follows:

$$
C2(s,i,y) = \begin{cases} 100\frac{rating(s,i,y)}{\sum_{e \in E} rating(s,i,e)} & \text{if } y \neq neutral \wedge \sum_{e \in E} rating(s,i,e) > 0 \\ 100 & \text{if } y = neutral \wedge \sum_{e \in E} rating(s,i,e) = 0 \\ 0 & \text{otherwise} \end{cases}
$$

Afterwards, the average percentage for each participant over all stimuli is computed.

In addition to *C1* and *C2*, *emotion ratings* are used. Six real-valued variables (rating: 0-8) represent how highly rated an emotion was for a given image. The values were retrieved by performing the following calculations: For each emotion, the real value given to the respective emotion for each image-participant pair is collected. Then, the average rating over all images per participant is calculated for that emotion. Note that no value could be included for neutral, as neutral in our study was represented as the absence of ratings.

Finally, seven real-valued variables (0%-100%) represent – for each of the emotions – the percentages of the above described ratings over the sum of all ratings given for an image. These variables are the *emotion percentages*. To retrieve these values, we calculate the average percentage of the total given to the respective emotion for each participant over all stimuli. Values for neutral are calculated as in *C1* and *C2*.

For the questionnaires, six ordinal variables are used to refer to each of the six studied emotions – anger, disgust, fear, happiness, sadness and surprise.

Outlier detection was performed with SPSS' build-in function on both the emotion rating task and the questionnaire data. For the emotion rating task, two strong outliers were identified and excluded from further analysis. For the questionnaire data, no strong outliers were found. Therefore, all results we report in this paper are based on the analysis of data for 38 test subjects.

A Shapiro-Wilk test for normality showed that all dependent variables were normally distributed. Having established this, we ran the following ANOVAs, from which some results will be illustrated in Section 4:

Correctness (C1 and C2): $7 \times 2 \times 2 \times 2$ (emotion × poser gender × age group × subject gender) mixed ANOVA.
Emotion Ratings and Percentages: $7 \times 2 \times 2 \times 2$ (emotion × poser gender × age group × subject gender) mixed multivariate ANOVA.
Questionnaire Variables: $2 \times 2 \times 2 \times 2 \times 2$ (subject gender × age group × target gender × questionnaire type × belief type) mixed multivariate ANOVA with 6 dependent variables, one per emotion.

All statistical analysis was carried out using SPSS Statistics, Version 22.0, and all post-hoc analysis was performed with a two-tailed *t*-test.

4   Results and Discussion

We begin by analyzing the subjects' performance on the emotion rating task. First, we show the mean values for both correctness measures for each emotion. The results can be seen in Table 1. To further illustrate the behavior of the subjects on the task, we plot in Figure 1 the average percentages of ratings assigned to each emotion.

As can be seen in Table 1, the subjects in our study showed a good overall performance on the emotion rating task when looking at the correctness results. An exception was participants' performance on neutral expressions, with correctness values of only 43.74% for both C1 and C2. This finding could be explained by task design: While all other emotional expressions could be given an intensity and rated along with other emotions, for neutrality this option was not given. As soon as a subject rated any other emotion with any intensity, the given image could not be rated as neutral anymore.

Interestingly, the results for correctness measure *C1* suggest a certain hierarchy: With a mean of 97.00%, subjects performed best at recognizing happiness compared to any other emotion, a result that is consistent with Beaupré and Hess (2006). Disgust, sadness, and surprise follow thereafter in the hierarchy, with respective means of 81.45%, 82.79%, and 86.17%. They are followed by anger at 71.67%, which is in turn followed by fear at 58.33%. At the bottom of the hierarchy are the neutral expressions. We see similar results for correctness measure *C2*, except for sadness and surprise for which the order was inverted. This hierarchical organization of the agreements on emotion ratings is consistent with the findings by Biehl et al. (1997).

Emotion	mean (C1)	mean (C2)
Anger	71.67%	70.26%
Disgust	81.45%	77.18%
Fear	**58.33%**	**60.65%**
Happiness	**97.00%**	**94.91%**
Sadness	82.79%	79.94%
Surprise	86.17%	77.43%
Neutral	43.74%	43.74%

Table 1: Mean values for expressed emotion on correctness measure C1 (Correct emotion ranked highest) and correctness measure C2 (Proportional rating of correct emotion).

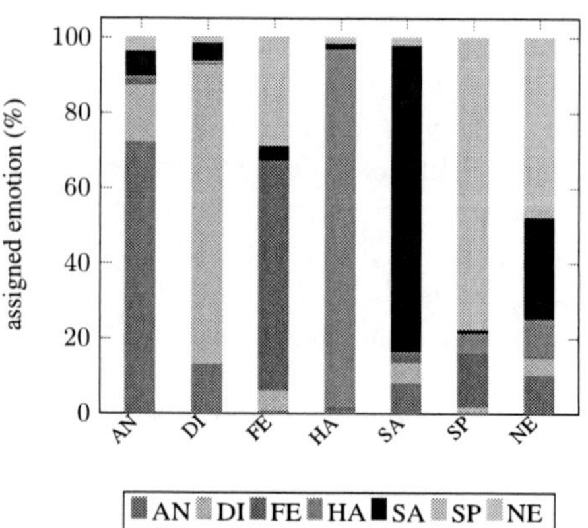

Figure 1: Average percentage of rating assigned to each emotion per expressor emotion.

Moreover, our results show that participants are outstandingly good at detecting happiness, with 97.00% and 94.91% for *C1* and *C2*, respectively. These numbers could be explained by the fact that happiness is the only strictly positive emotion in the set – the other emotions are all negative or ambiguous – and since distinguishing between positive and negative emotions is easier than discriminating between several options, happiness recognition is a relatively easy task.

Furthermore, as can be seen from Table 4, our subjects performed rather poorly at detecting emotional expressions of fear in human faces. In 41.67% of the cases where the expressed emotion was fear, another emotion was rated highest by the participants. Also, 39.35% of the rating points that were given to faces expressing fear were not given to fear but to one or more of the other emotions.

The emotion rating data shows that older subjects assign higher ratings of disgust to all emotions expressed. An interaction of emotion $\times$ age group with $p = .001$ ($F(6, 204) = 3.915$) for disgust was found. Post-hoc analysis shows that, on average, the older age group assigned a higher rating of disgust (6.21) to expressions of disgust than the younger age group (5.26). This effect was significant at $p = .008$. This outcome is consistent with the findings by Calder et al. (2003). No further age differences were found in our study.

To illustrate the effect of gender upon the rating task, we plot in Figures 2 and 3 the average percentages of ratings assigned to each emotion for each combination of subject gender and expressor gender.

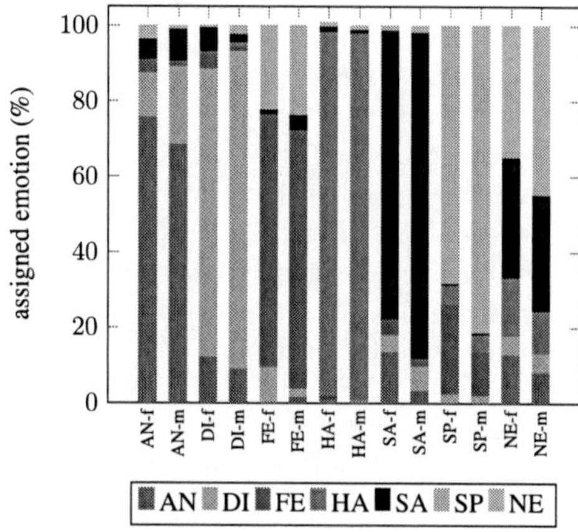

Figure 2: Average percentage of rating assigned to each emotion per expressor emotion and expressor gender for female subjects.

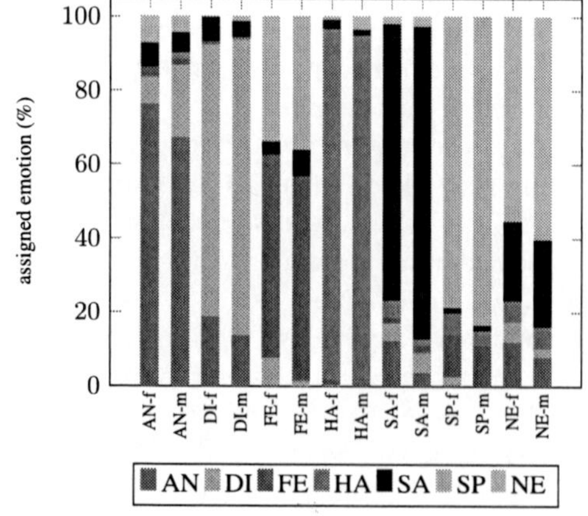

Figure 3: Average percentage of rating assigned to each emotion per expressor emotion and expressor gender for male subjects.

Contrary to what is found in Krems et al. (2015), in our study *both* genders assigned higher ratings of anger to *all* emotions expressed by female actors – on average 1.10 compared to 0.93 for male expressors ($p = .000$; $F(1, 34) = 15.537$). This can also be seen in Figures 2 and 3 – in both figures the value of anger is higher in the female bars than in the male bars (except for male subjects rating happiness, where a slight trend in the opposite direction is observed).

Furthermore, our analysis of fear and surprise expressions gives the following insight on the recognition of these two expressions: As in Tomkins and McCarter (1964), subjects confuse expressions of fear and surprise. However, they do this in gender-specific ways: Men predict more surprise, while women predict more fear. For the emotion ratings, an interaction was found for expressor gender $\times$ subject gender $\times$ emotion with $p = .004$ and $F(6, 204) = 3.300$. The post-hoc test shows that the mean rating given to fear by female subjects was 2.07, while the mean rating by male raters was 1.06. This effect is significant with $p = 0.012$. Females expressing surprise are rated as significantly more afraid if the rater is female.

For the emotion percentages, an interaction was found for emotion $\times$ subject gender. The significance values were $p = .013$ ($F(6, 204) = 2.760$) for fear and $p = .006$ ($F(6, 204) = 3.086$) for surprise. A post-hoc analysis shows that, for images of surprise, women assign higher percentages of fear than men do. For the female group, the mean percentage of fear assigned to surprise was 17.76%, men assigned 10.99% on average ($p = .044$). For images of fear, women assigned significantly less surprise than men did. Women on average assigned 23.07% of surprise to images of fear, whereas men on average assigned 35.03% surprise ($p = .041$).

Another interaction was detected for expressor gender $\times$ subject gender. For this interaction there is a significant effect at $p = .042$ ($F(1, 34) = 4.457$) for the percentage of fear rated. The post-hoc test reveals that on average images of women were rated as 14.19% fearful by female subjects, whereas male subjects on average assigned 10.37% fear to these images. This effect was significant with $p = .008$.

Moreover, an effect was found for the interaction of emotion $\times$ expressor gender $\times$ subject gender with $p = .005$ and $F(6, 204) = 3.163$. The percentage of ratings of fear given to female expressors posing surprise was significantly higher ($p = .012$) for female subjects (23.64%) than for male subjects (11.50%). Further, female subjects shown expressions of surprise assigned a significantly higher percentage of the ratings to fear if the expressor is female on average 23.64% to female expressors and 11.87% to male expressors ($p = .001$). It seems therefore that male subjects overcompensated by rating high values of surprise on both expressions of surprise and fear, while female subjects compensated by rating fear highly on expression of surprise and fear. This was especially true for female subjects rating female expressors.

The analysis of our questionnaire data also showed significant effects for fear, suggesting that subjects believe women are more prone to fear. For all emotions except anger, women were believed to experience and express these emotions more frequently than male targets do. The difference was especially large for fear – the average rating for male targets was 2.96, while it reached 4.95 for female targets. This was significant with $p = .000$ and $F(1, 34) = 46.289$. Plant et al. (2000) demonstrated that subjects prefer making predictions which are in accord with their own stereotypes, which could therefore serve as a possible explanation for our results.

Emotion	mean (express)	mean (experience)	p-value	$F(1, 34)$
Anger	3.88	4.46	.000	24.590
Disgust	3.48	3.92	.000	22.238
Fear	3.29	4.26	.000	42.219
Happiness	4.86	5.03	.169	1.975
Sadness	3.50	4.47	.000	32.870
Surprise	3.79	4.06	.054	3.991

Table 2: Means and significance values of the average rating by belief type and emotion.

Additionally, as can be seen in Table 2, our questionnaire data shows that all emotions are believed to be expressed less than they are experienced, suggesting that everyone is hiding emotions. A main effect of belief type was found for the 4 negative emotions anger, disgust, fear and sadness, all significant with $p = .000$. For all emotions, on average beliefs about experienced emotion are rated higher than beliefs about expressed emotions. The difference is especially high for anger, fear and sadness – three negative emotions – which indicates that people hide negative emotions more than positive emotions.

5 Conclusion

The goal of this study was to investigate gender and age differences in the recognition of emotions in facial expressions in a new cultural context. An emotion recognition study with subjects from the Danish population and two different age groups – followed by 2 questionnaires studying personal beliefs and cultural stereotypes – was conducted.

Consistent with relevant literature, the following findings were identified. First, emotions can be ordered by agreement hierarchy. Second, subjects show a good overall performance on the emotion rating task, especially for the emotion of happiness. Third, subjects perform the worst at detecting fear. And fourth, older subjects assign higher ratings of disgust.

In addition, we find that in our study *both* genders assign higher ratings of anger to *all* emotions expressed by female actors. This is in opposition to Krems et al. (2015), who found that women rated other womens' neutral faces as anger expressions. Furthermore, our subjects confuse expressions of fear and surprise, but in different, gender-specific manners: While men predict more surprise, women predict more fear. Our results show that, overall, gender plays an important role for the perception and recognition of emotions in facial expressions for Danish subjects, but in a different way than was found in Krems et al. (2015) among American subjects. Our results indicate that claims made about gender-specific differences in emotion recognition must take cultural factors into account.

This aspect could be studied in a more specific way in the future by investigating a possible correlation between measures of gender equality, perceived stereotypes and gender variation of emotion perception. Moreover, a separate experiment could be conducted to further examine the effects we have found concerning fear and surprise.

Another line of further investigation could deal with the difference between individual and collectivist cultures. Danish and American are in fact both considered individualist cultures. Interesting differences may arise when looking at data from a collectivist one, for example Japanese.

Finally, our study focuses on the recognition of emotions in static pictures. A much more complex, but certainly necessary domain in which emotions should be studied experimentally is that of videos, in which the understanding of emotions happens through the perception of multimodal expressions – facial expressions and speech.

Acknowledgements

We would like to thank the anonymous reviewers for their useful comments. Furthermore, we would like to thank all the participants who agreed to volunteer for our study.

References

Martin G. Beaupré and Ursula Hess. 2005. Cross-cultural emotion recognition among canadian ethnic groups. *Journal of Cross-Cultural Psychology*, 36(3):355–370.

Martin G. Beaupré and Ursula Hess. 2006. An ingroup advantage for confidence in emotion recognition judgments: The moderating effect of familiarity with the expressions of outgroup members. *Personality and Social Psychology Bulletin*, 32(1):16–26.

Michael Biehl, David Matsumoto, Paul Ekman, Valerie Hearn, Karl Heider, Tsutomu Kudoh, and Veronica Ton. 1997. Matsumoto and ekman's japanese and caucasian facial expressions of emotion (jacfee): Reliability data and cross-national differences. *Journal of Nonverbal Behavior*, 21(1):3–21.

Andrew J. Calder, Jill Keane, Tom Manly, Reiner Sprengelmeyer, Sophie Scott, Ian Nimmo-Smith, and Andrew W. Young. 2003. Facial expression recognition across the adult life span. *Neuropsychologia*, 41(2):195–202.

Charles Darwin, Paul Ekman, and Phillip Prodger. 1998. *The expression of the emotions in man and animals*. Oxford University Press, USA.

Paul Ekman and Wallace V. Friesen. 1978. *Manual for the facial action coding system*. Consulting Psychologists Press.

Paul Ekman, Wallace V. Friesen, Maureen O'Sullivan, Anthony Chan, Irene Diacoyanni-Tarlatzis, Karl Heider, Rainer Krause, William Ayhan LeCompte, Tom Pitcairn, Pio E. Ricci-Bitti, et al. 1987. Universals and cultural differences in the judgments of facial expressions of emotion. *Journal of personality and social psychology*, 53(4):712.

Paul Ekman. 1994. Strong evidence for universals in facial expressions: a reply to russell's mistaken critique.

Hillary Anger Elfenbein and Nalini Ambady. 2003. Universals and cultural differences in recognizing emotions. *Current Directions in Psychological Science*, 12(5):159–164.

Richard A Fabes and Carol Lynn Martin. 1991. Gender and age stereotypes of emotionality. *Personality and social psychology bulletin*, 17(5):532–540.

Judith A. Hall and David Matsumoto. 2004. Gender differences in judgments of multiple emotions from facial expressions. *Emotion*, 4(2):201.

Jaimie Arona Krems, Steven L. Neuberg, Gabrielle Filip-Crawford, and Douglas T. Kenrick. 2015. Is she angry?(sexually desirable) women see anger on female faces. *Psychological science*, 26(11):1655–1663.

Aleix Martinez and Shichuan Du. 2012. A model of the perception of facial expressions of emotion by humans: Research overview and perspectives. *The Journal of Machine Learning Research*, 13(1):1589–1608.

Sebastiaan Mathôt, Daniel Schreij, and Jan Theeuwes. 2012. Opensesame: An open-source, graphical experiment builder for the social sciences. *Behavior research methods*, 44(2):314–324.

David Matsumoto and Paul Ekman. 1989. American-japanese cultural differences in intensity ratings of facial expressions of emotion. *Motivation and Emotion*, 13(2):143–157.

David Matsumoto, Theodora Consolacion, Hiroshi Yamada, Ryuta Suzuki, Brenda Franklin, Sunita Paul, Rebecca Ray, and Hideko Uchida. 2002. American-japanese cultural differences in judgements of emotional expressions of different intensities. *Cognition & Emotion*, 16(6):721–747.

David Matsumoto. 1991. Cultural influences on facial expressions of emotion. *Southern Journal of Communication*, 56(2):128–137.

David Matsumoto. 2005. Scalar ratings of contempt expressions. *Journal of Nonverbal Behavior*, 29(2):91–104.

Aire Mill, Jüri Allik, Anu Realo, and Raivo Valk. 2009. Age-related differences in emotion recognition ability: a cross-sectional study. *Emotion*, 9(5):619.

E. Ashby Plant, Janet Shibley Hyde, Dacher Keltner, and Patricia G. Devine. 2000. The gender stereotyping of emotions. *Psychology of Women Quarterly*, 24(1):81–92.

James A. Russell. 1994. Is there universal recognition of emotion from facial expressions? a review of the cross-cultural studies. *Psychological bulletin*, 115(1):102.

Fraser W Smith and Philippe G Schyns. 2009. Smile through your fear and sadness transmitting and identifying facial expression signals over a range of viewing distances. *Psychological Science*, 20(10):1202–1208.

Silvan S. Tomkins and Robert McCarter. 1964. What and where are the primary affects? some evidence for a theory. *Perceptual and motor skills*, 18(1):119–158.

Nim Tottenham, James W Tanaka, Andrew C. Leon, Thomas McCarry, Marcella Nurse, Todd A. Hare, David J. Marcus, Alissa Westerlund, BJ Casey, and Charles Nelson. 2009. The nimstim set of facial expressions: judgments from untrained research participants. *Psychiatry research*, 168(3):242–249.

A Recurrent and Compositional Model for Personality Trait Recognition from Short Texts

Fei Liu♠*, Julien Perez♡ and Scott Nowson♣*
♠The University of Melbourne, Victoria, Australia
♡Xerox Research Centre Europe, Grenoble, France
♣Accenture Centre for Innovation, Dublin, Ireland
fliu3@student.unimelb.edu.au julien.perez@xrce.xerox.com
scott.nowson@accenture.com

Abstract

Many methods have been used to recognise author personality traits from text, typically combining linguistic feature engineering with shallow learning models, e.g. linear regression or Support Vector Machines. This work uses deep-learning-based models and atomic features of text, the characters, to build hierarchical, vectorial word and sentence representations for trait inference. This method, applied to a corpus of tweets, shows state-of-the-art performance across five traits compared with prior work. The results, supported by preliminary visualisation work, are encouraging for the ability to detect complex human traits.

1 Introduction

Techniques falling under the umbrella of "deep-learning" are increasingly commonplace in the space of Natural Language Processing (NLP) (Manning, 2016). Such methods have been applied to a number of tasks from part-of-speech-tagging (Ling et al., 2015) to sentiment analysis (Socher et al., 2013). Essentially, each of these tasks is concerned with learning representations of language at different levels. The work we outline here is no different in essence, though we choose perhaps the highest level of representation – that of the author of a given text rather than the text itself. This task, modelling people from their language, is one built on the long-standing foundation that language use is known to be influenced by sociodemographic characteristics such as gender and personality (Tannen, 1990; Pennebaker et al., 2003). The study of personality traits in particular is supported by the notion that they are considered temporally stable (Matthews et al., 2003), and thus our modelling ability is enriched by the acquisition of more data over time.

Computational personality recognition, and its broader applications, is becoming of increasing interest with workshops exploring the topic (Celli et al., 2014; Tkalčič et al., 2014). The addition of personality traits in the PAN Author Profiling challenge at CLEF in 2015 (Rangel et al., 2015) is further evidence. Much prior literature in this field has used some variation of enriched bag-of-words; e.g. the "Open vocabulary" approach (Schwartz et al., 2013). This is understandable as exploring the relationship between word use and traits has delivered significant insight into aspects of human behaviour (Pennebaker et al., 2003). Different levels of representation of language have been used such as syntactic, semantic, and higher-order such as the psychologically-derived lexica of the Linguistic Inquiry and Word Count (LIWC) tool (Pennebaker et al., 2015). One drawback of this bag-of-linguistic-features approach is that considerable effort can be spent on feature engineering. Another is an unspoken assumption that these features, like the traits to which they relate, are similarly stable: the same language features always indicate the same traits. However, this is not the case. As Nowson and Gill (2014) have shown, the relationship between language and personality is not consistent across all forms of communication and that it is more complex. In order to better explore this complexity in this work we propose a novel deep-learning feature-engineering-free modelisation of the problem of personality trait recognition. The task is framed

This work is licensed under a Creative Commons Attribution 4.0 International Licence. Licence details: http://creativecommons.org/licenses/by/4.0/

*Work carried out at Xerox Research Centre Europe

Proceedings of the Workshop on Computational Modeling of People's Opinions, Personality, and Emotions in Social Media,
pages 20–29, Osaka, Japan, December 12 2016.

as one of supervised sequence regression based on a joint atomic representation of the text: specifically on the character and word level. In this context, we are exploring short texts. Typically, classification of such texts tends to be particularly challenging for state-of-the-art BoW based approaches due, in part, to the noisy nature of such data (Han and Baldwin, 2011). To cope with this we propose a novel recurrent and compositional neural network architecture, capable of constructing representations at character, word and sentence level. The paper is structured as follows: after we consider previous approaches to the task of computational personality recognition, including those which have a deep-learning component, we describe our model. We report on two sets of experiments, the first of which demonstrates the effectiveness of the model in inferring personality for users, while the second reports on the short text level analysis. In both settings, the proposed model achieves state-of-the-art performance across five personality traits.

2 Related Work

Early work on computational personality recognition (Argamon et al., 2005; Nowson and Oberlander, 2006) used SVM-based approaches and manipulated lexical and grammatical feature sets. Today, according to the organisers (Rangel et al., 2015) "most" participants to the PAN 2015 Author Profiling task still use a combination of SVM and feature engineering. Data labelled with personality data is sparse (Nowson and Gill, 2014) and there has been more interest in reporting novel feature sets. In the PAN task alone[1] there were features used from multiple levels of representation on language. Surface forms were present in word, lemma and character n-grams, while syntactic features included POS tags and dependency relations. There were some efforts of feature curation, such as analysis of punctuation and emoticon use, along with the use of latent semantic analysis for topic modelling. Another popular feature set is the use of external resources such as LIWC (Pennebaker et al., 2015) which, in this context, represents over 20 years of psychology-based feature engineering. When applied to tweets, however, LIWC requires further cleaning of the data (Kreindler, 2016).

Deep-learning based approaches to personality trait recognition are, unsurprisingly given the typical size of data sets, relatively few. The model detailed in Kalghatgi et al. (2015) presents a neural network based approach to personality prediction of users. In this model, a Multilayer Perceptron (MLP) takes as input a collection of hand-crafted grammatical and social behavioral features from each user and assigns a label to each of the 5 personality traits. Unfortunately no evaluation of this work, nor details of the dataset, were provided. The work of Su et al. (2016) describes a Recurrent Neural Network (RNN) based system, exploiting the turn-taking of conversation for personality trait prediction. In their work, RNNs are employed to model the temporal evolution of dialog, taking as input LIWC-based and grammatical features. The output of the RNNs is then used for the prediction of personality trait scores of the participants of the conversations. It is worth noting that both works utilise hand-crafted features which rely heavily on domain expertise. Also the focus is on the prediction of trait scores on the user level given all the available text from a user. In contrast, not only can the approach presented in this paper infer the personality of a user given a collection of short texts, it is also flexible to predict trait scores from a single short text, arguably a more challenging task considering the limited amount of information.

The model we present in Section 3.2 is inspired by Ling et al. (2015), who proposed a character-level word representation learning model under the assumption that character sequences are syntactically and semantically informative of the words they compose. Based on a widely used RNN named long short-term memory network (LSTM) (Hochreiter and Schmidhuber, 1997), the model learns the embeddings of characters and how they can be used to construct words. Inspired by this, Yang et al. (2016) introduced Hierarchical Attention Networks where the representation of a document is hierarchically built up. The work of (Ling et al., 2015) provides a way to construct words from their constituent characters (Character to Word, C2W) while Yang et al. (2016) describe a hierarchical approach to building representations of documents from words to sentences, and eventually to documents (Word to Sentence to Document, W2S2D). In this work, inspired by the above works, we present a hierarchical model situated between the above two models, connecting characters, words and sentences, and ultimately personality traits

---

[1] Due to space consideration we are unable to cite the individual works.

(Character to Word to Sentence for Personality Trait, `C2W2S4PT`).

3   Proposed Model

To motivate our methodology, we review a commonly-used approach to representing sentences and discuss some of its limitations and motivation. Then, we propose the use of a compositional model to tackle the identified problems.

3.1   Current Issues and Motivation

One classical approach for applying deep learning models to NLP problems involves word lookup tables where words are typically represented by dense real-valued vectors in a low-dimensional space (Socher et al., 2013). In order to obtain a sensible set of embeddings, a common practice is to train on a large corpus in an unsupervised fashion, e.g. Word2Vec (Mikolov et al., 2013). Despite the success in capturing syntactic and semantic information with such word vectors, there are two practical problems with such an approach (Ling et al., 2015). First, due to the flexibility of language, previously unseen words are bound to occur regardless of how large the unsupervised training corpus is. The problem is particularly serious for text extracted from social media platforms such as Twitter and Facebook due to the noisy nature of user-generated text – e.g. typos, ad hoc acronyms and abbreviations, phonetic substitutions, and even meaningless strings (Han and Baldwin, 2011). Second, the number of parameters for a model to learn is overwhelmingly large. Assume each word is represented by a vector of d dimensions, the total size of the word lookup table is $d \times |V|$ where $|V|$ is the size of the vocabulary which tends to scale to the order of hundreds and thousands. Again, this problem is even more pronounced in noisier domain such as short text generated by online users. To address the above issues, we adopt a compositional character to word model described in the next section.

From the personality perspective, character-based features have been widely adopted in trait inference, such as character n-grams(González-Gallardo et al., 2015; Sulea and Dichiu, 2015), emoticons (Nowson et al., 2015; Palomino-Garibay et al., 2015), and character flooding (Nowson et al., 2015; Giménez et al., 2015). Motivated by this and the issues identified above, we propose in the next section a compositional model that operates hierarchically at the character, word and sentence level, capable of harnessing personality-sensitive signals buried as deep as the character level.

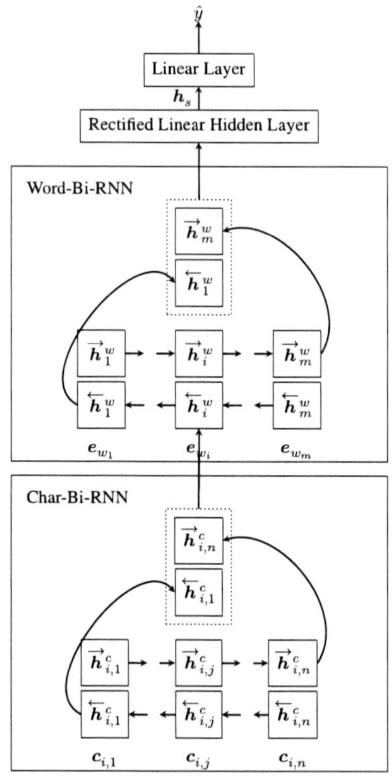

Figure 1: Illustration of the `C2W2S4PT` model. Dotted boxes indicate concatenation.

3.2   Character to Word to Sentence for Personality Traits

To address the problems identified in Section 3.1, we propose to extend the compositional character to word model first introduced by Ling et al. (2015) wherein the representation of each word is constructed, via a character-level bi-directional RNN (Char-Bi-RNN), from its constituent characters. The constructed word vectors are then fed to another layer of word-level Bi-RNN (Word-Bi-RNN) and a sentence is represented by the concatenation of the last and first hidden states of the forward and backward Word-RNNs respectively. Eventually, a feedforward neural network takes as input the representation of a sentence and returns a scalar as the prediction for a specific personality trait. Thus, we name the model `C2W2S4PT` (Character to Word to Sentence for Personality Traits) which is illustrated in Figure 1. Specifically, suppose we have a sentence s consisting of a sequence of words $\{w_1, w_2, \ldots, w_i, \ldots, w_m\}$.

We define a function $\mathrm{c}(w_i, j)$ which takes as input a word w_i, together with an index j and returns the one-hot vector representation of the jth character of the word w_i. Then, to get the embedding $c_{i,j}$ of the character, we transform $\mathrm{c}(w_i, j)$ by: $c_{i,j} = E_c \mathrm{c}(w_i, j)$ where $E_c \in \mathbb{R}^{d \times |C|}$ and $|C|$ is the size of the character vocabulary. Next, in order to construct the representation of word w_i, the sequence of character embeddings $\{c_{i,1}, \ldots, c_{i,n}\}$ is taken as input to the Char-Bi-RNN (assuming w_i is comprised of n characters). In this work, we employ gated recurrent unit (GRU) (Cho et al., 2014) as the recurrent unit in the Bi-RNNs, given that recent studies indicate that GRU achieves comparable, if not better, results to LSTM (Chung et al., 2014).[2] Concretely, the forward pass of the Char-Bi-RNN is carried out using the following:

$$\overrightarrow{z}^{c}_{i,j} = \sigma(\overrightarrow{W}^{c}_{z} c_{i,j} + \overrightarrow{U}^{c}_{hz} \overrightarrow{h}^{c}_{i,j-1} + \overrightarrow{b}^{c}_{z}) \tag{1}$$

$$\overrightarrow{r}^{c}_{i,j} = \sigma(\overrightarrow{W}^{c}_{r} c_{i,j} + \overrightarrow{U}^{c}_{hr} \overrightarrow{h}^{c}_{i,j-1} + \overrightarrow{b}^{c}_{r}) \tag{2}$$

$$\overrightarrow{\tilde{h}}^{c}_{i,j} = \tanh(\overrightarrow{W}^{c}_{h} c_{i,j} + \overrightarrow{r}^{c}_{i,j} \odot \overrightarrow{U}^{c}_{hh} \overrightarrow{h}^{c}_{i,j-1} + \overrightarrow{b}^{c}_{h}) \tag{3}$$

$$\overrightarrow{h}^{c}_{i,j} = \overrightarrow{z}^{c}_{i,j} \odot \overrightarrow{h}^{c}_{i,j-1} + (1 - \overrightarrow{z}^{c}_{i,j}) \odot \overrightarrow{\tilde{h}}^{c}_{i,j} \tag{4}$$

where $\odot$ is the element-wise product, $\overrightarrow{W}^{c}_{z}, \overrightarrow{W}^{c}_{r}, \overrightarrow{W}^{c}_{h}, \overrightarrow{U}^{c}_{hz}, \overrightarrow{U}^{c}_{hr}, \overrightarrow{U}^{c}_{hh}$ are the parameters for the model to learn, and $\overrightarrow{b}^{c}_{z}, \overrightarrow{b}^{c}_{r}, \overrightarrow{b}^{c}_{h}$ the bias terms. The backward pass, the hidden state of which is symbolised by $\overleftarrow{h}^{c}_{i,j}$, is performed similarly, although with a different set of GRU weight matrices and bias terms. It should be noted that both the forward and backward Char-RNN share the same character embeddings. Ultimately, w_i is represented by the concatenation of the last and first hidden states of the forward and backward Char-RNNs: $e_{w_i} = [\overrightarrow{h}^{c}_{i,n}; \overleftarrow{h}^{c}_{i,1}]^{\top}$. Once all the word representations e_{w_i} for $i \in [1, n]$ have been constructed from their constituent characters, they are then processed by the Word-Bi-RNN, similar to Char-Bi-RNN but on word level with word rather than character embeddings:

$$\overrightarrow{z}^{w}_{i} = \sigma(\overrightarrow{W}^{w}_{z} e_{w_i} + \overrightarrow{U}^{w}_{hz} \overrightarrow{h}^{w}_{i-1} + \overrightarrow{b}^{w}_{z}) \tag{5}$$

$$\overrightarrow{r}^{w}_{i} = \sigma(\overrightarrow{W}^{w}_{r} e_{w_i} + \overrightarrow{U}^{w}_{hr} \overrightarrow{h}^{w}_{i-1} + \overrightarrow{b}^{w}_{r}) \tag{6}$$

$$\overrightarrow{\tilde{h}}^{w}_{i} = \tanh(\overrightarrow{W}^{w}_{h} e_{w_i} + \overrightarrow{r}^{w}_{i} \odot \overrightarrow{U}^{w}_{hh} \overrightarrow{h}^{w}_{i-1} + \overrightarrow{b}^{w}_{h}) \tag{7}$$

$$\overrightarrow{h}^{w}_{i} = \overrightarrow{z}^{w}_{i} \odot \overrightarrow{h}^{w}_{i-1} + (1 - \overrightarrow{z}^{w}_{i}) \odot \overrightarrow{\tilde{h}}^{w}_{i} \tag{8}$$

where $\overrightarrow{W}^{w}_{z}, \overrightarrow{W}^{w}_{r}, \overrightarrow{W}^{w}_{h}, \overrightarrow{U}^{w}_{hz}, \overrightarrow{U}^{w}_{hr}, \overrightarrow{U}^{w}_{hh}$ are the parameters for the model to learn, and $\overrightarrow{b}^{w}_{z}, \overrightarrow{b}^{w}_{wr}, \overrightarrow{b}^{w}_{h}$ the bias terms. In a similar fashion to how a word is represented, we construct the sentence embedding by concatenation: $e_s = [\overrightarrow{h}^{w}_{m}; \overleftarrow{h}^{w}_{1}]^{\top}$. Lastly, to estimate the score for a particular personality trait, we top the Word-Bi-RNN with an MLP which takes as input the sentence embedding e_s and returns the estimated score $\hat{y}_s$: $h_s = \text{ReLU}(W_{eh} e_s + b_h)$ and then $\hat{y}_s = W_{hy} h_s + b_y$ where ReLU is the REctified Linear Unit defined as $\text{ReLU}(x) = \max(0, x)$, W_{eh}, W_{hy} the parameters for the model to learn, b_h, b_y the bias terms, and h_s the hidden representation of the MLP. All the components in the model are jointly trained with *mean square error* being the objective function: $L(\theta) = \frac{1}{n} \sum_{i=1}^{n} (y_{s_i} - \hat{y}_{s_i})^2$ where y_{s_i} is the ground truth personality score of sentence s_i and θ the collection of all embedding and weight matrices and bias terms for the model to learn.

3.2.1 Multitask Learning

While the dimensions of personality in any single model are designed to be independent of one another, there are often strong correlations between traits (Matthews et al., 2003). Understanding that such correlations exist, we ask whether it is beneficial to train a model capable of simultaneously predicting multiple highly correlated personality traits. To support this, we report the Pearson correlations of our dataset (see section 4.1) in Table 1 where EXT, STA, AGR, CON and OPN are abbreviations

---

[2] We performed additional experiments which confirmed this finding. Therefore due to space considerations, we do not report results using LSTMs here.

	EXT	STA	AGR	CON	OPN
EXT		0.295 ***	0.257 **	0.216 **	0.057
STA	0.295 ***		0.351 ***	0.091	0.045
AGR	0.257 **	0.351 ***		0.035	0.039
CON	0.216 **	0.091	0.035		0.174 *
OPN	0.057	0.045	0.039	0.174 *	

Note: *** $p \leqslant 0.001$, ** $p \leqslant 0.01$, * $p \leqslant 0.05$

Table 1: Pearson correlations for the five personality traits

for Extroversion, Emotional Stability (the inverse of Neuroticism), Agreeableness, Conscientiousness and Openness respectively. This gives us confidence that there are at least linear relationships between individual traits which could potentially be exploited by multitask learning (Caruana, 1997). Inspired by this and building on top of the compositional model, we propose a multitask learning model which shares the Char-Bi-RNN and Word-Bi-RNN components but has personality-trait-specific final layers, to predict multiple correlated personality traits simultaneously. Concretely, while Char-Bi-RNN and Word-Bi-RNN remain the same as described in Section 3.2, we utilise a collection of personality-trait-specific final layers: $h_{p,s} = \text{ReLU}(W_{peh}e_s + b_{ph})$ and then $\hat{y}_{p,s} = W_{phy}h_{p,s} + b_{py}$ where $p \in \{\text{EXT, STA, AGR, CON, OPN}\}$, $W_{peh}, W_{phy}, b_{ph}, b_{py}$ are the trait-specific weight matrices and bias terms, and loss functions: $L_p(\theta_p) = \frac{1}{n}\sum_{i=1}^{n}(y_{p,s_i} - \hat{y}_{p,s_i})^2$ where $L_p(\theta_p)$ is the loss function for a specific personality trait p. Note that, apart from the Bi-RNN embedding and weight matrices and bias terms, θ_p now also includes the trait-specific weight matrices W_{peh}, W_{phy} and bias terms b_{ph}, b_{py}. The model is then jointly trained using the sum of the loss functions: $L(\theta) = \sum_{p \in P} L_p(\theta_p)$ where P is a collection of (correlated) personality traits and $\theta = \bigcup_{p \in P} \theta_p$.

4 Experiments and Results

We report two sets of experiments: the first a comparison at the user level between our feature-engineering-free approach and current state-of-the-art models which rely on linguistic features; the second designed to evaluate the performance of the proposed model against other feature-engineering-free approaches on individual short texts. We show that in both settings, i.e., against models with or without feature engineering, our proposed model achieves better results across all personality traits.

4.1 Dataset

We use the English data from the PAN 2015 Author Profiling task dataset (Rangel et al., 2015), collected from Twitter and consisting of 14, 166 tweets and 152 users. For each user there is a set of tweets (average $n = 100$) and gold standard personality labels. The five trait labels – scores between -0.5 and 0.5 – are calculated following the author's self-assessment responses to the short Big 5 test, BFI-10 (Rammstedt and John, 2007) which is the most widely accepted and exploited scheme for personality recognition and has the most solid grounding in language (Poria et al., 2013).

In our experiments, each tweet is tokenised using Twokenizer (Owoputi et al., 2013), in order to preserve hashtag-preceded topics and user mentions. Unlike the majority of the language used in a tweet, URLs and mentions are used for their targets, and not their surface forms. Therefore each text is normalised by mapping these features to single characters (e.g., *@username* $\rightarrow$ @, *http://t.co/* $\rightarrow$ ^). Thus we limit the risk of modelling, say, character usage which was not directly influenced by the personality of the author.

4.2 Evaluation Method

Due to the unavailability of the test corpus – withheld by the PAN 2015 organisers – we compare the k-fold cross-validation performance ($k = 5$ or 10) on the available dataset. Performance is measured using Root Mean Square Error (RMSE) on either the tweet level or user level depending on the granularity of the task: $RMSE_{tweet} = \sqrt{\frac{\sum_{i=1}^{T}(y_{s_i} - \hat{y}_{s_i})^2}{T}}$ and $RMSE_{user} = \sqrt{\frac{\sum_{i=1}^{U}(y_{user_i} - \hat{y}_{user_i})^2}{U}}$ where T and U are the total numbers of tweets and users in the corpus, y_{s_i} and $\hat{y}_{s_i}$ the true and estimated personality trait score of the ith tweet, similarly y_{user_i} and $\hat{y}_{user_i}$ are their user-level counterparts. Each tweet in the dataset inherits the same five trait scores as assigned to the author from whom they were drawn. $\hat{y}_{user_i} = \frac{1}{T_i} \sum_{j=1}^{T_i} \hat{y}_{s_j}$ where T_i refers to the total number of tweets of $user_i$. In Section 4.3 and 4.4, we present the results measured at the user and tweet level using $RMSE_{user}$ and $RMSE_{tweet}$ respectively. It is important to note that, to enable direct comparison, we use exactly the same dataset and evaluation metric $RMSE_{user}$ as in the works of (Sulea and Dichiu, 2015; Mirkin et al., 2015; Nowson et al., 2015).

4.3 Personality Trait Prediction at User Level

We test the proposed models on the dataset described in Section 4.1 and train our model to predict the personality trait scores based purely on the text with no additional features supplied. To demonstrate the effectiveness of the proposed model, we evaluate the performance on the user level against models incorporating linguistic and psychologically motivated features. This allows us to directly compare the performance of current state-of-the-art models and C2W2S4PT. For 5-fold cross-validation, we compare to the tied-highest ranked (under evaluation conditions) of the PAN 2015 submissions (Sulea and Dichiu, 2015).[3] For 10-fold cross-validation, we similarly choose the work by ranking and metric reporting (Nowson et al., 2005). As here, these works predicted scores on text level, and averaged for each user. Therefore, we include subsequent work which reports results on concatenated tweets – a single document per user (Mirkin et al., 2015). We also show the most straightforward baseline Average Baseline which assigns the average of all the scores to each user. C2W2S4PT is trained with Adam (Kingma and Ba, 2014) and hyper-parameters: $\boldsymbol{E}_c \in \mathbb{R}^{50 \times |C|}$, $\overrightarrow{\boldsymbol{h}}_{i,j}^{\,c}$ and $\overleftarrow{\boldsymbol{h}}_{i,j}^{\,c} \in \mathbb{R}^{256}$, $\overrightarrow{\boldsymbol{h}}_i^{\,w}$ and $\overleftarrow{\boldsymbol{h}}_i^{\,w} \in \mathbb{R}^{256}$, $\boldsymbol{W}_{eh} \in \mathbb{R}^{512 \times 256}$, $\boldsymbol{b}_h \in \mathbb{R}^{256}$, $\boldsymbol{W}_{hy} \in \mathbb{R}^{256 \times 1}$, $b_y \in \mathbb{R}$, dropout rate to the embedding output: 0.5, batch size: 32. Training is performed until 100 epochs are reached. The $RMSE_{user}$ results are shown in Table 2.

RNN-based models outperform the previous state of the art In the 5-fold cross-validation group, C2W2S4PT - Multitask All is superior to the baselines, achieving better performance in three traits (tying the remaining traits). This is worth noting considering the model is trained jointly on all five traits. Even greater improvement is attained by training on fewer personality traits with state-of-the-art performance achieved mostly by C2W2S4PT. In terms of the performance measured by 10-fold cross-validation, the dominance of the RNN-based models is even more pronounced with C2W2S4PT outperforming the two selected baseline systems across all personality traits. Overall, in comparison to the previous state-of-the-art models in both groups, C2W2S4PT not only outperforms them – by a significant margin in the case of 10-fold cross-validation – but it also achieves so without any hand-crafted features, underlining the soundness of the approach.

4.4 Personality Trait Prediction at Single Tweet Level

Although user-level evaluation is the common practice, we choose tweet-level performance to study the models' capabilities to infer personality at a lower granularity level. To support our evaluation, a number of baselines were created. To facilitate fair comparison, the only feature used is the surface form of the text. Average Baseline, the most straightforward baseline, assigns the average of all the scores to each tweet. Also, two BoW systems, namely, Random Forest and SVM Regression, have been implemented for comparison. For these two BoW-based baseline systems, we perform grid search to find the best hyper-parameter configuration. For SVM Regression, the hyper-parameters include: kernel $\in \{\text{linear}, \text{rbf}\}$ and $C \in \{0.01, 0.1, 1.0, 10.0\}$ whereas for Random Forest, the number of trees is chosen from the set $\{10, 50, 100, 500, 1000\}$.

Additionally, two simpler RNN-based models, namely Bi-GRU-Char and Bi-GRU-Word, which only work on character and word level respectively but share the same structure of the final MLP classifier ($\boldsymbol{h}_s$ and $\hat{y}_s$), have also been presented in contrast to the more sophisticated character to word composi-

---

[3] Cross-validation $RMSE_{user}$ performance is not reported for the other top system (Álvarez-Carmona et al., 2015).

k	Model	EXT	STA	AGR	CON	OPN
—	Average Baseline	0.166	0.223	0.158	0.151	0.146
5	Sulea and Dichiu (2015)	0.136	0.183	0.141	0.131	0.119
	C2W2S4PT	**0.131**	**0.171**	**0.140**	**0.124**	**0.109**
	C2W2S4PT - Multitask STA&AGR	✕	0.172	0.140	✕	✕
	C2W2S4PT - Multitask AGR&CON	✕	✕	**0.138**	**0.124**	✕
	C2W2S4PT - Multitask All	0.136	0.177	0.141	0.128	0.117
10	Mirkin et al. (2015)	0.171	0.223	0.173	0.144	0.146
	Nowson et al. (2015)	0.153	0.197	0.154	0.144	0.132
	C2W2S4PT	**0.130**	**0.167**	**0.137**	**0.122**	**0.109**
	C2W2S4PT - Multitask STA&AGR	✕	0.168	0.140	✕	✕
	C2W2S4PT - Multitask AGR&CON	✕	✕	0.138	0.123	✕
	C2W2S4PT - Multitask All	0.136	0.175	0.140	0.127	0.115

Table 2: $RMSE_{user}$ across five traits. **Bold** highlights best performance. ✕ indicates N/A.

Model	EXT	STA	AGR	CON	OPN
Average Baseline	0.163	0.222	0.157	0.150	0.147
SVM Regression	0.148	0.196	0.148	0.140	0.131
Random Forest	0.144	0.192	**0.146**	0.138	0.132
Bi-GRU-Char	0.150	0.202	0.152	0.143	0.137
Bi-GRU-Word	0.147	0.200	**0.146**	0.138	0.130
C2W2S4PT	**0.142**	**0.188**	0.147	**0.136**	**0.127**
C2W2S4PT - Multitask STA&AGR	✕	**0.189**	0.146	✕	✕
C2W2S4PT - Multitask AGR&CON	✕	✕	0.146	0.136	✕
C2W2S4PT - Multitask All	**0.142**	0.191	**0.146**	0.137	0.127

Table 3: $RMSE_{tweet}$ across five traits level. **Bold** highlights best performance. ✕ indicates N/A.

tional model C2W2S4PT. For training, C2W2S4PT inherits the same hyper-parameter configuration as described in Section 4.3. For Bi-GRU-Char and Bi-GRU-Word, we set the character and word embedding size to 50 and 256 respectively. Due to time constrains, we did not perform hyper-parameter fine-tuning for the RNN-based models and C2W2S4PT. The $RMSE_{tweet}$ of each effort, measured by 10-fold stratified cross-validation, is shown in Table 3.

C2W2S4PT achieves comparable or better performance with SVM Regression and Random Forest C2W2S4PT is state of the art in almost every trait with the exception of AGR. This demonstrates that C2W2S4PT generates at least reasonably comparable performance with SVM Regression and Random Forest in the feature-engineering-free setting on the tweet level and it does so without exhaustive hyper-parameter fine-tuning.

C2W2S4PT outperforms the RNN-based models This success can be attributed to the model's capability of coping with arbitrary words while not forgetting information due to excessive lengths as can arise from representing a text as a sequence of characters. Also, given that C2W2S4PT does not need to maintain a large vocabulary embedding matrix as in Bi-GRU-Word, there are much fewer parameters for the model to learn (Ling et al., 2015), making it less prone to overfitting.

Multitask learning provides little benefits to performance Surprisingly, the model jointly trained on the weakest correlated pair, namely AGR&CON, achieves even better results than the one trained on the strongest correlated pair (STA&AGR). In fact, despite the noise introduced by training on non-correlated personality traits, there is little impact on the performance of the multitask-learning models and the model jointly trained on all 5 personality traits generates equally competitive performance.

4.5 Visualisation

To further investigate into the learned representations and features, we choose the `C2W2S4PT` model trained on a single personality trait and visualise the sentences with the help of PCA (Tipping and Bishop, 1999). We also experimented with t-SNE (Van der Maaten and Hinton, 2008) but it did not produce an interpretable plot. 100 tweets have been randomly selected (50 tweets each from either end of the EXT spectrum) with their representations constructed by the model. Figure 2 shows the scatter plot of the representations of the sentences reduced to a 2D space by PCA for the trait of Extraversion (EXT), selected as it is the most commonly studied and well understood trait. The figure shows clusters of both positive and negative Extraversion, though the former intersect the latter. For discussion we consider three examples as highlighted in Figure 2:

- POS7: *"@username: Feeling like you're not good enough is probably the worst thing to feel."*
- NEG3: *"Being good ain't enough lately."*
- POS20: *"o.O Lovely."*

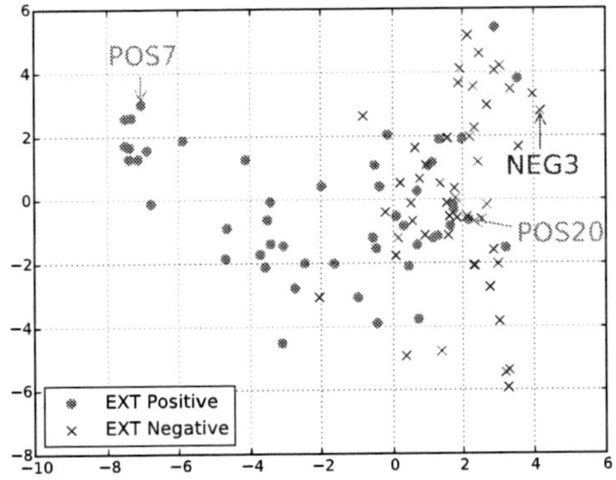

Figure 2: Scatter plot of sentence representations processed by PCA.

The first two examples (POS7 and NEG3) are drawn from largely distinct areas of the distribution. In essence the semantics of the short texts are the same. However, they both show linguistic attributes commonly understood to relate to Extraversion (Gill and Oberlander, 2002): POS7 is longer and, with the use of the second person pronoun, is more inclusive of others; NEG3 on the other hand is shorter and self-focused, aspects indicative of Introversion. The third sentence, POS20, is a statement from an Extravert which appears to map to an Introvert space. Indeed, while short, the use of "Eastern" style, non-rotated emoticons (such as *o.O*) has also been shown to relate to Introversion on social media (Schwartz et al., 2013). This is perhaps not the venue to consider the implications of this further, although one explanation might be that the model has uncovered a flexibility often associated with Ambiverts (Grant, 2013). However, it is important to consider that the model is indeed capturing well-understood dimensions of language yet with no feature engineering.

5 Discussion and Future Work

Overall, the results in the paper support our methodology: `C2W2S4PT` not only provides state-of-the-art results on the user level, but also performs reasonably well when adapted to the short text level compared to other widely used models in the feature-engineering-free setting. However, interpretation of the performance of the multitask experiments is less straightforward. At text level (as per Table 3) the results are almost identical whether modelling traits individually, all together, or with differing prior relationships. Perhaps it is the case that simple linear correlations do not adequately explain the relationships between traits when mediated via language use. It could also be that our model captures a more complex, non-linear relationship or some notion of latent variables. It is clear that this requires further investigation, though this will likely require an additional dataset, as with only 150 authors, the distribution of scores is somewhat limited. One advantage of our approach which requires validation is that lack of feature engineering should support language independence. Preliminary tests on the Spanish data from the PAN 2015 Author Profiling dataset show promising results. To further examine this property of the proposed model, we plan to adopt TwiSty (Verhoeven et al., 2016), a recently introduced corpus consisting of 6 languages and labelled with MBTI type indicators (Myers and Myers, 2010). However, due to time constraints, we leave this exercise for future work.

References

Miguel A. Álvarez-Carmona, A. Pastor López-Monroy, Manuel Montes y Gómez, Luis Villaseñor-Pineda, and Hugo Jair Escalante. 2015. INAOE's participation at PAN'15: Author Profiling task—Notebook for PAN at CLEF 2015. In *Working Notes Papers of the CLEF 2015 Evaluation Labs*.

Shlomo Argamon, Sushant Dhawle, Moshe Koppel, and James W. Pennebaker. 2005. Lexical predictors of personality type. In *Proceedings of the 2005 Joint Annual Meeting of the Interface and the Classification Society of North America*.

Rich Caruana. 1997. Multitask learning. *Machine Learning*, 28(1):41–75.

Fabio Celli, Bruno Lepri, Joan-Isaac Biel, Daniel Gatica-Perez, Giuseppe Riccardi, and Fabio Pianesi. 2014. The workshop on computational personality recognition 2014. In *Proc. ACMMM*, pages 1245–1246, Orlando, USA.

Kyunghyun Cho, Bart Van Merriënboer, Dzmitry Bahdanau, and Yoshua Bengio. 2014. On the properties of neural machine translation: Encoder-decoder approaches. *arXiv preprint arXiv:1409.1259*.

Junyoung Chung, Caglar Gulcehre, KyungHyun Cho, and Yoshua Bengio. 2014. Empirical evaluation of gated recurrent neural networks on sequence modeling. *arXiv preprint arXiv:1412.3555*.

Alastair J. Gill and Jon Oberlander. 2002. Taking Care of the Linguistic Features of Extraversion. In *Proc. CogSci*, pages 363–368, Fairfax, USA.

Maite Giménez, Delia Irazú Hernández, and Ferran Pla. 2015. Segmenting Target Audiences: Automatic Author Profiling Using Tweets—Notebook for PAN at CLEF 2015. In *Working Notes Papers of the CLEF 2015 Evaluation Labs*.

Carlos E. González-Gallardo, Azucena Montes, Gerardo Sierra, J. Antonio Núñez-Juárez, Adolfo Jonathan Salinas-López, and Juan Ek. 2015. Tweets Classification Using Corpus Dependent Tags, Character and POS N-grams—Notebook for PAN at CLEF 2015. In *Working Notes Papers of the CLEF 2015 Evaluation Labs*.

Adam M. Grant. 2013. Rethinking the extraverted sales ideal: The ambivert advantage. *Psychological Science 24(6)*, 24(6):1024–1030.

Bo Han and Timothy Baldwin. 2011. Lexical normalisation of short text messages: Makn sens a #twitter. In *Proc. ACL*, pages 368–378, Portland, Oregon, USA.

Sepp Hochreiter and Jürgen Schmidhuber. 1997. Long short-term memory. *Neural computation*, 9(8):1735–1780.

Mayuri Pundlik Kalghatgi, Manjula Ramannavar, and Nandini S. Sidnal. 2015. A neural network approach to personality prediction based on the big-five model. *International Journal of Innovative Research in Advanced Engineering (IJIRAE)*, 2(8):56–63.

Diederik Kingma and Jimmy Ba. 2014. Adam: A method for stochastic optimization. *arXiv preprint arXiv:1412.6980*.

Jon Kreindler. 2016. Twitter psychology analyzer api and sample code. `http://www.receptiviti.ai/blog/twitter-psychology-analyzer-api-and-sample-code/`. Accessed: 2016-09-30.

Wang Ling, Chris Dyer, Alan W Black, Isabel Trancoso, Ramon Fermandez, Silvio Amir, Luis Marujo, and Tiago Luis. 2015. Finding function in form: Compositional character models for open vocabulary word representation. In *Proc. EMNLP*, pages 1520–1530, Lisbon, Portugal.

Christopher D Manning. 2016. Computational linguistics and deep learning. *Computational Linguistics*.

Gerald Matthews, Ian J. Deary, and Martha C. Whiteman. 2003. *Personality Traits*. Cambridge University Press, second edition. Cambridge Books Online.

Tomas Mikolov, Ilya Sutskever, Kai Chen, Greg Corrado, and Jeff Dean. 2013. Distributed representations of words and phrases and their compositionality. In *Proc. NIPS*, pages 3111–3119, Stateline, USA.

Shachar Mirkin, Scott Nowson, Caroline Brun, and Julien Perez. 2015. Motivating personality-aware machine translation. In *Proc. EMNLP*, pages 1102–1108, Lisbon, Portugal.

Isabel Myers and Peter Myers. 2010. *Gifts differing: Understanding personality type*. Nicholas Brealey Publishing.

Scott Nowson and Alastair J. Gill. 2014. Look! Who's Talking? Projection of Extraversion Across Different Social Contexts. In *Proceedings of WCPR14, Workshop on Computational Personality Recognition at ACMM (22nd ACM International Conference on Multimedia)*.

Scott Nowson and Jon Oberlander. 2006. The Identity of Bloggers: Openness and gender in personal weblogs. In *AAAI Spring Symposium, Computational Approaches to Analysing Weblogs*.

Scott Nowson, Jon Oberlander, and Alastair J. Gill. 2005. Weblogs, genres and individual differences. In *Proc. CogSci*, pages 1666–1671.

Scott Nowson, Julien Perez, Caroline Brun, Shachar Mirkin, and Claude Roux. 2015. XRCE Personal Language Analytics Engine for Multilingual Author Profiling. In *Working Notes Papers of the CLEF 2015 Evaluation Labs*.

Olutobi Owoputi, Brendan O'Connor, Chris Dyer, Kevin Gimpel, Nathan Schneider, and Noah A. Smith. 2013. Improved part-of-speech tagging for online conversational text with word clusters. In *Proc. NAACL*, pages 380–390, Atlanta, USA.

Alonso Palomino-Garibay, Adolfo T. Camacho-González, Ricardo A. Fierro-Villaneda, Irazú Hernández-Farias, Davide Buscaldi, and Ivan V. Meza-Ruiz. 2015. A Random Forest Approach for Authorship Profiling—Notebook for PAN at CLEF 2015. In *Working Notes Papers of the CLEF 2015 Evaluation Labs*.

James W Pennebaker, Kate G Niederhoffer, and Matthias R Mehl. 2003. Psychological aspects of natural language use: Our words, our selves. *Annual Review of Psychology*, 54:547–577.

J. W. Pennebaker, R. L. Boyd, K. Jordan, and K. Blackburn. 2015. The development and psychometric properties of LIWC2015.

Soujanya Poria, Alexandar Gelbukh, Basant Agarwal, Erik Cambria, and Newton Howard, 2013. *Common Sense Knowledge Based Personality Recognition from Text*, pages 484–496.

Beatrice Rammstedt and Oliver P. John. 2007. Measuring personality in one minute or less: A 10-item short version of the big five inventory in english and german. *Journal of Research in Personality*, 41(1):203–212.

Francisco Rangel, Fabio Celli, Paolo Rosso, Martin Potthast, Benno Stein, and Walter Daelemans. 2015. Overview of the 3rd Author Profiling Task at PAN 2015. In *Working Notes Papers of the CLEF 2015 Evaluation Labs*.

H Andrew Schwartz, Johannes C Eichstaedt, Margaret L Kern, Lukasz Dziurzynski, Stephanie M Ramones, Megha Agrawal, Achal Shah, Michal Kosinski, David Stillwell, Martin E P Seligman, and Lyle H Ungar. 2013. Personality, Gender, and Age in the Language of Social Media: The Open-Vocabulary Approach. *PLOS ONE*, 8(9).

Richard Socher, Alex Perelygin, Jean Y Wu, Jason Chuang, Christopher D Manning, Andrew Y Ng, and Christopher Potts Potts. 2013. Recursive deep models for semantic compositionality over a sentiment treebank. In *Proc. EMNLP*, Seattle, USA.

Ming-Hsiang Su, Chung-Hsien Wu, and Yu-Ting Zheng. 2016. Exploiting turn-taking temporal evolution for personality trait perception in dyadic conversations. *IEEE/ACM Transactions on Audio, Speech, and Language Processing*, 24(4):733–744.

Octavia-Maria Sulea and Daniel Dichiu. 2015. Automatic profiling of twitter users based on their tweets. In *Working Notes Papers of the CLEF 2015 Evaluation Labs*.

Deborah Tannen. 1990. *You Just Dont Understand: Women and Men in Conversation*. Harper Collins, New York.

Michael E Tipping and Christopher M Bishop. 1999. Probabilistic principal component analysis. *Journal of the Royal Statistical Society: Series B (Statistical Methodology)*, 61(3):611–622.

Marko Tkalčič, Berardina De Carolis, Marco de Gemmis, Ante Odić, and Andrej Košir. 2014. Preface: Empire 2014. In *Proceedings of the 2nd Workshop Emotions and Personality in Personalized Services (EMPIRE 2014)*. CEUR-WS.org, July.

Laurens Van der Maaten and Geoffrey Hinton. 2008. Visualizing data using t-sne. *Journal of Machine Learning Research*, 9(2579-2605):85.

Ben Verhoeven, Walter Daelemans, and Barbara Plank. 2016. TwiSty: a multilingual twitter stylometry corpus for gender and personality profiling. In *Proc. LREC*, pages 1632–1637, Portorož, Slovenia.

Zichao Yang, Diyi Yang, Chris Dyer, Xiaodong He, Alex Smola, and Eduard Hovy. 2016. Hierarchical attention networks for document classification. In *Proc. NAACL*, pages 1480–1489, San Diego, USA.

Distant supervision for emotion detection using Facebook reactions

Chris Pool
Anchormen, Groningen
The Netherlands
c.pool@anchormen.nl

Malvina Nissim
CLCG, University of Groningen
The Netherlands
m.nissim@rug.nl

Abstract

We exploit the Facebook reaction feature in a distant supervised fashion to train a support vector machine classifier for emotion detection, using several feature combinations and combining different Facebook pages. We test our models on existing benchmarks for emotion detection and show that *employing only information that is derived completely automatically*, thus without relying on any handcrafted lexicon as it's usually done, we can achieve competitive results. The results also show that there is large room for improvement, especially by gearing the collection of Facebook pages, with a view to the target domain.

1 Introduction

In the spirit of the brevity of social media's messages and reactions, people have got used to express feelings minimally and symbolically, as with hashtags on Twitter and Instagram. On Facebook, people tend to be more wordy, but posts normally receive more simple "likes" than longer comments. Since February 2016, Facebook users can express specific emotions in response to a post thanks to the newly introduced *reaction feature* (see Section 2), so that now a post can be wordlessly marked with an expression of say "joy" or "surprise" rather than a generic "like".

It has been observed that this new feature helps Facebook to know much more about their users and exploit this information for targeted advertising (Stinson, 2016), but interest in people's opinions and how they feel isn't limited to commercial reasons, as it invests social monitoring, too, including health care and education (Mohammad, 2016). However, emotions and opinions are not always expressed this explicitly, so that there is high interest in developing systems towards their automatic detection. Creating manually annotated datasets large enough to train supervised models is not only costly, but also—especially in the case of opinions and emotions—difficult, due to the intrinsic subjectivity of the task (Strapparava and Mihalcea, 2008; Kim et al., 2010). Therefore, research has focused on unsupervised methods enriched with information derived from lexica, which are manually created (Kim et al., 2010; Chaffar and Inkpen, 2011). Since Go et al. (2009) have shown that happy and sad emoticons can be successfully used as signals for sentiment labels, *distant supervision*, i.e. using some reasonably safe signals as proxies for automatically labelling training data (Mintz et al., 2009), has been used also for emotion recognition, for example exploiting both emoticons and Twitter hashtags (Purver and Battersby, 2012), but mainly towards creating emotion lexica. Mohammad and Kiritchenko (2015) use hashtags, experimenting also with highly fine-grained emotion sets (up to almost 600 emotion labels), to create the large *Hashtag Emotion Lexicon*. Emoticons are used as proxies also by Hallsmar and Palm (2016), who use distributed vector representations to find which words are interchangeable with emoticons but also which emoticons are used in a similar context.

We take advantage of distant supervision by using Facebook reactions as proxies for emotion labels, which to the best of our knowledge hasn't been done yet, and we train a set of Support Vector Machine models for emotion recognition. Our models, differently from existing ones, exploit information which

This work is licenced under a Creative Commons Attribution 4.0 International Licence. Licence details: http://creativecommons.org/licenses/by/4.0/

Proceedings of the Workshop on Computational Modeling of People's Opinions, Personality, and Emotions in Social Media,
pages 30–39, Osaka, Japan, December 12 2016.

is *acquired entirely automatically*, and achieve competitive or even state-of-the-art results for some of the emotion labels on existing, standard evaluation datasets. For explanatory purposes, related work is discussed further and more in detail when we describe the benchmarks for evaluation (Section 3) and when we compare our models to existing ones (Section 5). We also explore and discuss how choosing different sets of Facebook pages as training data provides an intrinsic domain-adaptation method.

2 Facebook reactions as labels

For years, on Facebook people could leave comments to posts, and also "like" them, by using a thumbs-up feature to explicitly express a generic, rather underspecified, approval. A "like" could thus mean "I like what you said", but also "I like that you bring up such topic (though I find the content of the article you linked annoying)".

Figure 1: Facebook reactions

In February 2016, after a short trial, Facebook made a more explicit *reaction* feature available world-wide. Rather than allowing for the underspecified "like" as the only wordless response to a post, a set of six more specific reactions was introduced, as shown in Figure 1: `Like, Love, Haha, Wow, Sad` and `Angry`. We use such reactions as proxies for emotion labels associated to posts.

We collected Facebook posts and their corresponding reactions from public pages using the Facebook API, which we accessed via the Facebook-sdk python library[1]. We chose different pages (and therefore domains and stances), aiming at a balanced and varied dataset, but we did so mainly based on intuition (see Section 4) and with an eye to the nature of the datasets available for evaluation (see Section 5). The choice of which pages to select posts from is far from trivial, and we believe this is actually an interesting aspect of our approach, as by using different Facebook pages one can intrinsically tackle the domain-adaptation problem (See Section 6 for further discussion on this). The final collection of Facebook pages for the experiments described in this paper is as follows: `FoxNews, CNN, ESPN, New York Times, Time magazine, Huffington Post Weird News, The Guardian, Cartoon Network, Cooking Light, Home Cooking Adventure, Justin Bieber, Nickelodeon, Spongebob, Disney`.

For each page, we downloaded the latest 1000 posts, or the maximum available if there are fewer, from February 2016, retrieving the counts of reactions for each post. The output is a JSON file containing a list of dictionaries with a timestamp, the post and a reaction vector with frequency values, which indicate how many users used that reaction in response to the post (Figure 2). The resulting emotion vectors must then be turned into an emotion label.[3]

In the context of this experiment, we made the simple decision of associating to each post the emotion with the highest count, ignoring `like` as it is the default and most generic reaction people tend to use. Therefore, for example, to the first post in Figure 2, we would associate the label `sad`, as it has the highest score (284) among the meaningful emotions we consider, though it also has non-zero scores for other emotions. At this stage, we didn't perform any other entropy-based selection of posts, to be investigated in future work.

```
[
  {
    "created_time": "2016-06-19T01:40:00+0000",
    "message": "Walt Disney World representatives said
    they plan to put up fencing and signs at all resorts
    and waterways.",
    "reactions": [5073, 4483, 60, 22, 54, 284, 170, 0]
  }
],
[
  {
    "created_time": "2016-06-19T01:00:00+0000",
    "message": "Charlene and Joseph Handrik face more
    than 550 counts of animal cruelty.",
    "reactions": [2256, 1011, 16, 6, 123, 409, 691, 0]
  }
],
```

Figure 2: Sample of resulting JSON file. The order of values/reactions is `total, like, love, haha, wow, sad, angry, thankful`.[3]

---

[1] https://pypi.python.org/pypi/facebook-sdk
[3] Note that `thankful` was only available during specific time spans related to certain events, as Mother's Day in May 2016.

3 Emotion datasets

Three datasets annotated with emotions are commonly used for the development and evaluation of emotion detection systems, namely the *Affective Text* dataset, the *Fairy Tales* dataset, and the *ISEAR* dataset. In order to compare our performance to state-of-the-art results, we have used them as well. In this Section, in addition to a description of each dataset, we provide an overview of the emotions used, their distribution, and how we mapped them to those we obtained from Facebook posts in Section 3.4. A summary is provided in Table 1, which also shows, in the bottom row, what role each dataset has in our experiments: apart from the development portion of the Affective Text, which we used to develop our models (Section 4), all three have been used as benchmarks for our evaluation.

3.1 Affective Text dataset

Task 14 at SemEval 2007 (Strapparava and Mihalcea, 2007) was concerned with the classification of emotions and valence in news headlines. The headlines where collected from several news websites including Google news, The New York Times, BBC News and CNN. The used emotion labels were `Anger, Disgust, Fear, Joy, Sadness, Surprise`, in line with the six basic emotions of Ekman's standard model (Ekman, 1992). Valence was to be determined as positive or negative. Classification of emotion and valence were treated as separate tasks. Emotion labels were not considered as mututally exclusive, and each emotion was assigned a score from 0 to 100. Training/developing data amounted to 250 annotated headlines (*Affective development*), while systems were evaluated on another 1000 (*Affective test*). Evaluation was done using two different methods: a fine-grained evaluation using Pearson's *r* to measure the correlation between the system scores and the gold standard; and a coarse-grained method where each emotion score was converted to a binary label, and precision, recall, and f-score were computed to assess performance. As it is done in most works that use this dataset (Kim et al., 2010; Chaffar and Inkpen, 2011; Calvo and Mac Kim, 2013), we also treat this as a classification problem (coarse-grained). This dataset has been extensively used for the evaluation of various unsupervised methods (Strapparava and Mihalcea, 2008), but also for testing different supervised learning techniques and feature portability (Mohammad, 2012).

3.2 Fairy Tales dataset

This is a dataset collected by Alm (2008), where about 1,000 sentences from fairy tales (by B. Potter, H.C. Andersen and Grimm) were annotated with the same six emotions of the Affective Text dataset, though with different names: `Angry, Disgusted, Fearful, Happy, Sad`, and `Surprised`. In most works that use this dataset (Kim et al., 2010; Chaffar and Inkpen, 2011; Calvo and Mac Kim, 2013), only sentences where all annotators agreed are used, and the labels `angry` and `disgusted` are merged. We adopt the same choices.

3.3 ISEAR

The ISEAR (International Survey on Emotion Antecedents and Reactions (Scherer and Wallbott, 1994; Scherer, 1997)) is a dataset created in the context of a psychology project of the 1990s, by collecting questionnaires answered by people with different cultural backgrounds. The main aim of this project was to gather insights in cross-cultural aspects of emotional reactions. Student respondents, both psychologists and non-psychologists, were asked to report situations in which they had experienced all of seven major emotions (`joy, fear, anger, sadness, disgust, shame` and `guilt`). In each case, the questions covered the way they had appraised a given situation and how they reacted. The final dataset contains reports by approximately 3000 respondents from all over the world, for a total of 7665 sentences labelled with an emotion, making this the largest dataset out of the three we use.

3.4 Overview of datasets and emotions

We summarise datasets and emotion distribution from two viewpoints. First, because there are different sets of emotions labels in the datasets and Facebook data, we need to provide a mapping and derive a subset of emotions that we are going to use for the experiments. This is shown in Table 1, where in the "Mapped" column we report the final emotions we use in this paper: anger, joy, sadness, surprise. All labels in each dataset are mapped to these final emotions, which are therefore the labels we use for training and testing our models.

Second, the distribution of the emotions for each dataset is different, as can be seen in Figure 3. In Figure 4 we also provide the distribution of the emotions anger, joy, sadness, surprise per Facebook page, in terms of number of posts (recall that we assign to a post the label corresponding to the majority emotion associated to it, see Section 2).

Table 1: Emotion labels in existing datasets, Facebook, and resulting mapping for the experiments in this work. The last row indicates which role each dataset has in our experiments.

Affective Text	Fairy tales	ISEAR	Facebook	Mapped
Anger	Angry-Disgusted	Anger	Angry	anger
Disgust	Angry-Disgusted	Disgust		anger
Fear	Fearful	Fear		
Joy	Happy	Joy	Haha, Love	joy
Sadness	Sad	Sadness	Sad	sadness
Surprise	Suprised		Wow	surprise
		Shame		
		Guilt		
development/test	test	test	train	

We can observe that for example pages about news tend to have more sadness and anger posts, while pages about cooking and tv-shows have a high percentage of joy posts. We will use this information to find the best set of pages for a given target domain (see Section 5).

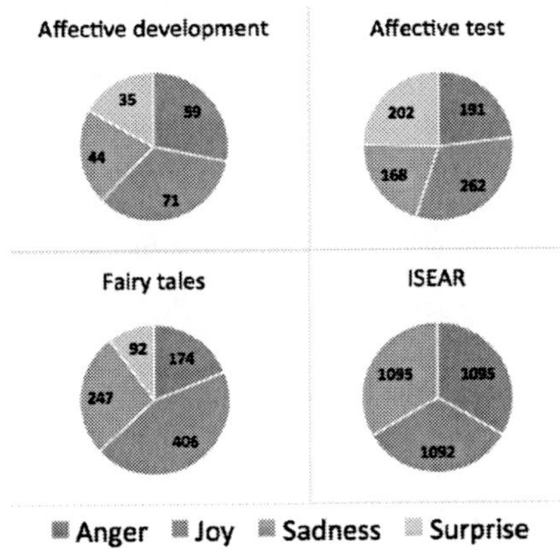

Figure 3: Emotion distribution in the datasets   Figure 4: Emotion distribution per Facebook page

4   Model

There are two main decisions to be taken in developing our model: (i) which Facebook pages to select as training data, and (ii) which features to use to train the model, which we discuss below. Specifically, we first set on a subset of pages and then experiment with features. Further exploration of the interaction between choice of pages and choice of features is left to future work, and partly discussed in Section 6. For development, we use a small portion of the Affective data set described in Section 3.1, that is the portion that had been released as development set for SemEval's 2007 Task 14 (Strapparava and Mihalcea, 2007), which contains 250 annotated sentences (*Affective development*, Section 3.1). All results reported in this section are on this dataset. The test set of Task 14 as well as the other two datasets described in Section 3 will be used to evaluate the final models (Section 4).

4.1 Selecting Facebook pages

Although page selection is a crucial ingredient of this approach, which we believe calls for further and deeper, dedicated investigation, for the experiments described here we took a rather simple approach. First, we selected the pages that would provide training data based on intuition and availability, then chose different combinations according to results of a basic model run on development data, and eventually tested feature combinations, still on the development set.

For the sake of simplicity and transparency, we first trained an SVM with a simple bag-of-words model and default parameters as per the Scikit-learn implementation (Pedregosa et al., 2011) on different combinations of pages. Based on results of the attempted combinations as well as on the distribution of emotions in the development dataset (Figure 3), we selected a *best model* (**B-M**), namely the combined set of `Time, The Guardian` and `Disney`, which yields the highest results on development data. `Time` and `The Guardian` perform well on most emotions but `Disney` helps to boost the performance for the `Joy` class.

4.2 Features

In selecting appropriate features, we mainly relied on previous work and intuition. We experimented with different combinations, and all tests were still done on *Affective development*, using the pages for the best model (**B-M**) described above as training data. Results are in Table 2. Future work will further explore the simultaneous selection of features and page combinations.

Standard textual features We use a set of basic text-based features to capture the emotion class. These include a tf-idf bag-of-words feature, word (2-3) and character (2-5) ngrams, and features related to the presence of negation words, and to the usage of punctuation.

Affect Lexicons This feature is used in all unsupervised models as a source of information, and we mainly include it to assess its contribution, but eventually do not use it in our final model.

We used the NRC10 Lexicon because it performed best in the experiments by (Mohammad, 2012), which is built around the emotions `anger, anticipation, disgust, fear, joy, sadness,` and `surprise`, and the valence values `positive` and `negative`. For each word in the lexicon, a boolean value indicating presence or absence is associated to each emotion. For a whole sentence, a global score per emotion can be obtained by summing the vectors for all content words of that sentence included in the lexicon, and used as feature.

Word Embeddings As additional feature, we also included Word Embeddings, namely distributed representations of words in a vector space, which have been exceptionally successful in boosting performance in a plethora of NLP tasks.We use three different embeddings:

- *Google embeddings*: pre-trained embeddings trained on Google News and obtained with the skip-gram architecture described in (Mikolov et al., 2013). This model contains 300-dimensional vectors for 3 million words and phrases.

- *Facebook embeddings*: embeddings that we trained on our scraped Facebook pages for a total of 20,000 sentences. Using the `gensim` library (Řehůřek and Sojka, 2010), we trained the embeddings with the following parameters: window size of 5, learning rate of 0.01 and dimensionality of 100. We filtered out words with frequency lower than 2 occurrences.

- *Retrofitted embeddings*: Retrofitting (Faruqui et al., 2015) has been shown as a simple but efficient way of informing trained embeddings with additional information derived from some lexical resource, rather than including it directly at the training stage, as it's done for example to create sense-aware (Iacobacci et al., 2015) or sentiment-aware (Tang et al., 2014) embeddings.[4] In this work, we retrofit general embeddings to include information about emotions, so that emotion-similar words can get closer in space. Both the Google as well as our Facebook embeddings were retrofitted with

---

[4]Training emotion-aware embeddings is a strategy that we plan to explore in future work.

lexical information obtained from the NRC10 Lexicon mentioned above, which provides emotion-similarity for each token. Note that differently from the previous two types of embeddings, the retrofitted ones do rely on handcrafted information in the form of a lexical resource.

4.3 Results on development set

We report precision, recall, and f-score on the development set. The average f-score is reported as *micro-average*, to better account for the skewed distribution of the classes as well as in accordance to what is usually reported for this task (Mohammad and Kiritchenko, 2015).

Table 2: Results on the development set (*Affective development*). *avg f* is the micro-averaged f-score.

Feature	anger prec,rec,f	joy prec,rec,f	sadness prec,rec,f	surprise prec,rec,f	avg f
Tf-idf	0.57,0.22,0.32	0.44,0.51,0.47	0.41,0.25, 0.31	0.22,0.49,0.30	0.368
Lexicon	0.28,0.08,0.13	0.43,0.37,0.40	0.31,0.30, 0.30	0.20,0.51,0.29	0.297
Token n-grams(2,5)	0.00,0.00,0.00	1.00,0.01,0.03	0.00,0.00, 0.00	0.17,1.00,0.29	0.172
Character n-grams(2,5)	0.50,0.03,0.06	0.39,0.73,0.51	0.38,0.07, 0.12	0.17,0.31,0.22	0.325
All features	0.40,0.03,0.06	0.35,0.97,0.52	0.62,0.11, 0.19	1.00,0.03,0.06	0.368
Google (G) embeddings	0.41,0.49,0.45	0.56,0.46,0.51	0.48,0.57, 0.52	0.22,0.17,0.19	0.445
Facebook (FB) embeddings	0.33,0.15,0.21	0.31,0.45,0.37	0.23,0.11,0.15	0.20,0.31,0.24	0.273
Retrofitted G-embeddings	0.36,0.20,0.26	0.42,0.48,0.45	0.30,0.25, 0.27	0.20,0.34,0.26	0.330
Retrofitted FB-embeddings	0.07,0.02,0.03	0.34,0.86,0.49	0.36,0.09,0.15	0.17,0.03,0.05	0.321
Tf-idf + G-emb	0.42,0.46,0.44	0.45,0.49,0.47	0.49,0.41, 0.44	0.29,0.26,0.27	0.426
All features + G-emb	0.63,0.29,0.40	0.43,0.83,0.56	0.46,0.27, 0.34	0.33,0.17,0.23	0.450
All features − Lexicon + G-emb	0.62,0.34,0.44	0.43,0.85,0.57	0.57,0.30, 0.39	0.36,0.14,0.20	**0.469**

From Table 2 we draw three main observations. First, a simple tf-idf bag-of-word mode works already very well, to the point that the other textual and lexicon-based features don't seem to contribute to the overall f-score (0.368), although there is a rather substantial variation of scores per class. Second, Google embeddings perform a lot better than Facebook embeddings, and this is likely due to the size of the corpus used for training. Retrofitting doesn't seem to help at all for the Google embeddings, but it does boost the Facebook embeddings, leading to think that with little data, more accurate task-related information is helping, but corpus size matters most. Third, in combination with embeddings, all features work better than just using tf-idf, but removing the Lexicon feature, which is the only one based on hand-crafted resources, yields even better results. Then our best model (**B-M**) on development data relies *entirely on automatically obtained information*, both in terms of training data as well as features.

5 Results

In Table 3 we report the results of our model on the three datasets standardly used for the evaluation of emotion classification, which we have described in Section 3.

Our **B-M** model relies on subsets of Facebook pages for training, which were chosen according to their performance on the development set as well as on the observation of emotions distribution on different pages and in the different datasets, as described in Section 4. The feature set we use is our best on the development set, namely all the features plus Google-based embeddings, but excluding the lexicon. This makes our approach completely independent of any manual annotation or handcrafted resource. Our model's performance is compared to the following systems, for which results are reported in the referred literature. Please note that no other existing model was re-implemented, and results are those reported in the respective papers.

Kim et al. (2010)   experiment with four different unsupervised techniques that rely on lexicon-derived information. In Table 3 we report the scores for their best average performing approach, namely a

CNMF-based categorical classification. They made the decision not to deal with `surprise` because this emotion is not present in the ISEAR dataset.

Strapparava and Mihalcea (2008) experiment with several models based on a core LSA model and, in their best performing model (`LSA-all emotion words`) whose results we report in Table 3, also use information from lexical resources both in their general (WordNet (Fellbaum, 1998)) and emotion-aware (WordNet Affect (Strapparava et al., 2004)) form.

Danisman and Alpkocak (2008) adopt a supervised approach, training a model using the ISEAR dataset and testing it on the Affective text dataset. They only report results per category in terms of f-score, without further specification of how precision and recall contribute.

We have mentioned that the selection of Facebook pages is relevant and can be also thought of as a tool for domain adaptation in accordance with the characteristics of the target domains/datasets (see also Section 2 and Figures 3–4). Although we believe that such an interesting aspect will require deeper investigation (see also Section 6), we preliminary test this assumption by developing and comparing two more models: a model that uses a combination of pages that we expect will perform best on the Fairy Tales dataset (**FT-M**), and a model that uses a combination of pages that should perform best on the ISEAR dataset (**ISE-M**). The feature set is kept the same for all three models.

FT-M The sentences in the Fairy Tales dataset are quite different compared to the news headlines in the development set. Looking at the distribution in this dataset, as can be seen in Figure 3, `Joy` is the most frequent class. We selected the pages `HuffPostWeirdNews`, `ESPN` and `CNN` for this model especially looking at the performance for the emotions that are most frequent in this dataset.

ISE-M As described in Section 3.3, the sentences in the ISEAR collection are also different compared to the two other datasets. Looking at the distribution in Figure 3 and according to performance on relevant emotions (we took into account the absence of `Surprise` in this dataset), we selected the pages `Time`, `The Guardian` and `CookingLight` for this model.

In Table 3 we report results for all of the models mentioned above. We indicate averages only for our models, since not all approaches deal with the same sets of emotions and we cannot easily compute them. We discuss results both in terms of how our models fair with respect to other systems as reported the literature, as well as how they compare to one another with a view to the selection of Facebook pages.

Compared to other systems, our models are globally competitive, given that **B-M** is entirely unsupervised. Overall, the unsupervised but heavily lexicon-based best model of (Kim et al., 2010) performs well on all emotions, excluding surprise, which they do not address (thus also making their classification task slightly easier). Differently from existing systems, our models appear rather balanced in terms of performance on the different emotions as well as in precision and recall, and are able to deal well with the variance of the datasets.

On the Affective Text dataset, we have the highest precision for all emotions but `joy`, though on this emotion our models have very good recall. The highest recall for all emotions for this dataset is reported in (Strapparava and Mihalcea, 2008), together with extremely low precision. Such skewed performance for all emotions can only be explained if different emotion-specific models were trained rather than a single multiclass model, but this is not described as such in the paper. The authors state that their models are completely unsupervised, which is true in terms of training data, but they nevertheless augment them with information derived from hand-crafted resources.

On the Fairy Tales dataset, (Kim et al., 2010) Chaffar and Inkpen (2011) also used the Fairy tales dataset to evaluate a supervised model using features like bag-of-words, N-grams and lexical emotion features, but report cross-validated results using accuracy only, and are therefore harder to compare.

On the ISEAR dataset, which is the largest, our models perform best for all emotions but `anger`, for which however we achieve the highest precision with all our models.

From the perspective of comparing our models, we do not observe any real correlation between our actual best performances and the models designed to best perform on a given dataset. For example, **B-M**

Table 3: Results on test datasets according to **P**recision, **R**ecall and **F**-score.

	Affective test			Fairy Tales			ISEAR		
	P	R	F	P	R	F	P	R	F
anger									
B-M	0.50	0.35	**0.41**	0.33	0.04	0.07	0.72	0.06	0.11
FT-M	**0.51**	0.30	0.38	0.27	0.02	0.04	0.57	0.10	0.17
ISE-M	0.48	0.35	0.40	0.36	0.05	0.08	**0.74**	0.06	0.11
(Strapparava and Mihalcea, 2008)	0.06	**0.88**	0.12						
(Kim et al., 2010)	0.29	0.26	0.28	**0.77**	**0.56**	**0.65**	0.41	**0.99**	**0.58**
(Danisman and Alpkocak, 2008)			0.24						
joy									
B-M	0.39	0.85	0.54	0.49	0.77	0.60	0.41	0.79	0.53
FT-M	0.41	0.77	0.54	0.49	0.69	0.58	**0.42**	0.63	0.50
ISE-M	0.39	0.82	0.53	0.48	**0.81**	0.60	0.40	**0.83**	**0.54**
(Strapparava and Mihalcea, 2008)	0.19	**0.90**	0.31						
(Kim et al., 2010)	**0.77**	0.58	**0.65**	**0.80**	0.76	**0.78**	0.39	0.01	0.01
(Danisman and Alpkocak, 2008)			0.50						
sadness									
B-M	0.51	0.21	0.30	0.43	0.39	0.41	0.50	**0.39**	**0.44**
FT-M	**0.53**	0.28	0.37	0.50	0.24	0.33	**0.79**	0.28	0.41
ISE-M	0.49	0.21	0.29	0.43	0.34	0.38	0.51	0.38	**0.44**
(Strapparava and Mihalcea, 2008)	0.12	**0.87**	0.22						
(Kim et al., 2010)	0.50	0.45	**0.48**	**0.71**	**0.82**	**0.77**	0.37	0.01	0.25
(Danisman and Alpkocak, 2008)			0.37						
surprise									
B-M	0.20	0.05	0.08	0.12	0.04	0.06			
FT-M	0.25	0.17	**0.20**	**0.14**	**0.33**	**0.19**			
ISE-M	**0.27**	0.08	0.12	0.17	0.04	0.07			
(Strapparava and Mihalcea, 2008)	0.08	**0.95**	0.14						
(Kim et al., 2010)									
(Danisman and Alpkocak, 2008)									
AVERAGE (micro f-score)									
B-M	0.409			0.459			0.411		
FT-M	**0.412**			0.408			0.336		
ISE-M	0.405			**0.460**			**0.422**		

was expected to perform best on the Affective Text, but it is outperformed by **FT-M** in the precision of detecting anger and sadness, and overall for the detection of surprise. Generally, by looking at averages, it seems that our best performing model across datasets is **ISE-M**. However, the extremely large variance among scores for the same emotion on the three datasets, highlights the differences among such datasets and the need to better tailor training data to different domains. The large discrepancy in detecting different emotions in the same dataset also deserves further investigation. We discuss such issues further in the next section, with a view to future work.

6   Discussion, conclusions and future work

We have explored the potential of using Facebook reactions in a distant supervised setting to perform emotion classification. The evaluation on standard benchmarks shows that models trained as such, especially when enhanced with continuous vector representations, can achieve competitive results without relying on any handcrafted resource. An interesting aspect of our approach is the view to domain adaptation via the selection of Facebook pages to be used as training data.

We believe that this approach has a lot of potential, and we see the following directions for improvement. Feature-wise, we want to train emotion-aware embeddings, in the vein of work by Tang et al. (2014), and Iacobacci et al. (2015). Retrofitting FB-embeddings trained on a larger corpus might also be successful, but would rely on an external lexicon.

The largest room for yielding not only better results but also interesting insights on extensions of this approach lies in the choice of training instances, both in terms of Facebook pages to get posts from, as well as in which posts to select from the given pages. For the latter, one could for example only select posts that have a certain length, ignore posts that are only quotes or captions to images, or expand posts by including content from linked html pages, which might provide larger and better contexts (Plank et al., 2014). Additionally, and most importantly, one could use an entropy-based measure to select only posts that have a strong emotion rather than just considering the majority emotion as training label. For the former, namely the choice of Facebook pages, which we believe deserves the most investigation, one could explore several avenues, especially in relation to *stance*-based issues (Mohammad et al., 2016). In our dataset, for example, a post about Chile beating Colombia in a football match during the Copa America had very contradictory reactions, depending on which side readers would cheer for. Similarly, the very same political event, for example, would get very different reactions from readers if it was posted on Fox News or The Late Night Show, as the target audience is likely to feel very differently about the same issue. This also brings up theoretical issues related more generally to the definition of the emotion detection task, as it's strongly dependent on personal traits of the audience. Also, in this work, pages initially selected on availability and intuition were further grouped into sets to make training data according to performance on development data, and label distribution. Another criterion to be exploited would be *vocabulary overlap* between the pages and the datasets.

Lastly, we could develop single models for each emotion, treating the problem as a multi-label task. This would even better reflect the ambiguity and subjectivity intrinsic to assigning emotions to text, where content could be at same time joyful or sad, depending on the reader.

Acknowledgements

In addition to the anonymous reviewers, we want to thank Lucia Passaro and Barbara Plank for insightful discussions, and for providing comments on draft versions of this paper.

References

Ebba Cecilia Ovesdotter Alm. 2008. *Affect in text and speech*. ProQuest.

Rafael A Calvo and Sunghwan Mac Kim. 2013. Emotions in text: dimensional and categorical models. *Computational Intelligence*, 29(3):527–543.

Soumaya Chaffar and Diana Inkpen. 2011. Using a heterogeneous dataset for emotion analysis in text. In *Advances in Artificial Intelligence*, pages 62–67. Springer.

Taner Danisman and Adil Alpkocak. 2008. Feeler: Emotion classification of text using vector space model. In *AISB 2008 Convention Communication, Interaction and Social Intelligence*, volume 1, page 53.

Paul Ekman. 1992. An argument for basic emotions. *Cognition & emotion*, 6(3-4):169–200.

Manaal Faruqui, Jesse Dodge, Sujay Kumar Jauhar, Chris Dyer, Eduard Hovy, and Noah A. Smith. 2015. Retrofitting word vectors to semantic lexicons. In *Proceedings of the 2015 Conference of the North American Chapter of the Association for Computational Linguistics: Human Language Technologies*, pages 1606–1615, Denver, Colorado, May–June. Association for Computational Linguistics.

Christiane Fellbaum. 1998. *WordNet*. Wiley Online Library.

Alec Go, Richa Bhayani, and Lei Huang. 2009. Twitter sentiment classification using distant supervision. *CS224N Project Report, Stanford*, 1:12.

Fredrik Hallsmar and Jonas Palm. 2016. Multi-class sentiment classification on twitter using an emoji training heuristic. Technical report, KTH/Skolan för datavetenskap och kommunikation (CSC). University essay.

Ignacio Iacobacci, Mohammad Taher Pilehvar, and Roberto Navigli. 2015. Sensembed: learning sense embeddings for word and relational similarity. In *Proceedings of ACL*, pages 95–105.

Sunghwan Mac Kim, Alessandro Valitutti, and Rafael A Calvo. 2010. Evaluation of unsupervised emotion models to textual affect recognition. In *Proceedings of the NAACL HLT 2010 Workshop on Computational Approaches to Analysis and Generation of Emotion in Text*, pages 62–70. Association for Computational Linguistics.

Tomas Mikolov, Ilya Sutskever, Kai Chen, Greg S Corrado, and Jeff Dean. 2013. Distributed representations of words and phrases and their compositionality. In *Advances in neural information processing systems*, pages 3111–3119.

Mike Mintz, Steven Bills, Rion Snow, and Dan Jurafsky. 2009. Distant supervision for relation extraction without labeled data. In *Proceedings of the Joint Conference of the 47th Annual Meeting of the ACL and the 4th International Joint Conference on Natural Language Processing of the AFNLP: Volume 2 - Volume 2*, ACL '09, pages 1003–1011, Stroudsburg, PA, USA. Association for Computational Linguistics.

Saif M Mohammad and Svetlana Kiritchenko. 2015. Using hashtags to capture fine emotion categories from tweets. *Computational Intelligence*, 31(2):301–326.

Saif M. Mohammad, Svetlana Kiritchenko, Parinaz Sobhani, Xiaodan Zhu, and Colin Cherry. 2016. A dataset for detecting stance in tweets. In *Proceedings of 10th edition of the the Language Resources and Evaluation Conference (LREC)*, Portorož, Slovenia.

Saif Mohammad. 2012. Portable features for classifying emotional text. In *Proceedings of the 2012 Conference of the North American Chapter of the Association for Computational Linguistics: Human Language Technologies*, pages 587–591, Montréal, Canada, June. Association for Computational Linguistics.

Saif M. Mohammad. 2016. Sentiment analysis: Detecting valence, emotions, and other affectual states from text. In Herb Meiselman, editor, *Emotion Measurement*. Elsevier.

F. Pedregosa, G. Varoquaux, A. Gramfort, V. Michel, B. Thirion, O. Grisel, M. Blondel, P. Prettenhofer, R. Weiss, V. Dubourg, J. Vanderplas, A. Passos, D. Cournapeau, M. Brucher, M. Perrot, and E. Duchesnay. 2011. Scikit-learn: Machine learning in Python. *Journal of Machine Learning Research*, 12:2825–2830.

Barbara Plank, Dirk Hovy, Ryan T McDonald, and Anders Søgaard. 2014. Adapting taggers to twitter with not-so-distant supervision. In *COLING*, pages 1783–1792.

Matthew Purver and Stuart Battersby. 2012. Experimenting with distant supervision for emotion classification. In *Proceedings of the 13th Conference of the European Chapter of the Association for Computational Linguistics*, pages 482–491. Association for Computational Linguistics.

Radim Řehůřek and Petr Sojka. 2010. Software Framework for Topic Modelling with Large Corpora. In *Proceedings of the LREC 2010 Workshop on New Challenges for NLP Frameworks*, pages 45–50, Valletta, Malta, May. ELRA. http://is.muni.cz/publication/884893/en.

Klaus R Scherer and Harald G Wallbott. 1994. Evidence for universality and cultural variation of differential emotion response patterning. *Journal of personality and social psychology*, 66(2):310.

Klaus R Scherer. 1997. The role of culture in emotion-antecedent appraisal. *Journal of personality and social psychology*, 73(5):902.

Liz Stinson. 2016. Facebook reactions, the totally redesigned like button, is here. *Wired*. http://www.wired.com/2016/02/facebook-reactions-totally-redesigned-like-button/.

Carlo Strapparava and Rada Mihalcea. 2007. Semeval-2007 task 14: Affective text. In *Proceedings of the 4th International Workshop on Semantic Evaluations*, pages 70–74. Association for Computational Linguistics.

Carlo Strapparava and Rada Mihalcea. 2008. Learning to identify emotions in text. In *Proceedings of the 2008 ACM symposium on Applied computing*, pages 1556–1560. ACM.

Carlo Strapparava, Alessandro Valitutti, et al. 2004. Wordnet affect: an affective extension of wordnet. In *LREC*, volume 4, pages 1083–1086.

Duyu Tang, Furu Wei, Nan Yang, Ming Zhou, Ting Liu, and Bing Qin. 2014. Learning sentiment-specific word embedding for Twitter sentiment classification. In *Proceedings of the 52nd Annual Meeting of the Association for Computational Linguistics*, volume 1, pages 1555–1565.

A graphical framework to detect and categorize diverse opinions from online news

Ankan Mullick
Department of Computer
Science and Engineering
IIT Kharagpur, India

Pawan Goyal
Department of Computer
Science and Engineering
IIT Kharagpur, India

Niloy Ganguly
Department of Computer
Science and Engineering
IIT Kharagpur, India

`{ankan, pawang, niloy}@cse.iitkgp.ernet.in`

Abstract

This paper proposes a framework to extract diverse opinionated sentences within a given news article, by introducing the concept of diversity in a graphical model for opinion detection. We conduct extensive evaluation and find that the proposed modification leads to impressive improvements in performance and makes the final results of the model more usable. The proposed method (OP-D) not only performs much better than the other techniques used for opinion detection and introducing diversity, but is also able to select opinions from different categories (Asher et al., 2009). By developing a classification model which categorizes the identified sentences into various opinion categories, we find that OP-D is able to push opinions from different categories uniformly among the top opinions.

1 Introduction

Online publishing houses desire to develop engagement of users around the articles published on their websites. An important aspect of user engagement is commenting on the article and subsequently building up a conversation around it. In order to facilitate meaningful conversation, an option might be to identify and highlight *specific relevant portions* of the article, which may act as a seed for such conversation. For ensuring wide engagement, it would be best if the sentences chosen are opinions expressed in the article, as unlike factual statements, opinions might easily kick-start discussions. Further, to be able to engage a wide range of audience, it would be helpful if each chosen sentence expresses different context than the other. In general, all opinions are not of the same type. Opinions can be categorized into various categories and sub-categories (Asher et al., 2009), and it would be ideal if the extracted opinions cover multiple such categories. Some examples of these categories are provided below:

1) **Report** : e.g., *Christie's staffs have denied Zimmer's allegation.*

2) **Judgment** : e.g., *McGreevey's lover was being paid 11000 Dollar even though he was wildly unqualified for the position.*

3) **Advise** : e.g., *Let's shoot at the opposition not our own troops, one Insider pleaded.*

4) **Sentimental** : e.g., *So why do so many people enjoy ridiculing my New Jersey One word Jealousy?*

Opinion analysis has been a major field of study in natural language processing and data mining for many years. Several works such as (Kim and Hovy, 2006; Qadir, 2009; Scholz and Conrad, 2013; Yu and Hatzivassiloglou, 2003) focus on opinion mining. Opinion mining is very similar to subjectivity classification where subjective nature indicates the tendency of expressing one's thoughts and opinions. Work has been done in the past for developing classifiers (Wiebe and Riloff, 2005) which separate subjective sentences from objective ones, using several features present in the sentences. (Soni et al., 2014) describes how to predict certainty (factuality) of text (e.g., tweet) by using keywords collected from source introducing predicates (cues) and groups (Saurí, 2008). These models focus only on the local context (takes no global context into account) from a sentence to measure its subjectivity. Side by side, there have been works where graphical models have been proposed to capture the global context, where the sentences are treated as nodes in the graph and a similarity measure between sentences is defined to

This work is licenced under a Creative Commons Attribution 4.0 International Licence. Licence details: `http://creativecommons.org/licenses/by/4.0/`

Proceedings of the Workshop on Computational Modeling of People's Opinions, Personality, and Emotions in Social Media,
pages 40–49, Osaka, Japan, December 12 2016.

build this graph. While some of the approaches use PageRank to model each node in a similar manner (Erkan and Radev, 2004), HITS framework has also been used that establishes a relationship between opinions and supporting facts by modeling opinions as hubs and facts as authorities (Rajkumar et al., 2014).

None of these works, however, focus on finding diverse opinions from an article. Experiments on MPQA and Yahoo datasets (both are English datasets) show that this leads to a sub-optimal performance, while trying to extract the most opinionated sentences in a news article. The graphical models end up choosing similar sentences - which is not ideal to enable wide-ranging user engagement. We, therefore, attempt to modify a variant of graphical model proposed in (Rajkumar et al., 2014) to introduce diversity. The basic idea of our approach is that once a node (sentence) is selected as an opinion because of a high hub score (as per the HITS framework used in (Rajkumar et al., 2014)), we can discount the hub scores for the nodes it links to, as these might be sub-opinions supporting the main opinion, and discounting their hub scores might improve diversity. We find that this simple modification to the earlier framework leads to impressive improvement in performance for (i) Classifying opinions and facts, and (ii) Identifying diverse opinion categories in both datasets. Extensive experimental results are reported to show that as a result of this modification, the output opinions can be used more meaningfully. Note that the proposed technique is unique from the general work on diversity (Carbonell and Goldstein, 1998; Munson et al., 2009; Zhu et al., 2007; Mei et al., 2010) in that we introduce diversity in a model with two different kinds of nodes in the document graph, as opposed to the other algorithms, which treat all the sentences equally.

Further, to understand the distribution of extracted opinions from online news in various categories, e.g., Report, Judgment, Advise and Sentiment etc. (Asher et al., 2009), we develop an opinion classification model. While classification of opinions into various sentiment levels such as positive, negative and neutral has been tried (Saggionα and Funk, 2010; Yu et al., 2008), automated classification of opinions into various categories is not available. Analysis using the opinion classification model shows that our algorithm (OP-D) actually adds diversity even at the category level by selecting opinions from different opinion categories.

2 Extracting Diverse Opinions: OP-D

The proposed algorithm for extracting diverse opinions from news articles comprises of three steps: (i) Extracting features and assigning a score to indicate opinionatedness of a sentence. (ii) Building up the fact-opinion graph, applying HITS algorithm and identifying highly opinionated sentences. (iii) Identifying diverse opinionated sentences (i.e. report, judgment, advise, sentiment).

(i) Feature Extraction: We extract an extensive set of features at the sentence level to classify a sentence as an opinion / fact using a binary Naïve Bayes (NB) classifier. The features used include: (a) count of the strong polar words, weak polar words in the sentence (Wiebe et al., 1999), (b) polarity of the root verb of the sentence, (c) presence of *aComp*, *xComp* and *advMod* dependencies (Qadir, 2009), (d) opinionated n-grams (Wiebe et al.,), (e) presence of modal verbs, (f) presence of pronouns, (g) opinionated words (e.g., 'should', 'always', 'anyone', 'if' etc.). From LIWC (Pennebaker et al., 2001) we collected words belonging to the categories - 'feel', 'swear', 'certain', 'percept', 'time', as their presence in the sentence can make it more subjective or objective. A list of positive and negative polar words was used from MPQA opinion lexicon. Stanford dependency parser (De Marneffe et al., 2006) was utilized to compute the dependencies for each sentence within the news article. After those features are extracted from sentences, the Weka implementation[1] of the Naïve Bayes classifier is used to calculate the probability for each sentence to be an opinion, based on the presence of the above features.

(ii) Graph Formation and Hub-Authority Calculation: In this step, a graph is generated considering each sentence as a node. The scores from the NB classifier are used to assign the initial hub scores to the sentences in the graph. In HITS, edges flow from Hubs to Authorities, so an edge between two nodes (S_i to S_j) is given a higher weight W_{ij} if the source sentence has a high probability of being an opinion (probability value obtained from the NB classifier, which is also used to initialize the hub score of this

---

[1]http://www.cs.waikato.ac.nz/ml/weka/

sentence as $H_i(0)$ and Initial Authority-score as 1- $H_i(0)$.), the cosine similarity between these sentences (Sim_{ij}) is high and the number of sentences separating i and j, ($dist_{ij}$) is small. The weight function, W_{ij} [2] is as following

$$W_{ij} = H_i^3(0) \cdot Sim_{ij} \cdot (0.2 + \frac{1}{dist_{ij}}) \tag{1}$$

We now consider only the top $k\%$ of the edges, having the highest weights in the graph.

Once we have established a hub-authority structure in the document, we compute the hub and authority scores of every node in the graph by applying the HITS algorithm Ideally, the 'important' opinion sentences would obtain high hub scores because such sentences usually are stressed more in the article by using supporting facts *or* other related sentences; this results in high number of outgoing edges from these opinion sentences. Sentences supporting these opinions, similarly, should get high authority score.

Algorithm 1 OP-D Algorithm (output: k sentences)

1: **procedure** OP-D
2:     **for** All sentences **do**   ▷ Initialization
3:         hubscore ← value_ by_ NB_ classifier
4:         authscore ← 1 −hubscore
5:         Take top k% edges with edge weight 1 (thresholded). Set other edge weights to 0.
6:     **end for**
7:     **while** Root Mean Squared Error $< \epsilon$ **do**   ▷ ϵ was set to 0.0001
8:         Update hubscore(h) & authscore(a)
9:         h ← $AA^T h$; a ← $A^T Aa$ ▷ A:Adjacency Matrix
10:     **end while**
11:     **while** NoOfSentencesChosen $<$ k **do**
12:         Sort the hub_scores and select the max
13:         Rank this maximum in final list
14:         Decrease the hub_score of the authorities of max_hub
15:     **end while**
16: **end procedure**

(iii). Ensuring Diversity: To introduce the notion of diversity in this framework, let us assume that we have selected a node i with the highest Hub score H_i as the opinion to be retrieved; and let node j be one of the authorities which has contributed to its hubness. Since we want the results to be more diverse, we decrease the hub scores of these nodes before selecting the next sentence with the highest hub score. The hub score of the authority (node j) is decremented by a fraction of the edge weight from hub (node i) to authority (node j), i.e.,

$$H_j \leftarrow H_j - \lambda.W_{ij} \tag{2}$$

where λ is a constant, H_j is the hub score of the authority node j and W_{ij} is the weight of the edge from node (hub) i to node (authority) j. The decrement ensures that these sentences do not get selected immediately when picking up the node with the next highest hub score. This process is repeated until we have selected the required number of opinionated sentences from the document. Steps are shown in **Algorithm 1**- *Opinion Diversity* (**OP-D**).

3   Dataset

To investigate the effectiveness of the proposed framework, experiments are conducted using two different datasets, a) the standard Multi-Perspective Question Answering (MPQA) dataset (contains 535 documents) and b) 120 news articles crawled from Yahoo news. Each document is a news article pertaining to some topic. In the MPQA dataset, each sentence is classified as either opinionated or factual by checking for the presence of certain subjective elements as annotated by the authors of the corpus (Wiebe

---

[2] In our approach W_{ij} is defined using parameters (Similar to (Rajkumar et al., 2014))

Table 1: Statistics of the MPQA and Yahoo datasets

Used	No.of Documents	Average length (no.of sentences) of an article	Average fraction of opinion sentences/article
Dataset	MPQA / Yahoo	MPQA / Yahoo	MPQA / Yahoo
Total	535 / 120	20.8 / 31	0.486 / 0.527
Train	435 / 95	20.2 / 31.4	0.49 / 0.524
Test	100 / 25	23.1 / 27	0.48 / 0.537

et al., 2005). For the Yahoo dataset, we get each sentence annotated manually using volunteers, different from the authors[3]. Statistics of these datasets, including the training-test splits, are provided in **Table 1.**

4   Experimental Framework and Results

From the 535 documents in the MPQA dataset, we randomly select 100 documents for the test set. Similarly, 25 documents are selected randomly from the Yahoo dataset for testing. Note that training and test splits are required for the first stage NB classifier. We first perform 5-fold cross validation experiments on the training sets. Then the entire training set is used to train the NB classifier and the results are reported on the test set.

Table 2: Variation of precision and recall for different k (% of edges) and weight (w) for OP-D

k(%)	$(P,R)@3$ wt=w MPQA	$(P,R)@5$ wt=w MPQA	$(P,R)@3$ w=1/0 MPQA	$(P,R)@5$ w=1/0 MPQA	$(P,R)@3$ wt=w Yahoo	$(P,R)@5$ wt=w Yahoo	$(P,R)@3$ w=1/0 Yahoo	$(P,R)@5$ w=1/0 Yahoo
5%	0.6, 0.23	0.61, 0.37	0.64, 0.23	0.61, 0.39	0.72, 0.22	0.64, 0.33	0.75, 0.24	0.65, 0.34
10%	0.66, 0.27	0.63, 0.42	**0.73, 0.32**	**0.69, 0.45**	0.75, 0.25	0.68, 0.34	**0.79, 0.26**	**0.7, 0.36**
20%	0.63, 0.25	0.61, 0.38	0.66, 0.26	0.64, 0.4	0.7, 0.22	0.66, 0.34	0.72, 0.23	0.67, 0.34
30%	0.6, 0.23	0.58, 0.39	0.62, 0.24	0.61, 0.4	0.64, 0.18	0.61, 0.31	0.65, 0.19	0.63, 0.31
40%	0.59, 0.23	0.58, 0.39	0.61, 0.24	0.59, 0.4	0.59, 0.17	0.58, 0.17	0.61, 0.19	0.60, 0.29

Parameter Fixing: The parameters that we needed to fix for the proposed algorithm were: weight of the edges (absolute (wt) or thresholded (1/0)), k for the top $k\%$ edges if thresholded weights are used and the constant λ in Equation 2. **Table 2** shows results obtained by OP-D for different k and weight. In all the cases, we find that we get better results when the weight is properly thresholded rather than taking the absolute weight - we follow that henceforth. $k = 10$ performs the best, so we take top 10% of the edges. **Figure 1** shows how the precision and recall values vary for different choices of λ using 5-fold cross validation for all the experiments reported. Since the best results are obtained for $\lambda = 20$, that has been fixed for all the experiments.

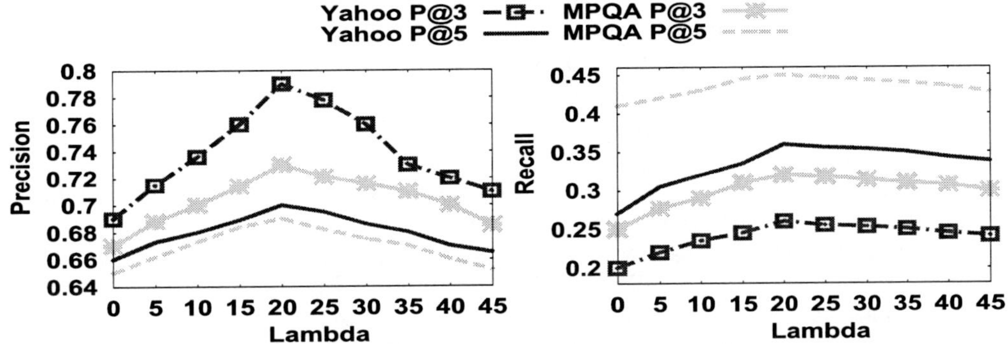

Figure 1: Variation of precision ($P@3$ and $P@5$) and recall ($R@3$ and $R@5$) for different values of λ.

---

[3]90 of these articles were obtained from Rajkumar et al. (2014). We increased this set to 120 articles. Inter-annotator agreement (Cohen κ) is 0.71.

Baselines: We use the following baselines for comparison:

a). **Random Baseline:** Each sentence is randomly assigned to one of the two classes, opinion or fact[4]. red We choose 3 and 5 sentences randomly to evaluate P@3 and P@5.

b). **Naïve Bayes (NB):** The next baseline is the first stage sentence-level classifier, as described earlier. We also experimented with Logistic Regression, SMO (Sequential Minimal Optimization), Support Vector Machine (SVM), Repeated Incremental Pruning - Java version (JRip) as well as other classifiers, however NB gave the best results and was used as a baseline.

c). **HITS (Rajkumar et al., 2014):** We use the method proposed by (Rajkumar et al., 2014) as another baseline. Note that the first two stages of our approach are similar to (Rajkumar et al., 2014) except that we use a more extensive set of features as well as the network is unweighted. We verified that these modifications indeed lead to performance gain, and used the modified approach as the baseline.

d). **FactJudge (Soni et al., 2014):** FactJudge proposes a method to detect factuality of tweet. We use the factuality score given by this approach as a baseline to detect opinions, i.e., higher the factuality score, lower is the probability of being an opinion.

Evaluation Metrics: We use precisions $P@3$, $P@5$ and recalls $R@3$, $R@5$ as the evaluation measures, as we would like to obtain the best 3 or 5 opinions from the document. We perform a series of evaluations to compare the proposed approach with other baselines. In the first evaluation, we verify if the top 3 or 5 sentences returned by the algorithm are actually opinions. We also report the recall at top 3 or 5 places. We consider only those files (86 out of 100 for MPQA and 23 out of 25 for Yahoo) for testing which have at least one opinion.

Table 3: Comparison results of the proposed OP-D framework with other baselines on MPQA and Yahoo datasets

Number Of Article	Method Dataset	$(P, R)@3$ (MPQA)	$(P, R)@5$ (MPQA)	$(P, R)@3$ (Yahoo)	$(P, R)@5$ (Yahoo)
5-fold cross	Random	0.5, 0.19	0.53, 0.3	0.54, 0.16	0.55, 0.26
validation	FactJudge	0.57, 0.19	0.56, 0.25	0.57, 0.15	0.57, 0.24
test on	NB	0.64, 0.28	0.63, 0.4	0.63, 0.17	0.62, 0.28
Training	HITS	0.67, 0.25	0.65, 0.41	0.69, 0.2	0.66, 0.27
data	**OP-D**	**0.73, 0.32**	**0.69, 0.45**	**0.79, 0.26**	**0.7, 0.36**
Testing On:	Random	0.52, 0.2	0.54, 0.32	0.53, 0.16	0.57, 0.27
MPQA	FactJudge	0.52, 0.19	0.53, 0.33	0.54, 0.15	0.54, 0.27
(86/100) ;	NB	0.62, 0.27	0.61, 0.4	0.65, 0.17	0.63, 0.29
Yahoo	HITS	0.66, 0.27	0.63, 0.4	0.69, 0.21	0.65, 0.32
(23/25)	**OP-D**	**0.72, 0.31**	**0.68, 0.44**	**0.81, 0.26**	**0.71, 0.38**

Performance: **Table 3** shows the comparison results for the two datasets. We see that the random baseline, along with (Soni et al., 2014) gives a precision close to 0.5. The first stage NB classifier performs better than these methods. The graphical framework (second stage) gives further improvements upon the NB classifier, and OP-D outperforms all these baselines consistently at least by 5%.

Performance on different buckets of opinion fraction: Since the fraction of opinions in each document varies, we wanted to investigate the performance at various sparsity levels and thus study the robustness of the proposed algorithm. The test datasets were divided into various buckets according to the fraction of opinionated sentence (sparse, medium and dense) in the document. The results shown in **Table 4** confirm that OP-D performs better consistently across various buckets. Specifically, even for the documents with small fraction of opinions, it is able to improve performance from the NB and HITS baselines. In general, for the documents with sparse opinions, the performance is poor (across methods) which is bringing down the overall performance. This needs detailed future inspection.

Diversity Experiment: While these evaluations establish that the top 3-5 sentences extracted by OP-D contain more opinions than the baselines, they do not provide insights into whether these selected opinions are more important and diverse topics with respect to the entire article. We, therefore, randomly select 50 MPQA articles and 25 Yahoo articles, provide all the sentences with gold standard opinion /

---

[4]Python "random" module has been used.

Table 4: Comparison results of precision and recall on different buckets of opinion fractions

Opinion Faction (Doc/Total)	Method	$(P, R)@3$ MPQA	$(P, R)@5$ MPQA	$(P, R)@3$ Yahoo	$(P, R)@5$ Yahoo
(0-0.3)(22/86) For MPQA;	Random	0.15, 0.28	0.19, 0.42	0.33, 0.23	0.31, 0.31
	FactJudge	0.17, 0.24	0.18, 0.43	0.34, 0.19	0.34, 0.39
	NB	0.26, 0.43	0.22, 0.64	0.43, 0.2	0.41, 0.4
(0-0.5)(7/23)	HITS	0.27, 0.46	0.22, 0.59	0.62, 0.33	0.56, 0.51
For Yahoo	**OP-D**	**0.41, 0.53**	**0.35, 0.72**	**0.67, 0.41**	**0.57, 0.58**
(0.3-0.65)(31/86) For MPQA;	Random	0.47, 0.18	0.5, 0.31	0.41, 0.08	0.53, 0.17
	FactJudge	0.45, 0.19	0.47, 0.32	0.54, 0.09	0.5, 0.14
	NB	0.54, 0.25	0.55, 0.38	0.625, 0.12	0.55, 0.17
(0.5-0.65)(8/23)	HITS	0.66, 0.25	0.6, 0.39	0.7, 0.14	0.6, 0.19
for Yahoo	**OP-D**	**0.72, 0.28**	**0.64, 0.41**	**0.75, 0.15**	**0.68, 0.22**
(0.65-1)(33/86) For MPQA;	Random	0.81, 0.16	0.84, 0.27	0.77, 0.19	0.8, 0.32
	FactJudge	0.81, 0.16	0.82, 0.27	0.56, 0.15	0.63, 0.27
	NB	0.92, 0.18	0.93, 0.3	0.81, 0.19	0.8, 0.3
(0.65-1)(9/23)	HITS	0.91, 0.18	0.91, 0.29	0.75, 0.18	0.76, 0.3
For Yahoo	**OP-D**	**0.93, 0.19**	**0.94, 0.31**	**0.96, 0.25**	**0.85, 0.34**

fact labels to the annotators, and ask them to label 5 opinions, which they feel are important as well as diverse topics to cover the entire article. Each article is provided to 3 annotators and we use a rank aggregation method to prepare a gold standard of 5 *important* and *diverse* opinions from these articles.

Table 5: Comparison results for the most diverse set of opinions

Method	$P@3(50)$ MPQA	$P@5(50)$ MPQA	$P@3(25)$ Yahoo	$P@5(25)$ Yahoo
NB	0.322	0.344	0.35	0.31
HITS	0.41	0.4	0.42	0.4
MMR(On NB)	0.387	0.36	0.41	0.38
MMR(On HITS)	0.465	0.44	0.48	0.46
Grasshopper(On NB)	0.384	0.38	0.39	0.37
Grasshopper(On HITS)	0.471	0.44	0.493	0.48
DivRank	0.485	0.473	0.51	0.49
OP-D	**0.584**	**0.571**	**0.63**	**0.61**

We now measure $P@3$ and $P@5$ (Total annotated important and diverse opinions per article is 5, so recall is a simple function of precision, therefore we omitted.) depending on what fraction of the top 3 or 5 sentences returned by various systems feature in the 5 *important* and *diverse* opinions, as selected by the annotators. We use the standard diversity algorithms, MMR (Carbonell and Goldstein, 1998) and Grasshopper (Zhu et al., 2007), both on the results of NB and HITS, as well as DivRank (Mei et al., 2010) as baseline algorithms for diversity. **Table 5** shows that OP-D outperforms other methods (sometimes even by **10%**) in detecting diverse opinions. While both MMR and Grasshopper are able to achieve improvement over both NB and HITS classifiers, the order of improvement by OP-D over HITS is much higher, indicating that decreasing the hub scores of the authority of the selected hubs results eventually in more diverse opinions getting selected.

A goodness test of algorithms would be if the chosen sentences fall uniformly under various categories and sub-categories - this may instill diverse type of user engagement. We took the top 5 sentences for 23 Articles from Yahoo Dataset detected by OP-D, DivRank, Grasshopper (on NB), Grasshopper (on HITS), MMR (on NB), MMR (on HITS) and then got each sentence (opinions) labeled by 2 anonymous human annotators for the category and subcategories it belongs to. Any tie has been settled by another annotator. **Figures 2** and **3** show the distribution of opinions detected by these algorithms into various categories and subcategories respectively[5]. Clearly, OP-D is able to select the opinionated sentences from various categories and subcategories much more uniformly than the other algorithms. OP-D achieves the highest Shannon entropy among all the baselines reinforcing that claim. The performance can be even better

---

[5]For the sake of space, Fig. 3 shows only the best 3 algorithms.

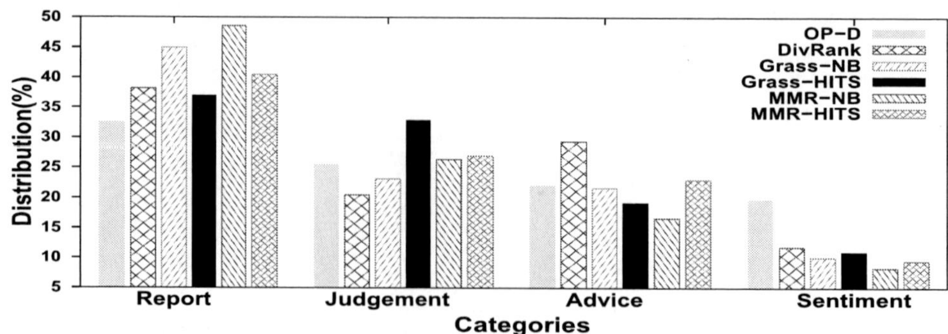

Figure 2: Distribution (Shannon Entropy) of opinions detected by OP-D (1.97), DivRank (1.88), Grasshopper on NB (1.82), Grasshopper on HITS (1.864), MMR on NB (1.73), MMR on HITS (1.8) into 4 broad categories.

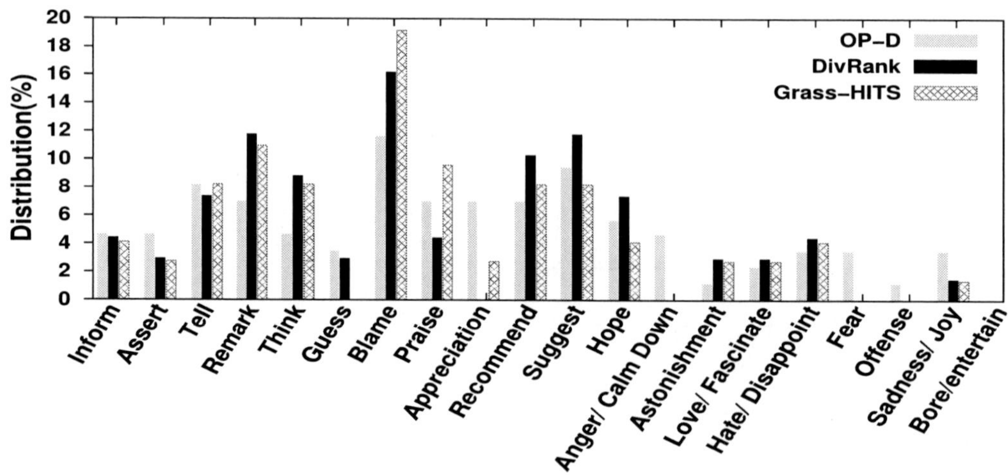

Figure 3: Distribution(Shannon Entropy) of opinions detected by best 3 methods- OP-D(4.05) DivRank(3.65),Grasshopper on HITS (S.E.= 3.63) into sub-categories.S.E. for Grasshopper on NB(3.54),MMR on NB(3.5),MMR on HITS(3.61).

appreciated if we can understand the overall distribution of opinions in an article. However, manually classifying all opinionated sentences is not possible - hence we build an automated classification model, which has been described in the next section.

5 Automatic Classification of Opinions into Opinion Categories

Dataset Preparation: 134 articles from MPQA and 29 articles from Yahoo dataset are taken randomly and have been annotated (with categories of opinion) manually using volunteers, different from the authors (Inter-annotator agreement Cohen κ is 0.8). Details of the datasets are provided in **Table 6**.

Table 6: Statistics of the Annotated MPQA and Yahoo dataset for automatic classification of opinion

Dataset	Sentences	Category	Sentences	Dataset	Sentences	Category	Sentences
MPQA	1237	Report	677	Yahoo	470	Report	216
		Judgment	247			Judgment	110
		Advise	132			Advise	79
		Sentiment	181			Sentiment	65

Features: We briefly describe the features used for automatic classification below:
(a) Sentence Length: Number of words in a sentence.

(b) Entropy of POS tags: After Parts of Speech (POS) tagging the sentence with Stanford POS tagger (De Marneffe et al., 2006), we take 14 POS tags (noun, pronoun, verb etc.) to calculate the Entropy of the probability distribution of POS tags in the sentence.

$$Entropy(i) = -\sum p_j * log_2(p_j) \tag{3}$$

(c) Positive, Negative and Neutral words: Number of positive, negative and neutral sentiment words. We checked it against standard positive, negative ((Rajkumar et al., 2014)) and neutral word set.

(d) Polarity of root verb: Polarity (+1, 0, -1) of the root verb is used as another feature.

(e) Average POS tag presence: We take average_word, average_letter_count, average_preposition, average_noun, average_pronoun, average_adjective, average_adverb for each category as features. For instance, average_noun for a category (e.g., reporting, advise etc) is computed as the average number of nouns per sentence of that category in the training set.

(f) Count of POS tags: Along with 5 different numeric features - count of noun, pronoun, adjective, adverb, preposition, we include 2 numeric features - count of weak adjectives and strong adjectives.

(g) Dependency Features: Count of adverbial clause modifier (advcl), adverb modifier (advmod), adjectival modifier (amod), clausal complement (ccomp), numeric modifier (num) dependencies are 5 numeric features (De Marneffe et al., 2006).

(h) Presence of Different Categories of Opinionated Words: From opinion groups and examples in (Asher et al., 2009), we collected words which are related to each of the four categories. Later we extended the wordset of each category by identifying similar words from wordnet (by calculating word similarity by path based approach) for Reporting, Judgment, Advice and Sentiment categories and created corresponding wordsets (4 binary features: 1 if word is present in the corresponding wordset, otherwise 0). Later, we manually checked every word in the wordset and removed words from the dataset which are not linked at all.

Classification Model: Initial datasets are imbalanced so we use SMOTE algorithm (Chawla et al., 2002) to make balanced datasets (w.r.t. number of reporting) and run several classifiers to obtain the best classification results. Repeated Incremental pruning - Java version (JRip), Logistic Regression (LR), Multi-Class Classifier (MCC), Naive Bayes (NB), Sequential Minimal Optimization (SMO), Support Vector Machine (SVM) available in Weka Toolkit (Hall et al., 2009) are used in the classification experiments.

Table 7: Comparison of 5-fold cross validation Accuracy (A), Precision (P), Recall (R), F1-Score (F) results for automatic classification of opinions for MPQA and Yahoo datasets.

Method	MPQA				Yahoo			
	A(%)	P	R	F	A(%)	P	R	F
JRip	**70.10**	**0.74**	**0.71**	**0.725**	**70.17**	**0.63**	**0.70**	**0.664**
LR	67.18	0.66	0.67	0.665	62.61	0.61	0.67	0.638
MCC	67.17	0.65	0.67	0.66	64.71	0.59	0.65	0.619
NB	53.68	0.51	0.54	0.525	50.42	0.55	0.51	0.53
SVM	53.12	0.53	0.53	0.53	64.3	0.5	0.64	0.561
SMO	65.73	0.68	0.66	0.67	68.48	0.59	0.68	0.632

Cross Validation: We first performed a 5-fold cross-validation using different classifiers. We achieve 70.1% accuracy, 0.74 precision (macro-average), 0.71 recall, 0.725 F-Score for MPQA and 70.17% accuracy, 0.63 precision (macro-average), 0.70 recall and 0.664 F-Score for Yahoo dataset for the task of opinion classification by the JRip classifier which produces better results than other five classifiers - Logistic Regression (LR), Multi-Class Classifier (MCC), Naive Bayes (NB), Sequential Minimal Optimization (SMO), Support Vector Machine (SVM). The results are shown in **Table 7.**

We now use this classifier to plot the opinion category distribution. We plot this distribution for top 3, 5 and 10 opinionated sentences retrieved by OP-D algorithm from the entire MPQA and Yahoo dataset. Then these top 3 (5 and 10) opinionated sentences are collected from each article into a set and the distribution of the set is plotted in **Figure 4**. We clearly observe that if we focus on the top 3 opinions only, OP-D is able to select uniformly from the four categories. However, as we look at top 5 or top 10 opinions, more opinions from Report category come in, which might be due to the fact that Report category is more prevalent in the dataset.

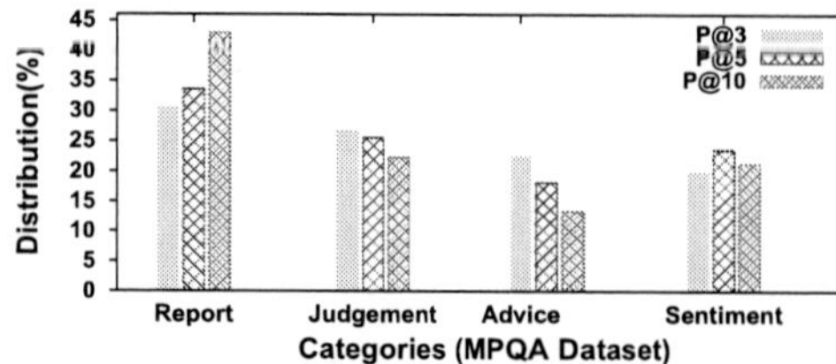
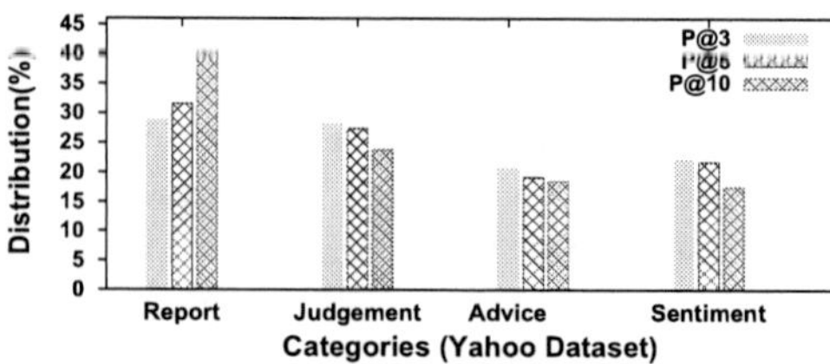

Figure 4: Distribution of opinion categories for top 3, 5 and 10 opinions retrieved by OP-D

6 Conclusion

In this paper, we first introduced diversity in a graphical framework to identify diverse and important opinions from a news article. Further, we built an automated classification model to classify the opinions into various opinion categories. Extensive evaluation establishes that the proposed modification helps in identifying the most diverse opinions from different opinion categories, giving a promising performance gain over the competing baselines. The top sentences returned by the algorithm can therefore be used to kick-start user discussions on a given news article. Building and deploying a system to that effect will be the immediate future step. Also, we would like to study more on how the distribution of opinions to facts, as well as across various opinion categories varies across various news categories.

References

Nicholas Asher, Farah Benamara, and Yvette Yannick Mathieu. 2009. Appraisal of opinion expressions in discourse. *Lingvisticæ Investigationes*, 32(2):279–292.

Jaime Carbonell and Jade Goldstein. 1998. The use of mmr, diversity-based reranking for reordering documents and producing summaries. In *Proceedings of the 21st annual international ACM SIGIR conference on Research and development in information retrieval*, pages 335–336. ACM.

Nitesh V. Chawla, Kevin W. Bowyer, Lawrence O. Hall, and W. Philip Kegelmeyer. 2002. Smote: synthetic minority over-sampling technique. *Journal of artificial intelligence research*, 16:321–357.

Marie-Catherine De Marneffe, Bill MacCartney, Christopher D Manning, et al. 2006. Generating typed dependency parses from phrase structure parses. In *LREC*, volume 6, pages 449–454.

Günes Erkan and Dragomir R Radev. 2004. Lexrank: Graph-based lexical centrality as salience in text summarization. *Journal of Artificial Intelligence Research*, 22:457–479.

Mark Hall, Eibe Frank, Geoffrey Holmes, Bernhard Pfahringer, Peter Reutemann, and Ian H Witten. 2009. The weka data mining software: an update. *ACM SIGKDD explorations newsletter*, 11(1):10–18.

Soo-Min Kim and Eduard Hovy. 2006. Extracting opinions, opinion holders, and topics expressed in online news media text. pages 1–8. ACL.

Qiaozhu Mei, Jian Guo, and Dragomir Radev. 2010. Divrank: the interplay of prestige and diversity in information networks. In *SIGKDD*, pages 1009–1018. Acm.

Sean A Munson, Daniel Xiaodan Zhou, and Paul Resnick. 2009. Sidelines: An algorithm for increasing diversity in news and opinion aggregators. In *ICWSM*.

James W Pennebaker, Martha E Francis, and Roger J Booth. 2001. Linguistic inquiry and word count: Liwc 2001. *Mahway: Lawrence Erlbaum Associates*, 71:2001.

Ashequl Qadir. 2009. Detecting opinion sentences specific to product features in customer reviews using typed dependency relations. eETTs '09, pages 38–43.

Pujari Rajkumar, Swara Desai, Niloy Ganguly, and Pawan Goyal. 2014. A novel two-stage framework for extracting opinionated sentences from news articles. *TextGraphs-9*, pages 25–33.

Horacio Saggionα and Adam Funk. 2010. Interpreting sentiwordnet for opinion classification. In *Proceedings of the seventh conference on international language resources and evaluation LREC10*.

Roser Saurí. 2008. *A factuality profiler for eventualities in text*. ProQuest.

Thomas Scholz and Stefan Conrad. 2013. Opinion mining in newspaper articles by entropy-based word connections. In *EMNLP*, pages 1828–1839.

Sandeep Soni, Tanushree Mitra, Eric Gilbert, and Jacob Eisenstein. 2014. Modeling factuality judgments in social media text. *ACL*.

Janyce Wiebe and Ellen Riloff. 2005. Creating subjective and objective sentence classifiers from unannotated texts. In *CICLingLing*, pages 486–497. Springer.

Janyce Wiebe, Theresa Wilson, and Matthew Bell. Identifying collocations for recognizing opinions. In *ACL-2001 Workshop*, pages 24–31.

Janyce M Wiebe, Rebecca F Bruce, and Thomas P O'Hara. 1999. Development and use of a gold-standard data set for subjectivity classifications. pages 246–253. ACL.

Janyce Wiebe, Theresa Wilson, and Claire Cardie. 2005. Annotating expressions of opinions and emotions in language. *Language resources and evaluation*, 39(2-3):165–210.

Hong Yu and Vasileios Hatzivassiloglou. 2003. Towards answering opinion questions: Separating facts from opinions and identifying the polarity of opinion sentences. pages 129–136. EMNLP.

Bei Yu, Stefan Kaufmann, and Daniel Diermeier. 2008. Exploring the characteristics of opinion expressions for political opinion classification. In *Proceedings of the 2008 international conference on Digital government research*, pages 82–91. Digital Government Society of North America.

Xiaojin Zhu, Andrew B Goldberg, Jurgen Van Gael, and David Andrzejewski. 2007. Improving diversity in ranking using absorbing random walks. In *HLT-NAACL*, pages 97–104. Citeseer.

Active learning for detection of stance components

Maria Skeppstedt[1], Magnus Sahlgren[2], Carita Paradis[3], Andreas Kerren[1]
[1]Computer Science Department, Linnaeus University, Växjö, Sweden
{maria.skeppstedt,andreas.kerren}@lnu.se
[2]Swedish Institute of Computer Science, Kista, Sweden
mange@sics.se
[3]Centre for Languages and Literature, Lund University, Lund, Sweden
carita.paradis@englund.lu.se

Abstract

Automatic detection of five language components, which are all relevant for expressing opinions and for stance taking, was studied: *positive sentiment*, *negative sentiment*, *speculation*, *contrast* and *condition*. A resource-aware approach was taken, which included manual annotation of 500 training samples and the use of limited lexical resources. Active learning was compared to random selection of training data, as well as to a lexicon-based method. Active learning was successful for the categories *speculation*, *contrast* and *condition*, but not for the two sentiment categories, for which results achieved when using active learning were similar to those achieved when applying a random selection of training data. This difference is likely due to a larger variation in how sentiment is expressed than in how speakers express the other three categories. This larger variation was also shown by the lower recall results achieved by the lexicon-based approach for sentiment than for the categories *speculation*, *contrast* and *condition*.

1   Introduction

In studies of automatic detection of opinions, it is typically assumed that there are substantial resources available in the form of annotated text corpora (Konstantinova et al., 2012; Socher et al., 2013). However, such large resources of annotated data cannot always be obtained, e.g., when crowd-sourced or community annotations are not possible or not desirable (Fort et al., 2011; Xia and Yetisgen-Yildiz, 2012). The aim of this study is, therefore, to explore the possibility to detect language components that are relevant for opinion mining and stance detection, when using very limited resources of manually annotated data.

Five language components, which are relevant as topic-independent components for expressing opinions and for stance taking, were investigated: *positive* and *negative* sentiment, *speculation*, *contrast* and *condition*. Sentiment analysis is an important component of stance detection, as knowledge of whether positive or negative sentiment is expressed towards a target of interest has been shown useful for the task of binary stance detection, i.e., stance taking *for* or *against* a certain target (Mohammad et al., 2016).

Speculation, *contrast* and *condition* were assessed as important components for stance taking, as they can all be used as modifications of opinions. For instance, an expression of *contrast* could indicate that opinions of different polarities are expressed, e.g., "I did enjoy reading some of this book, but the two tales in the middle dragged too much for me to be able to really recommend this book". A positive opinion that is expressed with *speculation* might be less positive, e.g., "His description of the 50's seems accurate and readers might enjoy the trip back in time". Finally, when a positive opinion is expressed in the context of a *condition*, it is not necessarily positive anymore, e.g., "If the plot had been more gripping, more intense, this would have worked perfectly".

2   Previous research

There is a large number of previous sentiment analysis studies, which use different techniques, corpora and task definitions (Täckström and McDonald, 2011; Wang et al., 2012). For instance, an accuracy of 0.85 was achieved when recursive neural networks were used to classify movie review sentences from the

This work is licensed under a Creative Commons Attribution 4.0 International Licence. Licence details: http:// creativecommons.org/licenses/by/4.0/

Proceedings of the Workshop on Computational Modeling of People's Opinions, Personality, and Emotions in Social Media,
pages 50–59, Osaka, Japan, December 12 2016.

Stanford Sentiment Treebank into the categories *positive* and *negative* sentiment. When the sentences were classified into a five-level scale of sentiment, with the category *neutral* included (Socher et al., 2013), an accuracy of 0.81 was achieved.

The three opinion modifying categories have all been defined in previous research. *Speculation* has, for instance, been defined as "the possible existence of a thing [that] is claimed – neither its existence nor its non-existence is known for sure" (Vincze, 2010). *Contrast* has been defined as "Contrast(α,β) holds when α and β have similar semantic structures, but contrasting themes, i.e. sentence topics, or when one constituent negates a default consequence of the other" (Reese et al., 2007). Finally, the category *condition* is defined within in Rhetorical Structure Theory as something which "presents a hypothetical, future, or otherwise unrealized situation" (Mann and Taboada, 2016).

There are several studies on speculation/uncertainty detection (Vincze et al., 2008; Farkas et al., 2010; Velupillai, 2012; Wei et al., 2013). On the SFU Review corpus, which consists of English consumer generated reviews of books, movies, music, cars, computers, cookware and hotels (Taboada and Grieve, 2004; Taboada et al., 2006), speculation cues, together with their scopes, have been annotated (Konstantinova et al., 2012). An F-score of 0.92 (Cruz et al., 2015) was achieved when training a support vector machine to automatically detect the annotated cues. The SFU Review corpus has also been annotated for contrasts and conditions (Taboada and Hay, 2008). Experiments have been carried out on the task of determining whether a sentence in this corpus contains an expression of *speculation, contrast* or *condition*. A classifier F-score of around 0.90 was achieved for *speculation*, around 0.60 for *contrast* and around 0.70 for *condition*, when using around 3,000 training samples (Skeppstedt et al., 2015).

The standard method to randomly select samples for training the machine learning models were used in all studies described above. However, instead of a random selection, it is possible to use an active selection of useful training data. Although there are some studies on the use of such active learning techniques for sentiment analysis (Li et al., 2012; Kranjc et al., 2015), few studies measure results for resource-aware approaches when using a very limited amount of manually annotated data. The usefulness of active learning for sentence-level detection of language components relevant when expressing stance, and when using a very limited amount of training data, is, therefore, the focus of this study.

3 Method

As the main resource-aware method for detecting the five categories studied, active learning was used. Lexicons of marker words for the categories were also incorporated when training the classifier. A baseline was formed by a simple look-up method that used these lexicons.

3.1 Corpora and lexicons

All classification experiments consisted of the task of sentence classification. That is, each training and testing sample consisted of a sentence and the models were trained to detect whether a sentence contained the category of interest or not. For exploring *negative* and *positive* sentiment, the previously mentioned corpus of 11,855 sentences (the Stanford Sentiment Treebank) that was annotated for sentiment was used (Socher et al., 2013). The annotations were collapsed into the three categories *positive, negative,* and *neutral*. These categories were then transformed into two binary text categorisation tasks: a) the detection of sentences that express *positive* sentiment in contrast to *negative* or *neutral*, and b) the detection of sentences that express *negative* sentiment in contrast to *positive* or *neutral*.

Data used for the other three categories consisted of the, above mentioned, corpora created by Konstantinova et al. (2012) and by Taboada and Hay (2008). Both of these two annotation projects were carried out on the 12,663 sentences included in the SFU Review corpus. The *speculation* category annotated by Konstantinova et al. and the *condition* category annotated by Taboada and Hay were used without modifications. The closely related categories *contrast* and *concession*, which were annotated by Taboada and Hay, were, however, merged into the one category that is here referred to as *contrast*. The annotations were transformed into three separate binary classifications tasks, i.e., the task to detect whether a sentence contained *speculation, contrast* and/or *condition*, respectively. The same procedure as used in the first of the CoNLL-2010 shared tasks (Farkas et al., 2010) for transforming the data into this format was applied. That is, if either the scope of a *speculation* cue or a segment annotated for *concession/contrast* or *condition* was present in a sentence, the sentence was categorised as belonging to this category (or categories, when several applied).

Limited-sized lexicons of marker words for the five categories were used. For positive and negative sentiment, SentiWordNet (Baccianella et al., 2010) was used to compile the lexicons. The 500 most positive and the 500 most negative words were extracted, and one annotator manually removed words from these lists that would not be considered as typically positive or negative in a movie review setting. Which words to extract as the most positive/negative was determined by ranking the words according to the difference between the positive and negative score of the SentiWordNet synset to which the word belonged. For words that belonged to several synsets, the score resulting in the best ranking on the the positive/negative list was used. The extraction and manual classification resulted in a final list of 373 markers for positive sentiment and 414 markers for negative sentiment.

The lexicons for *speculation* and *contrast* were based on marker words/constructions that have previously been listed by Konstantinova et al. (2012) and Velupillai et al. (2014), and by Reese et al. (2007), respectively. These markers were then used as seed words to expand the lists, by also adding their neighbours in a distributional semantics space to the lists (Sahlgren et al., 2016), as well as their synonyms from a traditional synonym lexicon (Oxford University Press, 2013). In the same fashion as for the sentiment words, the candidates on these expanded lists were then manually classified according to their suitability as marker words. This resulted in a list of 191 markers for *speculation*, and 39 for *contrast*. The *condition* category is a subset of what is defined as *speculation* by Konstantinova et al. (2012). The 26 markers used for this category were, therefore, compiled by manually extracting a subset of the *speculation* markers that were classified as suitable as markers for *condition*.

3.2 Machine learning and active learning methods used

Active learning is built on the idea to reduce the number of training samples required to train a machine learning classifier, by actively selecting useful samples from a pool of unlabelled data. Sample selection could, for instance, be based on the level of uncertainty for a classifier, on the level of disagreement among a number of different classifiers (Olsson, 2008, pp. 25–29), or on the expected model change when adding new data to the pool of labelled data (Tomanek, 2010). The sample selection method used in this study, *simple margin*, is based on expected model change. It is a computationally efficient approach for support vector machines, where the unlabelled sample closest to the separating hyperplane of the classifier is selected (Tong and Koller, 2002).

Support vector machines were used in all experiments, regardless of whether active or random selection of training samples was carried out. The Scikit-learn implementation of the SVC-class with a linear kernel was used (Pedregosa et al., 2011). For all approaches, except approach number four (see section 3.3, below), the machine learning features used were limited to unigrams and bigrams. For approach number four, the output of the lexicon-matching approach was also included as a feature. A minimum of two occurrences in the labelled data was used as a cut-off for including a bigram as a feature, and two occurrences in the entire data pool (labelled and unlabelled) was used as a cut-off for inclusion of unigrams. A corpus created through active selection instead of random selection is not representative of the true data distribution, and standard methods for parameter setting and feature selection do not give reliable results (Schohn and Cohn, 2000). Therefore, the default Scikit-learn SVC parameters were used, and the heuristics of limiting the number of features included to the n best was applied. An n equal to the number of samples was used, and, thereby the number of features was allowed to grow with an increasing number of training data samples. Which features were the best was, however, estimated by a χ^2-based feature selection.

3.3 Experiments

A total of five different approaches for detecting the categories investigated were compared, three methods based on active learning, one based on random sampling and one lexicon-matching approach:

(1) The *lexicon-matching* was the most basic approach. Sentences that contained a marker in any of the five compiled lexicons were classified as belonging to the category for which the lexicon was compiled.

(2) The second most basic approach was to use machine learning with random selection of data. (3) As the third approach, active learning based on *simple margin* for selecting a potentially useful training sample was used. An initial machine learning model was first trained on 30 randomly selected samples. Thereafter, the new training samples were chosen based on their distance to the separating hyperplane of the classifier. Two new training samples, i.e., the two samples closest to the separating hyperplane, were selected in each iteration. (4) The same active learning setup as for approach three was applied, but the output of the lexicon matching was used as one of the features for training the classifier. (5) The final approach was also identical to approach number three, but the initial seed set of 30 training samples was not randomly chosen. Instead, a set of 30 samples was selected, with the criterion of requiring each sample to contain a different marker from the lexicon compiled for this category. This follows previous work (Tomanek et al., 2007), in which results have been improved by the extraction of samples that contain known entities for forming the seed set. For the category *condition*, for which there were less than 30 items in the lexicon, the same lexicon item was used for selecting several seed samples.

3.4 Evaluation

A situation was simulated in which limited resources would be available to create an annotated corpus, and thereby a maximum of 500 annotated sentences would be available for training a classifier. Given a hypothetical annotation speed of 50 sentences per hour, it would be possible to construct such an annotated corpus in ten working hours. The five stance categories were evaluated separately, and separate binary classifiers were trained for each of the categories.

The work of the manual annotator was simulated by using the annotations in the corpora described above. Each corpus was split into two equally large sets: an evaluation set and a set to use as the pool of data from which training samples were to be selected. The pool of data from which samples were selected was thus used as simulated unlabelled data, and manual annotation of the selected samples was simulated by using the labelling available in the annotated corpus. The same randomly selected seed set of 30 training samples was used for all machine learning approaches, except for approach number five, for which the lexicons were used for selecting samples.

There is a large difference between the proportion of samples belonging to the minority category for the different categories. That is, a proportion of 24% for *speculation*, 8% for *contrast* and 4% for *condition*, compared to a proportion of 42% and 39% for *positive* and *negative* sentiment, respectively. In order to investigate whether potential differences between categories depend on these proportion differences, rather than on differences between how the categories are expressed, additional experiments were performed for modified versions of the *positive* and *negative* sentiment corpora. The original training data for the sentiment classifiers was modified to instead contain a 24% proportion of the minority category, i.e., the same proportion of minority category samples as the *speculation* category. This was achieved by removing a randomly selected set of instances that belonged to the minority category from the training data. That is, the instances classified as *positive* when investigating *positive* sentiment, and the instances classified as *negative* for *negative* sentiment.

For each of the seven data sets (five with original minority category frequencies and two with modified frequencies), the experiments were repeated 60 times, with a new random split into an evaluation set and into a pool of data from which to select training samples. For each of the 60 folds, a new randomly selected seed set (or a seed set selected based on the lexicon for approach number five) was used. Average precision, recall and F-score between the 60 folds were measured.

4 Results

Results for the five categories of stance are shown in Figures 1-4. The methods evaluated showed one trend for the two sentiment categories, and another trend for the three other categories.

For sentiment, results for active learning were very similar to those achieved when randomly sampling training data. When using 500 training samples, both methods achieved an average F-score of around 0.57 for detecting positive sentiment and an average F-score of around 0.52/0.53 for detecting negative sentiment. For the two versions of the sentiment corpora that had been modified to contain a lower

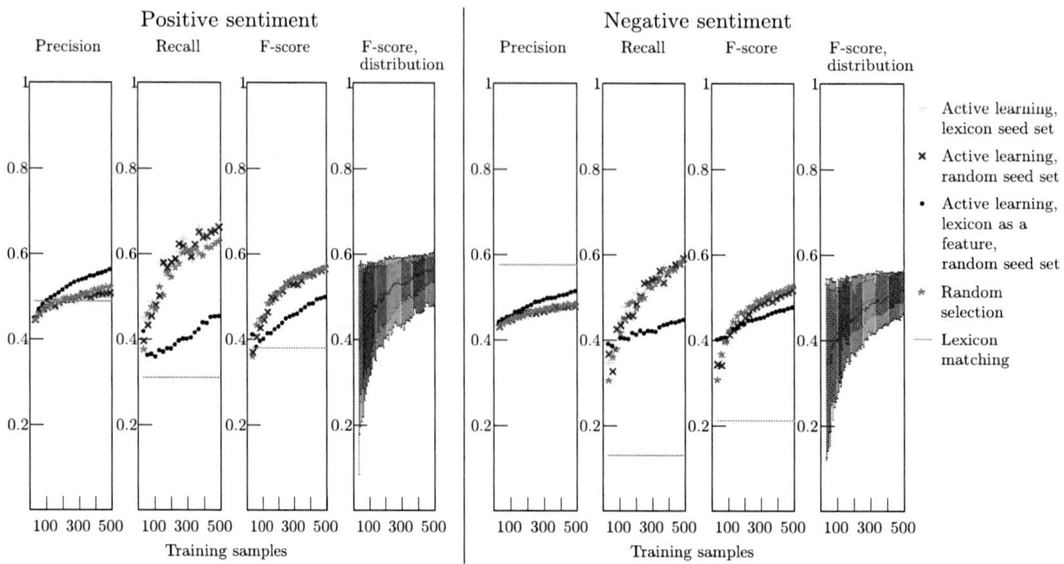

Figure 1: Results for the categories *positive* and *negative* sentiment. Average precision, recall and F-score for the 60 folds are shown. The bars for the distribution of F-score show the 5th to 95th percentile of the results for the 60 folds for *Active learning with a random seed set* and *Random selection*.

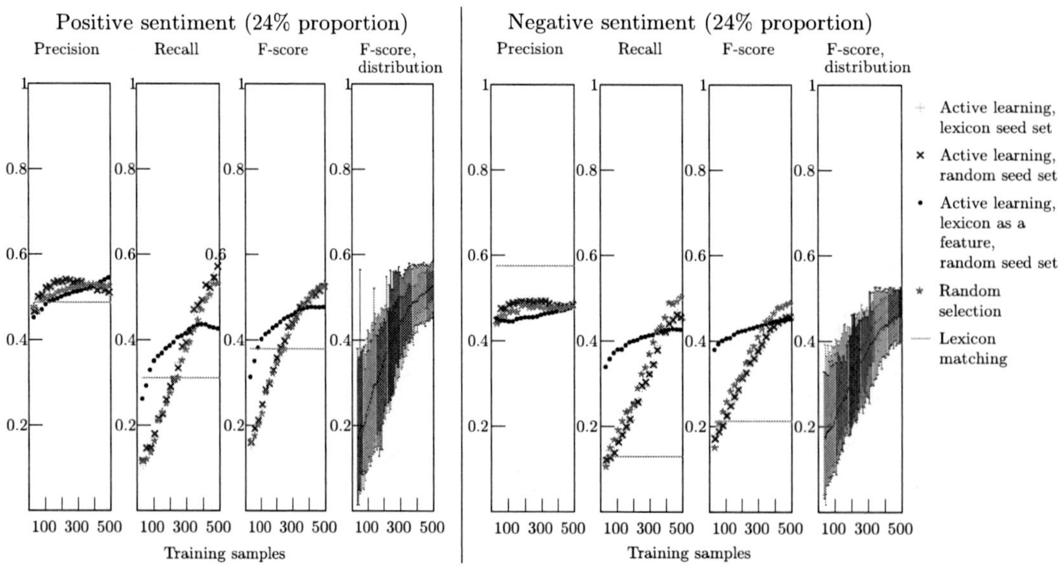

Figure 2: Results when the training data sets have been artificially modified to contain 24% of instances that belong to the minority categories, i.e., to the categories *positive* and *negative* sentiment, respectively. Average precision, recall and F-score for the 60 folds are shown. The bars for the distribution of F-score show the 5th to 95th percentile of the results for the 60 folds for *Active learning with a random seed set* and *Random selection*.

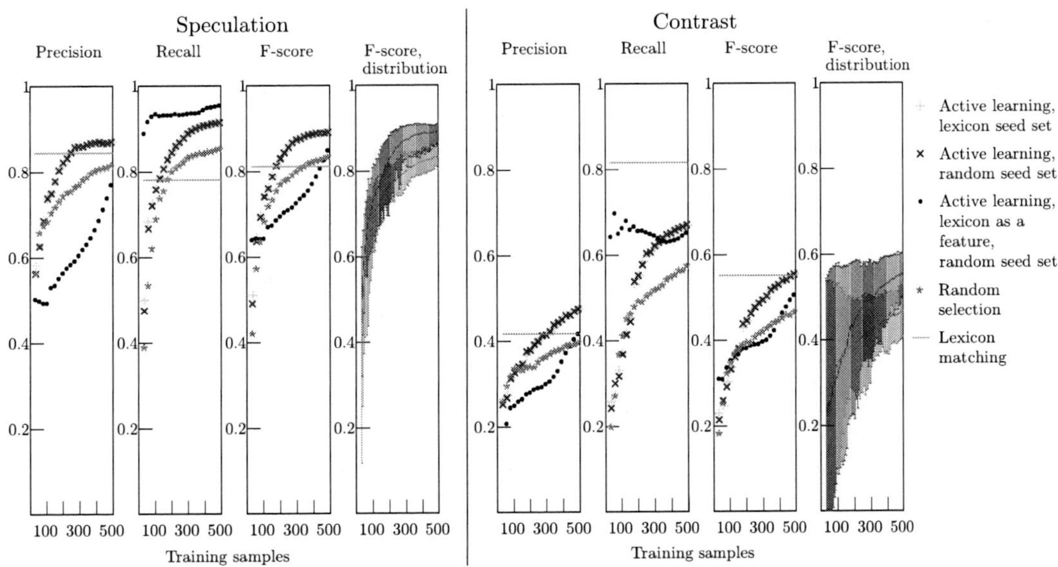

Figure 3: Results for the categories *speculation* and *contrast*. Average precision, recall and F-score for the 60 folds are shown. The bars for the distribution of F-score show the 5th to 95th percentile of the results for the 60 folds for *Active learning with a random seed set* and *Random selection*.

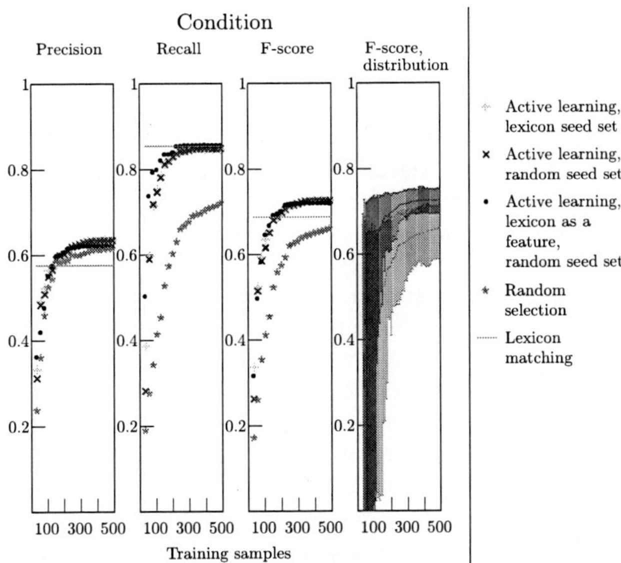

Figure 4: Results for the category *condition*. Average precision, recall and F-score for the 60 folds are shown. The bars for the distribution of F-score show the 5th to 95th percentile of the results for the 60 folds for *Active learning with a random seed set* and *Random selection*.

proportion of the minority categories, the same trend with similar results for active learning and random sampling was shown for *positive* sentiment, while random sample selection was slightly more successful than active learning for *negative* sentiment.

For *speculation*, *contrast* and *condition* on the other hand, active learning clearly outperformed random sampling. For *speculation*, an average F-score of 0.89 was achieved for active learning and an average F-score of 0.83 for random sampling, when using 500 training samples. The performance improvement for active learning started to level out already at 300 training samples for *speculation*, and at that point of measure, the difference between active learning and random selection of training samples was even larger. When using 500 training samples for *contrast*, an average F-score of 0.56 was achieved when using active learning and an average F-score of 0.47 for random sampling. The corresponding results for *condition* were an average F-score of 0.73 for active learning and 0.66 for random selection.

Another difference between these two groups of categories was the results of the lexicon-matching strategy. For *speculation* and *condition*, the lexicon matching performed in line with the classifier trained on randomly sampled data. For *contrast*, lexicon-matching outperformed the random sampling method and achieved results in line with the classifier trained on actively selected data using 500 training samples. However, the machine learning-based classifier showed a better balance between precision and recall.

The use of a seed set containing lexicon terms, instead of a randomly selected seed set, had almost no effect on the results. The use of the lexicon for generating features for training the classifier had a detrimental effect on the average F-score for all categories evaluated with a naturally occurring minority category proportion, except for *condition* for which it had no effect. For the sentiment categories, the use of the lexicon-matching feature led to a lower recall and a very limited increase in precision. The opposite results were observed for *speculation* and *condition*, with a much lower precision and an improvement in recall (for approximately the first 150 samples, a large improvement in recall). In contrast, when the sentiment corpora were modified to only contain 24% samples belonging to the minority category, the inclusion of lexicon-generated features led to a substantial improvement of results for very small data sets. Machine learning was, however, more successful when using 500 training samples.

5   Discussion

For this experiment, in which a very small training data set was used, active learning was successful for *speculation*, *contrast* and *condition*, but not for sentiment classification. This was observed regardless of which of the two minority category proportions for sentiment that was used. These differences are, therefore, likely to be due to a variation in how the different categories are expressed by the speakers.

Positive and *negative* sentiment are likely to be described with a larger set of words and constructions than the other three categories studied. This is indicated by the low recall results of the lexicon-matching approach for sentiment in comparison to the *speculation/contrast/condition* categories. Lower recall was achieved despite the fact that much larger lexical resources were used for detection of the sentiment categories. This larger variation in how the sentiment categories are expressed might be a reason why active learning did not have a positive effect for sentiment classification, since more variation in how a category is expressed results in a larger, natural, frequency of informative samples. This has the effect that a random selection of training samples for sentiment detection has a large probability of resulting in an informative sample being selected. For the three other categories, on the other hand, there is a lower probability that a randomly selected sample will be informative to the classifier, since there is a lower frequency of samples which contain information that is still unknown to the classifier.

The use of 500 training samples and an active learning approach gave results for *speculation* and *condition* that were in line with those previously achieved when more training data was used (Skeppstedt et al., 2015). Results for *contrast* were, however, slightly lower than those previously achieved. An active learning-based annotation effort of 500 samples, or possibly additional samples for *contrast*, would thus be the approach recommended for these three categories. For *contrast*, the same average F-score was achieved by lexicon-matching as for the classifier trained on 500 actively selected training samples. Although the compilation of a small lexicon of words and constructions signifying *contrast* is less time-consuming than the annotation of 500 sentences, the machine learning approach might be preferable, as it results in a better precision/recall balance.

In contrast, an F-score of 0.5 for detecting positive and negative sentiment is far from the results achieved in previous studies on the same classification task (Socher et al., 2013). A manual annotation of 11,855 sentences (including a more detailed annotation of 200,000 phrases in these sentences) was, however, required to achieve the average accuracy of above 0.8 that has been presented in previous studies. That is, an annotation effort that is far from reasonable in a project with limited resources. Whether to recommend such a limited-resource project to venture the construction of a sentence-level sentiment classifier, depends on the user requirements for this system. To be able to find around 60% of the sentences in which a negative or positive opinion is expressed, and to generate a list of such sentences of which around half are correctly categorised as positive/negative, is likely to be acceptable in some, but not all, circumstances. For sentiment, it is also less clear what training data selection method to recommended, since active and random sampling led to similar results.

It can be concluded that for the categories and text genre evaluated, i.e., the review genre, it is not worth the effort of compiling a limited lexical resource for selecting the seed set or for generating classifier features. However, the lexicons were useful for feature generation in the sentiment corpora with a smaller minority category proportion, when the data set contained up to around 300 training samples. It is, therefore, likely that lexical sentiment resources are more useful in a genre that lacks large resources of annotated data, and in which positive and negative sentiment is less frequently occurring.

5.1 Future work

Although the limited lexical resources compiled for this study did not contribute positively to the results for sentiment detection, it is still likely that an approach fully focusing on detection rules based on extensive and high-quality lexical resources could (i) either be a viable alternative to the machine learning models trained on limited data, which were explored here, or (ii) contribute positively when used as features for training a machine learning model. For instance, by compiling an extended version of SentiWordNet, and leveraging the sentiment scores of positive and negative terms in the resource, Dang et al. (2010) achieved precision and recall scores of around 80% for document level sentiment classification. Future work, therefore, includes the evaluation of such lexicon-based methods on sentence-level sentiment analysis, taking the resource-aware approach used in this study for evaluating its usefulness for projects with limited resources. In particular, there is previous research in which the active learning process has been improved by allowing the annotator to also rank features according to their importance to the category in question (Settles, 2011). Such an approach has the potential of being resource efficient, as it combines the process of compiling a sentiment lexicon with the process of creating labelled data that is useful for training a classifier.

6 Conclusion

Active learning was a successful strategy for three of the categories studied. When using 500 training samples and applying active learning, average F-scores of 0.89, 0.56, and 0.73 were achieved for detecting sentences containing *speculation*, *contrast* and *condition*, while the corresponding figures using random selection of training data were 0.83, 0.47, and 0.66.

For training classifiers to detect the categories *positive* and *negative* sentiment, however, similar results were achieved by active learning and random sampling of training data, an average F-score of 0.57 for detecting positive sentiment and an average F-score of around 0.52/0.53 for detecting negative sentiment. The reason for active learning not being successful for sentiment was not the high proportion of samples that belong to the minority categories in the sentiment corpora. Similar results were achieved when the training data set for sentiment was artificially modified to contain the same proportion of minority category samples as the corpus annotated for *speculation*. Instead, the difference is likely to be due to a larger variation in how *positive* and *negative* sentiment can be expressed, than in how speakers express *speculation*, *contrast* and *condition*. The larger variation in speakers' expressions for *positive* and *negative* sentiment is also indicated by the lower recall achieved by the lexicon-matching approach for sentiment than for the other three categories.

Acknowledgements

This work was funded by the StaViCTA project, framework grant "the Digitized Society – Past, Present, and Future" with No. 2012-5659 from the Swedish Research Council (Vetenskapsrådet).

References

Stefano Baccianella, Andrea Esuli, and Fabrizio Sebastiani. 2010. Sentiwordnet 3.0: An enhanced lexical resource for sentiment analysis and opinion mining. In *Proceedings of the Seventh International Conference on Language Resources and Evaluation (LREC'10)*, pages 2200–2204, Valletta, Malta, May. European Language Resources Association (ELRA).

Noa P. Cruz, Maite Taboada, and Ruslan Mitkov. 2015. A machine-learning approach to negation and speculation detection for sentiment analysis. *Journal of the Association for Information Science and Technology*, pages 526–558.

Yan Dang, Yulei Zhang, and HsinChun Chen. 2010. A lexicon-enhanced method for sentiment classification: An experiment on online product reviews. *IEEE Intelligent Systems*, 25(4):46–53.

Richárd Farkas, Veronika Vincze, György Móra, János Csirik, and György Szarvas. 2010. The CoNLL-2010 shared task: Learning to detect hedges and their scope in natural language text. In *Proceedings of the Fourteenth Conference on Computational Natural Language Learning*, pages 1–12, Stroudsburg, PA. Association for Computational Linguistics.

Karën Fort, Gilles Adda, Benoît Sagot, and Joseph Mariani. 2011. Crowdsourcing for language resource development: Critical analysis of amazon mechanical turk overpowering use. In *LTC, 5th Language and Technology Conference*.

Natalia Konstantinova, Sheila C.M. de Sousa, Noa P. Cruz, Manuel J. Maña, Maite Taboada, and Ruslan Mitkov. 2012. A review corpus annotated for negation, speculation and their scope. In *Proceedings of the Eight International Conference on Language Resources and Evaluation (LREC)*, pages 3190–3195, Istanbul, Turkey. European Language Resources Association (ELRA).

Janez Kranjc, Jasmina Smailović, Vid Podpečan, Miha Grčar, Martin Žnidaršič, and Nada Lavrač. 2015. Active learning for sentiment analysis on data streams: Methodology and workflow implementation in the clowdflows platform. *Information Processing & Management*, 51(2):187 – 203.

Shoushan Li, Shengfeng Ju, Guodong Zhou, and Xiaojun Li. 2012. Active learning for imbalanced sentiment classification. In *Joint Conference on Empirical Methods in Natural Language Processing and Computational Natural Language Learning*, pages 139–148, Jeju Island, Korea.

William C. Mann and Maite Taboada. 2016. Rhetorical structure theory, relation definitions. http://www.sfu.ca/rst/01intro/definitions.html (Accessed 2016-09-19).

Saif M Mohammad, Parinaz Sobhani, and Svetlana Kiritchenko. 2016. Stance and sentiment in tweets. *arXiv preprint arXiv:1605.01655*.

Fredrik Olsson. 2008. *Bootstrapping Named Entity Annotation by Means of Active Machine Learning*. Ph.D. thesis, University of Gothenburg. Faculty of Arts.

Oxford University Press. 2013. Oxford thesaurus of English. Digital Version 2.2.1 (156) on Mac OS X.

Fabian Pedregosa, Gaël Varoquaux, Alexandre Gramfort, Vincent Michel, Bertrand Thirion, Olivier Grisel, Mathieu Blondel, Peter Prettenhofer, Ron Weiss, Vincent Dubourg, Jake Vanderplas, Alexandre Passos, David Cournapeau, Matthieu Brucher, Matthieu Perrot, and Edouard Duchesnay. 2011. Scikit-learn: Machine learning in Python. *Journal of Machine Learning Research*, 12:2825–2830.

Brian Reese, Julie Hunter, Nicholas Asher, Pascal Denis, and Jason Baldridge. 2007. Reference manual for the analysis and annotation of rhetorical structure. timeml.org/jamesp/annotation_manual.pdf (accessed May 2015).

Magnus Sahlgren, Amaru Cuba Gyllensten, Fredrik Espinoza, Ola Hamfors, Jussi Karlgren, Fredrik Olsson, Per Persson, Akshay Viswanathan, and Anders Holst. 2016. The Gavagai living lexicon. In *Proceedings of the Conference on Language Resources and Evaluation*. European Language Resources Association (ELRA).

Greg Schohn and David Cohn. 2000. Less is More: Active Learning with Support Vector Machines. In *Proceedings of 17th International Conference on Machine Learning*, pages 839–846, San Francisco, CA, USA. Morgan Kaufmann.

Burr Settles. 2011. Closing the loop: Fast, interactive semi-supervised annotation with queries on features and instances. In *Proceedings of the Conference on Empirical Methods in Natural Language Processing (EMNLP)*, pages 1467–1478, Stroudsburg, PA, USA. Association for Computational Linguistics.

Maria Skeppstedt, Teri Schamp-Bjerede, Magnus Sahlgren, Carita Paradis, and Andreas Kerren. 2015. Detecting speculations, contrasts and conditionals in consumer reviews. In *Proceedings of the 6th Workshop on Computational Approaches to Subjectivity, Sentiment and Social Media Analysis*, pages 162–168, Stroudsburg, PA, USA, September. Association for Computational Linguistics.

Richard Socher, Alex Perelygin, Jean Wu, Jason Chuang, Christopher D. Manning, Andrew Y. Ng, and Christopher Potts. 2013. Recursive deep models for semantic compositionality over a sentiment treebank. In *Proceedings of the 2013 Conference on Empirical Methods in Natural Language Processing*, pages 1631–1642, Stroudsburg, PA, October. Association for Computational Linguistics.

Maite Taboada and Jack Grieve. 2004. Analyzing appraisal automatically. In *Proceedings of the AAAI Spring Symposium on Exploring Attitude and Affect in Text: Theories and Applications*, pages 158–161.

Maite Taboada and Montana Hay. 2008. The SFU review corpus. www.sfu.ca/ ˜mtaboada/research/SFU_Review_Corpus.html (accessed May 2015).

Maite Taboada, Caroline Anthony, and Kimberly Voll. 2006. Methods for creating semantic orientation dictionaries. In *Proceedings of 5th International Conference on Language Resources and Evaluation (LREC)*, pages 427–432, Genoa, Italy. European Language Resources Association (ELRA).

Oscar Täckström and Ryan McDonald. 2011. Discovering fine-grained sentiment with latent variable structured prediction models. In *Advances in Information Retrieval*, volume 6611 of *Lecture Notes in Computer Science*, pages 368–374. Springer Berlin Heidelberg.

Katrin Tomanek, Joachim Wermter, and Udo Hahn. 2007. Efficient annotation with the Jena ANnotation Environment (JANE). In *Proceedings of the Linguistic Annotation Workshop*, pages 9–16, Stroudsburg, PA, USA, June. Association for Computational Linguistics.

Katrin Tomanek. 2010. *Resource-Aware Annotation through Active Learning*. Ph.D. thesis, Technical University of Dortmund.

Simon Tong and Daphne Koller. 2002. Support vector machine active learning with applications to text classification. *J. Mach. Learn. Res.*, 2:45–66, March.

Sumithra Velupillai, Maria Skeppstedt, Maria Kvist, Danielle Mowery, Brian E Chapman, Hercules Dalianis, and Wendy W Chapman. 2014. Cue-based assertion classification for swedish clinical text–developing a lexicon for pyConTextSwe. *Artif Intell Med*, 61(3):137–44, Jul.

Sumithra Velupillai. 2012. *Shades of Certainty – Annotation and Classification of Swedish Medical Records*. Doctoral thesis, Department of Computer and Systems Sciences, Stockholm University, Stockholm, Sweden, April.

Veronika Vincze, György Szarvas, Richárd Farkas, György Móra, and János Csirik. 2008. The BioScope Corpus: Biomedical texts annotated for uncertainty, negation and their scopes. *BMC Bioinformatics*, 9 (Suppl 11):S9.

Veronika Vincze. 2010. Speculation and negation annotation in natural language texts: what the case of BioScope might (not) reveal. In *Proceedings of the Workshop on Negation and Speculation in Natural Language Processing*, pages 28–31, Stroudsburg, PA. Association for Computational Linguistics.

Hao Wang, Dogan Can, Abe Kazemzadeh, François Bar, and Shrikanth Narayanan. 2012. A system for real-time twitter sentiment analysis of 2012 U.S. presidential election cycle. In *Proceedings of the ACL 2012 System Demonstrations*, pages 115–120.

Zhongyu Wei, Junwen Chen, Wei Gao, Binyang Li, Lanjun Zhou, Yulan He, and Kam-Fai Wong. 2013. An empirical study on uncertainty identification in social media context. In *Proceedings of the 51st Annual Meeting of the Association for Computational Linguistics, ACL*, pages 58–62, Stroudsburg, PA. Association for Computational Linguistics.

Fei Xia and Meliha Yetisgen-Yildiz. 2012. Clinical corpus annotation: Challenges and strategies. In *The Third Workshop on Building and Evaluating Resources for Biomedical Text Mining (BioTxtM), an LREC Workshop*. Turkey.

Detecting Opinion Polarities using Kernel Methods

Rasoul Kaljahi
ADAPT Centre
School of Computing
Dublin City University, Ireland
`rasoul.kaljahi@adaptcentre.ie`

Jennifer Foster
ADAPT Centre
School of Computing
Dublin City University, Ireland
`jfoster@computing.dcu.ie`

Abstract

We investigate the application of kernel methods to representing both structural and lexical knowledge for predicting polarity of opinions in consumer product review. We introduce *any-gram kernels* which model lexical information in a significantly faster way than the traditional n-gram features, while capturing all possible orders of n-grams (n) in a sequence without the need to explicitly present a pre-specified set of such orders. We also modify the traditional tree kernel function to compute the similarity based on word embedding vectors instead of exact string match and present experiments using the new models.

1 Introduction

The automatic identification and analysis of opinion and sentiment in text (Pang and Lee, 2008) has emerged as a major natural language processing task in recent years, due in part to the abundance of opinions now available online. Initially, much of the focus of sentiment analysis research was on detecting the overall sentiment of documents and sentences (Pang et al., 2002). This kind of analysis is insufficient when the sentence or document contains multiple opinions directed towards multiple targets and the goal is to identify each of them individually. For example, a review of a laptop may discuss various features of the product such as battery life, speed and memory. While the review may carry a positive assessment of the laptop in general, the sentiment towards some of these aspects may be negative. *Aspect-based* sentiment analysis (ABSA) (Hu and Liu, 2004) aims to tackle this problem. In this work, we address the problem of aspect-based sentiment analysis and follow recent SemEval shared tasks in using consumer reviews of laptops and restaurants as our test domains.

The majority of machine learning approaches to sentiment analysis have relied on bag-of-n-grams (Pang and Lee, 2008). However, n-grams lead to large sparse feature sets which are not computationally efficient. Moreover, only a limited number of orders of n-grams (i.e. n) can be used and the choice of n requires tuning. To tackle this issue, we introduce *any-gram kernels* which 1) capture all orders of n-grams and 2) are faster while 3) performing at the same level as traditional n-gram features.

Recent research has shown that structural features extracted from syntactic analysis of text can boost the performance of surface-oriented models, by capturing information that these models cannot (Karlgren et al., 2010; Kiritchenko et al., 2014). For example, in *If you like spicy food get the chicken vindaloo.*, a lexicon-based model assigns a positive sentiment to the aspect term *spicy food* due to the nearby presence of *like* , whereas a syntax-based model has the potential to recognise that *like* does not convey an opinion when it is modified by *if*. We use tree kernels to model both the constituency and dependency structure of the sentences. This approach is more efficient than hand-crafted syntactic features, as it requires less engineering effort and is faster to develop.

Traditional tree kernel function computes the similarity of trees based on the exact string match of the node labels including words. This method overlooks the similarity between words which can be used interchangeably in the context. Plank and Moschitti (2013) address this problem by generalizing words

This work is licensed under a Creative Commons Attribution 4.0 International Licence. Licence details: `http://creativecommons.org/licenses/by/4.0/`

Proceedings of the Workshop on Computational Modeling of People's Opinions, Personality, and Emotions in Social Media,
pages 60–69, Osaka, Japan, December 12 2016.

using word clusters and latent semantic analysis (LSA). Word embeddings (Bengio et al., 2003), which have been used successfully in tasks involving similarity between words (Collobert and Weston, 2008; Mikolov et al., 2013; Baroni et al., 2014), are an alternative approach to obtain this generalization. We modify the tree kernel function so that the similarity of trees are computed based on the similarity of pre-trained word embedding vectors. We conduct experiments using the new kernel function and find that these similarities are not conclusively more useful than mere string matches.

2 Related Work

Although tree kernels have been previously used in sentiment analysis, no work has directly employed them in ABSA. The closest work has been carried out by Nguyen and Shirai (2015), who use tree kernels to first identify opinion words related to a given aspect term, which are then used in calculating the sentiment score for that aspect term. In sentence-level polarity prediction, Trindade et al. (2013) augment constituency tree kernels by inserting WordNet senses and contextual polarity of words as new nodes under terminal nodes. Agarwal et al. (2011) apply tree kernels with a customized tree format for tweets, instead of using parse trees, where tokens are gathered under a root node together with POS tags and a set of special tags used to represent the types of tokens (e.g. STOP for stop words). In document-level sentiment classification, Tu et al. (2012) combine constituency or dependency tree kernels with bag-of-word features. To represent documents, they use several minimal subtrees each of which contains at least one subjective word based on a sentiment lexicon.

Wiegand and Klakow (2010) employ tree kernels to represent constituency and predicate-argument structure (PAS) in finding opinion holders. They enrich these trees by inserting nodes with generalized concept labels such as location, opinion and person. Their results show that while augmenting the constituency trees is useful, PAS trees do not benefit from extra information. Their best tree kernel setting outperforms their hand-crafted features and their combination leads to a higher performance.

Syntax has also been used in sentiment analysis using hand-crafted features. Johansson and Moschitti (2013) build a set of classifiers and re-rankers for identification of opinion holders, opinion expressions and their polarity in the MPQA corpus (Wiebe et al., 2005). These systems exploit dependency paths within opinion expressions and between opinion holders and opinion expressions. They evaluate these systems extrinsically using a product attribute (aspect) polarity classifier on a product review dataset, which is similar to the task addressed here. This classifier uses syntactic path features from candidate attributes to sentiment words and identified opinion expressions. Dong et al. (2015) introduce a context-free grammar for sentiment in which positive and negative polarity symbols replace syntactic labels in non-terminals. They build a parser which learns this grammar using only sentences annotated with their polarity without any information about their syntactic structure. Socher et al. (2013) build a dataset of movie reviews automatically parsed and manually annotated for the polarity of each constituent. This dataset is then used to compute compositional vector representations of phrases in a neural network framework, which are then used as features in training a model to predict the polarity of each phrase.

Pre-trained word embeddings have previously been used by (Liu et al., 2015) in a similar task of aspect term extraction on the same dataset used here, as initial weights in neural network models and also as features in conditional random field models. Their results show that word embeddings can improve over the baselines of both of these models. To the best of our knowledge, our study is the first to use word embeddings in tree kernel computation.

3 Kernel Methods

Kernel methods provide a means to define custom similarity functions, called *kernel functions*, which can be used by some machine learning algorithms such as support vector machines (SVM) to calculate the similarity between two data points which are not represented as vectors of numbers. Tree kernels (Collins and Duffy, 2002; Moschitti, 2006) are examples of these functions that compute the similarity between two data points represented as trees, based on the number of common fragments between them. Therefore, the need for explicitly encoding an instance in terms of manually designed and extracted features is eliminated, while benefiting from a very high-dimensional feature space. This approach has

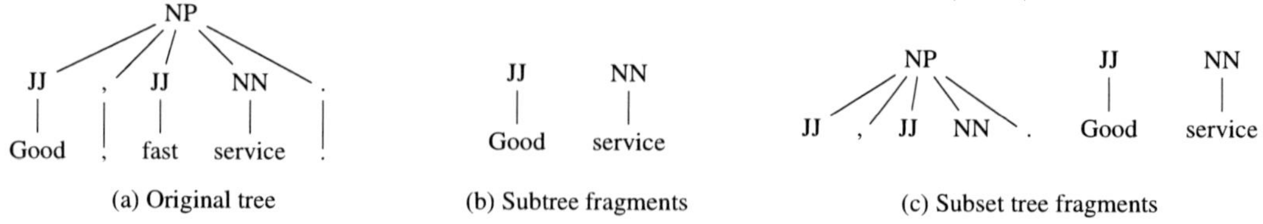

(a) Original tree   (b) Subtree fragments   (c) Subset tree fragments

Figure 1: A sample tree and examples of its *subtree* and *subset* tree fragments

shown to be effective in many NLP tasks including parsing and named entity recognition (Collins and Duffy, 2002), semantic role labelling (Moschitti, 2006), sentiment analysis (see §2) and machine translation quality estimation (Hardmeier et al., 2012; Kaljahi et al., 2014). In the following sections, we describe tree kernels and introduce *any-gram kernels* which are built on top of tree kernels. We also introduce a model which incorporates pre-trained word embedding vectors in tree kernel calculation.

3.1 Tree Kernels

The kernel function applied to tree pair T_1 and T_2 is defined as follows:

$$K(T_1, T_2) = \sum_{n_1 \in \{T_1\ nodes\}} \sum_{n_2 \in \{T_2\ nodes\}} \Delta(n_1, n_2) \tag{1}$$

where Δ calculates the similarity between every two nodes in the tree as follows (Moschitti, 2006):

$$\Delta(n_1, n_2) = \begin{cases} 0 \ : \ if\ pr_1 \neq pr_2 \\ 1 \ : \ if\ pr_1 = pr_2 \ \& \ n_1,\ n_2\ are\ pre\text{-}terminals \\ \prod_{j=1}^{nc}(\sigma + \Delta(c_{n_1}^j, c_{n_2}^j)) \ : \ otherwise \end{cases} \tag{2}$$

where pr_1 and pr_2 are the production rules rewriting n_1 and n_2 respectively, nc is the number of children of either node, as they have the same number of children because they have the same production rules, and $c_{n_1}^j$ is the jth child of node n_1. σ controls the type of tree fragments to be used: 0 is for *subtree* fragments which include a node in the tree with the whole sub-tree under it (Figure 1b) and 1 is for *subset* fragments which loosen this constraint by allowing the internal nodes as terminals, resulting in more substructures (Figure 1c). Moschitti (2006) introduces an efficient implementation within a SVM framework, where instead of all node pairs, the Δ function is applied only on similar node pairs.

3.2 Any-gram Kernels

N-gram features have been predominantly used in sentiment analysis and have shown to be very effective (Pang et al., 2002). While unigrams capture the individual sentiment-bearing words, higher orders of n-gram can also capture contextual information. However, there is no clear consensus as to what order of n-gram is the most effective in this task (Pang et al., 2002; Dave et al., 2003). Consequently, various orders should be empirically compared or combined together. Considering the sparsity of these features, especially in the higher orders, these approaches impose high computational costs. We propose *any-gram kernels*, which not only avoids this expense, but also models all orders of n-grams in a sequence. In this model, sentence tokens are arranged in a binary tree in such a way that all possible n-grams are captured by valid tree fragments, which are those extracted by subset tree kernels. Figure 2 shows an example of an n-gram tree and some of the tree fragments extracted from it acting as n-grams.

Adding a dummy X node under the left child helps extract unigrams (Figure 2b), as no valid tree fragment can consist of only one node. Bigrams are represented by tree fragments rooted at a two-children node with both of its children (Figure 2c). Trigrams are formed by tree fragments rooted at a two-children node with both of its children, and the children of the right child (Figure 2d). The n-grams for n>3 are represented in a similar way, which are not shown in Figure 2. As can be seen in Figure 2, a dummy *root* node is used to help extract the unigram for the first word of the sentence (*Good*). Note that

62

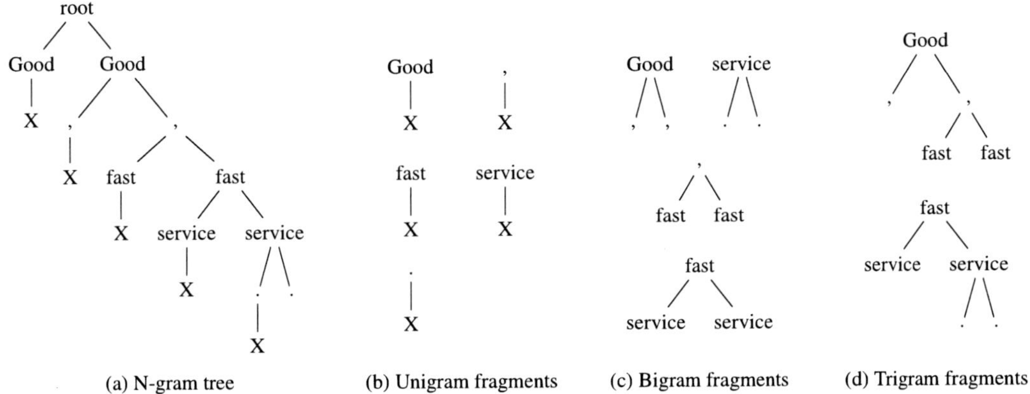

(a) N-gram tree   (b) Unigram fragments   (c) Bigram fragments   (d) Trigram fragments

Figure 2: N-gram tree for *Good, fast service.* and examples of its unigram, bigram and trigram fragments

these fragments are valid n-grams despite the duplicate nodes in them because no two different n-grams can be represented by a single such fragment. However, there are different fragments which represent a single n-gram. For example, the *Good-,* bigram is extracted with the fragment shown in Figure 2c as well as another one including the same fragment plus an X node under *Good* (not shown in the figure). These duplicates are inevitable but do not noticeably affect the performance. In total, the any-gram tree for a sentence of length N contains $3N + 1$ nodes. Another advantage of any-gram kernels is that other information (e.g. location of aspect term) can be plugged into the tree.

Any-gram kernels can be compared to string kernels (Lodhi et al., 2002) where the n-grams are not explicitly extracted for the learning algorithm but calculated using the string kernel function. The difference is that string kernels require the order of n-grams (n) to be fixed. Also, the tree kernel implementation of the any-gram kernels is faster as the tree kernels are computed in $O(K+M)$ average time, where K and M are the number of nodes of the two trees. When translated to the sentence length, the complexity of the any-gram kernel is $O(|s_1|+|s_2|)$ which is still linear to the sentence lengths $|s_1|$ and $|s_2|$, as the number of nodes in the any-gram tree of sentence s is $3|s|+1$ which is linear to the sentence length. However, the complexity of the string kernels is $O(n|s_1||s_2|)$.

3.3 Tree Kernels with Word Embeddings

The Δ presented in equation 2 computes the similarity of two production rules based on exact string match between the peer nodes in the rules. Consequently, similar but not identical tree fragments such as `JJ->amazing` and `JJ->wonderful` will be ruled out even though they can contribute to the similarity of two trees. Therefore, a mechanism which accounts for the similarity of nodes with different surface forms in this computation may be useful. To this end, we modify the Δ to compute the production rule similarity based on the similarity of the word embedding vectors of their peer node pairs.[1] Formally:

$$\Delta(n_1, n_2) = \begin{cases} 0 : if \ |pr_1|! = |pr_2| \ or \ \prod_{i=1}^{|pr_1|} t(n_{(pr_1)i}, n_{(pr_2)i}) = 0 \\ 1 : if \ n_1, \ n_2 \ are \ pre\text{-}terminals \ and \ \prod_{i=1}^{|pr_1|} t(n_{(pr_1)i}, n_{(pr_2)i}) = 1 \\ \prod_{j=1}^{nc}(\sigma + \Delta(c_{n_1}^j, c_{n_2}^j)) : otherwise \end{cases} \quad (3)$$

where pr_1 and pr_2 are the production rules rewriting n_1 and n_2 respectively, $|pr_1|$ and $|pr_2|$ are the number of nodes in the production rules, $n_{(pr_1)i}$ and $n_{(pr_2)i}$ are the ith peer nodes of the two production rules (e.g. *amazing* and *wonderful* as the 2nd nodes in the example production rules provided above) and t is a threshold function defined as follows:

---

[1]Obviously, exact match is used for the syntactic labels on the syntactic trees. For simplicity, we do not include this in the formal notation, but it can be easily addressed in the implementation.

63

	Laptop		Restaurant	
	Train	Test	Train	Test
# sentences	3045	800	3041	800
# aspect terms	2358	654	3693	1134
% positive	42%	52%	59%	65%
% negative	37%	20%	22%	17%
% neutral	19%	26%	17%	17%
% conflict[2]	2%	2%	2%	1%

Table 1: Number of sentences, aspect terms and their polarity distributions in the data sets

$$t(n_1, n_2) = \begin{cases} 0 & : \ if \ sim(V_{n_1}, V_{n_2}) < \theta \\ 1 & : \ if \ sim(V_{n_1}, V_{n_2}) \geq \theta \end{cases} \quad (4)$$

where V_{n_1} and V_{n_2} are the word embedding vectors of two input nodes, sim is a vector similarity function and θ is the similarity threshold above which the two nodes are considered equal for the kernel computation. With $\theta = 1$, the kernel value will be equal to the value of the traditional tree kernel.

Since all possible peer node pairs in the production rule pair need to be compared, unlike the traditional tree kernel, the worst-case complexity is increased to $O(N \times M)$, where N and M are the number of nodes in T_1 and T_2 respectively. To partially remedy this situation, we use dynamic programming where we store newly calculated production rule similarity as well as node similarity in a table for later use.

4 Experiments

Data We use the data released for Task 4 of SemEval 2014 (Pontiki et al., 2014) (called SE14 hereafter), which is concerned with ABSA. The data is in the form of consumer reviews from two domains: laptops and restaurants. Table 1 shows various characteristics of the data including the number of sentences and aspect terms and the percentage of each polarity type. As seen in Table 1, the restaurant dataset contains more aspect terms than the laptop ones, as most of its sentences have more than one aspect term. In terms of the polarity class distribution, the *conflict* polarity accounts for only a tiny portion of the aspect terms, whereas the *positive* polarity dominates the datasets except for the laptop training set where it has a similar share as the *negative* polarity. The proportion of *neutral* and *negative* polarities tend to be similar, which is also consistent across the four datasets.

Experiment Details To obtain the syntactic analysis of the data, we parse them into their constituency structures using a PCFG-LA parser (Petrov et al., 2006). The parser is trained on the entire Wall Street Journal section of the *Penn Treebank* (Marcus et al., 1993). We then obtain dependency parses by converting these constituency parses using the `Stanford` converter (de Marneffe and Manning, 2008). To apply tree kernels, we use the `SVMLight-TK` implementation (Moschitti, 2006)[3]. Based on a set of preliminary experiments, we use subset tree kernels and the *one-versus-one* (OVO) method to convert the binary output of the SVM to multi-class (positive, negative, neutral and conflict). The error/margin trade-off of the SVM (C) is tuned using development sets randomly extracted from the official training sets. For tree kernels with word embeddings, we use cosine similarity for sim in equation 4. The θ parameter is tuned on the development set, where the optimum value is selected from $\{0.7, 0.8, 0.9\}$. The pre-trained word vectors used are the publicly available ones trained using *GloVe* (Pennington et al., 2014) trained on 42B-token corpus of *Common Crawl* (1.9M vocabulary) with 300 dimensions.[4]

4.1 Word Any-gram Kernels

We start by modelling the word any-grams using traditional tree kernels, where for each aspect term, we take the any-gram tree formed using all tokens in the sentence in which the aspect term appears, as input

---

[2]The conflict polarity is used when both positive and negative sentiments are expressed towards the aspect term as in *Waiters are slow but sweet.*

[3]http://disi.unitn.it/moschitti/Tree-Kernel.htm

[4]http://nlp.stanford.edu/projects/glove/. We chose these word embeddings as they cover a wide range of domains and performed better than the other commonly used ones trained on 100GB Google News corpus using *word2vec*.

| | String Match | | | | Word Similarity | | | |
| | Laptop | | Restaurant | | Laptop | | Restaurant | |
	Dev	Test	Dev	Test	Dev	Test	Dev	Test
Majority	42.67	52.12	60.45	64.19	-	-	-	-
$HC_{ng_{1+2}}$	67.61	60.24	67.59	71.16	-	-	-	-
$NGTK_w$	65.04	60.24	67.26	70.72	64.78 (-)	62.08 (+)	68.40 (+)	70.99 (+)
$NGTK_s$	62.47	58.41	68.07	74.16	-	-	-	-
$NGTK_{w.s}$	**71.21**	**67.43**	70.99	**75.93**	**69.67 (-)**	**68.50 (+)**	**71.31 (+)**	**75.93 (=)**
$SyTK_c$	61.44	58.41	65.96	71.16	62.47 (+)	58.26 (-)	65.64 (-)	71.08 (-)
$SyTK_{c.s}$	68.64	65.44	70.02	**76.54**	67.87 (-)	66.06 (+)	69.69 (-)	75.84 (-)
$SyTK_d$	61.70	61.62	65.80	72.13	61.18 (-)	58.41 (-)	66.61 (+)	72.13 (=)
$SyTK_{d.s}$	65.81	65.44	69.37	75.22	65.81 (=)	64.98 (-)	69.37 (=)	74.96 (-)
$SyTK_{cs.ds}$	**68.89**	**67.13**	**71.96**	76.10	**68.38 (-)**	**68.35 (+)**	**70.99 (-)**	**76.46 (+)**
SE14 Best	-	70.48	-	80.95	-	-	-	-

Table 2: Accuracy of majority baseline, hand-crafted (HC) unigram+bigram features, any-gram kernel (NGTK) and syntax tree kernel systems (SyTK) and best SemEval 2014 system, evaluated on the laptop and restaurant development and test sets, based on exact string match and word embedding similarity

to our tree kernel algorithm. An example input tree is similar to the one shown in Figure 2 but with an AT node replacing the X node under the right child corresponding to an aspect term token (*service* in this example). The results are given in Table 2 ($NGTK_w$ under *String Match* column. The table also includes the performance of a majority baseline for comparison.

The second row of the table ($HC_{ng_{1+2}}$) contains the performance of an alternative system using hand-crafted unigrams and bigram features, containing 20K and 23K features for the laptop and restaurant datasets respectively. The performance of word any-gram kernels is on a par with the hand-crafted n-gram features (except on the laptop development set), although they are computationally cheaper and require much less engineering effort to select most useful orders and combination of orders of n-grams. We measured the time spent for the classification of both test sets using each model on the same machine. The average of three runs for $NGTK_w$ and $HC_{ng_{1+2}}$ were 50 and 490 ms respectively.[5] The comparison also suggest that higher orders of n-gram contained in the any-gram kernels are not useful in this task.

4.2 Constituency Tree Kernels

To use tree kernels for ABSA, the aspect terms need to be marked in the parse tree (Hovy et al., 2013), mainly to differentiate between multiple aspect terms in a sentence and also as information supplied to the algorithm. We tried a set of various formats for this purpose and decided to use one in which a node indicating aspect term (AT) is inserted above the pre-terminal node in the span of aspect term. The results for this format are presented in Table 2 under String Match column ($SyTK_c$) and an example tree is shown in Figure 3a. As can be seen, the constituency structure alone tends to be less effective than word n-grams.

4.3 Dependency Tree Kernels

While constituency trees can be readily used as input to tree kernels, dependency trees need to be restructured for this purpose, by moving the dependency labels from the arcs to nodes. We follow the format of Kaljahi et al. (2014), in which the nodes in the resulting trees are word forms and dependency relations, and we also included POS tags as they proved to be useful. In the resulting tree, a word is a child of its POS tag, which is in turn a child of its dependency relation to its head. The dependency relation is in turn the child of the head word. This continues until the root node. Aspect terms are represented by attaching an AT label to the dependency relations. Figure 3b depicts an example tree in this format and Table 2 shows its accuracy ($SyTK_d$) under String Match column. Dependency tree kernels tend to outperform the constituency ones. This may be an indication that relationships between words are more important than the hierarchical structure of in which they are arranged for this task.

---

[5]In fact, training and tuning time are also considerably lower. With the SVM that we use here, tree kernels have only the C parameter to be tuned, but the RBF kernels for hand-crafted features have the C and gamma parameters to be tuned.

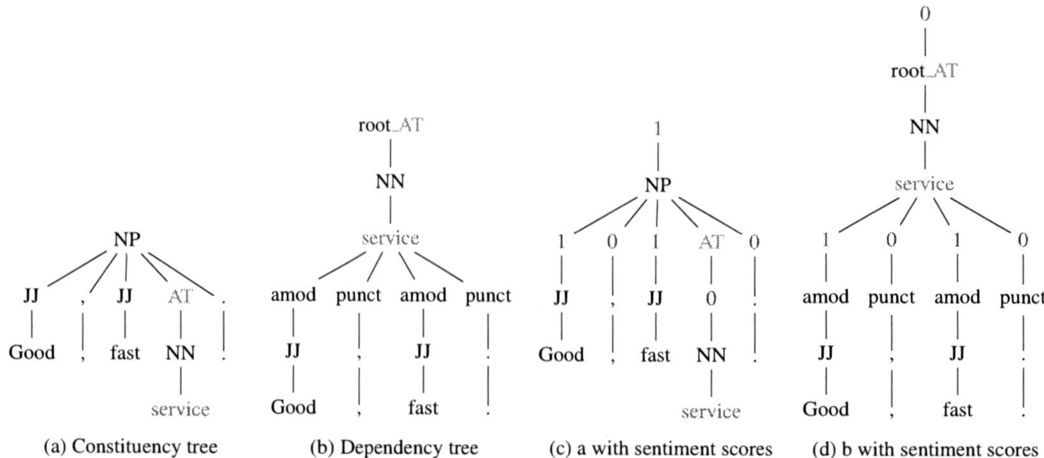

Figure 3: Sample plain constituency and dependency tree kernel representation for *Good, fast service.* (a and b) and with sentiment scores added (c and d)

4.4 Adding Sentiment Scores

Sentiment lexica assign a score to each word representing the polarity of its sentiment and are often constructed automatically or semi-automatically. We follow Wagner et al. (2014) in constructing a sentiment lexicon which is a combination of four commonly used lexica including *MPQA* (Wilson et al., 2005), *SentiWordNet* (Baccianella et al., 2010), *General Inquirer* [6] and *Opinion Lexicon* (Hu and Liu, 2004). The combined polarity score using their method is in the range [-4,4], where the sign of the score represents the polarity and its value expresses the strength of the sentiment it bears. However, to avoid sparsity, we use a coarse-grained set of three scores $\{-1, 0, 1\}$, for negative, neutral/unknown, positive polarities in the same order, which also turns out to perform better in our experiments.

Starting with the any-gram kernels, we replace the words with their sentiment polarity scores and replicate the experiments. Table 2 shows the performance of the resulting system (NGTK_s). According to the results, the sentiment score n-grams are more useful than the word n-grams for the restaurant dataset. However, the opposite seems to be true for the laptop dataset. When this system is combined with the word n-grams, the resulting system ($\text{NGTK}_{w.s}$ in Table 2 under String Match) significantly outperforms both of its components. Interestingly, the gain is more significant for the laptop dataset this time.

We now attempt to include sentiment scores in the parse trees. We experiment with various formats, including inserting the scores as nodes or replacing terminals with their scores in the original tree and combining the two trees. We also propagate them upwards in the tree to parent nodes until the root node, by assigning each node the majority score among all its children's positive and negative scores (neutral excluded).[7] In case of ties, the propagated score is set to neutral. Of the formats experimented with, the one with a single tree in which the scores are propagated and inserted as new nodes above their corresponding nodes outperformed others. An example tree is shown in Figure 3c. The propagated score for node NP is 1, as there are only two positive scores (1) among all its children (*good* and *fast*). Table 2 shows the accuracy of this setting ($\text{SyTK}_{c.s}$ under String Match column). Adding polarity scores substantially increases the performance, although the model complexity does not change significantly.

As in constituency tree kernels, we add sentiment scores to several positions in the dependency trees and find the best performance when they are inserted as nodes above the dependency relation nodes. For instance, in the example tree in Figure 3d, the polarity score for *fast* (1) is inserted as a node above its dependency relation node (amod) to its head (*service*). The accuracy obtained using these augmented trees is shown in Table 2 ($\text{SyTK}_{d.s}$ under String Match column).

---

[6]http://www.wjh.harvard.edu/~inquirer/

[7]We also tried using the average children score, which performed marginally lower than the majority score.

Interestingly, constituency and dependency tree kernels tend to perform closely, despite their different structures. While the latter slightly outperforms the former with plain trees, the former benefits more from the polarity scores. One reason can be that more structure is added to the constituency trees than to the dependency trees due to additional nodes for propagated scores.

Finally, we investigate the extent to which the different structures of constituency and dependency tree kernels complement each other by combining $SyTK_{c.s}$ and $SyTK_{d.s}$. The results are shown in Table 2 ($SyTK_{cs.ds}$ under String Match column). The laptop test set and the restaurant development sets benefit the most from the combination, while the other datasets do not see significant changes. This suggests that the complementarity of these two representations is dependent on the data. Compared to the any-gram kernels, the syntactic tree kernels perform slightly better on the restaurant dataset, but are outperformed on the laptop dataset, despite the any-gram kernels carrying less information and being simpler.

4.5 Using Word Embeddings

As described in §3.3 and §4, we replace word forms with word embeddings in kernel computation and use cosine similarity between them instead of exact string match between word forms. The *Word Similarity* column in Table 2 shows the performance of the systems replicated using this method. As can be seen, the changes are inconsistent, but in general the word embedding similarities tend to be helpful for any-gram kernels, contributing from 0.27 to 1.84 percentages of accuracy. However, most of the changes for syntactic tree kernels are negative, the sharpest being 3.21 percent for the laptop test set with $SyTK_d$.

Our analysis shows that the optimized similarity threshold tends to be as high as 0.9, while there is only about 500 type token pairs in each domain's dataset which are as similar. Interestingly, an overwhelming number of these pairs involve numbers and stop words. Perhaps, it would be worthwhile to examine word embeddings trained on a corpus in the same domain as the target data set instead of a large but general corpus, or those tuned to better capture sentimental facets of words. For example, with the word embedding used here, the cosine similarity between *good* and *bad* is 77%, which is higher than the similarity score of *superb* and *brilliant* which is 72%.

5 Discussion

Despite their simplicity and efficiency, the models built here achieve reasonably good performance. In fact, our best settings can take the third and fifth place among 31 systems submitted to the SE14 shared task (subtask 2 of task 4) for the laptop and restaurant domains respectively, although our goal here has not been to outperform the state of the art using these systems individually. Table 2 show the performance of the best system (Wagner et al., 2014) submitted to this shared task (*SE14 Best*), which achieves on average 4 points higher accuracy than the best systems built here. This system is built using n-grams and sentiment lexicon features. It combines the output of a rule-based system as features with bag-of-n-gram features. The rule-based system sums the polarity scores of all words around the aspect term in terms of token, discourse chunk and dependency path distance. Their bag-of-n-gram features target the aspect term context and combine word forms with polarity scores and part-of-speech tags. A similar speed test done for any-gram kernels in §4.1 shows that their system is 5 times slower than the tree kernel systems built here. To improve the state of the art, a combination strategy can be sought which effectively exploits the merits of both kinds of approaches.

6 Concluding Remarks

We have presented a series of experiments with tree kernels for aspect-based sentiment analysis and shown that a) tree kernels in the form of *any gram kernels* can be used as an efficient alternative to bag-of-ngrams, b) similarity based on word embeddings does not appear to be obviously superior to simple string match, c) constituency and dependency structure can be fruitfully combined, and d) it is always worth including information from sentiment lexica in the trees. A possible future work is to find methods to effectively combine tree kernels with state-of-the-art hand-crafted features.

Acknowledgements

This research is supported by Science Foundation Ireland in the ADAPT Centre (Grant 13/RC/2106) (www.adaptcentre.ie) at Dublin City University.

References

Apoorv Agarwal, Boyi Xie, Ilia Vovsha, Owen Rambow, and Rebecca Passonneau. 2011. Sentiment analysis of twitter data. In *Proceedings of the Workshop on Languages in Social Media*, pages 30–38.

Stefano Baccianella, Andrea Esuli, and Fabrizio Sebastiani. 2010. SentiWordNet 3.0: An Enhanced Lexical Resource for Sentiment Analysis and Opinion Mining. In *Proceedings of the Seventh Conference on International Language Resources and Evaluation (LREC'10)*.

Marco Baroni, Georgiana Dinu, and Germán Kruszewski. 2014. Don't count, predict! a systematic comparison of context-counting vs. context-predicting semantic vectors. In *Proceedings of the 52nd Annual Meeting of the Association for Computational Linguistics (Volume 1: Long Papers)*.

Yoshua Bengio, Réjean Ducharme, Pascal Vincent, and Christian Janvin. 2003. A neural probabilistic language model. *Journal of Machine Learning Research*, 3:1137–1155.

Michael Collins and Nigel Duffy. 2002. New Ranking Algorithms for Parsing and Tagging: Kernels over Discrete Structures, and the Voted Perceptron. In *Proceedings of ACL*, pages 263–270.

Ronan Collobert and Jason Weston. 2008. A unified architecture for natural language processing: Deep neural networks with multitask learning. In *Proceedings of the 25th International Conference on Machine Learning*, pages 160–167.

Kushal Dave, Steve Lawrence, and David M. Pennock. 2003. Mining the peanut gallery: Opinion extraction and semantic classification of product reviews. In *Proceedings of the 12th International Conference on World Wide Web*, pages 519–528.

Marie-Catherine de Marneffe and Christopher D. Manning. 2008. The Stanford typed dependencies representation. In *Proceedings of the COLING Workshop on Cross-Framework and Cross-Domain Parser Evaluation*, pages 1–8.

Li Dong, Furu Wei, Shujie Liu, Ming Zhou, and Ke Xu. 2015. A statistical parsing framework for sentiment classification. *Computational Linguistics*, 41(2):293–336.

C. Hardmeier, J. Nivre, and J. Tiedemann. 2012. Tree Kernels for Machine Translation Quality Estimation. In *Proceedings of WMT*, pages 109–113.

Dirk Hovy, Shashank Shrivastava, Sujay Kumar Jauhar, Mrinmaya Sachan, Kartik Goyal, Huying Li, Whitney Sanders, and Eduard Hovy. 2013. Identifying metaphorical word use with tree kernels. In *Proceedings of the First Workshop on Metaphor in NLP*, pages 52–57, Atlanta, Georgia, June. Association for Computational Linguistics.

Minqing Hu and Bing Liu. 2004. Mining and summarizing customer reviews. In *Proceedings of the Tenth ACM SIGKDD International Conference on Knowledge Discovery and Data Mining*, pages 168–177.

Richard Johansson and Alessandro Moschitti. 2013. Relational features in fine-grained opinion analysis. *Computational Linguistics*, 39(3):473–509.

Rasoul Samed Zadeh Kaljahi, Jennifer Foster, Raphael Rubino, and Johann Roturier. 2014. Quality Estimation of English-French Machine Translation: A Detailed Study of the Role of Syntax. In *Proceedings of COLING*, pages 2052–2063.

Jussi Karlgren, Gunnar Eriksson, Magnus Sahlgren, and Oscar Täckström. 2010. Between bags and trees–constructional patterns in text used for attitude identification. In *Advances in Information Retrieval*, pages 38–49.

Svetlana Kiritchenko, Xiaodan Zhu, Colin Cherry, and Saif Mohammad. 2014. Nrc-canada-2014: Detecting aspects and sentiment in customer reviews. In *Proceedings of the 8th International Workshop on Semantic Evaluation (SemEval 2014)*, pages 437–442.

Pengfei Liu, Shafiq Joty, and Helen Meng. 2015. Fine-grained opinion mining with recurrent neural networks and word embeddings. In *Proceedings of the 2015 Conference on Empirical Methods in Natural Language Processing*, pages 1433–1443.

Huma Lodhi, Craig Saunders, John Shawe-Taylor, Nello Cristianini, and Chris Watkins. 2002. Text classification using string kernels. *Journal of Machine Learning Research*, 2:419–444.

M. P. Marcus, B. Santorini, and M. A. Marcinkiewicz. 1993. Building a Large Annotated Corpus of English: the Penn Treebank. *Computational Linguistics*, 19(2):313–330.

Tomas Mikolov, Kai Chen, Greg Corrado, and Jeffrey Dean. 2013. Efficient estimation of word representations in vector space. In *Proceedings of Workshop at ICLR*.

Alessandro Moschitti. 2006. Making Tree Kernels practical for Natural Language Learning. In *Proceedings of EACL*, pages 113–120.

Thien Hai Nguyen and Kiyoaki Shirai. 2015. Aspect-based sentiment analysis using tree kernel based relation extraction. In *Computational Linguistics and Intelligent Text Processing - 16th International Conference, CICLing 2015, Proceedings, Part II*, pages 114–125.

Bo Pang and Lillian Lee. 2008. Opinion mining and sentiment analysis. *Foundations and trends in information retrieval*, 2(1-2):1–135.

Bo Pang, Lillian Lee, and Shivakumar Vaithyanathan. 2002. Thumbs up?: Sentiment classification using machine learning techniques. In *Proceedings of the ACL-02 Conference on Empirical Methods in Natural Language Processing - Volume 10*, pages 79–86.

Jeffrey Pennington, Richard Socher, and Christopher D. Manning. 2014. Glove: Global vectors for word representation. In *Empirical Methods in Natural Language Processing (EMNLP)*, pages 1532–1543.

Slav Petrov, Leon Barrett, Romain Thibaux, and Dan Klein. 2006. Learning Accurate, Compact and Interpretable Tree Annotation. In *Proceedings of COLING-ACL*.

Barbara Plank and Alessandro Moschitti. 2013. Embedding semantic similarity in tree kernels for domain adaptation of relation extraction. In *Proceedings of the 51st Annual Meeting of the Association for Computational Linguistics (Volume 1: Long Papers)*, pages 1498–1507.

Maria Pontiki, Dimitris Galanis, John Pavlopoulos, Harris Papageorgiou, Ion Androutsopoulos, and Suresh Manandhar. 2014. Semeval-2014 task 4: Aspect based sentiment analysis. In *Proceedings of the 8th International Workshop on Semantic Evaluation (SemEval 2014)*, pages 27–35.

Richard Socher, Alex Perelygin, Jean Wu, Jason Chuang, Christopher D. Manning, Andrew Ng, and Christopher Potts. 2013. Recursive deep models for semantic compositionality over a sentiment treebank. In *Proceedings of the 2013 Conference on Empirical Methods in Natural Language Processing*, pages 1631–1642, October.

Luis A. Trindade, Hui Wang, William Blackburn, and Niall Rooney. 2013. An enhanced semantic tree kernel for sentiment polarity classification. In *Proceedings of the 14th International Conference on Computational Linguistics and Intelligent Text Processing - Volume 2*, pages 50–62.

Zhaopeng Tu, Yifan He, Jennifer Foster, Josef van Genabith, Qun Liu, and Shouxun Lin. 2012. Identifying High-Impact Sub-Structures for Convolution Kernels in Document-level Sentiment Classification. In *Proceedings of ACL*, pages 338–343.

Joachim Wagner, Piyush Arora, Santiago Cortes, Utsab Barman, Dasha Bogdanova, Jennifer Foster, and Lamia Tounsi. 2014. Dcu: Aspect-based polarity classification for semeval task 4. In *Proceedings of the 8th International Workshop on Semantic Evaluation (SemEval 2014)*, pages 223–229.

Janyce Wiebe, Theresa Wilson, and Claire Cardie. 2005. Annotating expressions of opinions and emotions in language. *Language Resources and Evaluation*, 1(2):0.

Michael Wiegand and Dietrich Klakow. 2010. Convolution Kernels for Opinion Holder Extraction. In *Proceedings of NAACL-HLT*, pages 795–803.

Theresa Wilson, Janyce Wiebe, and Paul Hoffmann. 2005. Recognizing contextual polarity in phrase-level sentiment analysis. In *Proceedings of the Conference on Human Language Technology and Empirical Methods in Natural Language Processing*, pages 347–354.

Yuanbin Wu, Qi Zhang, Xuangjing Huang, and Lide Wu. 2009. Phrase dependency parsing for opinion mining. In *Proceedings of the 2009 Conference on Empirical Methods in Natural Language Processing*, pages 1533–1541, August.

Effects of Semantic Relatedness between Setups and Punchlines in Twitter Hashtag Games

Andrew Cattle   **Xiaojuan Ma**
Hong Kong University of Science and Technology
Department of Computer Science and Engineering
Clear Water Bay, Hong Kong
{acattle,mxj}@cse.ust.hk

Abstract

This paper explores humour recognition for Twitter-based hashtag games. Given their popularity, frequency, and relatively formulaic nature, these games make a good target for computational humour research and can leverage Twitter likes and retweets as humour judgments. In this work, we use pairwise relative humour judgments to examine several measures of semantic relatedness between setups and punchlines on a hashtag game corpus we collected and annotated. Results show that *perplexity*, *Normalized Google Distance*, and *free-word association-based features* are all useful in identifying "funnier" hashtag game responses. In fact, we provide empirical evidence that funnier punchlines tend to be more obscure, although more obscure punchlines are not necessarily rated funnier. Furthermore, the asymmetric nature of free-word association features allows us to see that while punchlines should be harder to predict given a setup, they should also be relatively easy to understand in context.

1 Introduction

Humour is ubiquitous in everyday language and important in social interactions. This has been recognized by the computing industry, as Google recently hired professional jokes writers to help make an upcoming AI assistant seem more natural (Stein, 2016). Beyond their applications in user interfaces (Morkes et al., 1998), the automatic identification, processing, or generation of humour also has applications in diverse fields such as sentiment analysis (Davidov et al., 2010) and computer-aided language acquisition (Ritchie et al., 2007).

While research into computational humour, and humour recognition in particular, has focused on humour as a classification task, humour recognition as a ranking task has received increased attention as of late. To this end, and to develop a more complete model of computational humour, this paper seeks to gain insights into the role of semantic relatedness between punchline and setup and its effects on perceived funniness. Specifically, we examine the semantic relationships between hashtag prompts (setups) and punchlines in Twitter hashtag games. We begin by introducing the task of humour recognition for Twitter hashtag games and describing the creation of an annotated hashtag game corpus. We then introduce multiple semantic relatedness measures including, to the best of our knowledge, the first uses of free word association datasets and Normalized Google Distance in computational humour. We evaluate the predictive power of these semantic relatedness measure for identifying the funnier or a pair of tweets. And finally we derive insights from our results. Although we will limit our analysis to a specific type of hashtag game, semantic relatedness should play a role in almost all humour.

Intuitively, punchlines should be relevant to setups, otherwise they become random non-sequiturs and thus are not funny. Therefore, we expect that punchlines which are very weakly semantically related to their setups will be judged as less humorous since the relevance of the punchline to the setup may be less readily apparent. Conversely, punchlines intuitively should not be obvious. Thus we expect that punchlines which are very strongly semantically related to their setups will be judged as less humorous since the punchline may be too straightforward.

This work is licensed under a Creative Commons Attribution 4.0 International Licence. Licence details: http://creativecommons.org/licenses/by/4.0/

Proceedings of the Workshop on Computational Modeling of People's Opinions, Personality, and Emotions in Social Media,
pages 70–79, Osaka, Japan, December 12 2016.

Ice, Ice Hockey #OlympicSongs @midnight
Smells Like Teen Sprint #OlympicSongs
Should I Sail? or Should I row? #OlympicSongs
I want to know what luge is #OlympicSongs @midnight
I'll tell you what I want, what I relay, relay want #OlympicSongs @midnight

Table 1: Sample responses for #OlympicSongs

Hashtag games, also known as hashtag wars, are a collaborative form of online play which is popular on social media sites, most notably Twitter. They work as follows. Participants write short humorous texts based around a common theme or topic, denoted using a hashtag. By including the common hashtag in their responses, participants can easily see each others responses in almost real time. Participants then compete to see who can come up with the funniest responses and amass the most likes and retweets (Sheridan, 2011). A sampling of responses to the hashtag #OlympicSongs is shown in Table 1. Although the games themselves date back to at least 2011, they have been popularized in recent years by the Comedy Central show *@midnight* through their nightly "Hashtag Wars" segment. These games present an attractive target for computational humour research because of their short length, high popularity, and relatively formulaic nature.

The types of hashtag prompts used in hashtag games are quite diverse. For example, #CollegeIn5Words and #MyLoveLifeIn3Words ask participants to describe a topic in a humorous way using a specified word limit. Other hashtags, such as #WhenIWasYourAge or #WrongReasonsToHaveKids, are even more open-ended as they specify a topic but do not place any other restrictions on responses.

This paper focuses on one of the most common genres of hashtag game in which participants take words or phrases associated with a source domain and modify them to include references to a target domain. For example, #OlympicSongs encourages participants to take song titles, song lyrics, etc. (the source domain) and modify them to include references to the Olympic Games (the target domain), as shown in Table 1. The formulaic nature of such hashtags makes them well suited for computational humour-related research, especially for investigating the relationships between punchlines and their se-tups. Typically, such modifications result in a pun, such as substituting "relay" for the phonetically similar "really" in the lyrics of the Spice Girls song "Wannabe" or substituting "sprint" for the orthographically similar "spirit" in the title of the Nirvana song "Smells like Teen Spirit". While the quality of such word play undoubtedly affects the perceived funniness of a tweet, this is beyond the scope of this paper.

2 Previous Work

Early work on computational humour focused more on humour generation in specific contexts, such as punning riddles (Binsted and Ritchie, 1994; Ritchie et al., 2007), humorous acronyms (Stock and Strapparava, 2002), or jokes in the form of "I like my X like I like my Y" (Petrovic and Matthews, 2013). Labutov and Lipson (2012) offered a slightly more generalized approach using Semantic Script Theory of Humour.

Recently, humour recognition has gained increasing attention. Taylor and Mazlack (2004) presented a method for recognizing wordplay in "Knock Knock" jokes. Mihalcea and Strapparava (2005) identified stylistic features, such as alliteration and antonymy, to identify humorous one-liners. Mihalcea and Pulman (2007) expanded on this approach, finding that human-centeredness and negative sentiment are both useful in identifying humorous one-liners as well as distinguishing satirical news articles from genuine ones. There is also the related task of irony identification (Davidov et al., 2010; Tsur et al., 2010; Reyes et al., 2012), which typically uses n-gram and sentiment features to distinguish ironic tweets from non-ironic ones.

Although humour recognition has by and large been presented as a classification task, Shahaf et al. (2015) and Radev et al. (2016) instead reframe humour recognition as a ranking task. Both works aim to identify the funnier of a pair of cartoon captions taken from submissions to The New Yorker's weekly Cartoon Caption Contest[1]. Each week, New Yorker readers are presented "a cartoon in need of a caption" and encouraged to submit their own humorous suggestions. Shahaf et al. (2015) found that simpler grammatical structures, less reliance on proper nouns, and shorter joke phrases all lead to funnier captions. Radev et al. (2016) showed that in addition to human-centeredness and sentiment, high LexRank score was a strong indication of humour, where LexRank is a graph-based text summarization technique introduced in Erkan and Radev (2004).

Works on cartoon caption contests serve as a logical starting point for hashtag game-related research. In both cases participants, who are members of the general public, are supplied with a common prompt which all submissions must relate to. In both cases submissions are short, humorous texts. As such, computational humour techniques designed for cartoon caption contests should be almost directly applicable to hashtag games.

Cartoon caption contests and hashtag games are similar in other ways, too. Both gather a large number of submissions; an average of 4,808 captions per cartoon (Shahaf et al., 2015) versus 11,278 responses per hashtag. Shahaf et al. (2015) and Radev et al. (2016) both noted that cartoon captions tended to hinge on similar jokes. While hashtag game responses also tended to hinge on similar jokes, this appeared to occur at a lower rate than in cartoon caption data, potentially due to hashtag game responses being visible to all participants as opposed to cartoon caption contests' closed submission system.

Despite their similarities, hashtag games offer several advantages over cartoon caption contests. First, setups are denoted using text-based hashtags, meaning they can be processed in a similar way to the responses. By comparison, cartoons, being a visual medium, require computer vision techniques in order to automatically extract setup-related features, adding system complexity. Furthermore, computer vision techniques are not yet sophisticated enough to reliably extract such features. This is why Shahaf et al. (2015) resorted to human annotations in order to extract context information from the cartoon prompts. Second, while works on cartoon captions have relied on Amazon Mechanical Turk (AMT)[2] or similar services to collect humour judgments for each caption (Shahaf et al., 2015; Radev et al., 2016), work on hashtag games can leverage built-in social media features such as likes or retweets to serve as humour judgments. Third, hashtag games enable researchers to explore humour in a social context by allowing access to an author's previous tweets as well as their social networks.

3 Data

The decentralized and transient nature of hashtag games presents a challenge to data collection. To alleviate this, we focus on hashtag games created by the Comedy Central show *@midnight* as part of their nightly "Hashtag Wars" segment. This ensures that each game has a sufficiently large number of active participants and provides a regular source of hashtag game prompts. In this work, we create a corpus of responses for four specific hashtags: #GentlerSongs, #OlympicSongs, #BoringBlockbusters, and #OceanMovies. These hashtags all occurred between April and August, 2016, and, as mentioned in Section 1, were chosen specifically for their formulaic nature.

3.1 Humour Judgments

Users on Twitter show their approval of a tweet through likes and retweets. Thus, we use these to infer humour judgments. More concretely, we compute, for each tweet, the sum of the number of likes and the number of retweets to act as funniness indicators. For each hashtag game, these sums, which we will refer to as the total likes, are compared to generate pairwise relative humour judgments, with the tweet that received more total likes being considered funnier than tweet with fewer.

In our dataset, total likes followed a Zipfian distribution with over 56% of all collected tweets obtaining zero total likes. To help reduce the effects of noise in the data as well as to ensure accuracy in our humour judgments, this paper only considers tweets which received at least seven total likes. Although Twitter

---

[1] http://contest.newyorker.com/
[2] https://mturk.com/

Hashtag	# of Tweets Collected	# of Tweet with ≥ 7 total likes	# of pairwise judgments (excluding ties)
#GentlerSongs	12,543	256	29,874
#OlympicSongs	8,778	460	100,175
#OceanMovies	12,189	327	49,638
#BoringBlockbusters	11,599	198	18,149
All	**45,109**	**1,241**	**197,836**

Table 2: Tweet counts and number of pairwise judgments by hashtag game

allows users to both like and retweet the same tweet, it does not provide an easy way to detect this. A threshold of seven total likes guarantees a tweet has been rated by at least four individuals. This helps to smooth out any unreliable judgments such as bots or misclicks and ensure a tweet has wide-spread humour appeal. This threshold resulted in 197,836 pairwise relative humour judgments, excluding ties, as shown in Table 2.

In general, liking or retweeting a tweet can be seen as an implicit approval, e.g. as a show of agreement, to save a tweet for future use, or as an act of curation (Boyd et al., 2010; Gorrell and Bontcheva, 2016). While it is easy to imagine scenarios where liking or retweeting is not an implicit approval, e.g. retweeting to provide context for a critique, at least in the case of hashtag games, such scenarios seem to be quite rare. In fact, e-commerce literature use retweets as "a measure of community interest" (Gilbert et al., 2013).

The act of retweeting is a complex phenomenon and is affected not only by linguistic but para-linguistic features such as URLs, hashtags, and mentions, as well as extra-linguistic factors such as number of followers (Suh et al., 2010). In order to control for these factors we omit all tweets containing URLs, photos, videos, hashtags (other than the relevant hashtag game prompt), or mentions (other than the @*midnight* account). This has the added benefit of ensuring that the humour of a tweet is indeed drawn from the tweet text itself rather than through a contrast between the text and a photo or news story.

Another potential shortcoming is that likes and retweets are not independent. More retweets mean a greater audience and thus potentially more likes. However, likes and retweet are both used to express appreciation of a tweet (Boyd et al., 2010; Gorrell and Bontcheva, 2016), and liking and retweeting are considered separate actions on Twitter. Some users may like a tweet without retweeting it while others may retweet without liking. Therefore, drawing humour judgments from only likes or only retweets would ignore a large portion of the available data. Furthermore, it would fail to capture scenarios where a user both likes and retweets the same tweet, which can be seen as an even stronger expression of appreciation than liking or retweeting alone. As mentioned above, since Twitter does not offer an easy way to tell when a user likes and retweets the same tweet, the easiest way to add weight such scenarios is through a simple sum.

As mentioned in Section 2, one potential alternative to using total likes as de facto humour judgments would be to collect gold standard pairwise humour judgments through AMT or similar service. While this may result in more trustworthy humour judgments, the collection process would be relatively time consuming and expensive. Furthermore, practical constraints may prevent researchers from obtaining pairwise judgments for all possible pairs. By comparison, like and retweet counts are built into the Twitter API[3] and require very little extra processing time or cost. Additionally, obtaining pairwise judgments for every possible pair is trivial. Although total likes is not a perfect metric for discerning humour, it still offers the easiest indication of how much users enjoyed a particular tweet. That said, an in-depth comparison of total likes versus gold standard humour judgments is a potential topic for future work.

---

[3] https://dev.twitter.com/

3.2 Punchline Annotation

It was necessary to first identify what the punchlines and setups in a tweet are in order to examine their semantic relatedness. As mentioned in Section 1, we focus on a specific type of hashtag game where well known quotes/lyrics/titles/etc. are taken from a source domain and modified with references to a target domain. Responses to #GentlerSongs and #OlympicSong tended to be variations on song titles or lyrics while responses to #OceanMovies and #BoringBlockbusters tended to be variations on movie titles.

A professional comedian and joke writer was invited to manually annotate the punchlines. Punchlines were loosely defined as the set of words which appear in a tweet that do not appear in original title/lyric, although the annotator was instructed to use their professional judgment in cases such as typos or minor misquotations. In fact, such situations were the reason we chose a human annotator over an automated approach involving partial text matching, although future works may explore this avenue. In cases where the annotator was unable to identify the original title/lyric, the tweet was omitted from the data. Setups were defined as the adjective part of the hashtag prompts, i.e. "gentler" for #GentlerSongs, "Olympic" for #OlympicSongs, etc.

4 Features

4.1 Measures of Semantic Relatedness

This paper considers five different measures of semantic relatedness. The first three measures are based on free word association (FWA) norms. Nelson et al. (1998) presented participants with a list of English words and instructed them "to write the first word that came to mind that was meaningfully related or strongly associated to the presented cue word." The proportion of respondents who produced word Y when presented with a cue word X is referred to as the forward strength from X to Y. It is important to note that forward strength is directional, i.e. participants may be more likely to produce "green" given the cue "grass" than to produce "grass" given the cue "green".

Due to the sparse nature of the FWA dataset, we define the *FWA strength* between two words as the product of the forward strengths along the shortest path between them. We compute this value by constructing a graph where each node U corresponds to a word in the Nelson et al. (1998) FWA norm vocabulary and each edge U, V has a weight proportional to $-log(f(U, V))$ where $f(U, V)$ is the forward strength between words U and V. The FWA strength is equal to $exp(cost(U, V))$ where $cost(U, V)$ is the cost of the shortest path from U to V according to Dijkstra's algorithm.

As we are interested in the semantic relationships between setups and punchline, we define $FWA_{forward}$ as the strength with which the setup conjures the punchline and $FWA_{backward}$ as the strength with which the punchline conjures the setup. Again, due to the directional nature of FWA, these values represent subtly different phenomena. We are also interested in how these measures interact so we define $FWA_{difference}$ as $FWA_{forward} - FWA_{backward}$.

The fourth measure is *Word2Vec similarity* (Mikolov et al., 2013), which we will simply refer to as Word2Vec. Word2Vec was trained using Gensim (Rehurek and Sojka, 2010) on English-language Wikipedia using a continuous bag-of-words model with feature vectors of dimensionality 400. Wikipedia was chosen as the training corpus in an attempt to capture world knowledge. We experimented with training Word2Vec on a 1,600,000 tweet corpus compiled in Go et al. (2009) but found it performed worse than Wikipedia, likely due to its relatively small sample size.

Finally, the fifth measure is the *Normalized Google Distance* (NGD) (Cilibrasi and Vitanyi, 2007). NGD represents the "normed semantic distance between the terms in question... in the cognitive space invoked by the usage of the terms on the world-wide-web as filtered by Google". In short, NGD offers an easy way to leverage not only the vast chunk of the word-wide-web indexed by Google but also the power of Google Search itself. Being a distance, NGD is unlike Word2Vec and FWA features in that smaller values represent stronger relationships.

We compute all measures between each tweet's setup and each word in the corresponding punchline, as defined in Section 3.2. We record the highest value pair, lowest value pair, and average value. It should be noted that specifically in the case of $FWA_{difference}$, $FWA_{difference}$ (highest) does not correspond to the setup/punch word pair with the greatest difference between $\text{FWA}_{\text{forward}}$ and $\text{FWA}_{\text{backward}}$ but rather the difference between $\text{FWA}_{\text{forward}}$ (highest) and $\text{FWA}_{\text{backward}}$ (highest).

4.2 Perplexity and POS Perplexity

We calculate the tweet-level *perplexity* and *POS perplexity* to serve as a baseline. This follows Shahaf et al. (2015) which found perplexity and POS perplexity to be simple yet effective methods for identifying the funnier of a pair of cartoon captions. Due to the similarities between cartoon captions and hashtag game responses noted in Section 2, we expect that perplexity should also be useful in identifying funnier hashtag game responses. Perplexity was calculated using 2-gram, 3-gram, and 4-gram language models trained using KenLM (Heafield et al., 2013) on English-language Wikipedia. POS perplexity was trained in a similar way but with each word in the training corpus being replaced by its respective POS tag according to NLTK[4]. As with Word2Vec, we experimented with language models trained on the same Go et al. (2009) tweet corpus tagged using Tweet NLP (Gimpel et al., 2011) but found it performed worse than Wikipedia.

Shahaf et al. (2015) note that funnier cartoon captions tend to use "simpler grammatical structure", i.e. have a lower POS perplexity. Their results for perplexity were less clear. While a lower perplexity, i.e. "less-distinctive language", was preferred when comparing captions with similar punchlines, a higher perplexity was preferred when comparing captions with different punchlines.

5   Results and Discussion

The statistics for each feature are shown in Table 3. Following Shahaf et al. (2015), results are shown as the percentage of pairs for which the higher value belonged to the funnier tweet, i.e. the tweet with more total likes. Values above 50% imply a positive correlation between that feature and perceived funniness, values below 50% imply a negative correlation. Significance was calculated using a two-sided Wilcoxon signed rank test. Since we consider multiple features, Holm-Bonferroni correction was employed to reduce the chance of a Type-I error. Although the reported results are close to the expectation by chance, 50%, many features showed a high degree of significance. Furthermore, these results are similar in magnitude to the results reported in Shahaf et al. (2015).

The results show that perplexity is relatively effective in identifying funnier tweets. This is in line with both our expectations and with the results of Shahaf et al. (2015). However, while Shahaf et al. (2015) found that lower perplexity was funnier only when comparing cartoon captions with similar punchlines, hashtag game responses with lower perplexity tended to be judged as funnier regardless of the similarity between tweets' punchlines. This indicates a preference for simpler vocabulary, possibly because a simpler vocabulary allows punchlines to be more easily understood.

In agreement with Shahaf et al. (2015), funnier tweets also tended to have slightly lower POS perplexity, indicating simpler grammatical structures. The relatively slight effect of POS perplexity compared to Shahaf et al. (2015), as well as the improved performance of the 2-gram language model over 3-grams and 4-grams, may be due to differences between the training and test corpora. Wikipedia and Twitter use very different styles of language. Although we expect that training language models on tweets, or even song lyrics, movie quotes, etc., would improve performance, as mentioned in Section 4.2 this would require an appropriate corpus and is a topic for future work.

Although we expected weaker relationships between setups and punchlines to be less humourous, the overall trend across all semantic relatedness measures was a notable preference for punchlines which are less related to setups (higher NGD, lower Word2Vec and FWA features). This seems counterintuitive at first as one would reasonably expect low NGD, high Word2Vec, or high FWA strengths to be funnier. However, this is not the case. One possible explanation is that, since we expect punchlines should be unexpected, punchlines with too low an NGD, too high a Word2Vec similarity, or too high FWA strengths may be too obvious and thus less funny. This is illustrated in Figure 1a which shows that while lower $\text{FWA}_{\text{backward}}$ scores do not necessarily result in funnier tweets, funnier tweets tend to have lower $\text{FWA}_{\text{backward}}$ scores. This is also reinforced by the fact that Word2Vec and $\text{FWA}_{\text{forward}}$ were the

---

[4]http://www.nltk.org/

Feature		% Funnier is Higher
Perplexity	(2-gram)	47.82**
	(3-gram)	47.88**
	(4-gram)	47.86**
POS Perplexity	(2-gram)	49.18**
	(3-gram)	49.47**
	(4-gram)	49.46**
$FWA_{forward}$	(highest)	48.42**
	(lowest)	48.40**
	(average)	48.61**
$FWA_{backward}$	(highest)	49.47**
	(lowest)	49.52
	(average)	49.38
$FWA_{difference}$	(highest)	48.38
	(lowest)	48.53**
	(average)	47.41**
Word2Vec	(highest)	49.63
	(lowest)	48.98**
	(average)	49.15**
NGD	(highest)	52.45**
	(lowest)	50.57**
	(average)	51.69**

Table 3: Percentage of caption pairs where funnier tweet contains the higher feature value. Significance according to a two-sided Wilcoxon signed rank test is indicated using *-notation (*$p \leq 0.05$, **$p \leq 0.005$, Holm-Bonferroni correction)

most predictive when considering the lowest value (least similar/weakest) setup/punch word pairs, while NGD was the most predictive when considering the highest (most distant) setup/punch word pairs.

Following the intuition that punchlines should be related to setups but should also not be obvious, one would expect that as NGD increases or Word2Vec/$FWA_{forward}$/$FWA_{backward}$ decrease, funniness should drop off after a certain point. While Figure 1a shows that this is not the case for $FWA_{backward}$, Figure 1b does seem to suggest it is for NGD. It may be the case that funnier punchlines are as obscure as possible while still having some recognizable connection to their corresponding setups. This would also help explain the increase in variance as $FWA_{backward}$ approaches 0; the less obvious the relation between punchline and setup is, the higher the upper bound on funniness but the greater the likelihood of the punchline not being understood. If this is the case it is not surprising that Word2Vec or FWA features failed to capture the expected drop off, nor that NGD succeeded in doing so, as they are trained on relatively small corpora compared to the amount of pages indexed by Google. Another advantage of NGD is that since Google is constantly indexing new pages, including news sites, NGD is able to capture emerging topical relationships that fixed corpora cannot, such as the controversy surrounding the Zika virus outbreak in Brazil during the 2016 Rio Olympic Games.

While both NGD and Word2Vec are symmetric, FWA features are not. Following the intuitions that punchlines should be unexpected and that punchlines should have some relation to the setup, one would expect that punchlines with low $FWA_{forward}$ but high $FWA_{backward}$ would be deemed funnier. A relatively weak $FWA_{forward}$ would suggest the punchline is unexpected given the setup while a relatively strong $FWA_{backward}$ would suggest the relationship between the punchline and the setup is easily recognizable. In other words, a punchline should be difficult to think of yourself while easy to understand.

Not only does this intuition appear to be correct but $FWA_{difference}$ is more predictive than $FWA_{forward}$ or $FWA_{backward}$ alone. Although the funniest tweets had an $FWA_{difference}$ of near 0, Figure 1c clearly shows that tweets with a negative $FWA_{difference}$ have a much greater potential to be judged as funny compared

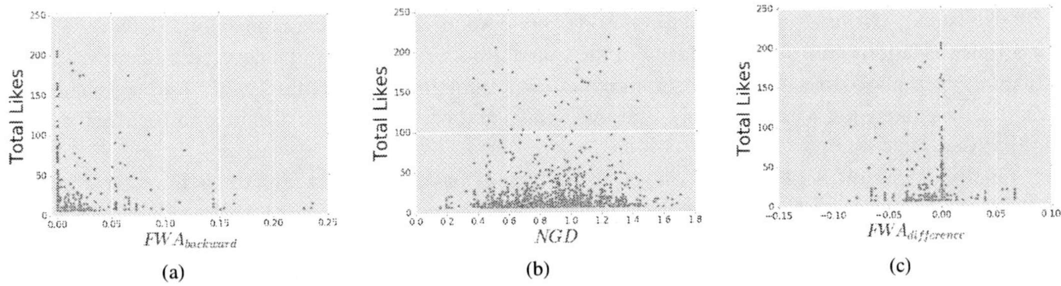

Figure 1: Total likes by (a) $FWA_{backward}$, (b) NGD, and (c) $FWA_{difference}$

to tweets with a positive one. However there is a trade-off between $FWA_{difference}$ and $FWA_{backward}$. As $FWA_{difference}$ becomes more negative, either $FWA_{forward}$ has to become smaller or $FWA_{backward}$ has to become larger. While decreasing $FWA_{forward}$ might actually increase funniness, the danger is that if $FWA_{backward}$ becomes too large then the tweet would become less funny.

One shortcoming of the FWA dataset is its relatively small vocabulary and sparse connectedness. For the hashtag #GentlerSongs, valid paths from the setup, "gentler", to at least one punch word were found in only 61.16% of tweets. Valid paths from some punch word to the setup occurred in only 49.72% of tweets. Only 21.03% of tweets had both. Obviously, this lack of coverage limits the widespread effectiveness of FWA features as well as the confidence with which we can view the results.

Finally, although we examine the highest, lowest, and average value per tweet for each of our five semantic measures, with the exception of NGD, all results were within a single percentage point of each other. This lack of variance can be at least partly attributed to the fact that punchlines in our dataset tended to be very short, averaging only 1.37 words per tweet.

6 Conclusions and Future Work

In this paper we explored the effects of semantic relatedness between setup and punchlines in Twitter hashtag games. To this end, we collected responses for four different hashtag games created by the Comedy Central show @*midnight* and used like/retweet counts to form pairwise relative humour judgments. We investigated five potential semantic relatedness measures and found perplexity, NGD, and $FWA_{difference}$ to be the most consistent indicators of funniness.

Additionally, we have provided empirical evidence of a preference against obvious jokes with funnier tweets tending to show weaker semantic relationships using symmetric measures of relatedness (NGD and Word2Vec). The asymmetric nature of the FWA features allows us to compare how easy it is to produce a punchline given only the setup versus how easy it is to recognize the connection between a punchline and a setup. Interestingly, we show that while punchlines should be easier to recognize than they are to produce, punchlines which are overall harder to recognize still tend to be judged as funnier.

Although this work represents only a first step towards a full humour recognition system, we believe semantic relatedness between setups and punchlines is worthy of further examination. Furthermore, we believe the task of humour recognition for Twitter hashtag games in general is an extremely promising area for computational humour research.

This paper focused on a relatively small subset of responses for only four different hashtag games, all relating to either songs or movies. Examining more tweets across a more diverse set of hashtag game prompts would allow for more easily generalized results. This work would be further improved by automatic punchline identification. The reliance on human punchline annotations prevents this work from being applied to a larger dataset. Additionally, while FWA feature results are promising, a lack of coverage means it is unlikely that FWA features will see wide spread use. However, they do suggest that asymmetrical measures of semantic relatedness deserve further examination.

In this work we defined the punchline as the deviation from the source domain (song titles or lyrics in the case of #GentlerSongs and #OlympicSongs; movie title in the case of #OceanMovies and #Boring-

Blockbusters). However, a tweet's humour does not come from such deviations alone. Quality of puns, multiple deviations, and even popularity of the source title/lyric can all affect perceived funniness. These features present obvious next steps for computational humour research into Twitter hashtag games. We expect their inclusion would not only improve results and but also lead to a more comprehensive model of hashtag game humour.

Finally, while this work focused on a specific type of hashtag game which tends to attract formulaic responses, hashtag games can be more complex. Word count related hashtags like #CollegeIn5Words, #MyLoveLifeIn3Words, etc. as well as open-ended hashtags like #WhenIWasYourAge, #WrongReasonsToHaveKids, etc. do not follow such formulas and thus present a significantly larger challenge to humour recognition. We intend to explore such hashtags in future works.

References

Binsted, K. & Ritchie, G. (1994) An implemented model of punning riddles. In *Proceedings of the Twelfth National Conference on Artificial Intelligence (Vol. 1)*. AAAI.

Boyd, D., Golder, S., & Lotan, G. (2010, January). Tweet, tweet, retweet: Conversational aspects of retweeting on twitter. In *System Sciences (HICSS), 2010 43rd Hawaii International Conference on (pp. 1-10)*. IEEE.

Cilibrasi, R. L., & Vitanyi, P. M. (2007). The google similarity distance. In *IEEE Transactions on knowledge and data engineering, 19(3), 370-383*.

Davidov, D., Tsur, O., & Rappoport, A. (2010, July). Semi-supervised recognition of sarcastic sentences in twitter and amazon. In *Proceedings of the fourteenth conference on computational natural language learning (pp. 107-116)*. ACL.

Erkan, G., & Radev, D. (2004). LexRank: Graph-based lexical centrality as salience in text summarization. In *Journal of Artificial Intelligence Research, 22, 457-479*.

Gilbert, E., Bakhshi, S., Chang, S., & Terveen, L. (2013, April). I need to try this?: a statistical overview of pinterest. In *Proceedings of the SIGCHI conference on human factors in computing systems (pp. 2427-2436)*. ACM.

Gimpel, K., Schneider, N., O'Connor, B., Das, D., Mills, D., Eisenstein, J., Heilman, M., Yogatama, D., Flanigan, F., & Smith, N. A. (2011, June). Part-of-speech tagging for twitter: Annotation, features, and experiments In *Proceedings of the 49th Annual Meeting of the Association for Computational Linguistics: Human Language Technologies: short papers-Volume 2 (pp. 42-47)*. ACL.

Go, A., Bhayani, R., & Huang, L. (2009). Twitter sentiment classification using distant supervision *CS224N Project Report, Stanford, 1, 12.*.

Gorrell, G., & Bontcheva, K. (2016). Classifying twitter favorites: like, bookmark, or thanks?. In *Journal of the Association for Information Science and Technology, 67(1), 17-25*.

Heafield, K., Pouzyrevsky, I., Clark, J. H., & Koehn, P. (2013, August) Scalable Modified Kneser-Ney Language Model Estimation. In *ACL (2) (pp. 690-696)*.

Labutov, I., & Lipson, H. (2012, July). Humor as circuits in semantic networks. In *Proceedings of the 50th Annual Meeting of the Association for Computational Linguistics: Short Papers-Volume 2 (pp. 150-155)*. ACL.

Mihalcea, R., & Pulman, S. (2007, February). Characterizing humour: An exploration of features in humorous texts. In *International Conference on Intelligent Text Processing and Computational Linguistics (pp. 337-347)*. Springer Berlin Heidelberg.

Mihalcea, R., & Strapparava, C. (2005, October). Making computers laugh: Investigations in automatic humor recognition. In *Proceedings of the Conference on Human Language Technology and Empirical Methods in Natural Language Processing (pp. 531-538)*. ACL.

Mikolov, T., Sutskever, I., Chen, K., Corrado, G., & Dean, J. (2013). Distributed representations of words and phrases and their compositionality. *Advances in neural information processing systems*.

Morkes, J., Kernal, H. K., & Nass, C. (1998, April). Humor in task-oriented computer-mediated communication and human-computer interaction. In *CHI 98 Conference Summary on Human Factors in Computing Systems (pp. 215-216)*. ACM.

Nelson, D. L., McEvoy, C. L., & Schreiber, T. A. (1998). The University of South Florida word association, rhyme, and word fragment norms. http://www.usf.edu/FreeAssociation/.

Petrovic, S., & Matthews, D. (2013, August). Unsupervised joke generation from big data. In *ACL (2) (pp. 228-232)*.

Radev, D., Stent, A., Tetreault, J., Pappu, A., Iliakopoulou, A., Chanfreau, A., de Juan, P., Vallmitjana, J., Jaimes, A., Jha, R., & Mankoff, B. (2016). Humor in Collective Discourse: Unsupervised Funniness Detection in the New Yorker Cartoon Caption Contest. In *Proceedings of the Tenth International Conference on Language Resources and Evaluation (LREC 2016)*. ELRA.

Rehurek, R., & Sojka, P. (2010) Software framework for topic modelling with large corpora. In *Proceedings of the LREC 2010 Workshop on New Challenges for NLP Frameworks*.

Reyes, A., Rosso, P., & Buscaldi, D. (2012). From humor recognition to irony detection: The figurative language of social media. *Data & Knowledge Engineering, 74, 1-12*.

Ritchie, G., Manurung, R., Pain, H., Waller, A., Black, R., & O'Mara, D. (2007). A practical application of computational humour. In *Proceedings of the 4th International Joint Conference on Computational Creativity (pp. 91-98)*.

Shahaf, D., Horvitz, E., & Mankoff, R. (2015, August). Inside jokes: Identifying humorous cartoon captions. In *Proceedings of the 21th ACM SIGKDD International Conference on Knowledge Discovery and Data Mining (pp. 1065-1074)*. ACM.

Sheridan, Rob. (2011, September 15). The Enthusiast: Hashtag Games [Web log post]. Retrieved from http://6thfloor.blogs.nytimes.com/2011/09/15/the-enthusiast-hashtag-games/?_r=0

Stein, Scott. (2016, October 10). Google Assistant uses joke writers from Pixar and The Onion Retrieved from https://www.cnet.com/news/google-hired-pixar-and-onion-joke-writers-for-assistant/

Stock, O., & Strapparava, C. (2002). HAHAcronym: Humorous agents for humorous acronyms. *Stock, Oliviero, Carlo Strapparava, and Anton Nijholt. Eds, 125-135*.

Suh, B., Hong, L., Pirolli, P., & Chi, E. H. (2010, August). Want to be retweeted? large scale analytics on factors impacting retweet in twitter network. In *Social Computing (SocialCom), 2010 IEEE Second International Conference on Social Computing (pp. 177-184)*. IEEE.

Taylor, J., & Mazlack, L. (2004, August). Computationally recognizing wordplay in jokes. In *Proceedings of CogSci (Vol. 2004)*.

Tsur, O., Davidov, D., & Rappoport, A. (2010, May). ICWSM-A Great Catchy Name: Semi-Supervised Recognition of Sarcastic Sentences in Online Product Reviews. In *ICWSM*.

Generating Sentiment Lexicons for German Twitter

Uladzimir Sidarenka and **Manfred Stede**
Applied Computational Linguistics
UFS Cognitive Science
University of Potsdam / Germany
{sidarenk|stede}@uni-potsdam.de

Abstract

Despite substantial progress made in developing new sentiment lexicon generation (SLG) methods for English, the task of transferring these approaches to other languages and domains in a sound way still remains open. In this paper, we contribute to the solution of this problem by systematically comparing semi-automatic translations of common English polarity lists with the results of the original automatic SLG algorithms, which were applied directly to German data. We evaluate these lexicons on a corpus of 7,992 manually annotated tweets. In addition to that, we also collate the results of dictionary- and corpus-based SLG methods in order to find out which of these paradigms is better suited for the inherently noisy domain of social media. Our experiments show that semi-automatic translations notably outperform automatic systems (reaching a macro-averaged F_1-score of 0.589), and that dictionary-based techniques produce much better polarity lists as compared to corpus-based approaches (whose best F_1-scores run up to 0.479 and 0.419 respectively) even for the non-standard Twitter genre. All reimplementations of the compared systems and the resulting lexicons of these methods are available online at https://github.com/WladimirSidorenko/SentiLex.

1 Introduction

Sentiment lexicons play a crucial role in many existing and emerging opinion mining applications. Not only do they serve as a valuable source of features for supervised classifiers (Mohammad et al., 2013; Zhu et al., 2014) but they also achieve competitive results when used as the main component of a sentiment analysis system (Taboada et al., 2011). Due to this high impact and tremendous costs of building such lexicons manually, devising new algorithms for an automatic generation of polarity lists has always been an area of active research in the sentiment analysis literature (Liu, 2012, pp. 79-91). Nevertheless, despite some obvious progress in this field (Cambria et al., 2016), the applicability of these approaches to other languages and text genres still raises questions: It is, for instance, unclear whether simply translating the existing English sentiment resources would produce better results than applying the methods that were initially proposed for their creation directly to the target language. Furthermore, for automatic systems which draw their knowledge from lexical taxonomies, such as WORDNET (Miller, 1995), it remains unanswered whether these approaches would also work for languages in which such resources are much smaller in size, and, even if they would, whether the resulting lexicons would then be general enough to carry over to more colloquial texts. Finally, for methods which derive their polarity lists from text corpora, it is not clear whether these approaches would still yield an acceptable quality when operating on inherently noisy input data.

In this paper, we try to analyze these and other problems in detail, using the example of German Twitter. More precisely, given a collection of German microblogs with manually labeled polar terms and prior polarities of these expressions, we want to find an SLG method that can best predict these terms and their semantic orientation. For this purpose, we compare the existing German sentiment lexicons

This work is licenced under a Creative Commons Attribution 4.0 International License. License details: http://creativecommons.org/licenses/by/4.0/

Proceedings of the Workshop on Computational Modeling of People's Opinions, Personality, and Emotions in Social Media,
pages 80–90, Osaka, Japan, December 12 2016.

(most of which were semi-automatically translated from popular English resources) with the results of common automatic dictionary- and corpus-based SLG approaches.

We begin our study by describing the data set which will be used in our evaluation. Afterwards, in Section 3, we introduce the metrics with which we will assess the quality of various polarity lists. Then, in Section 4, we evaluate three most popular existing German sentiment lexicons—the German Polarity Clues (Waltinger, 2010), SentiWS (Remus et al., 2010), and Zurich Polarity List of Clematide and Klenner (2010), subsequently comparing them with popular automatic SLG approaches in Section 5. Finally, after estimating the impact of different seed sets on the automatic methods and performing a qualitative analysis of their entries, we draw our conclusions and outline directions for future research in the final part of this paper.

To avoid unnecessary repetitions, we deliberately omit a summary of related work, since most of the popular SLG algorithms will be referenced in the respective evaluation sections anyway. We should, however, note that, apart from the research on the automatic lexicon generation, our study is also closely related to the experiments of Andreevskaia and Bergler (2008) and the "Sentiment Analysis in Twitter" track of the SemEval competition (Nakov et al., 2013; Rosenthal et al., 2014; Rosenthal et al., 2015). In contrast to the former work, however, where the authors trained a supervised classifier on one domain and applied it to another in order to determine the polarities of the sentences, we *explicitly model a situation where no annotated training data are available*, thus looking for the most general unsupervised SLG strategy which performs best regardless of the target domain, and we also *evaluate these strategies on the level of lexical phrases only*. Furthermore, unlike in the SemEval track, where the organizers also provided participants with sufficient labeled in-domain training sets and then asked them to predict the contextual polarity of pre-annotated polar expressions in the test data, we *simultaneously try to predict polar terms and their prior polarities, learning both of them without supervision*.

2 Data

We perform our evaluation on the publicly available Potsdam Twitter Sentiment corpus (PotTS; Sidarenka, 2016).[1] This collection comprises 7,992 microblogs pertaining to the German federal elections, general political life, papal conclave 2013, as well as casual everyday conversations. Two human experts annotated these posts with polar terms and their prior polarities,[2] reaching a substantial agreement of 0.75 binary κ (Cohen, 1960).[3] We used the complete data set labeled by one of the annotators as our test corpus, getting a total of 6,040 positive and 3,055 negative terms including multi-word expressions. However, since many of these expressions were emoticons, which, on the one hand, were a priori absent in common lexical taxonomies due to their colloquial nature and therefore not amenable to dictionary-based SLG systems but, on the other hand, could be easily captured by regular expressions, we decided to exclude non-alphabetic smileys altogether from our study. This left us with a set of 3,459 positive and 2,755 negative labeled terms (1,738 and 1,943 unique expressions respectively), whose κ-agreement run up to 0.59. Besides the test set, we selected a small subset of 400 tweets from the other annotator and used it as development data for tuning the hyper-parameters of the tested approaches.[4]

3 Evaluation Metrics

A central question to our experiments are the evaluation metrics that we should use for measuring lexicon quality. Usually, this quality is estimated either *intrinsically* (i.e., taking a lexicon in isolation and immediately assessing its accuracy) or *extrinsically* (i.e., considering the lexicon within the scope of a bigger application such as a supervised classifier which utilizes lexicon's entries as features).

---

[1] We use version 0.1.0 of this corpus.

[2] The annotators had been asked to judge the semantic orientation of a term irrespective of its possible negations. They could, however, consider the context for determining whether a particular reading of a polysemous word in the text was subjective or not.

[3] A detailed inter-annotator agreement study of this corpus is provided in (Sidarenka, 2016).

[4] That way, we only used the labeled corpus for evaluation or parameter optimization, other resources—GermaNet (Hamp and Feldweg, 1997) and the German Twitter Snapshot (Scheffler, 2014)—were used for training the methods.

Traditionally, intrinsic evaluation of English sentiment lexicons amounts to comparing these polarity lists with the General Inquirer (GI; Stone, 1966)—a manually compiled set of 11,895 words annotated with their semantic categories—by taking the intersection of the two resources and estimating the percentage of matches in which automatically induced polar terms have the same polarity as the GI entries. This evaluation method, however, is somewhat problematic: First of all, it is not easily transferable to other languages, since even a manual translation of the GI lexicon is not guaranteed to cover all language- and domain-specific polar expressions. Secondly, due to the intersection, this method does not penalize for a low recall so that a lexicon consisting of just two terms $good^+$ and bad^- will have the highest possible score, often surpassing polarity lists with a greater number of entries. Finally, this comparison does not account for polysemy. As a result, an ambiguous word only one of whose (possibly rare) senses is subjective will always be ranked the same as a purely polar term.

Unfortunately, an extrinsic evaluation does not always provide a solution in this case, since, depending on the type of the extrinsic system (e.g., a document classifier), it might still presuppose a large data set for training other system components and, furthermore, might yield overly high scores, which, however, are mainly due to these extrinsic modules rather than the quality of the lexicons themselves.

Instead of using these approaches, we opt for a direct comparison of the induced polarity lists with an existing annotated corpus, since this type of evaluation allows us to solve at least three of the previously mentioned issues: It does account for the recall, it does accommodate polysemous words,[5] and it does preclude intermediate components which might artificially boost the results. In particular, in order to check a lexicon against the PotTS data set, we construct a case-insensitive trie (Knuth, 1998, pp. 492–512) from the lexicon entries and match this trie against the contiguously running corpus text,[6] simultaneously comparing it with the actual word forms and lemmas of corpus tokens.[7] A match is considered correct iff the matched entry absolutely corresponds to the (possibly lemmatized) expert's annotation and has the same polarity as the one specified by the human coder. That way, we estimate the precision, recall, and F_1-score for each particular polarity class (positive, negative, and neutral), considering all words absent in the lexicons (not annotated in the corpus) as neutral.

4 Semi-Automatic Lexicons

We first apply the above metric to estimate the quality of the existing German resources: the German Polarity Clues (GPC; Waltinger, 2010), SentiWS (SWS; Remus, 2010), and the Zurich Polarity List (ZPL) of Clematide and Klenner (2010).

The GPC set comprises 10,141 subjective entries automatically translated from the English sentiment lexicons Subjectivity Clues (Wilson et al., 2005) and SentiSpin (Takamura et al., 2005), with a subsequent manual correction of these translations, and several synonyms and negated terms added by the authors. The SWS lexicon includes 1,818 positively and 1,650 negatively connoted terms, also providing their part-of-speech tags and inflections (resulting in a total of 32,734 word forms). Similarly to the GPC, the authors used an English sentiment resource—the GI lexicon of Stone et al. (1966)—to bootstrap their polarity list, manually revising these automatic translations afterwards. In addition to that, Remus et al. (2010) also expanded their set with words and phrases frequently co-occurring with positive and negative seed lexemes using collocation information obtained from a corpus of 10,200 customer reviews and the German Collocation Dictionary (Quasthoff, 2010). Finally, the Zurich Polarity List features 8,000 subjective entries taken from GERMANET synsets (Hamp and Feldweg, 1997). These synsets were manually annotated with their prior polarities by human experts. Since the authors, however, found the number of polar adjectives obtained that way insufficient for running further classification experiments, they automatically enriched this lexicon with more attributive terms by analyzing conjoined corpus collocations using the method of Hatzivassiloglou and McKeown (1997).

---

[5]Recall that the annotators of the PotTS data set were asked to annotate a polar expression iff its actual sense in the respective context was polar.

[6]In other words, we successively compare lexicon entries with the occurrences of corpus tokens in the same linear order as these occurrences appear in the text.

[7]We use the TREETAGGER of Schmid (1995) for lemmatization.

Lexicon	Positive Expressions			Negative Expressions			Neutral Terms			Macro F_1	Micro F_1
	Precision	Recall	F_1	Precision	Recall	F_1	Precision	Recall	F_1		
GPC	0.209	0.535	0.301	0.195	0.466	0.275	0.983	0.923	0.952	0.509	0.906
SWS	0.335	0.435	0.379	0.484	0.344	**0.402**	0.977	0.975	0.976	0.586	0.952
ZPL	0.411	0.424	0.417	0.38	0.352	0.366	0.977	0.979	0.978	0.587	0.955
GPC ∩ SWS ∩ ZPL	**0.527**	0.372	**0.436**	**0.618**	0.244	0.35	0.973	**0.99**	**0.982**	**0.589**	**0.964**
GPC ∪ SWS ∪ ZPL	0.202	**0.562**	0.297	0.195	**0.532**	0.286	**0.985**	0.917	0.95	0.51	0.901

Table 1: Evaluation of semi-automatic German sentiment lexicons.
GPC – German Polarity Clues (Waltinger, 2010), SWS – SentiWS (Remus et al., 2010), ZPL – Zurich Polarity Lexicon (Clematide and Klenner, 2010)

For our evaluation, we tested the three lexicons in isolation and also built their union and intersection in order to check for "synergy" effects. The results are shown in Table 1. As can be seen from the statistics, with a few exceptions, the highest scores for all classes as well as the best macro- and micro-averaged F_1-measures are achieved by the intersection of all three lexicons. On the other hand, as expected, the highest recall of polar expressions (and consequently the best precision at recognizing neutral terms) is attained by the union of these resources. The only case where individual lexicons are able to outperform these combinations is observed for the F_1-score of the negative class, where both SentiWS and ZPL show better results than their intersection, which is mainly due to the higher recall of these two polarity lists.

5 Automatic Methods

A natural question which arises upon the evaluation of the existing semi-automatic resources is how well fully automatic methods can perform in comparison with these lexicons. Traditionally, automatic SLG algorithms have been grouped into dictionary- and corpus-based ones, with their own complementary strengths and weaknesses. Dictionary-based approaches, for instance, incorporate distilled linguistic knowledge from a typically manually labeled lexical database, but lack any domain specificity. Corpus-based methods, on the other hand, can operate directly on unannotated in-domain data, but often have to deal with an extreme noisiness of their input. Since it was unclear which of these properties would have a stronger impact on the net results, we decided to reimplement the most commonly used algorithms from both of these paradigms and evaluate them on the PotTS corpus.

5.1 Dictionary-Based Approaches

For dictionary-based methods, we adopted the systems proposed by Hu and Liu (2004), Blair-Goldensohn et al. (2008), Kim and Hovy (2004), Esuli and Sebastiani (2006), as well as the min-cut and label-propagation approaches of Rao and Ravichandran (2009), and the random-walk algorithm described by Awadallah and Radev (2010).

The first of these works (Hu and Liu, 2004) expanded a given set of seed terms with known semantic orientations by propagating polarity values of these terms to their WORDNET synonyms and passing reversed polarity scores to the antonyms of these words. Later on, this idea was further refined by Blair-Goldensohn et al. (2008), who obtained polarity labels for new terms by multiplying a score vector $\vec{v}$ containing the orientation scores of the known seed words (-1 for negative expressions and 1 for positive ones) with an adjacency matrix A constructed for the WORDNET graph. With various modifications, the core idea of passing the polarity values through a lexical graph was adopted in almost all of the following dictionary-based works: Kim and Hovy (2004), for instance, computed the polarity class for a new word w by multiplying the prior probability of this class with the likelihood of the word w occurring among the synonyms of the seed terms with the given semantic orientation, choosing at the end the polarity which maximized this equation. Other ways of bootstrapping polarity lists were proposed by Esuli and Sebastiani (2006), who created their SENTIWORDNET resource using a committee of Rocchio and SVM classifiers trained on successively expanded sets of polar terms; Rao and Ravichandran (2009), who adopted the min-cut approach of Blum et al. (2004), also comparing it with the label-propagation algorithm of Zhu and Ghahramani (2002); and, finally, Awadallah and Radev (2010), who used a random walk method by estimating the polarity of an unknown word as the difference between an average number of steps a random walker had to make in order to reach a term from the positive or negative set.

Since some of these approaches relied on different seed sets or pursued different objectives (two- versus three-way classification), we decided to unify their settings and interfaces for the sake of our experiments. In particular, we were using the same translated seed list of Turney and Littman (2003) for all methods, expanding this set by 10 neutral terms ("neutral" *neutral*, "sachlich" *objective*, "technisch" *technical*, "finanziell" *financial* etc.).[8] Additionally, we enhanced all binary systems to ternary classifiers, so that each tested method could differentiate between positive, negative, and neutral terms. In the final step, we applied these methods to GERMANET (Hamp and Feldweg, 1997)—a German equivalent of the English WORDNET (Miller, 1995), which, however, is much smaller in size, having 20,792 less synsets for the three common parts of speech (nouns, adjectives, and verbs) than the Princeton resource.

Lexicon	# of Terms	Positive Expressions			Negative Expressions			Neutral Terms			Macro F_1	Micro F_1
		Precision	Recall	F_1	Precision	Recall	F_1	Precision	Recall	F_1		
SEED SET	20	**0.771**	0.102	0.18	0.568	0.017	0.033	0.963	**0.999**	**0.981**	0.398	**0.962**
HL	5,745	0.161	0.266	0.2	0.2	0.133	0.16	0.969	0.96	0.965	0.442	0.93
BG	1,895	0.503	0.232	**0.318**	0.285	0.093	0.14	0.968	0.991	0.979	**0.479**	0.959
KH	356	0.716	0.159	0.261	0.269	0.044	0.076	0.965	0.997	**0.981**	0.439	**0.962**
ES	39,181	0.042	**0.564**	0.078	0.033	**0.255**	0.059	**0.981**	0.689	0.81	0.315	0.644
RR$_{mincut}$	8,060	0.07	0.422	0.12	0.216	0.073	0.109	0.972	0.873	0.92	0.383	0.849
RR$_{lbl-prop}$	1,105	0.567	0.176	0.269	**0.571**	0.046	0.085	0.965	0.997	**0.981**	0.445	**0.962**
AR	23	0.768	0.1	0.176	0.568	0.017	0.033	0.963	**0.999**	**0.981**	0.397	**0.962**
HL ∩ BG ∩ RR$_{lbl-prop}$	752	0.601	0.165	0.259	0.567	0.045	0.084	0.965	0.997	**0.981**	0.441	**0.962**
HL ∪ BG ∪ RR$_{lbl-prop}$	6,258	0.166	0.288	0.21	0.191	0.146	**0.165**	0.97	0.958	0.964	0.446	0.929

Table 2: Evaluation of dictionary-based approaches.
HL – Hu and Liu (2004), BG – Blair-Goldensohn et al. (2008), KH – Kim and Hovy (2004), ES – Esuli and Sebastiani (2006), RR – Rao and Ravichandran (2009), AR – Awadallah and Radev (2010)

The results of this evaluation are shown in Table 2. This time, the situation is much more varied, as different systems can achieve best results on just some aspects of certain classes but can hardly attain best overall scores in all categories. This is, for instance, the case for the positive and negative polarities, where the best precision scores are reached by the seed set in the first case and the label propagation algorithm of Rao and Ravichandran (2009) in the second case. However, with respect to the recall, both of these polarity lists perform notably worse than the approach of Esuli and Sebastiani (2006). Yet other systems—the matrix-vector method of Blair-Goldensohn et al. (2008) and the union of the three overall top-scoring systems respectively—reach the highest F_1-scores for these two classes. Nevertheless, we can still notice three main tendencies in this evaluation: *i*) the method of Esuli and Sebastiani (2006) generally gets the highest recall of polar terms and, consequently, achieves the best precision in recognizing neutral words, but suffers from a low precision for the positive and negative polarities; *ii*) simultaneously five systems attain the same best F_1-scores on recognizing neutral terms, which, in turn, leads to the best micro-averaged F_1-results for all polarity classes; and, finally, *iii*) the system of Blair-Goldensohn et al. (2008) shows the best macro-averaged performance. This approach, however, is extremely susceptible to its hyper-parameter settings (in particular, we considered the maximum number of times the initial vector $\vec{v}$ was multiplied with the adjacency matrix A as such a parameter and noticed a dramatic decrease of method's scores after the fifth iteration).

5.2 Corpus-Based Approaches

An alternative way to generate polarity lists is to use corpus-based approaches. In contrast to dictionary-based methods, these systems typically operate immediately on raw texts and are, therefore, virtually independent of any manually annotated linguistic resources. This flexibility, however, might come at the cost of a reduced accuracy due to an inherent noisiness of the unlabeled data. The most prominent representatives of this class of algorithms are the approaches proposed by Takamura et al. (2005), Velikovich et al. (2010), Kiritchenko et al. (2014), and Severyn and Moschitti (2015), which we briefly describe in this section.

---

[8] All translated seed sets are provided along with the source code for this paper.

Drawing on the pioneering work of Hatzivassiloglou and McKeown (1997), in which the authors expanded an initial list of polar adjectives by analyzing coordinately conjoined terms from a text corpus, Takamura et al. (2005) enhanced this algorithm, extending it to other parts of speech and also incorporating semantic links from WORDNET in addition to the co-occurrence statistics extracted from the corpus. After representing the final set of terms as an electron lattice, whose edge weights corresponded to the contextual and semantic links between words, the authors computed the most probable polarity distribution for this lattice by adopting the Ising spin model from statistical mechanics.

The approach of Velikovich et al. (2010) was mainly inspired by the label-propagation algorithm of Rao and Ravichandran (2009), with the crucial difference that, instead of taking an averaged sum of the adjacent neighbor values when propagating the label scores through the graph, the authors took the maximum of these scores in order to prune unreliable, noisy corpus links. Similarly, Kiritchenko et al. (2014) built on the method of Turney and Littman (2003) and computed polarity scores for new words by taking the difference of their PMI associations with noisy labeled positive and negative classes. Finally, Severyn and Moschitti (2015) trained a supervised SVM classifier on a distantly labeled data set and included the top-ranked unigram and bigram features in their final lexicon.

For our evaluation, we applied these methods to the German Twitter Snapshot (Scheffler, 2014)—a collection of 24 M microblogs gathered in April, 2013, constructing the collocation graph from the lemmatized word forms of this corpus and only considering words which appeared at least four times in the analyzed data. We again were using the TREETAGGER of Schmid (1995) for lemmatization and GERMANET (Hamp and Feldweg, 1997) for deriving semantic links between word vertices for the method of Takamura et al. (2005).

Lexicon	# of Terms	Positive Expressions			Negative Expressions			Neutral Terms			Macro F_1	Micro F_1
		Precision	Recall	F_1	Precision	Recall	F_1	Precision	Recall	F_1		
SEED SET	20	**0.771**	0.102	0.18	**0.568**	0.017	0.033	0.963	**0.999**	**0.981**	0.398	**0.962**
TKM	920	0.646	**0.134**	**0.221**	0.565	**0.029**	**0.055**	**0.964**	0.998	**0.981**	**0.419**	**0.962**
VEL	60	0.764	0.102	0.18	**0.568**	0.017	0.033	0.963	0.999	0.98	0.398	**0.962**
KIR	320	0.386	0.106	0.166	**0.568**	0.017	0.033	0.963	0.996	0.979	0.393	0.959
SEV	60	0.68	0.102	0.177	**0.568**	0.017	0.033	0.963	**0.999**	**0.981**	0.397	**0.962**
TKM ∩ VEL ∩ SEV	20	**0.771**	0.102	0.18	**0.568**	0.017	0.033	0.963	**0.999**	**0.981**	0.398	**0.962**
TKM ∪ VEL ∪ SEV	1,020	0.593	**0.134**	0.218	0.565	**0.029**	**0.055**	**0.964**	0.998	0.98	0.418	**0.962**

Table 3: Evaluation of corpus-based approaches.
TKM – Takamura et al. (2005), VEL – Velikovich et al. (2010), KIR – Kiritchenko et al. (2014), SEV – Severyn and Moschitti (2015)

The results of these experiments are shown in Table 3. This time, we can observe a clear superiority of Takamura et al.'s method, which not only achieves the best recall and F_1 in recognizing positive and negative items but also attains the highest micro- and macro-averaged results for all three polarity classes. The cardinality of the other induced lexicons, however, is much smaller than the size of Takamura et al.'s polarity list. Moreover, these lexicons also show absolutely identical scores for the negative expressions as the original seed set. Since these results were somewhat unexpected, we decided to investigate the reasons for possible problems. As it turned out, the macro-averaged F_1-values of these methods were rapidly going down on the held-out development set as the number of their induced polar terms increased. Since we considered the lexicon size as one of the hyper-parameters of the tested approaches, we immediately stopped populating these lexicons when we noticed a decrease in their results. As a consequence, only the highest-ranked terms (all of which had the positive polarity) were included in the final lists.

One of the reasons for such rapid quality decrease was the surprisingly high positive bias of the initial seed set: While converting the original seed list of Turney and Littman (2003) to German, we translated the English word "correct" as "richtig". This German word, however, also has another reading which means *real* (as in *a real fact* or *a real sports car*) and which was much more frequent in the analyzed snapshot, often appearing in an unequivocally negative context, e.g., "ein richtiger Bombenanschlag" (*a real bomb attack*) or "ein richtiger Terrorist" (*a real terrorist*). As a consequence of this, methods relying on distant supervision had to deal with an extremely unbalanced training set (the automatically labeled corpus that we distantly obtained for the approach of Kiritchenko et al. (2014) using these seeds, for instance, had 716,210 positive versus 92,592 negative training instances).

6   Effect of Seed Sets

Since the set of the initial seed terms appeared to play an important role for at least three of the tested methods, we decided to analyze the impact of this factor in more detail by repeating our experiments with the seed lists proposed by Hu and Liu (2004), Kim and Hovy (2004), Esuli and Sebastiani (2006), and Remus et al. (2010). For this purpose, we manually translated the seed sets of Hu and Liu (2004) and Kim and Hovy (2004) into German. Since the authors, however, only provided some examples of their seeds without specifying the full lists, we filled up our translations with additional polar terms to match the original cardinalities. A different procedure was applied to obtain the seed set of Esuli and Sebastiani (2006)—since this resource comprised a vast number of neutral terms (the authors considered as neutral all words from the General Inquirer lexicon which were not marked there as either positive or negative), we automatically translated the neutral subset of these seeds with the help of a publicly available translation site (http://www.dict.cc), using the first suggestion returned by this service for each original English term.

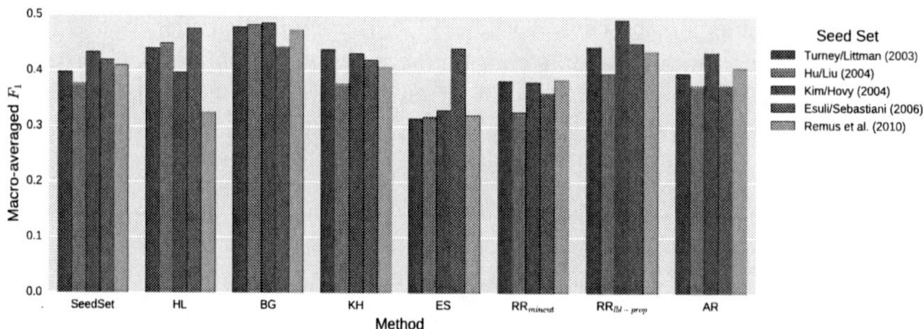

Figure 1: Macro-averaged F_1-scores of the dictionary-based approaches with different seed sets.

The updated results for the dictionary-based approaches with the alternative seed sets are shown in Figure 1. This time, we again can notice superior scores achieved by the method of Blair-Goldensohn et al. (2008), which not only performs better than the other systems on average but also seems to be less susceptible to the varying quality and size of the different seed lists. The remaining methods typically achieve their best macro-averaged results with either of the two top-scoring polarity sets—the seed list of Kim and Hovy (2004) or the seed set of Esuli and Sebastiani (2006). This is, for instance, the case for the method of Kim and Hovy (2004) and the min-cut approach of Rao and Ravichandran (2009), whose performance with the native Kim-Hovy seed set is on par with their results achieved using the Turney-Littman seeds. The label-propagation and random walk algorithms can even strongly benefit from the seeds provided by Kim and Hovy (2004). The remaining two methods—Hu and Liu (2004) and Esuli and Sebastiani (2006)—work best in combination with the initial polarity set proposed by Esuli and Sebastiani (2006).

A slightly different situation is observed for the corpus-based approaches as shown in Figure 2. Except for the method of Takamura et al. (2005), all three remaining methods—Velikovich et al. (2010), Kiritchenko et al. (2014), and Severyn and Moschitti (2015)—show very similar (though not identical) scores. Moreover, these scores are also very close to the results achieved by the respective seed sets without any expansion. The primary reasons for this were again the positive bias of the distantly labeled tweets and the consequently premature stopping of the expansion.

Following the suggestion of one of the reviewers, we additionally included two more seed sets in our evaluation: gold precision and emoticons. The former list contained just two polar terms—"gut" ($good^+$) and "schlecht" (bad^-)—which showed an almost perfect precision on the PotTS data set.[9] The

---

[9]Unfortunately, we could not include more terms in this seed set due to a high lexical ambiguity of other polar words. Even in our proposed prototypical seed list, one of the terms—"gut" (*good*)—could have another rather rare reading (*manor*) when used as a noun.

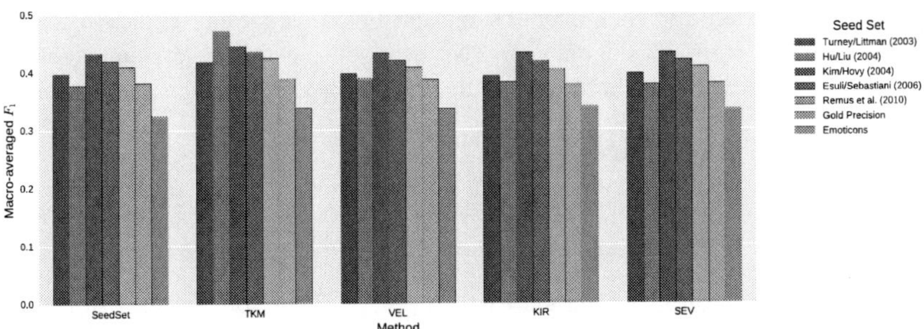

Figure 2: Macro-averaged F_1-scores of the corpus-based approaches with different seed sets.

latter seed set consisted of two regular expressions: one for capturing positive smileys and another one for matching negative emoticons. As can be seen form the figure, these lists, however, could hardly outperform any of our initially used seed sets.

7 Analysis of Entries

Besides investigating the effects of different hyper-parameters and seeds, we also decided to have a closer look at the actual results produced by the tested methods. For this purpose, we extracted ten highest scored entries (not counting the seed terms) from each automatic lexicon and summarized them in Table 4.

Rank	HL	BG	KH	ES	RR^{**}_{mincut}	$RR_{lbl\text{-}prop}$	TKM	VEL	KIR	SEV
1	perfekt *perfect*	fleißig *diligent*	anrüchig *indecent*	namenlos *nameless*	planieren *to plane*	prunkvoll *splendid*	Stockfotos *stock photos*	Wahlkampfgeschenk *election gift*	Suchmaschinen *search engines*	Scherwey *Scherwey*
2	mustergültig *immaculate*	böse *evil*	unecht *artificial*	ruhelos *restless*	Erdschicht *stratum*	sinnlich *sensual*	BMKS65 *BMKS65*	Ordensgeschichte *order history*	#gameinsight *#gameinsight*	krebsen *to crawl*
3	vorbildlich *commendable*	beispielhaft *exemplary*	irregulär *irregular*	unbewaffnet *unarmed*	gefallen *please*	pompös *ostentatious*	Ziya *Ziya*	Indologica *Indologica*	#androidgames *#androidgames*	kaschieren *to conceal*
4	beispielhaft *exemplary*	edel *noble*	drittklassig *third-class*	interesselos *indifferent*	Zeiteinheit *time unit*	unappetitlich *unsavory*	Shoafoundation *shoah found.*	Indologie *Indology*	Selamat *selamat*	Davis *Davis*
5	exzellent *excellent*	tüchtig *proficient*	sinnlich *sensual*	reizlos *unattractive*	Derivat *derivate*	befehlsgemäß *as ordered*	T1199 *T1199*	Energieverbrauch *energy consumption*	Pagi *Pagi*	#Klassiker *#classics*
6	exzeptionell *exceptional*	emsig *busy*	unprofessionell *unprofessional*	würdelos *undignified*	Oberfläche *surface*	vierschrötig *beefy*	Emilay55 *Emilay55*	Schimmelbildung *mold formation*	#Sparwelt *#savingsworld*	Nationalismus *nationalism*
7	außergewöhnlich *extraordinary*	eifrig *eager*	abgeschlagen *exhausted*	absichtslos *unintentional*	Essbesteck *cutlery*	regelgemäß *regularly*	Eneramo *Eneramo*	Hygiene *hygiene*	#Seittest *#Seittest*	Kraftstoff *fuel*
8	außerordentlich *exceptionally*	arbeitsam *hardworking*	gefällig *pleasing*	ereignislos *uneventful*	ablösen *to displace*	wahrheitsgemäß *true*	GotzeID *GotzeID*	wasserd *waterp*	Gameinsight *Gameinsight*	inaktiv *idle*
9	viertklassig *fourth-class*	mustergültig *exemplary*	mustergültig *exemplary*	regellos *irregular*	Musikveranstaltung *music event*	fettig *greasy*	BSH65 *BSH65*	heizkostensparen *saving heating costs*	#ipadgames *#ipadgames*	8DD *8DD*
10	sinnreich *ingenious*	vorbildlich *commendable*	unrecht *wrong*	fehlerfrei *accurate*	Gebrechen *afflictions*	lumpig *shabby*	Saymak. *Saymak.*	Referenzarchitekturen *reference architectures*	Fitnesstraining *fitness training*	Mailadresse *mail address*

Table 4: Top ten polar terms produced by the automatic methods.
*** – the min-cut method of Rao and Ravichandran (2009) returns an unsorted set*

As can be seen from the table, the approaches of Hu and Liu (2004), Blair-Goldensohn et al. (2008), Kim and Hovy (2004), as well as the label-propagation algorithm of Rao and Ravichandran (2009) produce almost perfect polarity lists. The SENTIWORDNET approach of Esuli and Sebastiani (2006), however, already features some spurious terms (e.g., "absichtslos" *unintentional*) among its top-scored entries. Finally, the min-cut approach of Rao and Ravichandran (2009) returns a set of mainly objective terms, which, however, is rather due to the fact that this method performs a cluster-like partitioning of the lexical graph without ranking the words assigned to a cluster.

An opposite situation is observed for the corpus-based systems: The top-scoring polarity lists returned by these approaches not only include many apparently objective terms but are also difficult to interpret in general, as they contain a substantial number of slang and advertising terms (e.g., "BMKS65", "#gamein-sight", "#androidgames" etc.). This again supports the hypothesis that an extreme content noisiness of the input domain might pose considerable difficulties to sentiment lexicon generation methods.

8   Conclusions and Future Work

Based on the above observations and our experiments, we can formulate the main conclusions that we come to in this paper as follows:

- semi-automatic translations of common English polarity lists notably outperform automatic SLG approaches that are applied directly to non-English data;

- despite their allegedly worse ability to accommodate new domains, dictionary-based methods are still superior to corpus-based systems (at least in terms of the proposed intrinsic evaluation), provided that a sufficiently big lexical taxonomy exists for the target language;

- a potential weakness of the dictionary-based algorithms, however, is their susceptibility to different hyper-parameter settings and the size and composition of the initial seed sets;

- nevertheless, the effect of the seed sets might be even stronger for the corpus-based approaches which rely on distant supervision, if the resulting noisy labeled training set becomes highly unbalanced.

In this respect, there appears to be a great need for a corpus-based method which can both benefit from in-domain data and be resistant to non-balanced training sets; and we are, in fact, currently working on such an algorithm. By taking advantage of the recent advances in deep learning and distributional semantics, we aim to show an efficient way of getting suitable vector representations for polar terms and generating high-quality sentiment lexicons from these automatically learned vectors.

Acknowledgments

We thank the anonymous reviewers for their suggestions and comments.

References

Alina Andreevskaia and Sabine Bergler. 2008. When specialists and generalists work together: Overcoming domain dependence in sentiment tagging. In *ACL 2008, Proceedings of the 46th Annual Meeting of the Association for Computational Linguistics, June 15-20, 2008, Columbus, Ohio, USA*, pages 290–298. The Association for Computer Linguistics.

Ahmed Hassan Awadallah and Dragomir R. Radev. 2010. Identifying text polarity using random walks. In Jan Hajic, Sandra Carberry, and Stephen Clark, editors, *ACL 2010, Proceedings of the 48th Annual Meeting of the Association for Computational Linguistics, July 11-16, 2010, Uppsala, Sweden*, pages 395–403. The Association for Computer Linguistics.

Sasha Blair-Goldensohn, Tyler Neylon, Kerry Hannan, George A. Reis, Ryan Mcdonald, and Jeff Reynar. 2008. Building a sentiment summarizer for local service reviews. In *In NLP in the Information Explosion Era*.

Avrim Blum, John D. Lafferty, Mugizi Robert Rwebangira, and Rajashekar Reddy. 2004. Semi-supervised learning using randomized mincuts. In Carla E. Brodley, editor, *Machine Learning, Proceedings of the Twenty-first International Conference (ICML 2004), Banff, Alberta, Canada, July 4-8, 2004*, volume 69 of *ACM International Conference Proceeding Series*. ACM.

Nicoletta Calzolari, Khalid Choukri, Bente Maegaard, Joseph Mariani, Jan Odijk, Stelios Piperidis, Mike Rosner, and Daniel Tapias, editors. 2010. *Proceedings of the International Conference on Language Resources and Evaluation, LREC 2010, 17-23 May 2010, Valletta, Malta*. European Language Resources Association.

Erik Cambria, Björn W. Schuller, Yunqing Xia, and Bebo White. 2016. New avenues in knowledge bases for natural language processing. *Knowl.-Based Syst.*, 108:1–4.

Simon Clematide and Manfred Klenner. 2010. Evaluation and extension of a polarity lexicon for German. In *Proceedings of the First Workshop on Computational Approaches to Subjectivity and Sentiment Analysis*, pages 7–13.

Jacob Cohen. 1960. A coefficient of agreement for nominal scales. *Educational and Psychological Measurement*, 20(1):37–46.

Andrea Esuli and Fabrizio Sebastiani. 2006. SentiWordNet: a high-coverage lexical resource for opinion mining. Technical Report ISTI-PP-002/2007, Institute of Information Science and Technologies (ISTI) of the Italian National Research Council (CNR), October.

Birgit Hamp and Helmut Feldweg. 1997. GermaNet - a lexical-semantic net for German. In *In Proceedings of ACL workshop Automatic Information Extraction and Building of Lexical Semantic Resources for NLP Applications*, pages 9–15.

Vasileios Hatzivassiloglou and Kathleen McKeown. 1997. Predicting the semantic orientation of adjectives. In Philip R. Cohen and Wolfgang Wahlster, editors, *35th Annual Meeting of the Association for Computational Linguistics and 8th Conference of the European Chapter of the Association for Computational Linguistics, Proceedings of the Conference, 7-12 July 1997, Universidad Nacional de Educación a Distancia (UNED), Madrid, Spain.*, pages 174–181. Morgan Kaufmann Publishers / ACL.

Minqing Hu and Bing Liu. 2004. Mining and summarizing customer reviews. In Won Kim, Ron Kohavi, Johannes Gehrke, and William DuMouchel, editors, *KDD*, pages 168–177. ACM.

Soo-Min Kim and Eduard H. Hovy. 2004. Determining the sentiment of opinions. In *COLING 2004, 20th International Conference on Computational Linguistics, Proceedings of the Conference, 23-27 August 2004, Geneva, Switzerland.*

Svetlana Kiritchenko, Xiaodan Zhu, and Saif M. Mohammad. 2014. Sentiment Analysis of Short Informal Texts. *J. Artif. Intell. Res. (JAIR)*, 50:723–762.

Donald E. Knuth. 1998. *The Art of Computer Programming, Volume 3: (2Nd Ed.) Sorting and Searching*. Addison Wesley Longman Publishing Co., Inc., Redwood City, CA, USA.

Bing Liu. 2012. *Sentiment Analysis and Opinion Mining*. Synthesis Lectures on Human Language Technologies. Morgan & Claypool Publishers.

George A. Miller. 1995. WordNet: A Lexical Database for English. *Communications of ACM*, 38(11):39–41, November.

Saif M. Mohammad, Svetlana Kiritchenko, and Xiaodan Zhu. 2013. NRC-Canada: Building the State-of-the-Art in Sentiment Analysis of Tweets. *CoRR*, abs/1308.6242.

Preslav Nakov, Sara Rosenthal, Zornitsa Kozareva, Veselin Stoyanov, Alan Ritter, and Theresa Wilson. 2013. SemEval-2013 Task 2: Sentiment Analysis in Twitter. In *Second Joint Conference on Lexical and Computational Semantics (*SEM), Volume 2: Proceedings of the Seventh International Workshop on Semantic Evaluation (SemEval 2013)*, pages 312–320, Atlanta, Georgia, USA, June. Association for Computational Linguistics.

Uwe Quasthoff. 2010. *Deutsches Kollokationswörterbuch*. deGruyter, Berlin, New York.

Delip Rao and Deepak Ravichandran. 2009. Semi-supervised polarity lexicon induction. In Alex Lascarides, Claire Gardent, and Joakim Nivre, editors, *EACL 2009, 12th Conference of the European Chapter of the Association for Computational Linguistics, Proceedings of the Conference, Athens, Greece, March 30 - April 3, 2009*, pages 675–682. The Association for Computer Linguistics.

Robert Remus, Uwe Quasthoff, and Gerhard Heyer. 2010. SentiWS - A publicly available German-language resource for sentiment analysis. In Calzolari et al. (Calzolari et al., 2010).

Sara Rosenthal, Alan Ritter, Preslav Nakov, and Veselin Stoyanov. 2014. SemEval-2014 Task 9: Sentiment Analysis in Twitter. In *Proceedings of the 8th International Workshop on Semantic Evaluation (SemEval 2014)*, pages 73–80, Dublin, Ireland, August. Association for Computational Linguistics and Dublin City University.

Sara Rosenthal, Preslav Nakov, Svetlana Kiritchenko, Saif Mohammad, Alan Ritter, and Veselin Stoyanov. 2015. Semeval-2015 task 10: Sentiment analysis in twitter. In *Proceedings of the 9th International Workshop on Semantic Evaluation (SemEval 2015)*, pages 451–463, Denver, Colorado, June. Association for Computational Linguistics.

Tatjana Scheffler. 2014. A German Twitter Snapshot. In Nicoletta Calzolari, Khalid Choukri, Thierry Declerck, Hrafn Loftsson, Bente Maegaard, Joseph Mariani, Asunción Moreno, Jan Odijk, and Stelios Piperidis, editors, *Proceedings of the Ninth International Conference on Language Resources and Evaluation (LREC-2014), Reykjavik, Iceland, May 26-31, 2014.*, pages 2284–2289. European Language Resources Association (ELRA).

Helmut Schmid. 1995. Probabilistic part-of-speech tagging using decision trees. In *Proceedings of the ACL SIGDAT-Workshop*.

Aliaksei Severyn and Alessandro Moschitti. 2015. On the automatic learning of sentiment lexicons. In Rada Mihalcea, Joyce Yue Chai, and Anoop Sarkar, editors, *NAACL HLT 2015, The 2015 Conference of the North American Chapter of the Association for Computational Linguistics: Human Language Technologies, Denver, Colorado, USA, May 31 - June 5, 2015*, pages 1397–1402. The Association for Computational Linguistics.

Uladzimir Sidarenka. 2016. PotTS: The Potsdam Twitter Sentiment Corpus. In Nicoletta Calzolari, Khalid Choukri, Thierry Declerck, Sara Goggi, Marko Grobelnik, Bente Maegaard, Joseph Mariani, Hélène Mazo, Asunción Moreno, Jan Odijk, and Stelios Piperidis, editors, *Proceedings of the Tenth International Conference on Language Resources and Evaluation LREC 2016, Portorož, Slovenia, May 23-28, 2016.* European Language Resources Association (ELRA).

Philip J. Stone, Dexter C. Dunphy, Marshall S. Smith, and Daniel M. Ogilvie. 1966. *The General Inquirer: A Computer Approach to Content Analysis*. MIT Press, Cambridge, MA.

Maite Taboada, Julian Brooke, Milan Tofiloski, Kimberly D. Voll, and Manfred Stede. 2011. Lexicon-based methods for sentiment analysis. *Computational Linguistics*, 37(2):267–307.

Hiroya Takamura, Takashi Inui, and Manabu Okumura. 2005. Extracting semantic orientations of words using spin model. In Kevin Knight, Hwee Tou Ng, and Kemal Oflazer, editors, *ACL 2005, 43rd Annual Meeting of the Association for Computational Linguistics, Proceedings of the Conference, 25-30 June 2005, University of Michigan, USA*. The Association for Computer Linguistics.

Peter D. Turney and Michael L. Littman. 2003. Measuring praise and criticism: Inference of semantic orientation from association. *ACM Trans. Inf. Syst.*, 21(4):315–346.

Leonid Velikovich, Sasha Blair-Goldensohn, Kerry Hannan, and Ryan T. McDonald. 2010. The viability of web-derived polarity lexicons. In *Human Language Technologies: Conference of the North American Chapter of the Association of Computational Linguistics, Proceedings, June 2-4, 2010, Los Angeles, California, USA*, pages 777–785. The Association for Computational Linguistics.

Ulli Waltinger. 2010. GermanPolarityClues: A Lexical Resource for German Sentiment Analysis. In Calzolari et al. (Calzolari et al., 2010).

Theresa Wilson, Janyce Wiebe, and Paul Hoffmann. 2005. Recognizing contextual polarity in phrase-level sentiment analysis. In *HLT/EMNLP 2005, Human Language Technology Conference and Conference on Empirical Methods in Natural Language Processing, Proceedings of the Conference, 6-8 October 2005, Vancouver, British Columbia, Canada*. The Association for Computational Linguistics.

Xiaojin Zhu and Zoubin Ghahramani. 2002. Learning from labeled and unlabeled data with label propagation, cmu-cald-02-107. Technical report, Carnegie Mellon University.

Xiaodan Zhu, Svetlana Kiritchenko, and Saif Mohammad. 2014. Nrc-canada-2014: Recent improvements in the sentiment analysis of tweets. In *Proceedings of the 8th International Workshop on Semantic Evaluation (SemEval 2014)*, pages 443–447, Dublin, Ireland, August. Association for Computational Linguistics and Dublin City University.

Innovative Semi-Automatic Methodology to Annotate Emotional Corpora

Lea Canales
University of Alicante
Alicante (Spain)
`lcanales@dlsi.ua.es`

Carlo Strapparava
Fondazione Bruno Kessler
Trento (Italy)
`strappa@fbk.eu`

Ester Boldrini
University of Alicante
Alicante (Spain)
`eboldrini@dlsi.ua.es`

Patricio Martínez-Barco
University of Alicante
Alicante (Spain)
`patricio@dlsi.ua.es`

Abstract

Detecting depression or personality traits, tutoring and student behaviour systems, or identifying cases of cyber-bulling are a few of the wide range of the applications, in which the automatic detection of emotion is a crucial element. Emotion detection has the potential of high impact by contributing the benefit of business, society, politics or education. Given this context, the main objective of our research is to contribute to the resolution of one of the most important challenges in textual emotion detection task: the problems of emotional corpora annotation. This will be tackled by proposing a new semi-automatic methodology. Our innovative methodology consists in two main phases: (1) an automatic process to pre-annotate the unlabelled sentences with a reduced number of emotional categories; and (2) a refinement manual process where human annotators will determine which is the predominant emotion between the emotional categories selected in phase 1. Our proposal in this paper is to show and evaluate the pre-annotation process to analyse the feasibility and the benefits by the methodology proposed. The results obtained are promising and allow obtaining a substantial improvement of annotation time and cost and confirm the usefulness of our pre-annotation process to improve the annotation task.

1 Introduction

Automatic detection of affective states in text has wide range of applications for business, society, politics or education. This is because detecting emotions is becoming more and more important due to the fact that it has the potential of bringing substantial benefits for different sectors: example of this can be for instance detecting depression (Cherry et al., 2012), identifying cases of cyber-bullying (Dadvar et al., 2013), tracking well-being (Schwartz et al., 2013), or contributing to improve the student motivation and performance (Montero and Suhonen, 2014).

So far, many of the existing machine learning techniques for automatic detection of emotions are supervised; systems first infer a function from a set of examples labeled with the correct sentiment (this set of examples is called the training data or labelled corpus). After this, the model is able to predict the emotion of new examples. Hence, the training dataset employed in supervised machine learning algorithms is crucial to build accurate emotion detection systems that can generate reliable results.

The creation of a labelled corpus is not trivial, since detecting emotion in text can be difficult even for humans due to the influence of each own background that can influence emotion interpretation. Most relevant research carried out so far has shown that the amount of agreement between annotations when associating emotion to instances is significantly lower compared to other tasks such as Part-Of-Speech (POS) or Named Entity (NE) detection. This is due to the fact that manual annotations can be significantly influenced by a set of different factors such as clarity of instructions, difficulty of task, training of the annotators, and even by the annotation scheme (Mohammad, 2016). For this reason, in this paper an innovative semi-automatic methodology is proposed to resolve one of the most important challenges in textual emotion detection task: the problems of the annotation of an emotional corpus.

The methodology proposed in our research consists of two main phases: (1) an automatic process to pre-annotate the unlabelled sentences with a reduced number of emotional categories; and (2) a refine-

91

Proceedings of the Workshop on Computational Modeling of People's Opinions, Personality, and Emotions in Social Media,
pages 91–100, Osaka, Japan, December 12 2016.

ment manual process where human annotators will determine which is the predominant emotion between the emotional categories selected in phase 1.

By means of proposing innovation in terms of annotation methodology, our aim is to reduce the complexity of emotion annotation task through reducing the number of emotional categories automatically, since the influence of the number of coding categories on reliability estimation is really important. As Antoine et al. (2014) concluded, the agreement values increase significantly when the number of classes decreases. Hence, our hypothesis is that the decrease of complexity of emotion annotation task through the reduction of the number of emotional categories will allow us to improve the reliability on the task. This methodology will allow us annotating large amount of emotional data in any genre efficiently and with guarantee of high standards of reliability. Our proposal in this paper is to show and evaluate the pre-annotation process to analyse the feasibility and the benefits by the methodology proposed.

The rest of the paper is organised as follows. Section 2 presents the related work and a reflection on the pending issues. After this, the proposed method is described in detail in the Section 3. Then, Section 4 is aimed at showing the approaches proposed, the evaluation methodology, the results obtained and a discussion about these results. Finally, Section 5 details our conclusions and future works.

2   Related work

This section summaries the most relevant emotional corpora developed for emotion detection purposes, their features and how they have been developed. Our analysis on Emotion Detection is focused on detecting areas of improvement that we aim to contribute to tackle with our research.

According to research in psychology, there is a number of theories about how to represent the emotions that humans can perceive and express. Among these theories, some of them are focused on defining the set of the basic emotions (Ekman, 1992; Plutchik, 1980), although there is not an universal consensus about which set of emotions are the most basic. Nevertheless, most of the work in automatic detection of emotions in text has focused on the limited set of proposed basic emotions, since this allows reducing the cost in terms of time and money. Even though there also are approaches based on non-basic emotions.

Most of the emotional resources developed so far have been annotated manually, since, in this way, machine learning systems learn from human annotations that are generally more accurate. Among these resources, we can find corpora labelled with the six basic emotions categories proposed by Ekman such as: (Alm et al., 2005) annotated a sentence-level corpus of approximately 185 children stories with emotion categories; (Aman and Szpakowicz, 2007) annotated blog posts collected directly from Web with emotion categories and intensity; or (Strapparava and Mihalcea, 2007) annotated news headlines with emotion categories and valence.

As mentioned previously, there are corpora labelled with other small set of emotions by manually annotation like: (Neviarouskaya et al., 2009) corpus extracted 1,000 sentences from various stories; Emotiblog-corpus that consists of a collection of blog posts manually extracted from the Web and annotated with three annotation levels: document, sentence and element (Boldrini and Martínez-Barco, 2012); or EmoTweet-28 corpus that consists of a collection of tweets annotated with 28 emotion categories (Liew et al., 2016).

The common feature of these emotional corpora is that have been annotated manually, a hard and time-consuming task where the obtaining an agreement between annotations is a challenge, due to the subjectivity of the task and the need to invest in many resources to annotate large scale emotional corpora.

Consequently and with the aim of overcoming the cost and time consuming shortcoming of manual annotation, several emotional resources have recently been developed employing emotion word hashtags to create automatic emotional corpus on Twitter. (Mohammad, 2012a) describe how they created a corpus from Twitter post (Twitter Emotional Corpus - TEC) using this technique. In literature, several works can be found with the use emotion word hashtags to create emotional corpora from Twitter (Choudhury et al., 2012; Wang et al., 2012).

Thus, in Sentiment Analysis research community, the interest of developing amounts of emotional

This work is licensed under a Creative Commons Attribution 4.0 International Licence. Licence details: `http://creativecommons.org/licenses/by/4.0/`

corpora has increased because that would allow us to obtain better supervised machine learning systems. The use of emotion word hashtags as technique to label data is really simple and efficient in terms of time and cost; however, it can be applied on social networks and microblogging services exclusively because they are only used in these genres. For this reason, our objective is to develop a semi-automatic methodology for large-scale annotation of emotional corpora in any genre and with high standards of reliability.

3 Pre-annotation process

After a reflection on the pending issues, this section describes the pre-annotation process developed for improving the emotion annotation task. The section is divided into four subsections where the dataset employed and the main tasks carried out by the process are explained.

The process receives as input data a collection of unlabelled sentences/phrases and a set of emotions. The approach presented in this paper works with the Ekman's six basic emotions (Ekman, 1992), although the process can also be adapted for other set of group of emotions.

The overall pre-annotation process is described in Figure 1, which shows the two main steps the process: selecting emotional seed words and the association between emotions and sentences, explained in subsection 3.2 and subsection 3.3, respectively.

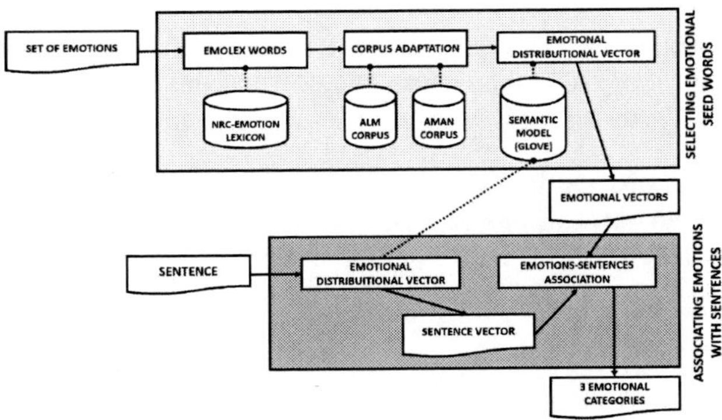

Figure 1: Overall pre-annotation process

3.1 Data

Regarding the corpora employed for the evaluation, this approach is assessed on two emotional corpora with sentence-level annotations: (i) Alm et al. (2005) corpus; and (ii) Aman and Szpakowicz (2007) corpus.

Alm corpus. This dataset consists in 1,580 annotated sentences from tales by the Grimm brothers, H.C. Andersen, and B. Potter. This corpus was annotated manually with an extended set of the Ekman's basic emotions (angry, disgusted, fearful, happy, sad, positively surprised and negatively surprised). For our evaluation, we employ the version of the corpus where the merged label set was used: anger-disgust, fear, joy, sadness, and surprise.

Aman corpus. This dataset contains sentence-level annotation of 4,000 sentences from blogs posts collected directly from Web. This resource was annotated manually with the six emotion categories proposed by Ekman and the emotion intensity (high, medium, or low).

These corpora are selected because of several reasons: (i) both corpora are manually annotated allowing us to compare automatic annotation to manual annotation; (ii) they are relevant to emotion detection task since they have been employed in many works to detect emotions (Keshtkar and Inkpen, 2010; Chaffar and Inkpen, 2011; Mohammad, 2012b); and (iii) these corpora allow us to test our approach about corpora with different sources of information: tales and blogs from Web. Thus, the usability and effectiveness of our approach can be checked.

3.2 Selecting Emotional Seed Words

In this section, the process of creation the emotional seed words employing an emotional resource is presented. This approach employs NRC Word-Emotion Association Lexicon (Emolex) (Version 0.92) (Mohammad and Turney, 2013) as emotional lexicon, although the process can be adapted to another resource annotated with emotions.

Emolex is a lexicon of general domain consisting of 14,000 English unigrams (words) associated with the Plutchik's eight basic emotions (Plutchik, 1980) (anger, fear, anticipation, trust, surprise, sadness, joy, and disgust) and two sentiments (negative and positive) compiled by manual annotation. We adopted them because: (i) it is general domain and it can be apply in different corpora; (ii) it is annotated a superset of Ekman's six basic emotions; and (iii) the most relevant feature of this resource is that the terms in this lexicon are carefully chosen to include some of the most frequent nouns, verbs, adjectives and adverbs.

The algorithm for the creation of the seed consists of:

- **Step 1 - Emolex words**: the process selects the Emolex words associated with only one of the Ekman's basic emotions to create an accurate seed without ambiguous words. Thus, each emotional category is represented by a bag of words. Figure 2 shows an example for ANGER, DISGUST and SADNESS emotions.

- **Step 2 - Corpus adaptation**: These bags of words are adapted to each corpus removing those words that not appear in the corpus. In this manner, the seed contains only the emotional words employed in the corpus to annotate. Figure 2 shows an example of the adaptation process for Alm corpus.

- **Step 3 - Emotional distributional vector**: Each seed is transformed into a distributional vector adding up the distributional vectors of each word contained in the seed. To achieve that, a GloVe model (Pennington et al., 2014) built from the lemmas and POS of the British National Corpus (BNC)[1] is employed. This model is explained in detail in Section 3.3.

Once the process is completed, each emotion is represented by a distributional vector, a real-valued vector that stores its semantic features. Moreover, the process also creates a vector for a NEUTRAL category with the Emolex words not associated with the Ekman's basic emotions.

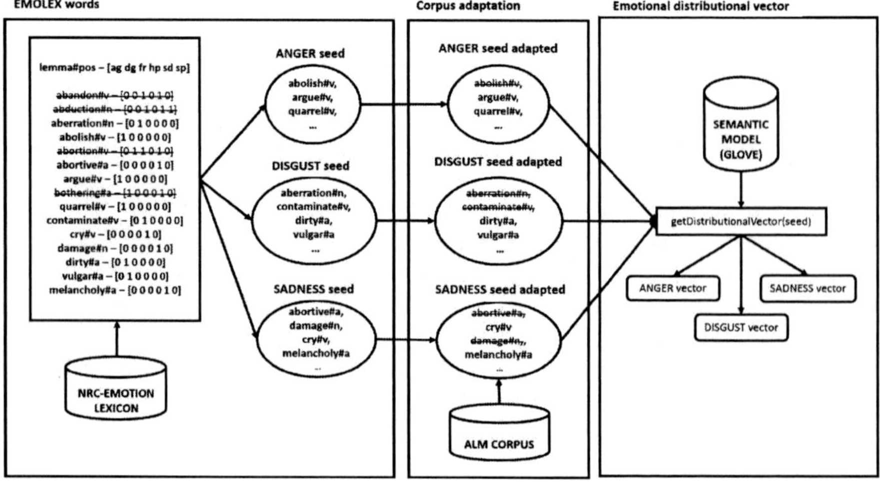

Figure 2: Creation of the emotional seed words for ANGER, DISGUST and SADNESS emotions (sample).

---

[1] http://www.natcorp.ox.ac.uk/

3.3 Associating Emotions with Sentences

After having the emotional seeds, the next step will consist in to associate the emotions represented by vectors with sentences, with the help of Distributional Semantics.

Distributional Semantic Models (DSM) are based on the assumption that the meaning of a word can be inferred from its usage. Therefore, these models dynamically build semantic representations (high-dimensional semantic vector spaces) through a statistical analysis of the contexts in which words occur[2]. Finally, each word is represented with a real-valued vector called word vector or *word embedding*.

Two are the main global families for learning word vectors: (1) global matrix factorization methods, and (2) local context windows methods. The methods based on local context windows poorly utilize the statistics of the corpus since they train on separate local context windows instead of on global co-occurrence counts and thus they are not as convenient as global matrix methods on word similarity task.

The association between the emotional seeds and the sentences of our proposal is based on the estimation the similarity among them. For this reason, in this paper we test a model based on global matrix factorization methods: GloVe (Pennington et al., 2014).

This model is run with the default settings, 300 dimensions and on the lemmas of the British National Corpus (BNC)[3] that can be considered as a balanced resource since it includes texts from different genres and domains

The process of the association consists of:

- **Step 1 - Emotional distributional vector**: each sentence is pre-processed (tokenization, lemmatization and Part-Of-Speech Tagger) using Stanford Core NLP (Manning et al., 2014) and then is represented by a distributional vector adding up the vectors of their words (noum, verbs, adjectives and adverbs). Figure 3 shows an example for the sentence *'The bear in great fury ran after the carriage'*.

- **Step 2 - Emotions-Sentences Association**: the process measure the similarity between the vector of the sentence and the vectors of each emotional category and associates the three emotions whose semantic similarity is higher. Figure 3 shows the pre-annotated emotions for the example sentence, among which is the emotion of the gold standard of Alm corpus: ANGER-DISGUST.

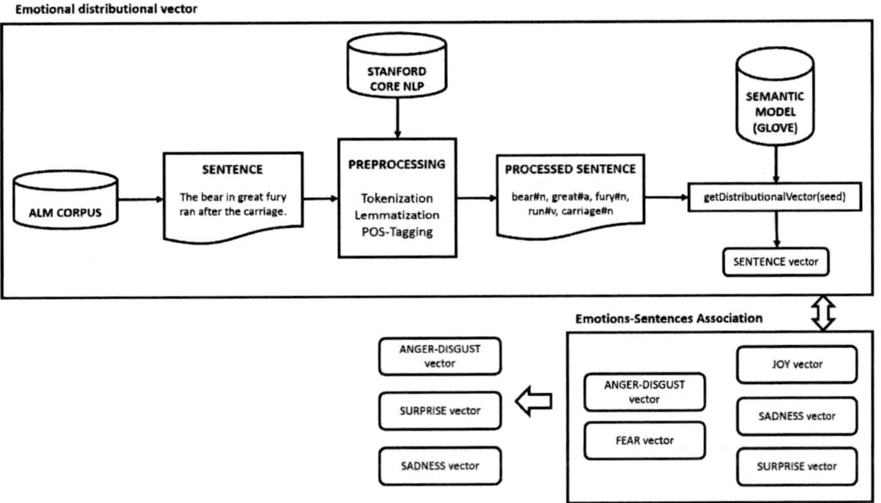

Figure 3: Association process between emotions and sentences with an example from Alm corpus.

---

[2]http://wordspace.collocations.de/doku.php/course:acl2010:start
[3]http://www.natcorp.ox.ac.uk/

At the end of the process, each sentence is annotated with the three emotional categories that are the ones more related to this sentence. The first phase of the methodology, the pre-annotation process, is finished with this step. Then, the second phase that consisting of a refinement manual process where human annotators will determine which is the predominant emotion would be developed. Although, this paper is focused on the evaluation of the pre-annotation process to evaluate the feasibility and the benefits by the methodology proposed before that the second phase be developed.

4   Evaluation

Once the pre-annotation process has been detailed, this section shows its evaluation.

Given the importance of the creation of an accurate seed in the pre-annotation process and the size of Emolex when it works with Ekman's basic emotions, three approaches have been evaluated employing different versions of Emolex (original, WordNet (WN) synonyms and Oxford synonyms). The extension process of Emolex is completely automatic and is explained in detail Section 4.1.

4.1   Enriched approaches by WordNet and Oxford synonyms

The enriched approaches employed consist in the extension of Emolex employing the synonyms of Word-Net (Version 3.0) (Miller, 1995) and the Oxford American Writer Thesaurus (Aubur et al., 2004).

In this process, each word contained in Emolex was looked up in WordNet/Oxford and the synonyms of all of senses were obtained and were added to the seed associated with the Emolex word. Figure 4 shows an example of the process employing WordNet. The word *alive* is contained in Emolex and has the emotion JOY associated. The process looks up *alive* in WordNet and obtains the synonyms of all of senses: *live*, *animated*, *active*, *alert* and *awake*. These synonyms are added to the seed of JOY emotion.

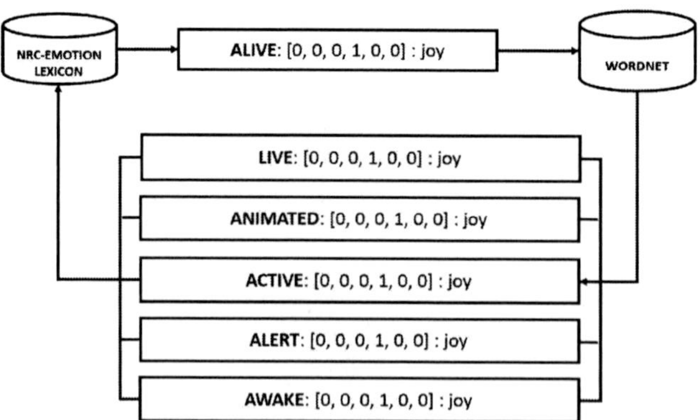

Figure 4: Process of the extension of Emolex by WordNet synonyms.

The enriched approaches run the same process than the original one, but employing the new versions of Emolex.

4.2   Evaluation Methodology

The pre-annotation process is assessed applying the measure of agreement between the gold standard of each corpus and our annotation. Since the pre-annotation process annotates the three emotional categories more related to each sentence, the evaluation process considers that there is an agreement if the correct emotion (the gold standard) is one of the three pre-annotated emotions. To achieve that, Cohen (1960) kappa and Krippendorff (2004) alpha are calculated. With both measures, we calculate the agreement based on a formula expressed in term of agreement (Cohen's kappa) and in terms of disagreement (Krippendorff's alpha). Since in metrics based on coefficients k, all disagreements are treated equally and disagreements are not all alike for semantic and pragmatic features (Artstein and Poesio, 2008), as the emotion detection task.

4.3 Results

The results obtained with both corpora are shown in Tables 1 and 2 below. Each table shows the Cohen's kappa and Krippendorff's alpha values obtained for each emotion employing the original and enriched approaches.

	Aman corpus					
	Cohen's Kappa			Krippendorff's Alpha		
	Original Appr.	WN Appr.	Oxford Appr.	Original Appr.	WN Appr.	Oxford Appr.
Anger	**0.50193**	0.39984	0.38544	**0.50199**	0.39991	0.38002
Disgust	0.35432	**0.56397**	0.53061	0.35033	**0.56386**	0.53061
Fear	**0.43424**	0.39342	0.26755	**0.43371**	0.39001	0.26252
Joy	**0.85897**	0.76931	0.71264	**0.85899**	0.76930	0.71251
Sadness	**0.51275**	0.45187	0.47945	**0.51280**	0.45188	0.47851
Surprise	**0.49255**	0.42098	0.38801	**0.48843**	0.41214	0.37709

Table 1: Cohen's kappa and Krippendorff's alpha values obtained by the Original Approach and the Enriched Approaches in the Comparison between their Annotations and the Gold of Aman Corpus.

	Alm corpus					
	Cohen's Kappa			Krippendorff's Alpha		
	Original Appr.	WN Appr.	Oxford Appr.	Original Appr.	WN Appr.	Oxford Appr.
Anger-Disgust	0.36762	0.53641	**0.56084**	0.34931	0.53655	**0.56043**
Fear	0.48990	0.58467	**0.59671**	0.48677	0.58481	**0.59667**
Joy	0.77948	0.75616	**0.79838**	0.77949	0.75523	**0.79823**
Sadness	0.59576	**0.72433**	0.57264	0.59566	**0.72424**	0.56721
Surprise	0.43095	0.38240	**0.44159**	0.42869	0.38251	**0.43351**

Table 2: Cohen's kappa and Krippendorff's alpha values obtained by the Original Approach and the Enriched Approaches in the Comparison between their Annotations and the Gold of Alm Corpus.

Several conclusions can be drown from Table 1. The results show the soundness of the original seed since they obtain the best results for most of the emotions except for DISGUST emotion. This can be due to the difficulty to distinguish between ANGER and DISGUST emotion in text even for humans since the results of these emotions are inverted in the enriched approaches. Thus, if we consider both emotions as an unique category, like on Alm corpus, these values would improve.

Regarding the rest of emotions, the values obtained by FEAR emotion are low, especially in the enriched approaches. This indicates that the seed of FEAR for Aman corpus not contains the words employed on blog posts to express FEAR emotion. But this could be improve it, including the words used in the blog posts in the seed. And about SURPRISE emotion, the results also are low although in this case it is coherent with many studies (Alm et al., 2005; Strapparava and Mihalcea, 2007).

About the conclusions on Alm corpus (Table 2), the enriched approach by Oxford synonyms demonstrates the improvements obtained by these synonyms since obtains the best results for most of emotions.

Taking into account that the pre-annotation have been carried out with a totally automatic process, the results on this corpus are considerably promising since the best approach obtains values higher 56% for the entire set of emotions except SURPRISE. Although, as we mentioned, these results are coherent with many studies. The lack of agreement in this emotion is due to the lack of para-linguistic information like tone, emphasis and facial expressions, relevant features for SUPRISE emotion.

4.4 Discussion

These results are interpreted taking into account that the gold standard of these corpora annotated manually (Aman and Alm corpus) achieved values of agreement less than 80%, the value needed to get a good reliability. Since there are cases in which the annotations of the gold standard seem questionable under a new review by humans. In these cases, our annotations can disagree with the gold standard but are considered errors of annotations and hence the agreement is worse.

Comparing both corpora, the results show that the pre-annotation process obtains better values on Alm corpus than on Aman data. This can be due to the genre of each corpus since the sentences on Aman corpus are from blog posts and the vocabulary employed is not formal and is not included in Emolex. Thus, the seed is less accurate than on Alm corpus, a corpus about children tales. Although, this is not a problem for our methodology since the pre-annotation process can be improved employing emotional lexicon adapted to different genres to create the seed. Hence, if the process employs a lexicon with the vocabulary employed on social media, the seed will be more accurate and the results will be improved.

Concerning the enriched approaches, the results show improvements on Alm corpus whereas on Aman corpus the best approach is the original one. This is related to the genre of the text because Oxford and Wordnet synonyms introduce noise on Aman corpus, since the vocabulary included in these resources is formal whereas the vocabulary employed in blog posts is informal.

5   Conclusion

As presented in the introductory section of this paper, the rationale beyond our research is the need to develop a methodology that allow us to tackle the annotation task of emotions with views on improving supervised learning techniques.

The paper presents an innovative semi-automatic methodology to annotate emotional corpora consisting of two main phases: (1) an automatic process to pre-annotate the unlabelled sentences with a reduced number of emotional categories; and (2) a refinement manual process where human annotators will determine which is the predominant emotion between the emotional categories selected in phase 1. A methodology adaptable to the genre of text and the set of emotions employed that will allow us the annotation of large amount of emotional data in any genre with efficiently and high standards of reliability.

The first evaluation performed for this innovative methodology confirms its feasibility and benefits since the agreements values are promising. Thus, our main conclusion is that the reduction of the number of categories could provide us benefits that will revert in positive impact in the emotion annotation task and therefore to improve the reliability on emotional corpora.

Taking into account the results obtained, our future work will be focused on developing a manual annotation task with the sentences pre-annotated by our automatic process to verify the benefits of the new methodology; analysis of the process to create a more accurate seed; and employing other emotional resources to create the seeds adapted to different genres and set of emotions.

Acknowledgements

This research has been supported by the FPI grant (BES-2013-065950) and the research stay grant (EEBB-I-16-11174) from the Spanish Ministry of Science and Innovation. It has also funded by the Spanish Government (DIGITY ref. TIN2015-65136-C02-2-R) and the Valencian Government (grant no. PROMETEOII/ 2014/001).

References

Cecilia Ovesdotter Alm, Dan Roth, and Richard Sproat. 2005. Emotions from text: Machine learning for text-based emotion prediction. In *Proceedings of the conference on HLT-EMNLP*, pages 579–586.

Saima Aman and Stan Szpakowicz. 2007. Identifying Expressions of Emotion in Text. In *Text, Speech and Dialogue*, pages 196–205.

Jean-yves Antoine, Jeanne Villaneau, and Anaïs Lefeuvre. 2014. Weighted Krippendorff's alpha is a more reliable metrics for multi- coders ordinal annotations: experimental studies on emotion, opinion and coreference annotation. In *Proceedings of the 14th Conference of the European Chapter of the Association for Computational Linguistics*, number 1, pages 550–559.

Ron Artstein and Massimo Poesio. 2008. Inter-coder Agreement for Computational Linguistics. *Comput. Linguist.*, 34(4):555–596.

David Aubur, Rae Armantrout, David Crystal, and Michael Dirda. 2004. *Oxford American Writer's Thesaurus*. Oxford University Press.

Ester Boldrini and Patricio Martínez-Barco. 2012. *EMOTIBLOG: A model to Learn Subjetive Information Detection in the New Textual Genres of the Web 2.0-Multilingual and Multi-Genre Approach-*. Ph.D. thesis.

Soumaya Chaffar and Diana Inkpen. 2011. Using a Heterogeneous Dataset for Emotion Analysis in Text. In *Proceedings of the 24th Canadian Conference on Advances in Artificial Intelligence*, Canadian AI'11, pages 62–67, Berlin, Heidelberg. Springer-Verlag.

Colin Cherry, Saif M. Mohammad, and Berry De Bruijn. 2012. Binary Classifiers and Latent Sequence Models for Emotion Detection in Suicide Notes. *Biomedical informatics insights*, 5(Suppl 1):147–154.

Munmun De Choudhury, Michael Gamon, and Scott Counts. 2012. Happy, Nervous or Surprised? Classification of Human Affective States in Social Media. In *Proceedings of the 6th International AAAI Conference on Weblogs and Social Media*.

J Cohen. 1960. A Coefficient of Agreement for Nominal Scales. *Educational and Psychological Measurement*, 20(1):37.

Maral Dadvar, Dolf Trieschnigg, Roeland Ordelman, and Franciska de Jong. 2013. Improving cyberbullying detection with user context. In *Advances in Information Retrieval*, pages 693–696.

Paul Ekman. 1992. An argument for basic emotions. *Cognition and Emotion*, pages 169–200.

Fazel Keshtkar and Diana Inkpen. 2010. A Corpus-based Method for Extracting Paraphrases of Emotion Terms. In *Proceedings of the NAACL HLT 2010 Workshop on Computational Approaches to Analysis and Generation of Emotion in Text*, CAAGET '10, pages 35–44, Stroudsburg, PA, USA. Association for Computational Linguistics.

Klaus Krippendorff. 2004. Content Analysis: An Introduction to Its Methodology. In *Content Analysis: An Introduction to Its Methodology*, chapter 11. Sage Publications.

Jasy Suet Yan Liew, Howard R. Turtle, and Elizabeth D. Liddy. 2016. EmoTweet-28: A Fine-Grained Emotion Corpus for Sentiment Analysis. In *Proceedings of the Tenth International Conference on Language Resources and Evaluation (LREC 2016)*.

Christopher D Manning, Mihai Surdeanu, John Bauer, Jenny Finkel, Steven J Bethard, and David McClosky. 2014. The {Stanford} {CoreNLP} Natural Language Processing Toolkit. In *Association for Computational Linguistics (ACL) System Demonstrations*, pages 55–60.

George A Miller. 1995. WordNet: A Lexical Database for English. *Communications of the ACM*, 38(11):39–41.

Saif M. Mohammad and Peter D. Turney. 2013. Crowdsourcing a Word-Emotion Association Lexicon. *Computation and Language*, 29 (3):436–465.

Saif Mohammad. 2012a. #Emotional Tweets. In *Proceedings of the First Joint Conference on Lexical and Computational Semantics*.

Saif Mohammad. 2012b. Portable Features for Classifying Emotional Text. In *Proceedings of the 2012 Conference of the North American Chapter of the Association for Computational Linguistics: Human Language Technologies*, pages 587–591, Montréal, Canada. Association for Computational Linguistics.

Saif M Mohammad. 2016. Sentiment Analysis: Detecting Valence, Emotions, and Other Affectual States from Text. In Herb Meiselman, editor, *Emotion Measurement*. Elsevier.

Calkin Suero Montero and Jarkko Suhonen. 2014. Emotion analysis meets learning analytics: online learner profiling beyond numerical data. In *Proceedings of the 14th Koli Calling International Conference on Computing Education Research*, pages 165–169.

Alena Neviarouskaya, Helmut Prendinger, and Mitsuru Ishizuka. 2009. Compositionality Principle in Recognition of Fine-Grained Emotions from Text. In *Proceedings of the Third International ICWSM Conference*, pages 278–281.

Jeffrey Pennington, Richard Socher, and Christopher D Manning. 2014. GloVe: Global Vectors for Word Representation. In *Empirical Methods in Natural Language Processing (EMNLP)*.

Robert Plutchik. 1980. A general psychoevolutionary theory of emotion. In *Theories of Emotion*, pages 3–33.

Hansen Andrew Schwartz, Johannes C. Eichstaedt, Margaret L. Kern, Lukasz Dziurzynski, Richard E. Lucas, Megha Agrawal, Gregory J. Park, Shrinidhi K. Lakshmikanth, Sneha Jha, Martin E. P. Seligman, and Lyle Ungar. 2013. Characterizing Geographic Variation in Well-Being Using Tweets. In *Proceedings of the International AAAI Conference on Weblogs and Social Media*.

Carlo Strapparava and Rada Mihalcea. 2007. Semeval-2007 task 14: Affective text. In *Proceedings of the 4th International Workshop on Semantic Evaluations*, pages 70–74.

Wenbo Wang, Lu Chen, Krishnaprasad Thirunarayan, and Amit P. Sheth. 2012. Harnessing Twitter "Big Data" for Automatic Emotion Identification. In *International Confernece on Social Computing (SocialCom)*.

Personality Estimation from Japanese Text

Koichi Kamijo
IBM Research - Tokyo
Chuo-ku, Tokyo
Japan
kamijoh@jp.ibm.com

Tetsuya Nasukawa
IBM Research - Tokyo
Chuo-ku, Tokyo
Japan
nasukawa@jp.ibm.com

Hideya Kitamura
Kansai University
Suita-shi, Osaka
Japan
kitamura.hideya@gmail.com

Abstract

We created a model to estimate personality trait from authors' text written in Japanese and measured its performance by conducting surveys and analyzing the Twitter data of 1,630 users. We used the Big Five personality traits for personality trait estimation. Our approach is a combination of category- and Word2Vec-based approaches. For the category-based element, we added several unique Japanese categories along with the ones regularly used in the English model, and for the Word2Vec-based element, we used a model called GloVe. We found that some of the newly added categories have a stronger correlation with personality traits than other categories do and that the combination of the category- and Word2Vec-based approaches improves the accuracy of the personality trait estimation compared with the case of using just one of them.

1 Introduction

There has been a growing interest in the analysis of text in social media. If you can determine the personality trait of a writer, you can apply the result to various purposes, such as how you should contact this person in the future and how you should advertise your products to them. However, most of these personality trait analyses have been done for English text only, with studies focusing on the Big Five (Yarkoni, 2010; McCrae and John, 1992; Golbeck et al., 2011), Needs (Yang and Li, 2013), and Values (Boyd et al., 2015; Chen et al., 2014). In this work, we analyze Japanese text to investigate the differences in personality trait analyses based on language by considering what kind of textual features in Japanese are relevant to personality trait, and report the results of our analysis on Big Five personality. Figure 1 shows the overview of our system for personality trait estimation. We perform a survey to determine personality trait while a crawler obtains the author's tweet data, as discussed in detail in Section 3. The survey results and tweet data are saved to a storage for later analysis. After a certain amount of data is gathered, we perform linguistic analysis on it and then calculate the correlation (relationship) between the analyzed data and the survey results, after which we can estimate the personality trait.

We discuss related work in Section 2, how we collected the training data in Section 3, our personality estimation model in Section 4, and the analysis results in Section 5. We conclude in Section 6 with a brief summary.

2 Related Work

Ever since the significance of the relationship between people's personality traits and the textual features of how they write or talk (Mairesse et al., 2007) became known, there have been attempts to analyze personality traits from written texts. Moreover, as some indices of personality traits (such as the Big Five model) have been standardized, workshops for shared tasks on computational personality recognition have been organized to evaluate features and learning techniques and even to compare the performances of systems for personality recognition on a common benchmark (Celli et al., 2013; Celli et al., 2014).

The Big Five model describes personality on the basis of five traits formalized as bipolar scales (Norman., 1963), namely:

This work is licenced under a Creative Commons Attribution 4.0 International License. License details: http://creativecommons.org/licenses/by/4.0/

Proceedings of the Workshop on Computational Modeling of People's Opinions, Personality, and Emotions in Social Media,
pages 101–109, Osaka, Japan, December 12 2016.

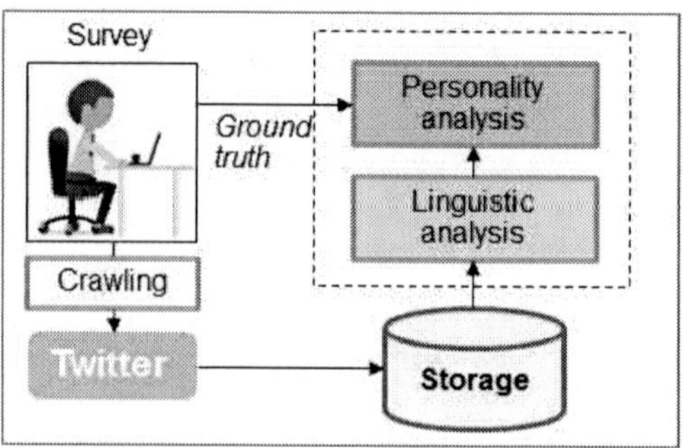

Figure 1: System overview of personality trait estimation model.

- **Agreeableness** (friendly vs. uncooperative)
- **Conscientiousness** (organized vs. careless)
- **Extraversion** (sociable vs. shy)
- **Neuroticism** (neurotic vs. calm)
- **Openness** (insightful vs. unimaginative)

Even though this Big Five model has been widely adopted on the global level, most of the personality recognition work has been conducted in English. Only a little work has been done on this area in the Japanese language, such as three papers written in Japanese (Fujikura et al., 2013; Okamoto et al., 2014; Okumura et al., 2015). This is problematic because the relationship between people's personality traits and textual features depends highly upon both language and cultural background. We therefore believe it is necessary to analyze the relationship in each language.

3   Collection of the Training Data

In order to determine the correlation between tweet data and the author's personality trait, we first performed a Web-based survey of personality trait diagnosis for authors having a certain amount of writing ($\geq$150 tweets) on Twitter (Fig. 1). Such surveys have previously been performed in English and Spanish, but we did this Japanese one separately, since the usage of the language, nationality, culture, and the like is so different. We announced our survey on our Facebook and home page as well as directly announcing the survey to Twitter users. The survey included a questionnaire for the Big Five Personality, Needs, and Values, including 50 questions for Big Five. The sources of the survey for Big Five and Values are (IPIP., 2016) and (Schwartz, 2003), respectively.

Values is typically defined as a network of ideas that a person views to be desirable and important (Boyd et al., 2015; Rokeach, 1973). This network, as developed by Schwartz (Schwartz, 1992; Schwartz, 2006; Schwartz, 2012), includes four high-level values (Self-transcendence, Conservation, Self-enhancement, Open to change) and ten values (Self-direction, Stimulation, Hedonism, Achievement, Power, Security, Conformity, Tradition, Benevolence, Universalism). Needs is typically defined as the relationship between human needs and the social value; it includes 12 profiles (Challenge, Closeness, Curiosity, Excitement, Harmony, Ideal, Liberty, Love, Practicality, Self-(expression), Stability, Structure) based on Kevin Ford's universal needs map (Ford, 2005).

Figure 2 shows examples of questions for Big Five, where respondents were asked to select one from "Strongly Agree", "Agree", "Neutral", "Disagree", or "Strongly Disagree". When the respondents completed the survey, they were provided with a quick personality diagnostic result, which functioned as an incentive for them to complete the survey. Figure 3 shows an example of the quick personality diagnostic result. Our system also collected respondents' tweet data and stored it for later analysis (Fig. 1). As these survey and tweet data include private data, they were securely stored and treated in our system so that they would not be exposed to the outside, and obviously they will not be published. We included a few dummy questions (e.g., the sixth question in Fig. 2) to exclude those who might have been answering

The survey questions are shown in a boxed figure:

1. I am the life of the party.
2. I feel little concern for others.
3. I am always prepared.
4. I get stressed out easily.
5. I have a rich vocabulary.
6. Sorry, another question to make sure you are still reading these. Select "Agree" for this one.

Figure 2: Survey example.

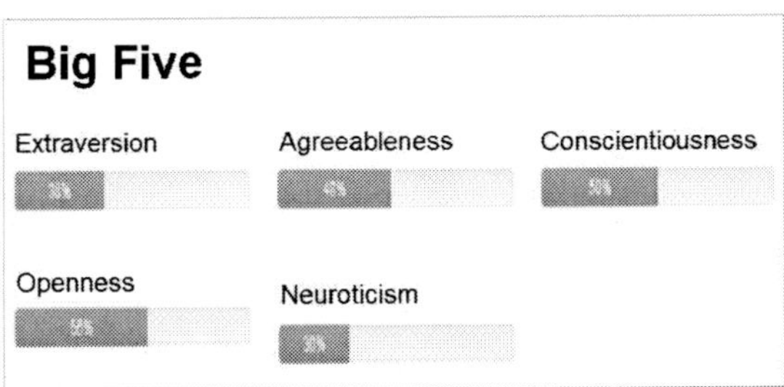

Figure 3: An example of the quick personality diagnostic result shown after the respondent completes the survey.

without looking at the questions. We collected training data for Big Five from 1,630 persons (n=1,630). Distribution of respondents' ages was 6.4% (under 18), 42.6% (18–24), 29.6% (25–34), 20.1% (35–54), and 1.3% (55+). Gender ratio was 61.9% (Male) and 38.1% (Female). Figure 4 shows the distribution of (a) the number of words in all respondents' tweets per user, (b) the number of tweets per user, and (c) the average of number of words per tweet. The averages of (a), (b), and (c) are 26092.6, 1315.0, and 20.5, respectively.

4 Personality Estimation Model

Two approaches were utilized to realize the estimation of personality traits from user text: a category-based approach and a Word2Vec-based one.

4.1 Category–based

We categorized Japanese expressions by referring to the English Linguistic Inquiry and Word Count (LIWC) (Pennebaker et al., 2001). Among the 68 categories in the LIWC2001 dictionary, we excluded the *Article* category, as articles do not exist in the Japanese language, and *Fillers*, which can hardly be distinguished from *Non-fluencies*. For the remaining 66 categories, we defined corresponding Japanese expressions to create a dictionary that we call Japanese Categories for Personality Identification (JCPI). We also implemented a mechanism to identify the emergence of each expression in the text using the language processing function of the IBM Watson Explorer Advanced Edition Analytical Components V11.0 ("WEX" hereinafter) (Zhu et al., 2014). To create the JCPI, instead of simply translating English expressions in the LIWC2001 dictionary, we have defined appropriate expressions for each category in the LIWC2001 by taking the Japanese nationality and culture into consideration and created various new categories and subcategories on the basis of this.

First, from the psychological viewpoint considering Japanese culture, we added the following six categories:

- *Event* (such as "festival", "fireworks")
- *Relax* (such as "hot spring", "healing")
- *Move* (such as "train", "commuting")
- *Position Conversion* (such as "career change", "change")

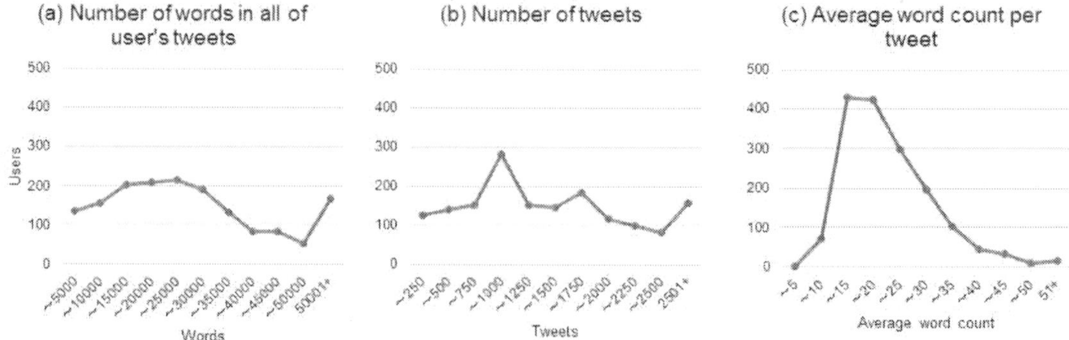

Figure 4: Statistical distribution data for survey respondents: (a) number of words in all a respondents' tweets, (b) number of tweets, (c) average word count per tweet.

- *Reading* (such as "read", "book")
- *Playing* (just "game" and "playing" only)

We also added the following four categories, including three Japanese-specific representations (excluding *Alphabet*):

- *Kanji* (Chinese character)
- *Hiragana* (cursive syllabary)
- *Katakana* (often used to express foreign proper nouns)
- *Alphabet*

Second, since Japanese does not have any *Prepositions*, we defined instead a *Particle* category for postpositional particles. Unlike in English, where word order plays an important role for indicating grammatical roles, as in the basic subject-verb-object pattern, word order in Japanese is flexible, and it is particles that play the more important role in terms of indicating the grammatical and semantic function of preceding words. In light of this importance of particles, we added the following subcategories:

- *Kakujoshi* (case markers: indicating subject, object, etc.)
- *Keijoshi* (binding particles: indicating inclusion, emphasis, etc.)
- *Fukujoshi* (adverbial particles: indicating degree, constraint, etc.)
- *Shuujoshi* (sentence-ending particles: indicating question, inhibition, etc.)

Finally, in the JCPI, we added the following subcategories to existing categories:

- To *Total_1st_person*: *Watashi* (such as "I" or "me", relatively formal), *Boku* (such as "I" or "me", relatively informal, mainly by boys), *Ore* (such as "I" or "me", informal, mainly by men)
- To *Causation*: *Good_causation* (such as "because of" or "achievements"), *Bad_causation* (such as "due to" or "caused by")
- To *Communication*: *Drinking_party* (such as "drinking" or "year-end party")
- To *Friends*: *Lover* (such as "boyfriend" or "girlfriend", relatively shallow relationship in Japan)
- To *Family*: *Children* (such as "son" or "daughter")
- To *Time*: *On_time* (such as "slow" or "late")

In all, we defined 89 categories including subcategories (n_c=89). The JCPI is not published, but part of it is discussed in (Yamamoto et al., 2016).

Table 1: Correlation between Big Five profiles and selected categories. *: newly added, *Italic*: $p < 0.01$, **bold**: $p < 0.001$.

	Kakujoshi*	Keijoshi*	Fukujoshi*	Drinking*	Hiragana*	Event*	Playing*	Motion	Job
A	**−0.128**	−0.071	*−0.082*	0.076	−0.038	**0.102**	**−0.148**	0.053	0.059
C	−0.037	0.027	−0.029	0.076	**−0.127**	0.047	*−0.084*	*0.082*	*0.088*
E	0.018	0.007	−0.059	**0.128**	−0.026	0.062	**−0.138**	*0.095*	**0.148**
N	**0.129**	**0.103**	−0.052	**0.124**	−0.065	−0.014	*−0.086*	**0.166**	**0.155**
O	**0.257**	**0.178**	0.014	−0.048	0.014	**−0.096**	0.025	0.047	0.079

4.2 Word2Vec–based

We also used a vector representation of words (Word2Vec), since the category-based approach covers words and patterns that are relatively short, while Word2Vec is expected to cover up-to-date sentences relatively longer than what the category-based approach covers. For this purpose, we selected GloVe (Pennington et al., 2014), which was developed by Stanford University. GloVe is trained on aggregated global word-word co-occurrence statistics from a large corpus described in (Pennington et al., 2014), and the resulting representations capture semantic similarities and differences in the words by which we can keep up with the latest and emerging vocabulary on social media. In GloVe, we used only Japanese words whose lengths were between two and ten characters (taking the performance at the training stage into consideration) for 125,129 words in all, and used vectors whose dimensions were 200 (n_w=200). We did not convert the words into regular or formal expressions but used them as they are, since the words as they are, not the converted words, are better for expressing personality.

5 Analysis

For analysis, we used data from 1,630 Twitter users collected by means of a survey. We excluded retweets and URL addresses.

We analyzed the correlations between categories and personality in the category-based approach first, and then between words and personality in the Word2Vec-based approach, and finally we estimated overall performance accuracy.

5.1 Correlation and Matching Analysis

First we analyzed the correlation between categories and profiles. For each author j, we first performed a morphological analysis of j's tweets using the WEX, counted the number of words/patterns included in each category i used in j's total tweets, and then divided each number by the number of words used in j's total tweets (defined as x_{ij}) to obtain $x_i = (x_{i1}, .., x_{in})^\top$, $i = 1, .., n_c$, where $^\top$ stands for Transpose. Also, we obtained a score vector, $s_k = (s_{k1}, .., s_{kn})^\top$, where s_{kj} ($0 \leq s_{kj} \leq 1$) is the ground truth score of j for profile k ($k = 1, .., n_s, n_s = 5$, which corresponds to Big Five file profiles) obtained from the survey. Then, we calculated Pearson's product-moment correlation coefficient (r), as well as p-value (p), between x_i and s_k. Table 1 shows the r and p values for selected categories including newly added categories/subcategories and categories whose correlation ($|r|$) is larger in one of the profiles. Correlations that were statistically significant for $0.001 \leq p < 0.01$ and $p < 0.001$ are in italics and bold, respectively. In Tables 1 and 2, **A,C,E,N,** and **O** stand for **Agreeableness, Conscientiousness , Extraversion, Neuroticism,** and **Openness**, respectively. From Table 1, we find the following:

- Subcategories of *Particle* (*Kakujoshi, Keijoshi*) have a strong relationship with **Agreeableness** (negatively), **Neuroticism** (positively), and **Openness** (positively). This suggests that agreeable people tend to be friendly and frank, so they often skip such formal particles, especially Kakujoshi. In contrast, neurotic people tend to be nervous and people who are open to experience tend to be highly educated, and both types rigidly use particles, even on social media platforms such as Twitter.
- *Drinking* has a strong positive relationship with **Extraversion** and **Neuroticism**. This suggests that extraverted people and neurotic people tend to drink, with others or alone.
- *Hiragana* has a strong negative relationship with **Conscientiousness**. This suggests that non-conscientious people tend to use Hiragana, which is often used for informal expressions.

Length	Number of words	The ratio of words used at least once by each author	Most frequently used word (MFUW)	Meaning of the MFUW	The ratio of the MFUW being used at least once by each author
10	3524	0.284	ありがとうございまし	Part of formal "thank you"	0.249
9	4683	0.387	コミュニケーション	"Communication"	0.108
8	7047	0.515	になってしまった	"has become …"	0.106
7	10019	0.627	と思ってたけど	"although I thought …"	0.086
6	14879	0.729	かもしれない	"may be"	0.091
5	19656	0.794	とりあえず	"for now"	0.091
4	26732	0.851	なかった	"never been", "did not"	0.074
3	22292	0.898	なくて	"never", "not", etc.	0.082
2	16297	0.933	れる	Auxiliary verb for passive, active, possible, or respect	0.123

Figure 5: Matching analysis between words in GloVe and in tweets.

- *Playing* has a strong negative relationship with **Agreeableness** and **Extraversion**. This suggests that non-agreeable or non-extraverted people tend to play indoor games alone. An important finding is that, although *Playing* includes just two words, 90% of the respondents (tweet authors) used either or both of the words in the *Playing* category at least once (not shown in table).
- *Job* has a strong positive relationship with **Extraversion** and **Neuroticism**. This suggests that extraverted people tend to discuss their working life with others and that neurotic people are worried about their jobs.

There are some prior works that examine the correlation between the LIWC categories and personality traits in English with a large dataset. For example, (Chen et al., 2014) used the data of 799 users on Reddit, a popular Web forum in the English-speaking world, to examine the correlations between LIWC categories and Values personality traits; the largest $|r|$ value was 0.184. Since the number of users is 1,630 in our case, it is not an accurate comparison, but still, these results are not much different from ours. Another example (Golbeck et al., 2011) used 50 users on Twitter data to study correlations between LIWC categories and Big Five personality traits, as well as to analyze its estimation performance. Its maximum $|r|$ value was 0.426, between **Openness** and *Work*, which is much larger than our case. However, the relative mean absolute (MAE) value for estimation performance with 10-fold cross validation was larger than our cases, as discussed in Section 5.2.

Next, we analyzed the matching between words in GloVe and in tweets. Figure 5 shows the number of words used for matching, the ratio of words used at least once by each author, the most frequently used word (MFUW), the meaning of the MFUW, and the ratio of the MFUW being used at least once by each author, for each length of the words in GloVe. From Fig. 5, we find the following:

- The ratio of words used at least once by each author simply increases as the word length decreases, and for length = 2, it is more than 90%, which is a very high ratio.

- The ratio of the MFUW being used at least once by each author is high even if the word length is long. This suggests that it does not depend on the length of the word but rather on what the word means. For example, the MFUW for the length of ten is a part of "thank you", which is frequently used in almost any circumstance.

5.2 Performance Analysis

Next, to examine the personality trait estimation accuracy of our model, we performed mean absolute error (MAE) and correlation (Corr) analysis to compare the trait scores calculated using our model with

Table 2: Performance comparison with (a) Category-based (new Japan-unique categories/subcategories only), (b) Category-based (All), (c) Word2Vec-based, and (d) Category-based + Word2Vec-based ((b)+(c)), average for each case, and mean and standard deviation of the survey scores.

	(a) Category (JP)		(b) Category (All)		(c) Word2Vec		(d) Category+W2V		ZeroR	mean	sd
	MAE	Corr	MAE	Corr	MAE	Corr	MAE	Corr	MAE		
A	0.1084	0.2003	0.1057	0.2958	0.1027	0.3278	0.1001	0.3602	0.1115	0.5792	0.1369
C	0.0977	0.1625	0.0962	0.2254	0.0941	0.2602	0.0939	0.2635	0.0999	0.4937	0.1248
E	0.1266	0.1682	0.1211	0.3227	0.1158	0.3862	0.1145	0.4005	0.1292	0.4791	0.1608
N	0.1220	0.2231	0.1186	0.3022	0.1147	0.3349	0.1122	0.3644	0.1258	0.3335	0.1572
O	0.1109	0.2719	0.1099	0.2591	0.1064	0.3067	0.1063	0.2817	0.1158	0.6225	0.1454
Avg.	0.1131	0.2052	0.1103	0.2810	0.1067	0.3231	0.1054	0.3341	0.1164	0.5016	0.1450

Table 3: Relative MAE comparison with (a) Category-based (new Japan-unique categories/subcategories only), (b) Category-based (All), (c) Word2Vec-based, (d) Category-based + Word2Vec-based , and Golbeck.

	(a) Category (JP)	(b) Category (All)	(c) Word2Vec	(d) Category+W2V	Golbeck
A	0.9715	0.9477	0.9213	0.8972	1.0053
C	0.9782	0.9630	0.9422	0.9401	0.9985
E	0.9804	0.9374	0.8968	0.8868	1.0000
N	0.9697	0.9428	0.9121	0.8921	0.9997
O	0.9577	0.9485	0.9183	0.9177	0.9999
Avg.	0.9715	0.9479	0.9181	0.9068	1.0008

the corresponding psychometric measures collected with the survey. Measurements were conducted for four cases:

(a) Category-based (newly added Japan-unique categories/subcategories only)
(b) Category-based (all categories/subcategories)
(c) Word2Vec-based
(d) Category-based + Word2Vec-based ((b) +(c))

For (a), we used just $\{x_i | i \in C_{new}\}$ for estimation, where C_{new} is the set of category numbers that belong to 24 categories and subcategories newly added for Japanese. For (b), we used all of the 89 categories and subcategories, i.e., $\{x_1, .., x_{n_c}\}$, for estimation. For (c), for each tweet, we counted the matched words from the longer ones in GloVe, created a vector for j by weighting the n_w-dimensional GloVe vector by the count and dividing the coefficients of the vector by the number of words used in j's total number of tweets, and obtained $y_i = (y_{i1}, .., y_{in})^\top, i = 1, .., n_w$, where y_{ij} is the coefficient for the i-th dimension of j. We then used $\{y_1, .., y_{n_w}\}$ for estimation. For (d), we used $\{x_1, .., x_{n_c}, y_1, .., y_{n_w}\}$ for estimation.

To estimate the score of each Big Five profile using the set of data described above for each case, we used a generalized linear regression model and performed 10-fold cross validation to calculate the MAE. Table 2 shows the results. In this table, "Corr" is the r value between survey score and estimated score, and "ZeroR" is the MAE when the average of the survey scores is used as the estimated score for all users. Also, "mean" and "sd" are the average and standard deviation of the survey score data for each profile. These values are posted in the table as references.

The results shown in Table 2 yielded the following findings:

- Japan-unique (sub)categories were effective for estimating personality, especially for profiles that have a strong correlation with newly added (sub)categories. For example, in the case of **Openness**, the MAE of (a) was improved (reduced) 4.2% from ZeroR, and (b) improved only 0.95% from (a).
- By using all of the (sub)categories, the MAEs improved for all of the profiles, with 4.4% at maximum (**Extraversion**), compared with just using Japan-unique (sub)categories. This suggests that there is still room for improvement by using categories other than Japan-unique (sub)categories.
- The MAEs of the Word2Vec-based case were better (smaller) than those of the category-based for all of the profiles, with 4.3% at maximum (**Extraversion**), which suggests that Word2Vec covers

several words including up-to-date words that appear in the tweet data.

- Combining the category-based and Word2Vec-based approaches yielded the best result for all of the profiles, with a maximum improvement of 2.6% (**Agreeableness**) compared with the Word2Vec-based case.

In addition, we calculated the relative MAE, which is calculated as MAE/ZeroR, for each case and compared it with the case of (Golbeck et al., 2011). We used relative MAE for comparison since MAE and ZeroR values vary according to the dataset. Although the number of users was just 50 and the training algorithm is a Gaussian process in the Golbeck case, we find that ours had a more accurate performance (smaller relative MAE), even with (a).

6   Conclusion and Future Work

We analyzed the performance of personality estimation from category-based and Word2Vec-based approaches and found that, in Japanese, some personality traits are more highly correlated with how an author writes than what he or she writes. This is demonstrated by the fact that the *Particle* category, which is unique to Japanese, strongly correlates with several Big Five profiles. This is an important discovery because, since the Japanese language does not consider the grammatical order of words in a sentence, as English does, it is up to the authors to decide how formally and logically they write on social media, and this results in the usage of particles, which also exposes their personality traits. Moreover, not just the use of function words like particles but also the way of expressing content words in Hiragana characters is highly correlated with some personality traits. This is also a new aspect based on the characteristics of the Japanese language that we were able to find.

We also found that the Word2Vec-based approach performed better than the category-based approach, and that the combination of the two had the best estimation performance. We conclude that GloVe includes several longer words that are recently often used in tweets, and that the category-based approach covers other short words that Word2Vec-based does not. Also, we found that, when using a large data set ($n = 1,630$), the relative MAE values are smaller than those in a prior work in English, even when only Japan-unique categories.

As future work, we intend to further improve the estimation accuracy by adding and optimizing the categories as well as by optimizing Word2Vec. Also, in the present analysis, we found categories that are effective uniquely for Japanese and effective for English as well. By expanding this analysis, we aim to build a multi-language model that can be applied regardless of the languages.

Acknowledgements

We thank the IBM Watson Personality Insights survey participants for providing us with valuable ground truth data as well as with tweet data.

IBM ®Watson Explorer Advanced Edition Analytical Components V11.0 and IBM Watson Personality Insights are trademarks of the International Business Machines Corporation in the U.S. and other countries.

References

Ryan L. Boyd, Steven R. Wilson, James W. Pennebaker, Michal Kosinski, David J. Stillwell, and Rada Mihalcea. 2015. Values in Words: Using Language to Evaluate and Understand Personal Values. In *Proceedings of the Ninth International AAAI Conference on Web and Social Media*:31–40.

Fabio Celli, Fabio Pianesi, David Stillwell, and Michal Kosinski. 2013. Workshop on Computational Personality Recognition (Shared Task). *AAAI Technical Report*, WS-13-01.

Fabio Celli, Bruno Lepri, Joan-Isaac Biel, Daniel Gatica-Perez, Giuseppe Riccardi, and Fabio Pianesi. 2014. The Workshop on Computational Personality Recognition 2014. In *Proceedings of the 22nd ACM international conference on Multimedia*, ACM:245–1246.

Jilin Chen, Gary Hsieh, Jalal U. Mahmud, and Jeffrey Nichols. 2014. Understanding individuals' personal values from social media word use. In *Proceedings of the 17th ACM conference on Computer supported cooperative work & social computing*, ACM:405–414.

Kevin Ford. 2005. Brands laid bare: Using market research for evidence-based brand management. John Wiley & Sons.

Shohei Fujikura, Yoshito Ogawa, and Hideaki Kikuchi. 2013. Automatic estimation of users' personality from speech dialog and Twitter. (in Japanese) In *Proceedings of the 19th Annual Conference of the Association for Natural Language Processing (NLP2013)*, 900–903.

Jennifer Golbeck, Cristina Robles, Michon Edmondson, and Karen Turner. 2011. Predicting personality from twitter. In *Privacy, Security, Risk and Trust (PASSAT) and 2011 IEEE Third International Conference on Social Computing (SocialCom), 2011 IEEE Third International Conference on* IEEE:149–156.

International Personality Item Pool. 2016. Administering IPIP Measures, with a 50-item Sample Questionnaire, `http://ipip.ori.org/new_ipip-50-item-scale.htm`.

Francois Mairesse, Marilyn A. Walker, Matthias R. Mehl, and Roger K. Moore. 2007. Using linguistic cues for the automatic recognition of personality in conversation and text. *Journal of Artificial Intelligence Research*, 30:457–500.

Robert R. McCrae and Oliver P. John. 1992. An introduction to the five - factor model and its applications. *Journal of Personality, 60*(2):175–215.

Warren T. Norman. 1963. Toward an adequate taxonomy of personality attributes: Replicated factor structure in peer nomination personality rating. *Journal of Abnormal and Social Psychology*, Vol. 66(6):574–583.

James W. Pennebaker, Martha E. Francis, and Roger J. Booth. 2001. Linguistic inquiry and word count: LIWC 2001. *Mahway: Lawrence Erlbaum Asso-ciates*, Vol. 71:1–21.

Takuma Okamoto, Kazuyuki Matsumoto, Minoru Yoshida, and Kenji Kita. 2014. Personality estimation from Twitter using a naive bayes method. (in Japanese) In *Proceedings of the 20th Annual Conference of the Association for Natural Language Processing (NLP2014)*, 1123–1125.

Noriyuki Okumura, Yusuke Kanamaru, and Manabu Okumura. 2015. Personality Estimation of Blog Authors based on Emotion Judgment and Big Five. (in Japanese) In *Proceedings of the 29th Annual Conference of the Japanese Society of Artificial Intellegence (JSAI2015)*, 4J1-5.

Jeffrey Pennington, Richard Socher, and Christopher D. Manning. 2014. Glove: Global Vectors for Word Representation. *EMNLP*, Vol. 14.:1532–43.

Milton Rokeach. 1973. The nature of human values. Vol. 438. New York: Free press.

Shalom H. Schwartz. 1992. Universals in the content and structure of values: Theoretical advances and empirical tests in 20 countries. *Advances in experimental social psychology* 25:1–65.

Shalom H. Schwartz. 2003. A proposal for measuring value orientations across nations. *Questionnaire Package of the European Social Survey*:259–290.

Shalom H. Schwartz. 2006. Basic Human Values: Theory, Measurement, and Applications. *Revue Francaise de Sociologie*, Vol. 47(4).

Shalom H. Schwartz, et al. 2012. Refining the theory of basic individual values.*Journal of Personality and Social Psychology* 103(4):663–688.

Masahiro Yamamoto, Tetsuya Nasukawa, Koichi Kamijo, and Hideya Kitamura. 2016. A Proposal of LIWC2001manual translation of policies and semi-automatic translation method. (in Japanese) In *Proceedings of the 22nd Natural Language Processing Annual Conference (NLP2016)*, D7-2.

Huahai Yang and Yunyao Li. 2013. Identifying user needs from social media. *IBM Research Report*, RJ10513 (ALM1309-013).

Tal Yarkoni. 2010. Personality in 100,000 words: A large-scale analysis of personality and word use among bloggers. *Journal of research in personality, 44*(3):363–373.

Wei-Dong Zhu, Bob Foyle, Daniel Gagne, Vijay Gupta, Josemina Magdalen, Amarjeet S Mundi, Tetsuya Nasukawa, Mark Paulis, Jane Singer, and Martin Triska. 2014. IBM Watson Content Analytics: *Discovering Actionable Insight from Your Content*, An IBM Redbooks publication, ISBN-10:0738439428.

Predicting Brexit:
Classifying Agreement is Better than Sentiment and Pollsters

Fabio Celli[1], Evgeny A. Stepanov[1], Massimo Poesio[2], Giuseppe Riccardi[1]
[1]Signals and Interactive Systems Lab, University of Trento, Italy
{fabio.celli,evgeny.stepanov,giuseppe.riccardi}@unitn.it
[2]School for Computer Science and Electronic Engineering, University of Essex, UK
poesio.essex.ac.uk

Abstract

On June 23rd 2016, UK held the referendum which ratified the exit from the EU. While most of the traditional pollsters failed to forecast the final vote, there were online systems that hit the result with high accuracy using opinion mining techniques and big data. Starting one month before, we collected and monitored millions of posts about the referendum from social media conversations, and exploited Natural Language Processing techniques to predict the referendum outcome. In this paper we discuss the methods used by traditional pollsters and compare it to the predictions based on different opinion mining techniques. We find that opinion mining based on agreement/disagreement classification works better than opinion mining based on polarity classification in the forecast of the referendum outcome.

1 Introduction

The outcome of the 2016 EU referendum did not only spell disaster for the UK government and the Remain campaign. It also amounted to a Press Release disaster for commercial pollsters. YouGov, Populus, ComRes, ORB, Ipsos-Mori and Survation, all failed to correctly predict the outcome. Of the larger pollsters, only TNS and Opinium correctly called the outcome, although still underestimating the Leave vote. This general failure, moreover, follows hard on the heels of similar failures in both the 2010 and 2015 General Elections, and public faith in commercial polling has taken another serious blow. By contrast, predictions using Natural Language Processing (NLP) and Computational Linguistics (CL) techniques, such as opinion mining, proved to be much more reliable. In what follows we will refer to opinion mining as the automatic task of assigning a polarity to a topic in context (Wiebe et al., 2005); to polarity classification and sentiment analysis as the tasks for the extraction of emotive polarity or scores from text; to agreement/disagreement classification as the task of recognizing the opinion of a message towards others in a thread (Wang and Cardie, 2014) or pairs of replying posts (Celli et al., 2016); and to stance classification as the task of recognizing the overall opinion of an author from text.

In this paper we discuss the methods used by traditional pollsters and compare them to the predictions based on different opinion mining techniques, in particular polarity classification and agreement/disagreement classification. We describe a system that predicted the outcome of the

This work is licensed under a Creative Commons Attribution 4.0 International Licence. Licence details:
http://creativecommons.org/licenses/by/4.0/

Proceedings of the Workshop on Computational Modeling of People's Opinions, Personality, and Emotions in Social Media,
pages 110–118, Osaka, Japan, December 12 2016.

referendum correctly to within one-tenth of a percentage point. Unlike many political prediction papers that provide post-hoc analyses (Gayo-Avello, 2012), our final prediction was publicly available the day before the referendum (i.e. 22nd of June) on our referendum monitoring web site; thus, it is indeed the prediction of the future result.

The rest of the paper is structured as follows: in Section 2 we report the techniques used by commercial pollsters to forecast the votes, in Section 3 we report related work on forecasts from social media using opinion mining. Section 4 describes the methodology we have used for data collection and the system for the prediction of the referendum outcome. In the same section we provide analyses of the representativeness of our data sources and the methods for topic labeling and automatic annotation of opinions. Finally, in Section 5 we analyze and compare polling and NLP-based predictions. We hope that the results and discussions presented in this paper will contribute to pushing NLP further in the exploitation of para-semantic analysis techniques to forecast and understand collective decisions.

2   Traditional Opinion Polling

Traditional commercial polling for the EU referendum in UK started in the months between the announcement of the referendum (January 22, 2013) and the referendum day (June 23, 2016). Although the UK government started a pro-Remain campaign in April 2016, opinion polls of voters in general tended to show roughly equal proportions in favor of remaining and leaving. Polls done in the weeks preceding the referendum showed majority being in favor of remaining, and the outcome of the referendum showed that there is a bias in the methods used by traditional opinion pollsters to sample and collect the data.

Known issues with traditional opinion polling techniques are related to demographic bias in the way voters are polled. Demographics-wise, post-referendum analyses showed that younger voters tended to support remaining in the EU, but are generally less likely to vote; whereas older people tended to support leaving, and they are less likely to use social media or reply to online polling. According to two out of three pollsters, managerial, professional and administrative workers were most likely to favor staying in the EU, while semi-skilled and unskilled workers, plus those reliant on benefits, were the largest demographics supporting leaving. University graduates were generally more likely to vote Remain compared to those with no qualifications. White voters were evenly split, and all ethnic minority groups leaned towards backing Remain. Support for remaining in the EU was known to be significantly higher in Scotland than it is in Great Britain as a whole, with Scottish voters saying they are generally more likely to vote.

The way voters are polled is known to affect the outcome. Traditional methods consisting of telephone polls usually based on small samples ranging from 1000 to 1500, and online polls are usually based on larger samples (from 2000 to 5000). Telephone polls have consistently found more support for remaining in the EU than online polls. Ipsos-Mori and ComRes argued that telephone polls are more reliable, but YouGov, which uses online polling, has criticized telephone polls because they have a high percentage of graduates, thus skewing the results towards Remain. A study by Populus concluded that telephone polls were likely to better reflect the state of public opinion. However, overall for the EU referendum, online polls seem to have had a

http://www.sense-eu.info
http://www.populus.co.uk/2016/03/polls-apart/

time window	Remain	Leave	undecided	sample	pollster	method
22 June	55%	45%	0%	4700	Populus	Online
20-22 June	51%	49%	0%	3766	YouGov	Online
20-22 June	49%	46%	5%	1592	Ipsos Mori	Phone
20-22 June	44%	**45%**	11%	3011	Opinium	Online
17-22 June	48%	42%	10%	1032	ComRes	Phone
16-22 June	41%	**43%**	16%	2320	TNS	Online
20 June	45%	44%	11%	1003	Survation	Phone
18-19 June	42%	**44%**	14%	1652	YouGov	Online
16-19 June	53%	46%	1%	800	ORB	Phone

Table 1: Overview of the results obtained and methods adopted by traditional pollsters for the referendum.

better prediction than phone polls .

Table 1 reports the results of the major commercial pollsters, with details on the sample size and the methods adopted. In the days before the referendum, only TNS and Opinium predicted the outcome correctly, both using online polling and a three day time window, or larger. But results are contradictory: Populus used online polling, and with a larger sample, but they focused on a one-day time window and their prediction failed. Moreover, YouGov gave a first correct prediction with online polls from June 18 to 19, and then failed using the same method with a larger sample collected between June 20 to 22.

Other pollsters based their predictions on various aggregations of the polls from different companies, adjusting for biases and gaps they have perceived in their methodology, such as the one between telephone and online polling. However, no pollster utilizing this methodology was able to predict the referendum outcome correctly.

3   Opinion Mining and Forecasting

Opinion mining based on sentiment analysis has become one of the most popular tasks in the last decade (Li and Wu, 2010) and many works have demonstrated how much it can be useful for recommendation systems (Zhang and Pennacchiotti, 2013) among other tasks. Opinion mining is traditionally performed by means of sentiment lexica or dictionaries (Cambria et al., 2012), although other methods based on semantics (Agarwal et al., 2015) or stylometry (Anchiêta et al., 2015) have been tested in recent years. One of the most popular applications of sentiment analysis to event forecasting is perhaps the works initiated by Bollen and colleagues on the prediction of the stock market from Twitter: they found strong correlations between collective mood states extracted from large-scale Twitter feeds and the value of the Dow Jones on a 3-days time window (Bollen et al., 2011). They also attempted to detect the public's response to the US presidential election and Thanksgiving day in 2008, successfully predicting the outcome with an accuracy of 86.7%.

More recent studies analyze political opinions and make political forecasts through sentiment analysis of social media: for example, O'Connor connected measures of public opinion from polls with sentiment measured from text and found strong correlations between public opinion and tweet texts (O'Connor et al., 2010). This highlights the potential of text streams as a

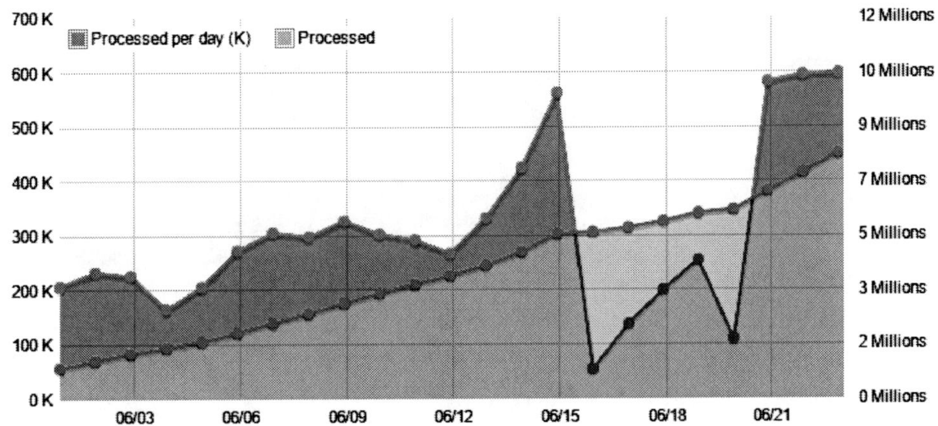

Figure 1: Data collected per day and overall from June 1, 2016 to the referendum date. The lower peaks correspond to the aftermath of the Cox's murder, followed by a news breakout on Brexit.

substitute fot or supplement to traditional polling. Other studies showed that the mere number of political party mentions accurately reflects the election results (Tumasjan et al., 2010). In a recent study, Burnap and colleagues used Twitter data to forecast the outcome of the 2015 UK General Election: they exploited sentiment analysis and prior party support to generate a forecast of parliament seat allocation that turned out to hit the final result with high accuracy (Burnap et al., 2016).

4   Prediction Methodology

Similar to other papers using social media for political predictions, such as (O'Connor et al., 2010), our methodology consists of collecting social media data and applying opinion mining techniques to predict the distribution of votes.

4.1   Data Collection for Referendum Monitoring

Starting from May 19, 2016 we crawled the web for conversations about Brexit using hand-crafted lists of keywords, hashtags and mentions (e.g. *EUreferendum*, *#Brexit*, and *@ukleave-eu*); and created daily data dumps. The conversations were collected from more than 4000 sources such as newspaper blogs, social network sites and other types of social media in 20 languages and from 14 countries of the European Union. The collected data was automatically processed with cross-language algorithms for extracting topics (Leave/Remain) and opinions towards them. Within the referendum monitoring time frame, we have collected and processed more than 8 million posts (see Figure 1), about 80% of which comes from Twitter. The portion of collected data used for the prediction will be made available on demand.

Requests can be made from the website http://sisl.disi.unitn.it

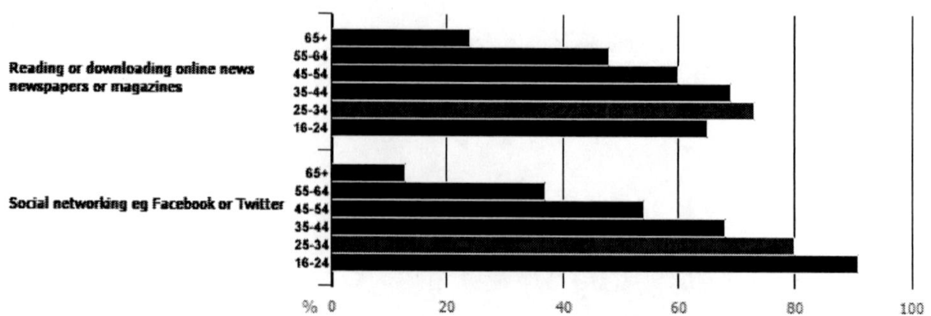

Figure 2: Percentage of online news readers and social network users by age. Source: ONS, year 2014.

Leave	Remain
euroscepticism,	SayYes2Europe, Remain,
#beLeave, #betteroffout, #britainout,	#bremain, #betteroffin , #leadnotleave,
#LeaveEU, #noTTIP, #TakeControl,	#Remain, #Stay, #strongerin, #ukineu,
#VoteLeave, #VoteNO, #voteout,	#votein, #voteremain, #VoteYES,
@end-of-europe, @leaveeuofficial,	#yes2eu, #yestoeu, #SayYes2Europe,
@NoThanksEU, @nothankseu,	
@ukleave-eu, @vote-leave	

Table 2: Sets of keywords, hashtags and mentions for assigning posts to Leave and Remain categories.

4.2 Representativeness of the Social Media Data for Political Predictions

How representative is the social media data of the voter demographics is a debated topic. As it is illustrated in Figure 2 that shows the distribution of social network and online news readers reported by the national UK statistic agency in 2014, not every age group is equally represented in social media. The same is also true for other demographic factors such as gender, race, social class, etc. An extensive work on 70 million tweets collected between 2011 and 2012 during Spanish and US presidential elections, showed that Twitter users who write about politics tend to be male, to live in urban areas, and to have extreme ideological preferences (Barberá and Rivero, 2014). Moreover, since there is usually no demographic information available in Twitter or other sources as meta data, sample representativeness is not easy to verify. Thus, it is inevitable that it will be biased. For predicting the outcome of Brexit referendum, we did not apply any techniques to account for UK voter demographics. We plan to address this in future work.

4.3 Leave/Remain Topic Labeling

As the first step, the posts in the collected data are automatically assigned Leave or Remain topics. The task is performed by means of simple hand-crafted rules that use keywords, hashtags

---

http://www.ons.gov.uk/

and mentions to map the posts to classes. If a post contains keywords, hashtags, or mentions for Leave and not for Remain, it is mapped to Leave; and if it contains keywords, hashtags or mentions for Remain and not for Leave, it is mapped to Remain. Unclassified posts were not used for the prediction. The sets of keywords, hashtags and mentions used for each class were selected such that they yield balanced probabilities. The sets for each class are given in Table 2.

4.4 Automatics Classification of Author's Opinions

Just assignment of a topic to a post is not enough for the prediction of authors' opinions. The authors' opinions towards topics could be predicted either as a sentiment polarity expressed in a post, or as an agreement or disagreement with the topic expressed in a post. In this section we describe the sentiment polarity prediction and the agreement/disagreement prediction systems that are used for posts classification.

4.4.1 Agreement/Disagreement

The system for the automatic labeling of posts with agreement/disagreement makes use of language independent stylometric features such as: character-based ratios of upper and lowercase letters, numbers, various punctuation marks and special characters; word-based ratios of URLs, Twitter mentions and hashtags, negative and positive emoticons. Additionally, the model considers ratios of character and word ngrams (bigrams to tetragrams). All the features have their numerical values between 0 and 1.

The model is trained and evaluated on the Italian CorEA corpus (Celli et al., 2014) using 66% of the data for training and 33% for evaluation. The corpus consists of about 2900 posts to online news articles that were manually annotated with respect to agreement, disagreement and neutrality/not applicability to the parent posts. The system was trained only on agreement and disagreement labels, removing neutral and not applicable cases. The inter-annotator agreement on two classes is k=0.85 and the manually annotated posts used for training and testing are approximately 2000. The task is cast as a regression with the well balanced bimodal distribution. The performance of the Support Vector Regressor (Shevade et al., 2000) on the CorEA test set has a Mean Absolute Error (MAE) of 0.32.

Even though the model is trained and tested on Italian data, the features are language independent: semantics of features such as emoticons and punctuation are similar at least across European languages; thus, we believe that the model is applicable to other languages as well.

4.4.2 Sentiment Polarity

The sentiment polarity prediction system is lexicon-based. We used OpenNER polarity lexicon to label each post as either negative, positive, or neutral. The posts classified as neutral were removed for the prediction. The performance of the system on the Movie Reviews 2.0 data set (Pang and Lee, 2004) has accuracy of 68.7%. Even though the system has moderate performance, it is in line to the state-of-the-art lexicon-based approaches to sentiment analysis.

5   Brexit Prediction, Analysis and Evaluation

We have predicted the outcome of the referendum from a subset of approximately 178 thousand posts in a time window of 2 days (June 20 and June 21). In this paper we compare two opinion

---

http://www.opener-project.eu

System	Leave		Remain	
	Counts	Percentages	Counts	Percentages
Baseline	178,722	(60.97%)	114,403	(39.03%)
Sentiment Polarity	63,788	(51.26%)	60,657	(48.74%)
Agreement/Disagreement	90,847	(51.79%)	84,560	(48.21%)
Referendum Outcome		51.9%		48.1%

Table 3: Counts and percentages for Leave and Remain as predicted by sentiment polarity prediction system (*polarity*) and agreement/disagreement prediction system (*agreement/disagreement*). Baseline is the counts of posts selected by hand-crafted rules. The referendum outcome is provided for the reference.

mining systems – the one based on sentiment polarity and the one based agreement/disagreement classification. The baseline is the volume of posts about Leave and Remain topics, obtained by topic labeling with the hand-crafted rules described in Section 4.3. For the final prediction of each system we compute the percentage of posts that are positive towards one class and negative towards the other. For example, the predicted percentage for Leave counts posts in agreement with Leave and in disagreement with Remain, and vice versa. Neutral posts are ignored (this is why the posts used by the NLP systems are fewer than the posts used for the baseline).

Predictions using each system are reported in Table 3. While sentiment polarity and agreement/disagreement systems yield correct predictions, we found that the baseline is significantly offset and overestimates Leave (60.97%). This suggests that people tend to write a lot about Leave, but mainly to criticize. The agreement/disagreement based prediction is more accurate than the sentiment polarity based prediction. One reason can be that the agreement/disagreement based system considers significantly more posts ($\approx$ 50K more) than the sentiment polarity system.

Our findings support the claim that NLP techniques such as opinion mining can be very useful to opinion polling and social media analytics, and that events such as a referendum can be predicted with high accuracy. However, a correct prediction is the result of a combination of many factors, where the time period is important as well as the analysis method. As literature reports, a time-window of 2 or 3 days is the best for a prediction, and we used a 2 days time-window like many pollsters. However, in this specific case, we were able to capture the moment when undecided people (estimated between 7% to 11% of voters) changed their minds towards Leave areas, while traditional pollsters were not. In the aftermath of the referendum, YouGov attributed the error in their predictions to this higher turnout in Leave-oriented areas not captured by their polls. In our opinion there are three reasons for the NLP techniques being able to produce more accurate predictions than traditional polling:

- NLP techniques can analyze much larger sample sizes. Traditional polls typically interview on average 1000 to 4000 individuals. By contrast, with NLP techniques we processed a minimum of 80K to 100K posts per day, and aggregation of this order produces compelling evidence.

- Traditional polling asks for the peoples behavioral intentions or opinions, whereas analyses carried out with NLP techniques try to infer opinions that motivate behavior. Modern cognitive science has established that direct questions about opinions and behavioral intentions may produce unreliable and invalid responses (Hufnagel and Conca, 1994). Asking subjects to fill questionnaires is only used when more indirect methods cannot be applied, such as measuring the time it takes to perform a task, or eye-tracking. NLP in this case represents such an indirect method, since it focuses on opinions that are some distance from the behavior.

- Data collected from social media and processed with NLP techniques may well cover posts coming from a wider range of geographical locations and demographic variety than pollster's surveys.

6 Conclusions

We have predicted the outcome of the Brexit referendum with high accuracy exploiting NLP techniques and outperforming a baseline based on the volume of posts. We analyzed some possible causes of this result, comparing our prediction to pollsters' surveys. Our findings are based just on one event, and require further study to be consolidated. To date, however, neither polling organizations nor the media have paid much attention to NLP methods for election and referendum forecasting, but the results of this work suggest that these methods, with all their limitations, can produce reliable forecasts.

At the very least, campaigners and the media alike should consider using NLP methods to compare with or complement the polls. While every new methodology is rightly treated with a degree of suspicion and while it is premature to expect traditional polling to disappear, there are grounds for both campaigners and the media to take NLP techniques seriously in the future.

Acknowledgements

The research leading to these results has received funding from the European Union - Seventh Framework Programme (FP7/2007-2013) under grant agreement n. 610916 - SENSEI. We would like to thank Websays for providing the data for the baseline.

References

Basant Agarwal, Soujanya Poria, Namita Mittal, Alexander Gelbukh, and Amir Hussain. 2015. Concept-level sentiment analysis with dependency-based semantic parsing: a novel approach. *Cognitive Computation*, 7(4):487–499.

Rafael T Anchiêta, Francisco Assis Ricarte Neto, Rogério Figueiredo de Sousa, and Raimundo Santos Moura. 2015. Using stylometric features for sentiment classification. In *Proc. of CICLing 2015*, pages 189–200.

Pablo Barberá and Gonzalo Rivero. 2014. Understanding the political representativeness of twitter users. *Social Science Computer Review*, pages 1–29.

Johan Bollen, Huina Mao, and Xiaojun Zeng. 2011. Twitter mood predicts the stock market. *Journal of Computational Science*, 2(1):1 – 8.

http://websays.com

Pete Burnap, Rachel Gibson, Luke Sloan, Rosalynd Southern, and Matthew Williams. 2016. 140 characters to victory? using twitter to predict the uk 2015 general election. *Electoral Studies*, 41:230–233.

Erik Cambria, Catherine Havasi, and Amir Hussain. 2012. Senticnet 2: A semantic and affective resource for opinion mining and sentiment analysis. In *Proc. of FLAIRS*, pages 202–207.

Fabio Celli, Giuseppe Riccardi, and Arindam Ghosh. 2014. Corea: Italian news corpus with emotions and agreement. In *Proc. of CLIC-it 2014*, pages 98–102.

Fabio Celli, Evgeny Stepanov, and Giuseppe Riccardi. 2016. Tell me who you are, i'll tell whether you agree or disagree: Prediction of agreement/disagreement in news blog. In *Proc. of NLPMJ*.

Daniel Gayo-Avello. 2012. "i wanted to predict elections with twitter and all i got was this lousy paper" – a balanced survey on election prediction using twitter data. *CoRR*, abs/1204.6441.

Ellen M Hufnagel and Christopher Conca. 1994. User response data: The potential for errors and biases. *Information Systems Research*, 5(1):48–73.

Nan Li and Desheng Dash Wu. 2010. Using text mining and sentiment analysis for online forums hotspot detection and forecast. *Decision Support Systems*, 48(2):354 – 368.

Brendan O'Connor, Ramnath Balasubramanyan, Bryan R Routledge, and Noah A Smith. 2010. From tweets to polls: Linking text sentiment to public opinion time series. pages 122–129.

Bo Pang and Lillian Lee. 2004. A sentimental education: Sentiment analysis using subjectivity summarization based on minimum cuts. In *Proc. of the ACL*.

Shirish Krishnaj Shevade, S Sathiya Keerthi, Chiranjib Bhattacharyya, and Karaturi Radha Krishna Murthy. 2000. Improvements to the smo algorithm for svm regression. *Neural Networks, IEEE Transactions on*, 11(5):1188–1193.

Andranik Tumasjan, Timm O Sprenger, Philipp G Sandner, and Isabell M Welpe. 2010. Election forecasts with twitter: How 140 characters reflect the political landscape. *Social Science Computer Review*, pages 1–17.

Lu Wang and Claire Cardie. 2014. Improving agreement and disagreement identification in online discussions with a socially-tuned sentiment lexicon. *Proc. of the ACL*, pages 97–102.

Janyce Wiebe, Theresa Wilson, and Claire Cardie. 2005. Annotating expressions of opinions and emotions in language. *Language resources and evaluation*, 39(2-3):165–210.

Yongzheng Zhang and Marco Pennacchiotti. 2013. Recommending branded products from social media. In *Proc. of ACM conference on Recommender Systems*, pages 77–84.

Sarcasm Detection : Building a contextual hierarchy

Taradheesh Bali
Centre of Exact Humanities
IIIT, Hyderabad
Telangana, India
taradheesh.bali@research.iiit.ac.in

Navjyoti Singh
Centre of Exact Humanities
IIIT, Hyderabad
Telangana, India
navjyoti@iiit.ac.in

Abstract

The conundrum of understanding and classifying sarcasm has been dealt with by the traditional theorists as an analysis of a sarcastic utterance and the ironic situation that surrounds it. The problem with such an approach is that it is too narrow, as it is unable to sufficiently utilize the two indispensable agents in making such an utterance, viz. the speaker and the listener. It undermines the necessary context required to comprehend a sarcastic utterance. In this paper, we propose a novel approach towards understanding sarcasm in terms of the existing knowledge hierarchy between the two participants, which forms the basis of the context that both agents share. The difference in relationship of the speaker of the sarcastic utterance and the disparate audience found on social media, such as Twitter, is also captured. We then apply our model on a corpus of tweets to achieve significant results and consequently, shed light on subjective nature of context, which is contingent on the relation between the speaker and the listener.

1 Introduction

Though deceptively simple for humans, it should come as no surprise that automatic recognition of sarcasm by machines is a highly complex task. Even more so when it is only through text, which is where even human annotators have struggled and have had differences of opinion as reported by Tsur et al. (2010). Computational detection of sarcasm, therefore, has been a more recent field of study. Davidov et al. (2010) made the first notable contribution through their semi-supervised classifier for tweets and Amazon product reviews. Since then a host of researches (González-Ibánez et al., 2011; Riloff et al., 2013; Barbieri et al., 2014) have primarily focused on lexical features, such as word frequency (to detect the most commonly occurring words in a sarcastic statement), conjunctively occurring noun and verb phrases, sentiment analysis of such phrases etc. In addition to these, González-Ibánez et al. (2011) included pragmatic features such as emoticons and in-reply-to user (though this only validated the interaction as a conversation). Similarly, Bamman and Smith (2015) also tried to make use of the two-fold relation between the author and the audience of a sarcastic utterance by maintaining a familiarity score between both. Joshi et al. (2015) lexical analysis a step further by harnessing the inter-sentential context incongruity. Sulis et al. (2016)

In this paper we provide a computational model built and structured on our proposed theoretical improvements to the framework for understanding sarcasm. Treating the sarcastic utterance as a multi-agent process between the speaker and the listener, we create a hierarchical knowledge structure for understanding their context. As a result, we are able to highlight and tackle the drawbacks of the past theories as well as computational attempts for understanding sarcasm. Recent studies have also tried to distinguish between verbal irony and sarcasm (Sulis et al., 2016) but for the scope of this paper we have treated them alike and both terms have been used interchangeably.

Rest of the paper is organized as follows. We first discuss related theoretical and computational work and their drawbacks in Section 2. Then Section 3 contains our proposed framework based on under-

This work is licensed under a Creative Commons Attribution 4.0 International Licence. Licence details: http://creativecommons.org/licenses/by/4.0/

Proceedings of the Workshop on Computational Modeling of People's Opinions, Personality, and Emotions in Social Media,
pages 119–127, Osaka, Japan, December 12 2016.

standing context through knowledge hierarchy. Section 3.1 introduces the belief contradiction. Section 4 comprises of our methodology for data extraction, interpretation and classification. Sections 5 and 6 contain analysis and future work respectively.

2 Related work

2.1 Theoretical work

The traditional view of sarcasm/verbal irony has been that in such an utterance the speaker means the opposite of what he says. Many significant works in that direction are based on the maxims proposed by Grice (1970) [1]. However, when understood in such a manner it is easy to see why a typical Gricean explanation based on the violation of his conversational implicatures would suffice. But on closer examination it appears that while sarcasm and irony both tend to follow the trend of violation of Gricean Maxims in most (not all) cases, so do metaphors as well. This is because his account treats both the phenomenon as deviations from Gricean conventions. Also according to the Gricean account of meaning inversion, where the speaker intends to convey opposite of what he said is incomplete because in cases other than assertions or declarative statements it is not always possible to construe the opposite of what is said. Opposite in different utterances can mean different things like negation of proposition, negation of predicate, negation of implicature etc. This is because the speaker can selectively target from a specific part of the speech act to its whole to express his opinion sarcastically. Additionally, in cases such as hyperbole, rhetorical questions or over-polite requests where the no maxim is directly violated the line becomes even more blurred. Moreover, such a theory gives no significant reason as to why a speaker would choose to convey what he intends in such a way instead of simply stating what he wants and is therefore a better fit for incongruity resolution rather than for understanding sarcasm. But then again his theory of implicatures was not specifically meant to deal with such problems (at least not initially (Grice, 1978)) but was more about defining maxims for more conventional conversations.

Since then there have two significant approaches towards explaining sarcasm, viz., the pretense based approach and the echoic mention approach, both disagree with the Gricean claim and treat sarcasm not merely as semantic inversion but also as an act of speaker's expression of his attitude. While people on each side have claimed and tried to justify their approach to be superior, the debate has subdued as recent hybrid approaches have emerged which incorporate some aspects from both sides have proven to be better suited to explaining the process.

The most basic claims of these theories are as follows -

- **The Echoic Theory** - According to the echoic mention theory, a sarcastic utterance is understood by the listener when he is able to detect that the speaker of such an utterance is mocking or expressing his attitude towards some previously stated proposition (Sperber, 1984). That proposition can either be explicitly expressed in the conversation before or be implied implicitly. But this definition of echo was deemed too narrow and was later expanded to include the allusion to established social norms as well (Kumon-Nakamura et al., 1995).

- **The Pretense Theory** - Grice, without giving any proper explanation, had suggested that the being ironic involves an act of pretense which the pretender intends the audience to catch. Fowler (1965) introduced the concept of two types of audience, where one on listening to a sarcastic utterance could not get past the literal meaning but the other who are a part of the inner circle. Clark and Gerrig (1984) build on Grice's and Fowler's approach towards sarcasm and postulate that when uttering a sarcastic statement U, the speaker S is pretending to be another person P to whom S ascribes the utterance to, and intends for the listener L to look past/understand this pretense and know S's opinion/emotional attitude towards U and how ridiculous U is and in turn tries to mock either both P and U. That person P can be either a real or an imaginary person who endorses the idea of U.

---

[1] Grice's four maxims of quality, quantity, relevance and manner

Kumon-Nakamura et al. (1995) and Camp (2012) have also provided two significant combined accounts which incorporate elements from both the pretense account as well as the echoic account.

2.1.1 Criticisms

The echo theorists mainly emphasise on the content of the sarcastic utterance and suggest that the pretense theory focuses more on the form of the utterance (Wilson, 2006). Conforming to the echo theory, an argument often made is that while most instances of sarcasm/verbal irony can be explained through pretense, it is not a necessary condition for all the occurrences. According to Wilson (2006), while pretense can successfully mimic the form of another speech act, the content which the speaker alludes to, a necessary component of any sarcastic utterance, can only be delivered through echo. As a result, a pretense account cannot capture the essential attributive element of the sarcastic utterance, and determine towards whom or what is the speaker directing his derogatory attitude. Currie (2006) while agreeing that attribution is an indispensable constituent of a sarcastic utterance he also points out that such attribution is not always because of echoic content. For example, in cases of parodic sarcasm, one need not necessarily imitate bring forward the content but rather it is the form in this case which generates the echo. Therefore, reminding effect that echoic theory banks upon can be explained through both reminiscence in content as well as in form.

A major flaw in the criticisms of the pretense accounts is that their definitions of pretense are very limited and often is the case that they use a definition of pretense which only suits their criticism of it. Pretense is a very powerful concept that can be applied to a variety of speech acts. If not applied precisely enough pretense theories such as Clark and Gerrig (1984) or Clark (1996) can lead to a very generic and noisy classification, where even though the points they make are correct they are neither necessary nor sufficient. For example, it is not always the case that I consider myself as a gullible audience first in order to see through the pretense and nor do I as an audience necessarily take part actively in the speaker's pretense as is suggested in their dual audience or joint-pretense theories respectively.

Popa-Wyatt (2014) illustrates that, although Kumon-Nakamura et al. (1995) and Camp (2012), have tried to merge the two theories and related aspects together, they are unable to reasonably explain the relation between echo and pretense, and the interplay between both when identifying a sarcastic utterance. Camp (2012) suggests that for understanding a sarcastic utterance an inversion of a pre-supposed normative scale takes place but remains fairly unclear on the meaning of pre-supposition of the said normative scale. Popa-Wyatt (2014) while criticising Walton's (1990) account of pretense for identifying the right target of sarcasm also uses the argument that it can't be assumed that one disbelieves what one pretends to believe. While her objection is correctly placed, she does not progress the argument significantly. Her account follows *abductive reasoning* [2] when explaining that there is some connection between the pretend defective thought and the real/conceivable thought (which is the target), whereas a sufficient theory should be able to properly explain this connection that they both share and also be able to answer the questions of how one invokes the other and why does this effect take place.

2.2 Computational work and drawbacks

One of the key contributions of this paper is that instead of treating the problem of detecting sarcasm as a mere lexical exercise, we have tried to model a system that tries to build an understanding of the whole process as a human would do. González-Ibáñez et al. (2011) have shown that even after including the significant pragmatic features such as emoticons but leaving out of account the context associated with a particular tweet results in misclassification. They admitted that the brevity of a tweet sometimes makes it necessary to include additional information about the interaction between the tweeters such as common ground and world knowledge.

Bamman and Smith (2015) tried to tackle this problem by incorporating a familiarity score between the speaker and the audience, which was a measure for how much interaction both the parties have had. They also maintained a historical profile of the author and the audience of the sarcastic comment with features such as maintaining a score for their historical salient terms or his historical topics, which again

---

[2] Abductive reasoning, is a form of logical inference which goes from an observation to a theory which accounts for the observation, ideally seeking to find the simplest and most likely explanation.

is similar to the previous word frequency models albeit with the inclusion/acknowledgement of author-audience interaction for the first time. Although these features helped in increasing the accuracy, they fail to provide any significant improvement when both the users had low familiarity score or historical background. The efficiency of their proposition gets diminished even further when even though both the speaker and listener have some common context but the speaker has made a sarcastic utterance for the first time.

In their paper Joshi et al. (2015) tried to capture context incongruity, with their premise being - *sarcasm is a contrast between positive sentiment word and a negative situation and vice versa* - an approach similar to that of Riloff et al. (2013), but while Riloff (2013) focused only on contrast between words bearing positive sentiment and a negative situation; Joshi (2015) also laid equal emphasis on contrast between noun phrases with negative sentiment juxtaposed with a positive situation (comprised of the verb phrase). Though their research helped in shedding new light on the matter, the scope of the definition for context that they use is very limited and as reported in their paper, led to errors in cases where the context was highly subjective and could not be detected from only a single tweet.

3   Proposed Framework

Knowledge and uncertainty, especially the hierarchy that it generates in multi-agent systems has been a serious area of enquiry in game theory and philosophy. Inside a conversation, what the participants know about each other and what the participants know about the knowledge of other participants Lee (2001) [3], all play a central role in how pretense is incorporated or acted out. Sarcastic pretense, as an act of speech, involves a fair degree of such higher order thinking, which can be understood to some degree by this vocabulary borrowed from game theory and epistemology. Also, one must note, that while the original treatment of these constructs deal with modelling agents in terms of bayesian rationality, we have no such unrealistic ambitions and are only using the broader framework to shed some light on the layers of perception that shape a speech act.

If the participants of a conversation are Speaker S and Listener L, then let us use B^s and B^l to denote the set and structure of beliefs held by them respectively. B_0^s, then, essentially represents the real identity of S, and similarly B_0^l for L. Given that, let us denote what S believes to be L's beliefs by B_1^s, ie. what L believes in accordance to B_0^l (and similarly B_1^l denote what L believes to be S's beliefs).

Likewise, B_2^s is what S believes about the beliefs held by L about S's beliefs, ie. B_2^s is the beliefs of S in accordance to S's perception of B_1^l. And similarly, for any i, B_i^s denotes what S believes about the beliefs about S held in B_{i-1}^l.

In these terms, sarcastic pretense can be viewed as an act of speech where the if S has spoken an utterance U pretending to be P, then

- U is not entirely aligned to S's beliefs, ie. B_0^s

- L is able to distinguish P from S, using U. ie. U is sufficient to distinguish between B_1^l and P

- S knows that L will be able to distinguish P from S using U, ie. U is sufficient to distinguish between B_2^s and P. Otherwise, if S is not certain that L will be able to distinguish, an explicit marker of pretense would be required to convey the intended message.

An important thing to note here is the speaker's intent behind the sarcastic utterance. The intent of the speaker behind an act of sarcastic pretense is for the audience to see-through the pretense, and hence, through our structure of belief hierarchy we are also able to differentiate between a lie and a sarcastic utterance, which an echoic account is unable to capture due to its focus being mainly on content.

---

[3]Mutual Knowledge - An event is mutual knowledge if all agents know that the event occurred. However, mutual knowledge by itself implies nothing about what agents know about other agents'knowledge: i.e. it is possible that an event is mutual knowledge but that each agent is unaware that the other agents know it has occurred.

Common Knowledge - There is common knowledge of p in a group of agents G when all the agents in G know p, they all know that they know p, they all know that they all know that they know p, and so on ad infinitum.

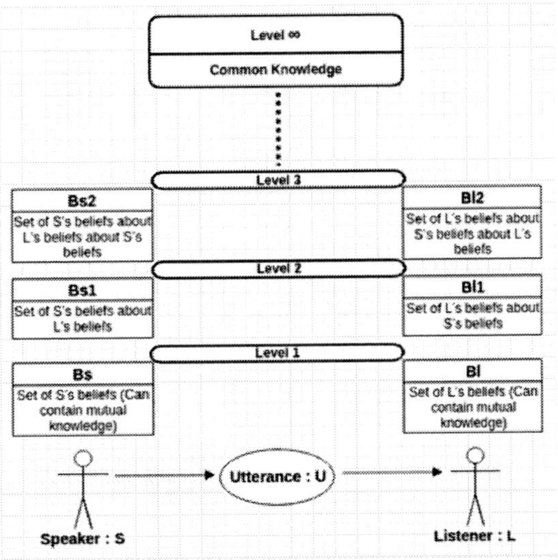

Figure 1: Knowledge Hierarchy

3.1 Belief Contradiction

One common drawback of the previous research on this topic is that it tries to isolate a sarcastic utterance from the conversation. Any conversation in general, not only on social media, has to have a speaker and an audience. The additional feature of conversations on social media is that much of it is public, especially on twitter. A tweet even when directed to a single user as a part of a conversation between two people who know each other is accessible to everyone who views it. Therefore, an uninitiated audience can also share their opinions on the matter with varying degrees of knowledge about the previous conversation. Such an unconventional structure can make the interpretation of a sarcastic utterance very difficult. As we have discussed above a joint account of pretense and echo is best suited for explaining the process of sarcasm. Besides, a better understanding of the process of pretense is required to explain how the speaker decides to carry out a pretense so that the audience that he is aiming for to see through the pretense understands it.

For a successful understanding of the pretense and subsequently the sarcasm/sarcastic intent behind my utterance, the audience has to recurse to the second level and validate, whether what I said either -

1. Contradicts or expresses a contrasting attitude towards B_1^l or,

2. Contradicts or expresses a contrasting attitude towards the beliefs in B^l (this set of beliefs can contain L's own bias as well as the established norms).

While for the listener to understand the sarcastic utterance he has to recurse to the second level, in order for the speaker of the sarcastic utterance to make sure that the listener understands the sarcastic utterance he has to recurse to the third level. Then if B_2^s is populated in respect to the attitude he wants to convey he utters the sentence. Otherwise with the additional functionality of written social media he can add a #sarcasm or #sarcastic in the end to make his attitude a common knowledge.

Consequently, the audience that has to understand the sarcastic utterance can broadly be divided into two classes :

Case 1 : B_1^l is not empty and U is in contrast

This means that both agents have either some established common knowledge before or some perceived/inferred knowledge that L possesses which was conveyed by S. In such a case, L compares U or its literal implicature against elements in B_1^l, and if the attitude expressed by S through U is in contrast with the relevant beliefs in B_1^l then there is increased likelihood that L understands the utterance U to be sarcastic.

Figure 2 shows S conveying and thereby, populating B_1^l with his (negative) emotional attitude. A literal (positive) understanding of the belief conveyed through U (Figure 3) shows S contrasting his previously conveyed belief. Thus, informing L about the increased probability of the U being sarcastic.

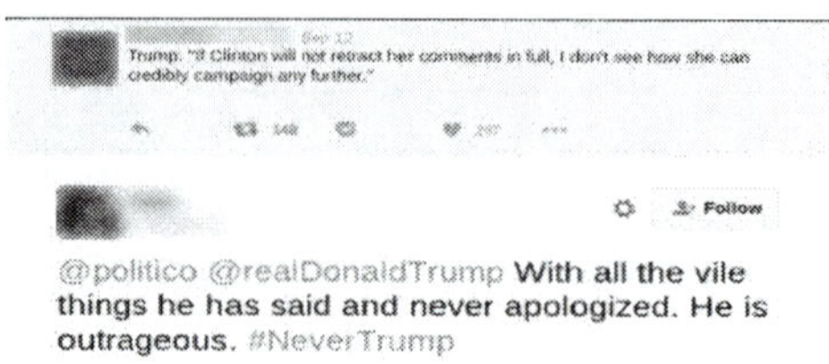

Figure 2: Belief conveyed in prior conversation

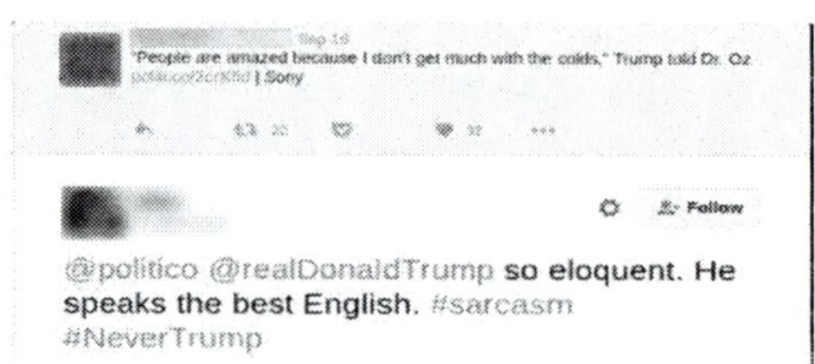

Figure 3: Belief contradiction through sarcastic utterance U

Case 2 : B_1^l is not empty but has no priors related to U OR B_1^l is empty

This means that either, L does not have any previous knowledge about U and related implicatures or he does not have any previous shared knowledge with S. In both the cases L has only B^l to rely upon in relation to U, therefore if the attitude expressed by S through U is now in contrast with relevant beliefs in B^l then there is increased likelihood that L understands the utterance U to be sarcastic.

Let us call both the audience L_1 and L_2 respectively.

4   Method

4.1   Data and its interpretation

To ensure that high precision tweets are chosen for the positive set we limit our scope only to those tweets which have #sarcasm or #sarcastic explicitly mentioned in them. We keep only English tweets with number of words ≥ 5, filter out hyperlinks or retweets. Tweets were mined using tweepy, a python library for accessing twitter API. A datapoint in this dataset will be our U (sarcastic utterance). In order to ensure that there is a communicative context we only choose those tweets that are in reply to another parent tweet say p. Cases where p is protected (inaccessible via API due to restricted permissions) were also accounted for and such dangling pairs, along with their references were cleaned from our dataset as a part of pre-processing. The user who has replied with the sarcastic tweet is S and the user to whose tweet he is replying to is L. We store all the hashtags used in both p and U, in a set H. These hashtags function as indicators of the topics that both are talking about. We then crawl and retrieve the most recent tweets of both the authors, which contain an element of H in order to populate B^s and B^l. Now we check if L and S have had any previous communication in relation to an element of H.

If yes, then it is Case 1 (with audience type L_1) and each such B_1^l is populated with a maximum of 10 tweets containing an element of H which S has tweeted to L.

If no, then it is Case 2 (with audience type L_2) and each such B^l is populated with a maximum of 10 tweets containing an element of H which either L has tweeted independently or have been tweeted by rest of the world. This is done because in this case either L could have explicitly tweeted his opinions on elements in H or we assume that his views even though not categorically expressed in any previous tweets are aligned with what the overall popular sentiment exhibits through the 10 most recent tweets (tweeted by the rest of the world) on topics in H. L's independent tweets represent his biases and the tweets from the rest of the world represent the norms.

For negative data the above mentioned process was repeated but for replies without an explicit #sarcasm or #sarcastic marker. Finally, the negative data was manually cross-verified and tweets with implicit sarcastic mentions were removed. We maintain a Reference Table for reference IDs for each type of tweet for both positive as well as the negative data. This table helps in cross-checking the negative data such that it does not overlap via any user, tweet or retweet with the positive data. This yields us total of 2000 conversational instances with a positive set of 1000 instances, 500 for each case, and an equal number of negative instances.

Table 1: Feature Set

Lexical	
Word Unigrams and Bigrams	For tweets of both S and L, we used unigrams and bigrams found in the training corpus.
Brown cluster unigrams	Again for both tweets S and L, we used brown clusters which helped us in grouping words used in similar contexts into the same cluster.
Part of Speech	Output of the POS tagger of CMU[4] of each lexical item in the tweet.
Pragmatic	
Capitalization	Number of capitalized letters.
Emoticons and Expressions	Number of emoticons and expressions such as lol, haha, :D
Frequent Expressions in sarcastic utterances	For sarcastic tweets of both S and L, we kept a list of top 100 words according to their tf-idf score. This feature indicated the presence of a such a word in the current tweets.
Contextual	
Belief Contradiction	Binary feature stating if a belief has been contradicted or not.

4.2 Classification

Similar to Bamman and Smith (2015), we adopted a binary logistic regression with l_2 regularization using 10 fold cross validation to do the binary classification task of marking tweets as SARCASTIC and NOT SARCASTIC. 8 folds out of 10 were used for training, 1 for tuning and remaining last was used for testing. Our baseline model, which predicted the most common of the two labels, gave an accuracy of 48%.

Our feature set is described in Table 1. We used three sets of features, namely, Lexical, Pragmatic, and Contextual. The lexical and pragmatic features are self-explanatory. As our contextual feature we used the proposed belief contradiction method. The noisy non-standard tokens in the data were normalized using the English Normalizer implemented by Sharma et al. (2016). We then used Stanford's Sentiment Analyzer (Socher et al., 2013) to calculate the sentiment of a tweet which we used as the belief of L / S regarding the topic and for the current tweet as well. These belief scores were normalized between -1

---

[4] www.cs.cmu.edu/~ark/TweetNLP/ (2011)

to 1, with -1 being very negative and 1 being very positive. The overall sentiment scores for B_1^l and B^l are calculated as the average of that set. A belief is deemed to be violated when it exudes a contrasting sentiment as compared to the sentiments of either B_1^l or B^l, depending on the type of audience.

Table 2: Results

Results Table	
Features	Accuracy
Lexical(Baseline)	71.2%
Lexical+Pragmatic	75.8%
Lexical+Pragmatic+Contextual	78.7%

5 Analysis

As Table 2 shows the impact of contextual features based on our belief contradiction method as it hugely improves the accuracy from baseline and therefore, is statistically significant. Also, we have addressed problems faced in previous researches, such as, Joshi et al. (2015), where samples containing highly subjective incongruity were misclassified. Our classifier correctly predicted most such samples, as it is able to capture the incongruence in cases where context is highly subjective and varies for a speaker in each interaction. For instances of Case 2, when the speaker and the audience have no previous context, Bamman and Smith (2015) model does not perform well. But our framework captures the violation of normative expectation through an overall recent sentiment score for such topics and hence, is able to correctly classify such instances as well.

6 Future Work

The number of features for lexical and pragmatic analyses could be increased and diversified to enhance our system. Also, while we were analysing the overall sentiment of a tweet, breaking a tweet into parts according to each topic could be done to analyse the sentiment of the speaker towards each topic. This could provide us with a better understanding of his beliefs on that topic. It also allows us to capture the sentiment contrast at a sub-tweet level rather than the whole tweet. In the future, this experiment can be extended to the sarcastic tweets of collections that have been used previously, for instance the one used in the shared task 11 of SemEval-2015 (Ghosh et al., 2015). The scope of this paper stretches beyond sarcasm detection in tweets only. Our model can also be incorporated in conversational chat bots to detect sarcasm in a user's reply and respond accordingly. The historical features that we propose can ameliorate the responses even for smart messaging services such as Google's Allo.

References

David Bamman and Noah A Smith. 2015. Contextualized sarcasm detection on twitter. In *Ninth International AAAI Conference on Web and Social Media*.

Francesco Barbieri, Horacio Saggion, and Francesco Ronzano. 2014. Modelling sarcasm in twitter, a novel approach. *ACL 2014*, page 50.

Elisabeth Camp. 2012. Sarcasm, pretense, and the semantics/pragmatics distinction. *Noûs*, 46(4):587–634.

Herbert H Clark and Richard J Gerrig. 1984. On the pretense theory of irony. *Journal of Experimental Psychology: General*, 113(1):121–126.

HH Clark. 1996. Using language cambridge university press cambridge.

Gregory Currie. 2006. Why irony is pretence. *The architecture of the imagination*, pages 111–33.

Dmitry Davidov, Oren Tsur, and Ari Rappoport. 2010. Semi-supervised recognition of sarcastic sentences in twitter and amazon. In *Proceedings of the fourteenth conference on computational natural language learning*, pages 107–116. Association for Computational Linguistics.

Henry Watson Fowler. 1965. Modern english usage (revised by sir ernest gowers).

Aniruddha Ghosh, Guofu Li, and Tony Veale. 2015. Semeval-2015 task 11: Sentiment analysis of figurative language in twitter.

Kevin Gimpel, Nathan Schneider, Brendan O'Connor, Dipanjan Das, Daniel Mills, Jacob Eisenstein, Michael Heilman, Dani Yogatama, Jeffrey Flanigan, and Noah A Smith. 2011. Part-of-speech tagging for twitter: Annotation, features, and experiments. In *Proceedings of the 49th Annual Meeting of the Association for Computational Linguistics: Human Language Technologies: short papers-Volume 2*, pages 42–47. Association for Computational Linguistics.

Roberto González-Ibánez, Smaranda Muresan, and Nina Wacholder. 2011. Identifying sarcasm in twitter: a closer look. In *Proceedings of the 49th Annual Meeting of the Association for Computational Linguistics: Human Language Technologies: short papers-Volume 2*, pages 581–586. Association for Computational Linguistics.

Herbert P Grice. 1970. *Logic and conversation*. na.

H Paul Grice. 1978. Further notes on logic and conversation. *1978*, 1:13–128.

Aditya Joshi, Vinita Sharma, and Pushpak Bhattacharyya. 2015. Harnessing context incongruity for sarcasm detection. In *Proceedings of the 53rd Annual Meeting of the Association for Computational Linguistics and the 7th International Joint Conference on Natural Language Processing*, volume 2, pages 757–762.

Sachi Kumon-Nakamura, Sam Glucksberg, and Mary Brown. 1995. How about another piece of pie: The allusional pretense theory of discourse irony. *Journal of Experimental Psychology: General*, 124(1):3.

Benny PH Lee. 2001. Mutual knowledge, background knowledge and shared beliefs: Their roles in establishing common ground. *Journal of pragmatics*, 33(1):21–44.

Mihaela Popa-Wyatt. 2014. Pretence and echo: towards an integrated account of verbal irony. *International Review of Pragmatics*, 6(1):127–168.

Ellen Riloff, Ashequl Qadir, Prafulla Surve, Lalindra De Silva, Nathan Gilbert, and Ruihong Huang. 2013. Sarcasm as contrast between a positive sentiment and negative situation. In *EMNLP*, volume 13, pages 704–714.

Arnav Sharma, Sakshi Gupta, Raveesh Motlani, Piyush Bansal, Manish Srivastava, Radhika Mamidi, and Dipti M Sharma. 2016. Shallow parsing pipeline for hindi-english code-mixed social media text. *arXiv preprint arXiv:1604.03136*.

Richard Socher, Alex Perelygin, Jean Y Wu, Jason Chuang, Christopher D Manning, Andrew Y Ng, and Christopher Potts. 2013. Recursive deep models for semantic compositionality over a sentiment treebank. In *Proceedings of the conference on empirical methods in natural language processing (EMNLP)*, volume 1631, page 1642. Citeseer.

Dan Sperber. 1984. Verbal irony: Pretense or echoic mention?

Emilio Sulis, Delia Irazú Hernández Farías, Paolo Rosso, Viviana Patti, and Giancarlo Ruffo. 2016. Figurative messages and affect in twitter: differences between# irony,# sarcasm and# not. *Knowledge-Based Systems*.

Oren Tsur, Dmitry Davidov, and Ari Rappoport. 2010. Icwsm-a great catchy name: Semi-supervised recognition of sarcastic sentences in online product reviews. In *ICWSM*.

Kendall L Walton. 1990. *Mimesis as make-believe: On the foundations of the representational arts*. Harvard University Press.

Deirdre Wilson. 2006. The pragmatics of verbal irony: Echo or pretence? *Lingua*, 116(10):1722–1743.

Social and Linguistic Behavior and its Correlation to Trait Empathy

Marina Litvak
Department of Software Engineering
Shamoon College of Engineering
Be'er Sheva, ISRAEL
marinal@sce.ac.il

Jahna Otterbacher
Social Information Systems
Open University of Cyprus
Nicosia, CYPRUS
jahna.otterbacher@ouc.ac.cy

Chee Siang Ang
School of Multimedia and Digital Arts
University of Kent
Kent, UK
C.S.Ang@kent.ac.uk

David Atkins
School of Multimedia and Digital Arts
University of Kent
Kent, UK
D.Atkins@kent.ac.uk

Abstract

A growing body of research exploits social media behaviors to gauge psychological characteristics, though *trait empathy* has received little attention. Because of its intimate link to the ability to relate to others, our research aims to predict participants' levels of empathy, given their textual and friending behaviors on Facebook. Using Poisson regression, we compared the variance explained in Davis' *Interpersonal Reactivity Index* (IRI) scores on four constructs (empathic concern, personal distress, fantasy, perspective taking), by two classes of variables: 1) post *content* and 2) *linguistic style*. Our study lays the groundwork for a greater understanding of empathy's role in facilitating interactions on social media.

1   Introduction

Empathy is an important component of social cognition that contributes to one's ability to understand and respond to the emotions of others, to succeed in emotional communication, and to promote pro-social behavior (Spreng, 2009). We explore the correlations between participants' levels of the various types of trait empathy, and their digital traces at Facebook, representing social media activities. To date, empathy has received little attention from social media and human factors researchers. Some work has been done toward understanding "empathic design" of online support communities (Brennan, Moore, & Smyth, 1991), (Tetzlaff, 1997), (Brennan & Ripich, 1994). However, surprisingly, empathy in social media in the context of day-to-day conversations or messaging has not been well studied.

In this work, we conceptualize empathy as a trait, operationalizing it within the context of our study. In the next subsections, we highlight the intimate relationship between empathy, communication, and friendship patterns, and present hypotheses to be tested. Finally, we explain why users' writing patterns are expected to provide a source of information with respect to their underlying levels of empathy, detailing our hypotheses of interest. We test these hypotheses by fitting the Poisson regression model with each IRI score as the outcome variable and a set of explanatory variables suitable for each hypothesis.

1.1   Davis' IRI

Davis' IRI (Davis, 1983) is a measure of trait empathy that considers a set of four distinct but related constructs. Each of the four subscales of the IRI—empathic concern (EC), fantasy subscale (FS), perspective taking (PT) and personal distress (PD)—was assessed with seven items on a five-point Likert

This work is licensed under a Creative Commons Attribution 4.0 International License. License details:
http://creativecommons.org/licenses/by/4.0/

Proceedings of the Workshop on Computational Modeling of People's Opinions, Personality, and Emotions in Social Media,
pages 128–137, Osaka, Japan, December 12 2016.

scale (1 = *does not describe me well* to 5 = *describes me very well*). The subscales that pertain to cognitive dimensions of empathy are the FS and the PT subscale. They measure the tendency to get caught up in fictional stories and imagine oneself in the same situations as fictional characters, and the tendency to take the psychological point of view of others, respectively. The EC and PD subscales measure the affective dimensions of empathy. Specifically, the EC measures sympathy and concern for others and is typically considered as an other-oriented emotional response in which attention is directed to the person in distress (Schroeder, et al, 1988). The PD scale considers a self-oriented emotional response in which attention is directed at one's negative emotions of distress and the reduction of these negative emotions. The IRI has demonstrated good intra-scale and test-retest reliability, and convergent validity is indicated by correlations with other established empathy scales (Davis, 1983).

1.2 Empathy in Social Media

Scholars such as Rogers (2003) have noted the abilities of highly empathic individuals to influence the opinions of others. This could also be the case in the context of social media, although it is unclear whether or not measures such as an individual's network size and frequency and types of activities could reflect this. On Facebook in particular, establishing a friendship is a mutual decision, meaning that both sides must confirm it in order to be connected. Intuitively, we can say that the creation of a "friendship" on Facebook is an indication that individuals are open to sharing with others. A previous study performed on a large and diverse dataset of Facebook participants in Bachrach et al. (2012) found significant relationships between their personality traits and the size and density of their friendship network, and their activity online. Kang and Lerman (2015) explored user effort and content diversity in social networks, with a commentary on cognitive constraints in social network activity. Given that little work on empathy in the social media literature, we found it necessary to establish the baseline relationship (if any) between network size, activity, and trait empathy.

H1a: The size of one's friendship network is correlated to her levels of empathy.

H1b: A user's level of activity (i.e., amount of written text) is correlated to her levels of empathy.

While level of activity depends on one's network size, there is also reason to believe that in some cases, people with smaller networks may engage actively with their close friends, thus producing higher levels of activity than those with a larger network. Therefore, we also examine the relationship between level of activity and empathy.

1.3 Empathy and writing patterns

The widespread use of writing therapy by psychologists (Pennebaker, 1997) confirms the tight relationship between writing characteristics and aspects of the self, such as empathy. We believe that the level of one's empathy influences one's writing. Therefore, we analyzed written content (in the form of posts and comments) in order to distinguish between users with different levels of empathy. Previous research (Pennebaker and King, 1999), (Mairesse and Walker, 2008) concluded that linguistic style is an independent and meaningful way of exploring personality and there is a strong correlation between language dimensions, measured by the Linguistic Inquiry and Word Count (LIWC), and personality factors. Our analysis focuses on LIWC Psychological (i.e., content) and Linguistic (i.e., style) measures (see Table 2), to test the following hypotheses:

H2a: Users whose social media texts express more socially oriented content are more empathic.

H2b: Users whose social media texts exhibit linguistic styles that engage others are more empathic.

2   Methodology

2.1   Data collection and preprocessing

We developed a Facebook application ("app") in order to carry out the following phases of our data collection: capturing each participant's digital traces during the previous 30 months, and administering a standardized test that measures different types of trait empathy. We analyzed participants' levels of trait empathy using Davis' IRI.[1]

The app captured participants' profile (upon their agreement), including the full list of their Facebook friends. In addition, the app tracked users' recent social activities: with whom and how frequently they interacted through "likes," "shares," and "comments" to others' posts. Then, the participant was prompted to complete the IRI. The participant could also invite friends to complete the survey and become new participants. As such, we employed an opportunistic sampling and snowballing method. Table 1 describes attributes that were collected while Figure 1 depicts the app flowchart.

In order to describe participants' language behaviors, we considered all textual communication (i.e., posts on one's own Facebook wall and comments left on the walls of others) that occurred during the previous 30 months. We used LIWC, which analyzes a text by counting word occurrences in psychologically meaningful categories such as negative versus positive emotion, or social versus cognitive processes (Pennebaker, Francis, & Booth, 2001). At the same time, LIWC computes attributes of linguistic style (e.g., the use of punctuation, the extent to which first-, second-, and third-person pronouns are used), otherwise known as stylometric features (Brizan, et al, 2015). Each participant's set of texts was processed using LIWC, in order to obtain scores on six psychological (i.e., content) measures, described in Table 2, and ten linguistic (i.e., style) measures. The style features included the participant's total word count and the mean number of words per post. Finally, we considered the proportion of words used belonging to each of the following categories: pronouns, verbs, adverbs, auxiliary (i.e., "helping") verbs, quantifiers, numbers, swearing, and punctuation.

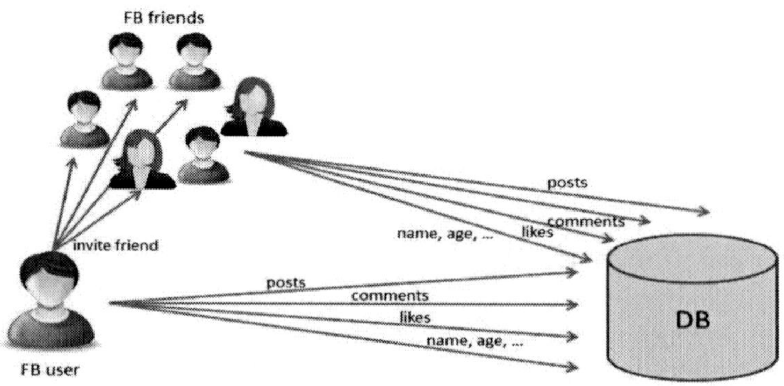

Figure 1: Data collection and system flowchart.

Table 1: Data collected via Facebook application.

Type	Attributes
Profile attributes	Location, Gender, Age
Analyzed profile attributes	Number of friends, Number of likes received from friends, Number of words of the comments received from friends
Trait Empathy Results	IRI Scores: Empathic Concern (EC), Fantasy Scale (FS), Perspective Taking (PT), Personal Distress (PD)

---

[1] The study was approved by the University of Kent's research ethics committee.

Table 2: LIWC Categories used to process participants' textual communications.

	LIWC category	Explanation	Key words (examples)
Psychological Processes / Content	Social processes	Communication related to family, friends, people	Daughter, husband, friend, neighbor, baby, boy, talk
	Affective processes	Positive or negative emotions, anger, sadness, anxiety, joy excitement	Love, sweet, happy, cried, ugly, nasty, hate, kill, annoy
	Cognitive mechanisms	Communication related to thought and reasoning	Think, know, consider, cause, should, would, guess
	Perceptual processes	Language describing observations and senses	Hear, feel, view, see, touch, listen
	Biological processes	Communication describing bodily functions	Eat, blood, pain, hands, spit, clinic, love, eat
	Relativity	Language describing motion, space, time	Area, bend, exit, arrive, go, down

2.1.1 Participants

A total of 334 Facebook users participated in the study. In the current analysis, we considered only the users who posted in English, such that their traces could be analyzed via LIWC, and who completed the IRI. We also restricted the dataset to include only individuals whose profiles indicated that they were 65 years old or younger. This was to ensure the integrity of the data. We did not filter short posts and did not distinguish between users using few words and ones using many words.

After applying the aforesaid restrictions, a total of 202 complete profiles were available for the analysis. Of these, 167 participants (82.7%) were female, with mean and median ages of 39.3 and 36.0 years, respectively. This gender imbalance can likely be attributed to the manner by which we incentivized participation. It is well established that there are gender-based differences with respect to empathy. Specifically, women reportedly score higher than men on all four subscales of the IRI (Davis, 1980). Therefore, in our analyses, we included gender as a control variable.

As expected, the distributions of the total number of friends as well as two measures of attention received from others (the number of likes received and the number of words commented on users' posts) were skewed to the right. The mean and median numbers of friends among participants were 304.1 and 238.5, respectively, while the mean and median numbers of likes per post were 16.3 and 13.0, respectively. Participants received a mean of 636, and a median of 257 words, in the comments posted by their friends.

2.1.2 Trait empathy

We considered our participants' scores on the four IRI scales by gender, given that previous studies report salient gender differences. The non-parametric Wilcoxon test reveals that, compared to male participants, females score significantly higher on measures of empathic concern and fantasy. However, no significant gender differences were revealed with respect to perspective-taking and personal distress. These gender differences are somewhat in line with previous research that has reported greater trait empathy overall (i.e., all IRI subscales) among women (Davis, 1980). As mentioned, we retain gender as a control variable in our regression analyses.

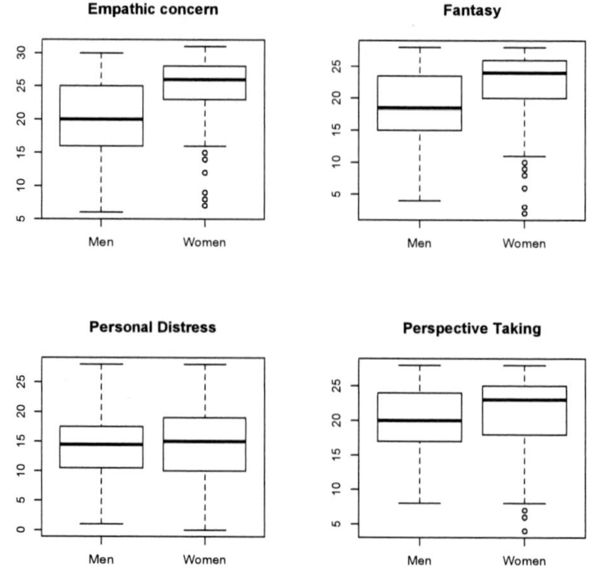

Figure 2: Distribution of IRI scores.

As shown in Figure 2, the median IRI scores for participants is as follows (men / women): EC (20 / 26), FS (18.5 / 24), PD (14.5 and 15), and PT (20 / 23).

2.2 Data analysis

In order to examine the relationship between users' Facebook behaviors and their trait empathy, we used Poisson regression models. Specifically, for each of the four IRI scores, we fit four models, in order to explore the explanatory power of four sets of variables:

- **Control**: Participant gender and age only;
- **Model 1**: The *content* of users' posts, namely, psychological processes exhibited in the text (social, affective, cognitive mechanisms, perception, biological, relativity);
- **Model 2**: The *linguistic style* of posts, namely, linguistic characteristics (total word count, words per post, pronouns, verbs, adverbs, auxiliary verbs, quantifiers, numbers, swearing, punctuation);
- **Model 3**: Measures of users' friendship network (namely, number of total friends and likes).

2.2.1 Poisson regression model

The Poisson regression model is a type of Generalized Linear Model (GLM). Such models use the logarithm link function in order to correlate the model predictors (explanatory variables) to the outcome variable, which is an expected frequency (incidence). In our case, the outcome variable is the IRI score, which ranges from 0 to 28 for each of the four subscales. The estimation of the Poisson models was conducted using the R statistical computing package[2]. For each of the models, we estimate the parameter and statistical significance of each explanatory variable. In addition, we gauged the degree to which the variance in the dependent variable (i.e., the level of empathy as measured by the relevant IRI score) is explained by the set of explanatory variables. To this end, we use Mittlböck's adjusted R^2, which is appropriate for evaluating Poisson regression models (Mittlböck, 2002).

---

[2] http://cran.r-project.org

3 Results and discussion

Table 3 shows that gender is correlated to three subscales of empathy. Specifically, female participants display higher levels of empathic concern, fantasy, and personal distress. Age is negatively correlated to the level of personal distress. In all three cases, the control variables do not explain a good deal of variance in the IRI scores. In the case of empathic concern, gender alone explains 13% of the variability (i.e., the R^2 of the model with gender as the only explanatory variable is 0.13).

Table 3: Model with control variables.

	Empathic concern	Fantasy	Perspective taking	Personal distress
Intercept	**2.9475*****	**3.0311*****	**2.9163*****	**3.0239*****
Gender	**0.1884****	**0.1864*****	0.05642	**0.1364****
Age	**0.002893***	-0.001945	0.003057	**-0.01181*****
R^2	0.1573	0.05931	0.03023	0.08097

***p-value < .001; *p-value < 0.1

Focusing on the model that includes the content of users' posts, we see an improvement in the explanatory power of our Poisson model for each of the four subscales of empathy (over the control model), as can be seen from Table 4. However, the most significant improvements are for EC and PT. Gender and social psychological processes in users' text account for just over 20% of the variance in EC score. In particular, female participants and those whose posts are more social (i.e., make references to people, friends and family) tend to score higher on the empathy scale of the IRI. This is expected, given that a user's attentional focus when using social processes within their text is likely to be oriented to others, which is encapsulated in the other-oriented empathic concern subscale. Likewise, the social and perception processes are significant correlates of the PT score. PT is a measure of the dispositional ability to consider the perspective of others.

Table 4: Model 1 - The content of users' posts.

	Empathic concern	Fantasy	Perspective taking	Personal distress
Intercept	**2.8755*****	**2.9714*****	**2.8797*****	**3.0160*****
Gender	**0.1513*****	**0.1614*****	0.02087	**0.1375****
Age	0.001361	-0.002870	0.001579	**-0.01210*****
Social	**0.008304***	0.003043	**0.007709***	-0.006554
Affect	-0.001940	0.0009739	-0.0007692	0.004469
Cogmech	0.0008126	0.0008076	-0.001549	-0.002789
Percept	0.01296	0.001750	**0.03029****	-0.01173
Bio	-0.002502	**0.02334***	-0.01211	0.008979
Relativ	0.002555	-0.001853	0.001692	0.007410
R^2	0.2051	0.08630	0.08241	0.09080

***p-value < .001; **p-value < .01; *p-value < 0.05

Thus, using language relating to social processes would likely enable users to take the perspective of others; they need information about their communication partner to take their perspective. Unsurprisingly, language referring to perceptual processes significantly correlates to trait PT. In order to take the perspective of another (i.e., to understand the issues, thoughts, and feelings of others) one needs to use perceptual processes. That said, the effect sizes are rather small to draw any definitive conclusions regarding the *H2a*.

Table 5 shows that for all four subscales of empathy, adding the stylistic characteristics of users' texts increases the proportion of variance explained. Interestingly, the use of auxiliary verbs significantly correlates to both greater cognitive and affective empathy (i.e., all IRI subscales), while pronouns significantly correlate to FS and PT. The fact that the number of words per post is significantly correlated to greater PD could refer to a need to express oneself (e.g., an opinion, complaint or need). However, the fact that the word counts of the participant's posts or comments are not correlated to other empathy measures approves that, in general, ***H1b*** is not supported.

A possible explanation can be found in Bachrach et al (2012)'s work, where all Big Five personality traits have demonstrated correlation to the activity level of users in Facebook, expressed by number of likes, uploaded photos, statuses, and more. It was found that extroverts are more likely to reach out and interact with other people on Facebook. Given that word counts of posts or comments are also self-generated content, it is arguably possible that a greater volume of written words is reflective of a more extroverted personality trait. However, there is no direct correlation between empathy and extraversion trait (Magalhães et al., 2012).

Table 5: Model 2 - The linguistic style of posts.

	Empathic concern	Fantasy	Perspective taking	Personal distress
Intercept	**2.962***	**2.969***	**2.867***	**2.990***
Gender	**0.1291**	**0.1355**	0.005643	**0.1482**
Age	0.002012	**-0.002920***	0.002114	**-0.01200***
Word count	-0.00003474	0.00004009	0.000007792	-0.00009535
Words per post	0.0005015	-0.000005146	-0.00002968	**0.002625**
Pronouns	0.004271	**0.007317***	**0.006648***	**-0.005947***
Verbs	-0.007095	**-0.01249***	-0.002170	-0.003509
Adverbs	-0.008531	0.007475	-0.002882	-0.001027
Aux verbs	**0.01662***	**0.01543***	**0.01538***	**0.02764**
Quantifiers	0.002737	-0.0007620	**-0.03161**	**-0.04031***
Numbers	0.002383	**0.02999***	0.006492	**0.05199***
Swearing	-0.008739	-0.008929	-0.04189	0.01032
Punctuation	**-0.0006776***	-0.0003195	0.000008210	-0.00004612
R^2	0.2540	0.1146	0.1009	0.1376

***p-value < .001; **p-value < .01; *p-value < 0.1

We observed a number of correlations between linguistic styles and empathy measures. Importantly, the use of pronouns is positively correlated with PT and FS, but negatively correlated with PD. The regular use of pronouns might indicate that a user is switching perspectives frequently within a session, which would in turn exercise perspective taking skills. Although communication partners are real, as opposed to a character in a novel, there is still a barrier between the user and his or her communication partner because they are not physically face-to-face. In a sense, this type of communication is surreal and may require some fantasy. Interestingly, the use of auxiliary verbs such as am, will, or have, is positively correlated with all empathy measures. Auxiliary verbs add functional meaning to the clause in which the auxiliary verb appears and thus can express tense and emphasis among other meanings. Therefore, these words function to create a more vivid sense of an action, which consequently would exercise more mental imagery. The use of our mental imagination capacities is inherent in the FS and PT subscales.

Further, greater words per post significantly correlating to greater personal distress could refer to a need to express oneself. Feelings of personal distress are uncomfortable and someone who is distressed has a reason that has evoked negative feelings in the first place. In the digital domain, one way of alleviating the distress would be to write about one's feelings as a cathartic exercise, or perhaps to express their point if in an argument or debate; both would likely require more words to achieve.
In sum, it is safe to say that users with varying levels of empathy do exhibit different linguistic styles when communicating in social media. Therefore, the results of our analysis support ***H2b***.
The number of available cases to fit model 3 was reduced to 169 participants (from 202), because some of the data regarding friends of participants could not be collected (most likely because it was protected by the respective Facebook users).

134

The total number of likes and comments received on posts, as well as number of friends were used in order to examine the relationship between these measures and empathy. As can be seen in Table 6, the number of likes on one's posts and total number of friends were not correlated to any of the four types of empathy. The volume of comments (measured as the total number of words of the comments) on one's posts is weakly correlated to PD, although the direction of the relationship is negative.
Therefore, we can conclude that **H1a** is not supported; network size alone is not a clear signal of an empathic personality.

A possible explanation of this finding might be that participants use Facebook to manage a large number of "weak ties" (people from different social circles) while still maintaining closer relationship with a smaller number of friends (see (Marsden 1987) and (Putnam 2001) for details). However, without quantifying the nature (weak vs strong) of each Facebook friend, we cannot test this explanation.
Still another possibility is the link between network size and narcissism, which is negatively correlated to empathy (see (Mehdizadeh, 2013) and (Buffardi and Campbell, 2008) for more explanations).

Table 6: Model 3 - Measures of user activity and interactions with friends.

	Empathic concern	Fantasy	Perspective taking	Personal distress
Intercept	**2.9638***	**3.0123***	**2.9443***	**2.9117***
Gender	**0.1953***	**0.1792***	0.06689	**0.08796***
Age	0.001214	-0.001493	0.001394	**-0.006859***
Friends	-0.003352	-0.002132	0.002311	-0.014941
Likes	0.007440	-0.009567	-0.004216	0.01942
R^2	0.1375	0.05622	0.01861	0.05250

***p-value < .001; ** p-value < 0.01; *p-value < 0.05

4 Conclusions and future work

Given the unprecedented scale of human connectivity realized through social media, with unforeseeable consequences on a global scale, it is timely to study the relationship of online interactions with such an important human characteristic as empathy. In this paper, we explored correlations between multiple behavioral cues on social media and empathy. We considered a snapshot of a user's Facebook data, collected over a given time interval, to understand how different behavioral cues correlate to the user's levels of empathy. In other words, we explore how other Facebook users might form impressions about someone's level of empathy based on his or her behavior. The main focus and novelty of our study was to explore whether the writing characteristics can describe the user in terms of empathy.

We learned that the relationship between participants' social media behaviors, friendships and interactions with others, and their levels of trait empathy is rather complex. While we began with hypotheses grounded in previous literature, we observed some unexpected correlations. In particular, it appears to be the case that not all interactions are equal; it is likely that simple traces of interaction such as "likes" and "commenting" may tell us different things about an individual's willingness and ability to engage others. Future work could probe deeper in order to understand how and why users exhibiting relatively high and low levels of empathy engage "the other".

We also generated some ideas for future work, including experimenting with more targeted linguistic features (such as modal and hypothetical verbs); using syntactic structure for a more complex measurement of style; building a cross-validated predictive model; analysis of other traits, e.g. narcissism, big five (BF) personality (and considering empathy as an aspect of agreeableness from the BF personality traits); distinguishing between friendship, acquaintances, and incidental/semi-random FB connections in our model; considering how empathy relates to the care/harm dimension of moral foundations theory; and exploring trolling (Buckels et al., 2014) as an opposite of empathy.

In summary, this paper has highlighted a few interesting research directions: the relationship between social media activities, communication patterns, and the human characteristic of empathy. Future work must focus on recruiting a larger sample of participants in order to obtain a more balanced representation of different cultural groups as well as gender representation. In addition, the study can be extended to inter-group interactions based on social classes, religions, nationality, and so on. An in depth understanding of inter-group interaction online and its relationship to empathy is an important direction of research, and would potentially provide insights to those who design social technology that would facilitate positive intergroup interactions, thus creating a more empathic online environment.

Acknowledgements

The authors would like to thank project students from the Software Engineering department of the Shamoon College of Engineering—Yoel Feuermann, Shahar Rotshtein, Sergey Sobolevsky, and Andrey Kozlov—for implementing the FB app, collecting and processing the dataset, and further technical support.
The authors also would like to thank the efforts of the three anonymous reviewers in providing thorough feedback on this work. In particular, we would like to acknowledge their suggestions for several interesting future directions, which are mentioned in the conclusion of the paper.

References

Bachrach, Y., Kosinski, M., Graepel, T., Kohli, P., and Stillwell, D. (2012). Personality and Patterns of Facebook Usage. In Proceedings of ACM Web Sciences 2012.

Brennan, P. F., Moore, S. M., & Smyth, K. A. (1991). ComputerLink: Electronic support for the home caregiver. Advances in Nursing Science , 13 (4), 14-27.

Brennan, P. and Ripich, S. (1994). Use of a homecare computer network by persons with AIDS. International Journal of Technology Assessment in Health Care , 10 (2), 258-272.

Brizan, D. G., Goodkind, A., Koch, P., Balagani, K., Phoha, V., & Rosenberg, A. (2015). Utilizing linguistically enhanced keystroke dynamics to predict typist cognition and demographics. International Journal of Human-Computer Studies , 82, 57-68.

Buckels, E. E., Trapnell, P. D., Paulhus, D. L. (2014). Trolls just want to have fun. Personality and individual Differences, 67, 97-102.

Buffardi, L. E. and Campbell, W. K. (2008). Narcissism and social networking websites. Personality and Social Psychology Bulletin , 34, 1303-1324.

Davis, M. H. (1980). A multidimensional approach to individual differences in empathy. JSAS Catalog of Selected Documents in Psychology , 85.

Davis, M. H. (1983). Measuring individual differences in empathy: Evidence for a multidimensional approach. Journal of Personality and Social Psychology , 44 (1), 113-126.

Kang, J-H and Lerman, K. (2015). User Effort and Network Structure Mediate Access to Information in Networks. arXiv preprint arXiv:1504.01760.

Mairesse, F. and Walker, M.A. (2008). Trainable Generation of Big-Five Personality Styles through Data-driven Parameter Estimation. In Proceedings of ACL-08: HLT, 165–173

Marsden, P.V. (1987). Core discussion networks of Americans. American Sociological Review, 122–131.

Magalhães E, Costa P, Costa M. J. (2012). Empathy of medical students and personality: evidence from the Five-Factor Model. Med Teach. 34(10), 807-812.

Mehdizadeh, S. (2013). Self-Presentation 2.0: Narcissism and Self-Esteem on Facebook. Cyberpsychology, Behavior, and Social Networking , 13 (4), 357-364.

Mittlböck, M. (2002). Caculating adjusted R2 measures for Poisson regression models. Computer Methods and Programs in Biomedicine , 68, 205-214.

Pennebaker, J. W. (1997). Writing about emotional experiences as a therapeutic process. Psychological Science , 8 (3), 162-166.

Pennebaker, J. W., King, L. A. (1999). Linguistic styles: Language use as an individual difference. Journal of Personality and Social Psychology, 77(6), 1296-1312.

Pennebaker, J., Francis, M., Booth, R. (2001). Linguistic Inquiry and Word Count (LIWC): LIWC 2001. Mahwah, NJ, USA: Erlbaum.

Putnam, R.D. Bowling alone: The collapse and revival of American community. Simon and Schuster, New York, 2001.

Rogers, E. (2003). The Diffusion of Innovations. New York: Free Press.

Schroeder, D. A., Dovidio, J. F., Sibicky, M. E., Matthews, L. L., & Allen, J. L. (1988). Empathy and helping behavior: Egoism or altruism. Journal of Experimental Social Psychology , 24, 333-353.

Spreng, R. M. (2009). The Toronto empathy questionnaire: Scale development and initial validation of a factor-analytic solution to multiple empathy measures. Journal of Personality Assessment , 91 (1), 62-71.

Tetzlaff, L. (1997). Consumer informatics in chronic illness. Journal of the American Medical Informatics Association , 4 (4), 285-299.

The Challenges of Multi-dimensional Sentiment Analysis
Across Languages

Emily Öhman and **Timo Honkela** and **Jörg Tiedemann**
University of Helsinki
`firstname.lastname@helsinki.fi`

Abstract

This paper outlines a pilot study on multi-dimensional and multilingual sentiment analysis of social media content. We use parallel corpora of movie subtitles as a proxy for colloquial language in social media channels and a multilingual emotion lexicon for fine-grained sentiment analyses. Parallel data sets make it possible to study the preservation of sentiments and emotions in translation and our assessment reveals that the lexical approach shows great inter-language agreement. However, our manual evaluation also suggests that the use of purely lexical methods is limited and further studies are necessary to pinpoint the cross-lingual differences and to develop better sentiment classifiers.

1   Introduction

Typically, sentiment analysis is modeled as a three-class classification task, marking utterances as either positive, negative or neutral. In some cases, this may be accompanied with a degree of polarity. However, that still treats the task as a one-dimensional one along the scale of general polarity. In this paper, we look at the challenge of a multi-dimensional approach in which we aim at a much more fine-grained classifications with eight distinct dimensions of emotion in addition to the classical sentiments of positive and negative polarity. These emotions are based on Plutchik's wheel of emotions (see Figure 1): anger, anticipation, disgust, fear, joy, sadness, surprise, and trust (Plutchik, 1980). Detecting fine-grained sentiment is important for practical applications as well as for theoretical reasons. In the context of social media, it is useful to know whether someone is, for instance, happy, angry or sad, rather than relying solely on positive or negative sentiments. This can be applied, for instance, for the detection of hate-speech or depression and can be used to monitor peoples well-being or social dynamics.

As sentiment analysis methods are often developed for English first and other languages second, it is necessary to know whether it is possible to transfer tools and resources from English to other languages to speed up the coverage of the linguistic diversity in the World. With the growing importance of social media in societal issues, as a marketing tool, opinion generator, and so forth, it is essential to be able to accurately classify sentiments and emotions also for languages other than English. For those reasons, we, therefore, focus on cross-lingual methods and multi-dimensional settings.

Previous work has focused on lexical approaches using indicator word lists that define cues for detecting certain types of sentiment. In our work, we are interested in studying the effectiveness of these purely lexical approaches and we emphasize their use across languages. We have previously conducted research on multidimensional sentiment analysis (Honkela et al., 2014) but not across language borders. Multilingual studies for conventional sentiment analysis have been done, e.g., for English and German by Denecke (2008) but not with the fine-grained multidimensional analysis. Other related studies using Plutchik's eight emotions are for example the Rule-based Emission Model by Tromp and Pechenizkiy (2014) and EmoTwitter which takes advantage of the NRC Word-Emotion Association Lexicon to produce visualizations for identifying enduring sentiments in tweets (Munezero et al., 2015).

This work is licensed under a Creative Commons Attribution 4.0 International License. License details: http://creativecommons.org/licenses/by/4.0/

Proceedings of the Workshop on Computational Modeling of People's Opinions, Personality, and Emotions in Social Media,
pages 138–142, Osaka, Japan, December 12 2016.

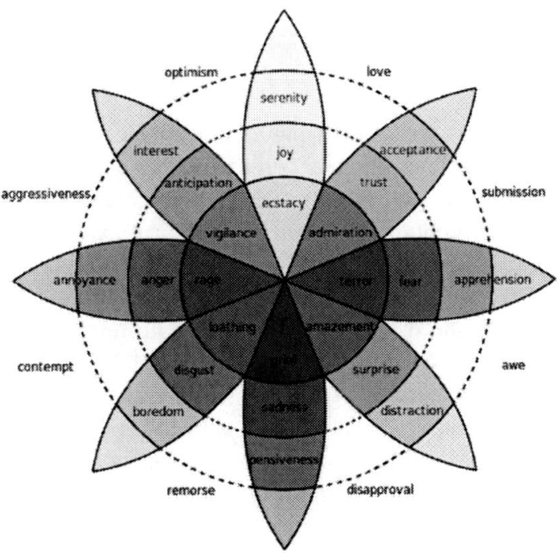

Figure 1: Plutchik's wheel of emotions [1]

One of the main research question we ask in our study is whether fine-grained sentiment and emotions are preserved across languages. Studies directly evaluating the preservation of sentiments in translation have often focused on comparing them with other methods such as whether it is better to translate the original text to English and analyze the English sentiments or to translate the lexicon from English to the "original" target language (work on Arabic (Salameh et al., 2015) and Chinese (Wan, 2008)). One study found that connotations change if texts are machine translated or manually translated and suggested that "further cross-lingual studies should not use parallel corpora to project annotations blindly" (Carpuat, 2015).

Related work does not provide a full picture of sentiment preservation in translation and we are interested in additional investigations with other data sets and setups. In particular, we would like to understand more clearly how sentiment preservation applies to the multidimensional task and whether there are differences between cases of similar versus less-related languages. For this purpose, we use lexicon-based methods and parallel data sets as a proxy for multilingual sentiment analyses on comparable texts. We also test the reliability of the purely lexical sentiment detection strategy using a small-scale manual evaluation.

The essential research questions we would like to ask are, hence, the following:

- To what extent is fine-grained sentiment preserved in translation? Are there differences between languages and their cultural embeddings?

- How reliable are purely lexical approaches in detecting multi-dimensional sentiments and emotions across languages?

To address the first question, we performed a small scale manual evaluation of movie subtitles to measure the correlation between detected sentiments in aligned subtitles. Using this set of manually classified utterances we then estimate the expected preservation of sentiment across specific language pairs. Finally, using those expectations we can measure the correlation with the automatic classification based on lexical look-up across languages to address our second question.

In the following, we first briefly describe the data sets and resources used in our study. Thereafter, we describe the manual evaluation of sentiment across languages and, finally, we discuss the results of

---

[1]Source: https://en.wikipedia.org/wiki/Contrasting_and_categorization_of_emotions

automatic multi-dimensional sentiment classification based on an existing lexical resource. We conclude with our main findings and prospects for future research.

2 Multilingual Data Resources

For our cross-lingual experiments we rely on publicly available parallel data sets. OPUS[2] provides large quantities of sentence-aligned multilingual corpora including a comprehensive collection of movie subtitles in various languages (Lison and Tiedemann, 2016). Movies certainly contain a lot of emotional contents and their predominantly colloquial style makes them a good proxy for social media data we aim at with our multidimensional sentiment analyzer.

As a comparison data set, we selected the Europarl parallel corpus (Tiedemann, 2012). Europarl represents a different genre and the translations come from professional sources, whereas the subtitle translations contain a much larger quantity of noise (due to the unreliability of user-generated / user-provided content, incomplete data sets as well as conversion and alignment errors). We are thus able to compare two different quality-levels of translation as well besides the comparison of two dissimilar genres. In both cases, we used 1.5 million lines of aligned sentences from the parallel corpora for each language, which we lemmatized using the Turku Finnish Dependency Parser for Finnish (Ginter et al., 2013) and UDPipe (Straka et al., 2016) for all other languages.

The emotion lexicon we apply is called the NRC Word-Emotion Association Lexicon (Mohammad and Turney, 2013). The lexicon is a list of originally English words and their crowd-sourced associations with Plutchik's eight basic emotions and two sentiments (Plutchik, 1980). The words have been translated by the creators of the lexicon using Google Translate. The number of annotated words per language vary between 4,043 and 14,182. We also translated the remaining words for the target languages in the same way bringing the total number of annotated words to 14,182 for all languages. The translation results were checked and, for the target languages, no clear translation errors were found making the full lexicon at least as good as the original version.

3 Multilingual Fine-Grained Sentiment Classification

In the following, we look at a purely lexicon-based approach to fine-grained sentiment analyses using the multilingual emotion lexicon presented in the previous section. For this, all lines in our data set are matched one-by-one with the items in the lexicon. The result of this process is a 10-dimensional vector for each line containing the counts of matched words that represent the sentiment or emotion of that particular dimension according to the lexicon. We can interpret the vectors in two different ways: (i) Any non-zero count indicates the presence of the sentiment in question (binarized interpretation), or, (ii) the counts represent the prevalence of the corresponding sentiments and emotions.

We can now measure the cross-lingual correlation between the sentiments detected by the lexicon-based approach by comparing the vectors created for each of the 1.5 million lines in each translation. We do this for both, the subtitle corpus and the Europarl corpus by means of individual emotions and sentiments and by means of a multidimensional comparison. For the former we apply the binarized interpretation and compute the percentage of matching sentiments detected across language borders. Table 1 lists the scores for each test case. Note that we discard all zero-score matches where no sentiment was detected in either language. This applies to the majority of lines and, therefore, would blur the picture.

The scores in the table show that for English-Finnish the subtitle data is more likely to match across languages than the Europarl data. For all the other pairs, this trend is reversed for all emotions and sentiments.

The most common emotions in the texts were the same for all languages: negative, positive, then fairly similar for trust, disgust, anger, fear, joy, sadness, and generally much lower for anticipation and surprise. This is most likely related to the higher cross-language agreement for these emotions: the more common a sentiment, the more chances of one language detecting it but it being missed by the other and therefore decreasing the cross-language agreement score.

---

[2]http://opus.lingfil.uu.se

Language	Emotion / Sentiment										
	pos.:	neg.:	anger:	anticip.:	disg.:	fear:	joy:	sad.:	surpr.:	trust:	ALL
Language	Movie Subtitles										
EN-FI	.6051	.4535	.7507	.8299	.7761	.7818	.8364	.7766	.8964	.7471	$0.752^{\pm0.232}$
EN-SV	.5709	.4744	.7897	.8310	.7817	.7948	.7710	.7865	.8922	.7631	$0.802^{\pm0.220}$
ES-PT	.6186	.4912	.7964	.8419	.8119	.7715	.8749	.7299	.9248	.8251	$0.746^{\pm0.231}$
Language	EuroParl										
EN-FI	.5670	.4613	.7733	.8138	.7839	.7805	.8240	.7755	.8914	.7434	$0.788^{\pm0.241}$
EN-SV	.3219	.4028	.7148	.6590	.7420	.6605	.7314	.6902	.7888	.4851	$0.665^{\pm0.213}$
ES-PT	.4172	.4480	.6849	.6934	.7815	.6783	.7352	.6501	.8278	.5570	$0.692^{\pm0.178}$
AVG:	.5168	.4552	.7516	.7782	.7795	.7446	.7955	.7348	.8702	.6868	

Table 1: Percentage of matched sentiments across languages according to lexicon-based classification. *ALL* refers to the averaged cosine similarity of the 10-dimensional sentiment vectors and the number in superscript gives the standard deviation observed in the data.

The cosine similarity scores indicate that the Finnish and English vectors are most dissimilar, with only slightly higher similarity scores for the English-Swedish pair. The Spanish-Portuguese scores, however, show higher similarity scores than either of the other two languages. One is tempted to conclude that this illustrates the cultural influences that determine the expressions of sentiments and emotions but we have to take these preliminary results with a grain of salt also based on the manual evaluation presented below, which indicates that purely lexicon-based methods are not reliable enough.

4 Manual Evaluation

In order to test the reliability of the lexicon-based method, we conducted a small scale manual evaluation on the same data set. For this, we randomly selected 100 lines of the aligned texts and annotated them by hand using Plutchik's eight emotions as well as their positive and negative sentiments.

	pos.:	neg.:	anger:	antic.:	disgust:	fear:	joy:	sad.:	surpr.:	trust:	AVG	COS
EN-FI	.923	.846	1.000	.897	.821	.923	1.000	.949	.872	.897	.913	.983
EN-SV	.909	.848	.970	.909	.788	.970	.970	.939	1.000	1.000	.930	.976

Table 2: Hand-annotation sentiment agreement across languages

Each line corresponds to one or more sentences from within a translation unit and we also considered previous and subsequent context for deciding proper classifications. We restricted ourselves to binary choices when marking one or more of the ten dimensions. Using scales for such human annotation would be an interesting extension that we would like to explore in future work. Each line was classified by two annotators and a third annotator was consulted in case of disagreement between the two.

As Table 2 shows, the manual annotation reveals that cross-language agreement is high for both language pairs and all emotions and sentiments. Using the manual annotation as gold standard we then computed precision and recall of the automatic classification. To our surprise (especially with respect to precision), both mesaures are extremely low (below 10%) for all emotions and sentiments. However, this may be caused due to the overall scarcity of emotions and our little data set in general. In order to understand better the true precision and recall of the automatic classification as compared to the hand-annotated data-set it would, of course, be highly beneficial to have a larger sample of hand-annotated data.

5 Conclusions and Discussions

The study of multilingual social media corpora is important as it provides, for instance, a possibility to compare how people in different parts of the world view various topics.

There is clearly a use for good lexicons in sentiment analysis. The extent to which these are utilized and the quality of the lexicon, especially if translated, is what influences the cross-language agreement ratings the most.

As the results show, a purely lexicon-based approach can tell us about the sentiments and emotions in a text, but that it is not as good as a gold standard. In this pilot study we can see that Spanish and Portuguese have higher cross-language agreement than English and Finnish, or English and Swedish. In the future it would be interesting to compare languages that are culturally more different such as English and Chinese, or English and Arabic or Japanese. This might reveal a clearer picture about the influence of cultural backgrounds on the expressions of emotions and sentiments in comparable texts.

With respect to our second research question, we are at this stage interested in how well lexical approaches are capable of detecting multidimensional sentiments using parallel data as a proxy for evaluation. For this, we assume that sentiments and emotions are preserved in translation and we verify this with a small-scale manual annotation. These initial results will guide us in future work to enhance the detection approach with more sophisticated methods based on supervised and semi-supervised machine learning techniques including cross-lingual representations and transfer models.

References

Marine Carpuat. 2015. Connotation in Translation. In Alexandra Balahur, Erik van der Goot, Piek Vossen, and Andrés Montoyo, editors, *WASSA@EMNLP*, pages 9–15. The Association for Computer Linguistics.

Kerstin Denecke. 2008. Using SentiWordNet for multilingual sentiment analysis. In *ICDE Workshops*, pages 507–512. IEEE Computer Society.

Filip Ginter, Jenna Nyblom, Veronika Laippala, Samuel Kohonen, Katri Haverinen, Simo Vihjanen, and Tapio Salakoski. 2013. Building a Large Automatically Parsed Corpus of Finnish. In Stephan Oepen, Kristin Hagen, and Janne Bondi Johannessen, editors, *NODALIDA*, volume 85 of *Linköping Electronic Conference Proceedings*, pages 291–300. Linköping University Electronic Press.

Timo Honkela, Jaakko Korhonen, Krista Lagus, and Esa Saarinen. 2014. Five-Dimensional Sentiment Analysis of Corpora, Documents and Words. In *Advances in Self-Organizing Maps and Learning Vector Quantization - Proceedings of the 10th International Workshop, WSOM 2014*, pages 209–218.

Pierre Lison and Jörg Tiedemann. 2016. OpenSubtitles2016: Extracting Large Parallel Corpora from Movie and TV Subtitles. In Nicoletta Calzolari, Khalid Choukri, Thierry Declerck, Sara Goggi, Marko Grobelnik, Bente Maegaard, Joseph Mariani, Hélène Mazo, Asunción Moreno, Jan Odijk, and Stelios Piperidis, editors, *LREC*. European Language Resources Association (ELRA).

Saif M. Mohammad and Peter D. Turney. 2013. Crowdsourcing a Word-Emotion Association Lexicon. 29(3):436–465.

Myriam Munezero, Calkin Suero Montero, Maxim Mozgovoy, and Erkki Sutinen. 2015. EmoTwitter - A Fine-Grained Visualization System for Identifying Enduring Sentiments in Tweets. In Alexander F. Gelbukh, editor, *CICLing (2)*, volume 9042 of *Lecture Notes in Computer Science*, pages 78–91. Springer.

Robert Plutchik. 1980. A general psychoevolutionary theory of emotion. *Theories of emotion*, 1:3–31.

Mohammad Salameh, Saif Mohammad, and Svetlana Kiritchenko. 2015. Sentiment after Translation: A Case-Study on Arabic Social Media Posts. In Rada Mihalcea, Joyce Yue Chai, and Anoop Sarkar, editors, *HLT-NAACL*, pages 767–777. The Association for Computational Linguistics.

Milan Straka, Jan Hajič, and Straková. 2016. UDPipe: Trainable Pipeline for Processing CoNLL-U Files Performing Tokenization, Morphological Analysis, POS Tagging and Parsing. In *Proceedings of the Tenth International Conference on Language Resources and Evaluation (LREC'16)*, Paris, France, May. European Language Resources Association (ELRA).

Jorg Tiedemann. 2012. Parallel Data, Tools and Interfaces in OPUS. In Nicoletta Calzolari (Conference Chair), Khalid Choukri, Thierry Declerck, Mehmet Ugur Dogan, Bente Maegaard, Joseph Mariani, Jan Odijk, and Stelios Piperidis, editors, *Proceedings of the Eight International Conference on Language Resources and Evaluation (LREC'12)*, Istanbul, Turkey, may. European Language Resources Association (ELRA).

Erik Tromp and Mykola Pechenizkiy. 2014. Rule-based Emotion Detection on Social Media: Putting Tweets on Plutchik's Wheel. *CoRR*, abs/1412.4682.

Xiaojun Wan. 2008. Using Bilingual Knowledge and Ensemble Techniques for Unsupervised Chinese Sentiment Analysis. In *Proceedings of the Conference on Empirical Methods in Natural Language Processing*, EMNLP '08, pages 553–561, Stroudsburg, PA, USA. Association for Computational Linguistics.

The Social Mood of News:
Self-reported Annotations to Design Automatic Mood Detection Systems

Firoj Alam, Fabio Celli, Evgeny A. Stepanov, Arindam Ghosh, and Giuseppe Riccardi
Department of Information Engineering and Computer Science,
University of Trento, Italy
{firoj.alam,fabio.celli,evgeny.stepanov,arindam.ghosh,giuseppe.riccardi}@unitn.it

Abstract

In this paper, we address the issue of automatic prediction of readers' mood from newspaper articles and comments. As online newspapers are becoming more and more similar to social media platforms, users can provide *affective* feedback, such as mood and emotion. We have exploited the self-reported annotation of mood categories obtained from the metadata of the Italian online newspaper *corriere.it* to design and evaluate a system for predicting five different mood categories from news articles and comments: indignation, disappointment, worry, satisfaction, and amusement. The outcome of our experiments shows that overall, bag-of-word-ngrams perform better compared to all other feature sets; however, stylometric features perform better for the mood score prediction of articles. Our study shows that self-reported annotations can be used to design automatic mood prediction systems.

1 Introduction and Background

Participating in social media has become a mainstream part of our daily lives – we read articles, comments, other people's statuses and provide feedback in terms of emotions through written content. Currently, newspapers are also being designed as social media platforms to facilitate users to provide their opinion along with emotional feedback. Since currently our social participation is mostly done through social media platforms, the online content, including social media and newspapers' content, is growing very rapidly. In (Turner et al., 2014) the authors estimate that by 2020 online content might reach 44 trillion gigabytes, including news articles and user generated content such as likes, dislikes, emotions, tastes, identities, and data collected by sensors (Liu, 2007).

Such increasing amount of digital data creates an unprecedented opportunities for businesses and individuals, as well as it poses new challenges to process and generate concrete summaries out of it. For example, everyday journalists need to deal with the large quantity of information whenever they need to prepare a historical/follow-up report or a summary from a large collection of documents. They might want to know how particular *topics* of a news are associated with *users' mood*. The importance of such studies and their use cases have also been reported in (Riccardi et al., 2015). The challenges include automatic processing of semi-structured or unstructured data in different dimensions such as linguistic style, interaction, sentiment, mood and other social signals. Finding the collective information of such signals requires automatic processing, which will be useful for various professionals, specifically psychologists and social and behavioral scientists. Among other affective dimensions, mood and sentiment are particularly important for the analysis the consumer behavior towards brands and products (Pang and Lee, 2008; Stieglitz and Dang-Xuan, 2013).

In the past few decades, the affective dimension of text has been mainly analyzed in terms of positive and negative polarity (Pak and Paroubek, 2010a; Kouloumpis et al., 2011; Cambria et al., 2016a), although more detailed dimensions are proven to be very useful. In particular, moods such as tension, depression, anger, vigor, fatigue, and confusion in tweets have been found to be good predictors of

---

This work is licensed under a Creative Commons Attribution 4.0 International Licence. Licence details:
http://creativecommons.org/licenses/by/4.0/.

Proceedings of the Workshop on Computational Modeling of People's Opinions, Personality, and Emotions in Social Media,
pages 143–152, Osaka, Japan, December 12 2016.

stock market exchanges (Bollen et al., 2011). It has also been demonstrated that it is possible to predict anger, sadness, and joy from LiveJournal blogs with performances up to 78% accuracy (Nguyen et al., 2010). Moreover, it is also possible to distinguish Twitter users who are likely to share content generating joy or amusement from the ones who are likely to share content generating sadness, anger or disappointment with an accuracy of around 61% (Celli et al., 2016). An increasing number of studies focuses on analyzing sentiment in terms of positive and negative polarity from a short text (microblog) (Akkaya et al., 2009; Paltoglou and Thelwall, 2010). From the automatic classification perspective, a research application SentiStrength utilizes a different source of information to assign a sentiment score to a short text (Thelwall et al., 2011; Stieglitz and Dang-Xuan, 2013). Such information includes word-list of sentiment, idioms, emoticons, negating words, linguistic rules and sentiment polarity classification algorithms.

To design automatic detection and classification systems a typical approach to generating reference annotation is to use either sentiment lexicon or automatic system (such as SentiStrength) (Bollen et al., 2011; Stieglitz and Dang-Xuan, 2013; Ferrara and Yang, 2015; Kim and Salehan, 2015), manual expert annotation *or* self-reported user annotation (Nguyen et al., 2014; Mishne and others, 2005). In (Cambria, 2016), the authors present a hybrid framework for sentiment analysis that includes a knowledge-based system and a machine learning module. Recent advances in knowledge-based NLP for sentiment analysis can be found in (Cambria et al., 2016b).

Self-reported mood annotation by the users of the blog posts has been previously addressed in (Go et al., 2009; Pak and Paroubek, 2010b; Pak and Paroubek, 2010b). In (Davidov et al., 2010), the authors use twitter hashtags as labels for designing an automatic classification system. A similar study has also been reported in (Kunneman et al., 2014). There are still many challenges in designing an automatic system using self-reported annotation because the annotations are not done in a consistent manner. Users annotate them based on their *self-perception*, and social media platforms are not designed following any psychological instruments or instructions. The obvious advantages of such annotations are that (1) they are cost-effective, and (2) they provide users' natural affective expressions.

In this work, our goal is to investigate whether such annotations can be useful for designing an automatic system. We investigate two different approaches to predict mood from articles and user comments: (1) regression to assign a score for *each mood category*, and (2) binary classification into a positive and negative mood. We comparatively evaluate the predictive power of different feature sets such as character, word, and part-of-speech ngrams, stylometric, and psycholinguistic features. Our study is in-line with the study presented in (Nguyen et al., 2014), where the authors investigate a different set of features along with different machine learning algorithms for feature selection and classification. However, our focus in on the prediction of mood on a continuous $[0..1]$ scale and the utilization of different sets of features. Moreover, we extract the feature from both articles and comments. Because text may contain a blend of emotional manifestations in separate parts, our goal is to obtain a fine-grained view on of a comment or an article in the form of 'emotional sphere'. Since mood can be expressed through certain idiosyncratic vocabulary and writing style, we make use of stylometric and psycholinguistic features.

The structure of the paper is as follows. In Section 2 we present the details of the data we use throughout experiments. Then, in Section 3 we report the experimental methodology, and in Section 3.2 the results of the experiments. Finally, discussions and conclusions appear in Sections 4 and 5, respectively.

2 Corpus

The data was collected from the most popular Italian daily newspapers – *Corriere della Sera*. The newspaper's web site is structured as a social media platform (Boyd et al., 2010). In particular, the platform of the Corriere (1) provides a semi-public profile[1] for each registered user, (2) articulates a list of users connected by an 'interest' relationship, (3) allows to view user's connections to other registered users, and (4) includes mood meta data reported by the readers as their 'self-perception'.

The annotations for moods are available at the article and author levels. Therefore, the mood scores for

---

[1]By semi-public we mean that for a user Corriere provides the average mood scores, the number of posted comments and votes, interests and the number of people following; however, no demographic information is provided.

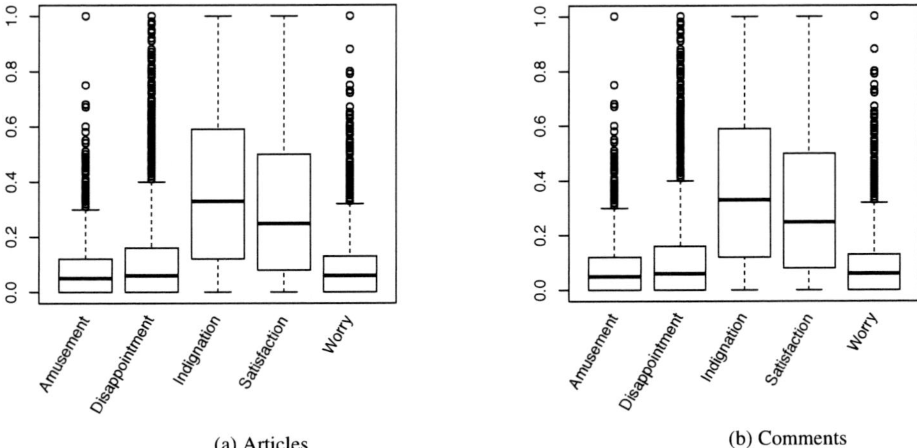

(a) Articles   (b) Comments

Figure 1: Box-plots for the reference mood scores of each mood category.

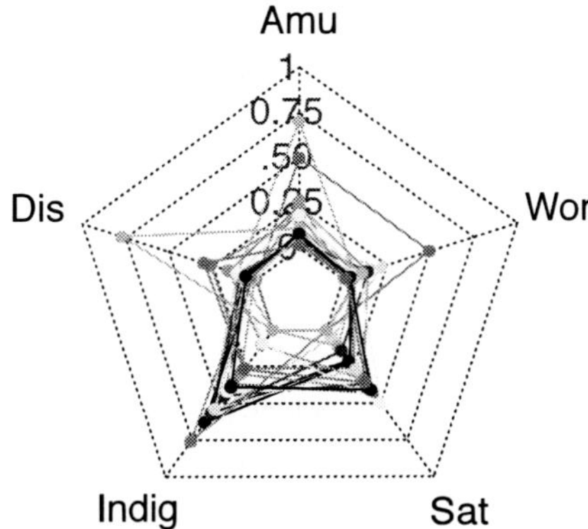

Figure 2: Spider plot of the reference mood scores from the selected comments. Amusement (Amu), Disappointment (Dis), Indignation (Indig), Satisfaction (Sat), Worry (Wor).

each article are directly obtained from the metadata as an average of the reported users' mood score for that article. Whereas the mood scores for comments are obtained from the mood scores of the posting user. Mood scores for users are part of users' personal profiles and describe all the moods they have declared after reading the articles. A portion of the corpus has also been used in (Celli et al., 2014; Celli et al., 2016) to study mood and the relation between mood, personality traits and interaction styles.

For this study, we have collected ≈ 2200 articles and $\approx 300K$ comments to them. The data was pre-processed to remove outliers for each mood category in both articles and comments. Outliers are defined as the mood scores that appear independently in each category. In Figure 1, for instance, for some articles we can observe outlier scores for amused, disappointed and worried. For comments, on the other hand, the outliers are for the satisfied category. Outliers for comments in the amused category have a score above 0.4, which are the scores above the upper outer fence in the boxplot.

In Figure 1, we present box-plots of the mood score distribution for the articles and comments, respectively. From the figures, we observe that the distribution of the mood categories for both articles and comments are similar. For example, for *indignation* and *satisfaction*, the scores of the data points vary between 0.1 to 0.6. From the data, we also observe that in many cases users tend to annotate articles when the content of an article represents the emotions of *indignation* or *satisfaction*.

A lexical analysis has been performed on articles and comments to understand the complexity of the task. We observe that for articles the average number of tokens is 550, with maximum $3,188$ and minimum 44 tokens. Whereas for comments, the average is 44 with a maximum of 285 and a minimum

145

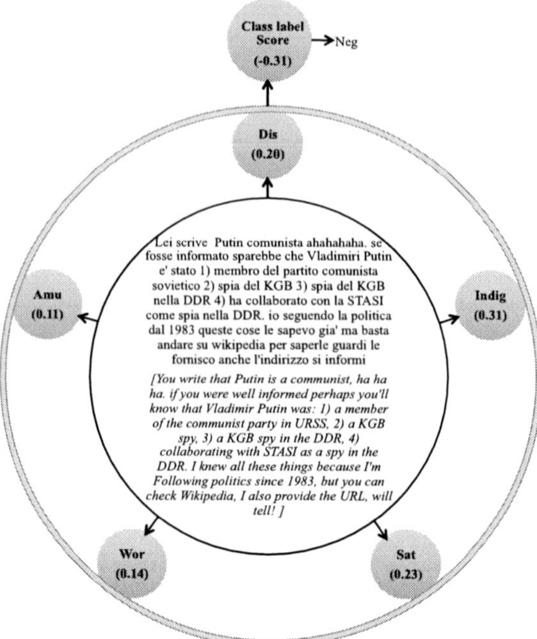

Figure 3: An example of self-reported annotation of a comment with mood scores and category (negative for this example). English translation is provided in italics.

of 1 token. A closer look at the comments with a higher number of tokens reveals that people usually talk about national issues such as economy, taxes, and environmental causes. There is a difference between article and comments in terms of language style. Naturally, the written style of the articles is more formal, whereas the text in comments is more noisy and informal as it contains repetitions, emoticons, jargon, abbreviations, non-standard grammar, and URLs. The noisy structure is very common in any social media conversation as also reported in (Nguyen et al., 2014; Alam et al., 2013).

In Figure 2, we present a spider-plot with reference mood scores from the selected comments, which range from 0 to 1. As can be seen in the figure, the mood scores for indignation and satisfaction are higher than for other categories.

For a better understanding of labels such as mood scores and category for comments and articles, in Figure 3 we provide an example of an annotated user comment. In the figure, the comment is labeled with five mood scores for five mood categories as reported by the user. These mood scores are then turned into a class label (see Section 3.2.2) as positive or negative.

The data is split into training, development, and test sets as 60%, 20%, and 20% respectively. The data partitioning will be made available together with the URL links to the articles on GitHub[2].

3   Methodology

For prediction of mood score and designing the classification system using both articles and comments, we experiment with different sets of features. The feature sets include bag-of-word-ngrams and bag-of-character-ngrams, part-of-speech ngrams, psycholinguistic, and stylometric features. In addition to studying predictive power of individual feature sets, we have also experimented with their feature level fusion. However, due to low performances, they are not reported.

For the mood score prediction task we use the Random Forests, whereas for the classification task we use Support Vector Machines (SVMs). The choice of algorithms for each task is motivated by our prior research on the topic, e.g. in (Celli et al., 2016) Random Forests outperform SVMs for the prediction

---

[2]https://github.com/nlpresources/Corriere-mood-data

task.

3.1 Features

Bag-of-word-ngram   We investigated the bag-of-word-ngrams, with $3 >= n >= 1$, and their logarithmic term frequencies (tf) multiplied with inverse document frequencies (idf) – tf-idf. Although the bag-of-words model has many drawbacks such as data sparsity and high dimensionality, it is the simplest and is known to work well for most text-based classification tasks. As bag-of-ngrams representation yields a large dictionary which increases computational cost, we have selected 5K most frequent ngrams.

Bag-of-character-ngram   Similar to the bag-of-word-ngrams, we also extracted and evaluated bag-of-character-ngrams, with $6 >= n >= 2$ and tf-idf transformation. The motivation for experimenting with this feature set is its success in sentiment classification task (Abbasi et al., 2008).

Part-of-Speech features (POS):   To extract POS features we used TextPro (Pianta et al., 2008) and designed the feature vector using bag-of-ngram representation, with $3 >= n >= 1$ and tf-idf transformation.

Stylometric Features   The use of stylometric features has its root in the domain of authorship identification (Yule, 1939; Abbasi and Chen, 2008; Bergsma et al., 2012; Cristani et al., 2012). Its use has also been reported for text categorization and discourse classification problems (Koppel et al., 2002; Celli et al.,). In authorship identification task, stylometric features are defined ias different groups such as lexical, syntactic, structural, content specific, idiosyncratic and complexity-based (Koppel et al., 2002; Abbasi and Chen, 2008; Cristani et al., 2012). In this work, we use the term *stylometric* to refer to the complexity-based[3] features reported in (Tanaka-Ishii and Aihara, 2015; Tweedie and Baayen, 1998). The used stylometric feature groups are listed in Table 1.

In addition to the features listed in Table 1, we also extract word and character based low-level features and projected them onto statistical functionals. These include counts of word-ngrams (2 to 3-grams) and character ngram (2 to 4-grams). The statistical functions include mean, median and standard deviation. The total number of the features in the set is 97.

Psycholinguistic Features   To extract the psycholinguistic features from the articles and comments we utilized the Linguistic Inquiry Word Count (LIWC) (Pennebaker et al., 2001), which is a knowledge-based system developed over the past few decades. The utility of these features has been studied in different research fields such as psychology and sociology, and they are frequently used to study relations between usage of word and attributes such as gender, age, personality, honesty, dominance, deception, and health (Mairesse et al., 2007; Tauszik and Pennebaker, 2010). The utility of these features has also been reported in (Nguyen et al., 2014; Alam and Riccardi, 2014; Danieli et al., 2015).

The types of LIWC features include the following:

- *General*: word count, average number of words per sentence, a percentage of words found in the dictionary and percentage of words longer than six letters and numerals.
- *Linguistic*: pronouns and articles.
- *Psychological*: affect, cognition, and biological phenomena.
- *Paralinguistic*: accents, fillers, and disfluencies.
- Personal concerns: work (e.g., job and majors), achievement (e.g., earn, hero, and win) and home (e.g., family).
- Punctuation marks and spoken categories such as assent (e.g., agree, OK and yes) nonfluencies (e.g., Er, hm and umm).

Since LIWC is a knowledge based system, it is packaged with dictionaries for different languages including Italian. In this paper, we use the Italian version of the dictionary (Alparone et al., 2004), which

---

[3]Also the terms constancy measure or lexical richness are used in literature.

Table 1: Stylometric features

General
• word count = N • dictionary size = V

Length-based features:
• Average word length • Short word ratio (length = 1-3) to N

Frequency-based Ratios
• Ratio of Hapax Legomena to N • Ratio of Hapac Dislegomena to N

Lexical Richness using transformations of N and V:
• Mean Word Frequency = N/V • Type-Token Ratio = V/N • Guiraud's $R = V/sqrt(N)$ • Herdan's $C = log(V)/log(N)$ • Rubet's $K = log(V)/log(log(N))$ • Maas $A = (log(N) - log(V))/log^{2(N)} = a^2$ • Dugast's $U = log^{2(N)}/(log(N) - log(V))$ • Lukjanenkov and Neistoj's $LN = (1 - V^2)/(V^2 * log(N))$ • Brunet's $W = N^{(V^{(-a)})}, a = 0.172$

Lexical Richness using Frequency Spectrum:
• Honore's $H = b(log(N)/a - (V(1, N)/V)), b = 100, a = 1$ • Sichel's $S = V(2, N)/V$ • Michea's $M = V/V(2, N)$ • Herdan's $V = sqrt(sum(V(i, N) * (V(i, N)/N)^2) - 1/V)$ • Yule's $K = a(-1/N + sum(V(i, N) * (V(i, N)/N)^2)), a = 1$ • Simpson's $D = sum(V(i, N)(V(i, N)/N)(V(i, N) - 1)/(N - 2))$ • Entropy $= V(i, N)(-log((V(i, N)/N))^s * (V(i, N)/N)^t, s = t = 1$
• Length ratios 30 features

contains 85 word categories. In addition, we have also extracted 5 general descriptors and 12 punctuation categories to yield a total of 102 features. The LIWC feature processing differs with respect to the type, which includes counts and relative frequencies (see (Tausczik and Pennebaker, 2010)).

3.2 Experiments

In this section, we report experiments on mood score prediction and mood classification. The development set is used for the preliminary experiments and final models are trained by joining training and development sets.

3.2.1 Mood Score Prediction Experiments and Results

For the mood score prediction experiments, we utilized Random Forests as a learning algorithm (Breiman, 2001). It is a decision tree based algorithm where instances and features are randomly sampled to generate several trees (forest). Then the score of the forest is computed by averaging the scores from the trees. For this experiment, the number of trees is set to 100. We did not optimize the number of trees for the task and plan to address this in the future.

We measure the performance of the mood score prediction system as Root Mean Square Error (RMSE). The performances of models are compared to the baseline that is produced by randomly generating the scores using Gaussian distribution with respect to the prior mean and standard deviation, as presented in Table 2.

In Table 2, we present the performances of different feature sets. The best results for the mood of

Table 2: Performance of the different feature sets on the test set as RMSE (lower is better). Baseline performances are produced by randomly selecting from the Gaussian distribution with respect to prior mean and standard deviation. Base: Baseline, W-ng: word ngram, C-ng: character ngram. Amusement (Amu), Disappointment (Dis), Indignation (Indig), Satisfaction (Sat), Worry (Wor).

	Article						Comments					
Class	Base	W-ng	C-ng	POS	Style	LIWC	Base	W-ng	C-ng	POS	Style	LIWC
Amu	0.130	0.100	0.100	0.102	0.120	0.102	0.170	0.118	0.118	0.119	0.119	0.120
Dis	0.150	0.108	0.112	0.116	0.128	0.120	0.180	0.126	0.127	0.127	0.128	0.128
Indig	0.380	0.266	0.274	0.280	0.247	0.278	0.350	0.245	0.244	0.246	0.246	0.247
Sat	0.370	0.267	0.276	0.271	0.166	0.275	0.230	0.165	0.164	0.165	0.165	0.166
Wor	0.130	0.095	0.096	0.099	0.118	0.099	0.170	0.118	0.117	0.118	0.118	0.118
Avg	0.230	0.167	0.172	0.174	**0.156**	0.175	0.220	**0.154**	**0.154**	0.155	0.155	0.156

the articles are obtained using stylometric features, and the second best results are obtained using word-ngrams. For the comments, on the other hand, the best results are obtained with the word- and character-ngrams. Moreover, for comments, all the feature sets produce close results. The reason for this might be the noisy nature of comment content, and part-of-speech tags, stylometric and LIWC features might not be able to capture significant information. Yet another reason might be high variation in comment length, thus high feature sparseness. In terms of the performance and the number of features, we speculate that stylometric features might be useful for cross-language/domain experiments.

Nevertheless, compared to the random baseline performances are statistically significant with paired t-test $p < 0.05$ for both articles and comments.

3.2.2 Mood Classification Experiments and Results

For the classification task, we first transformed the mood scores into binary classes such as positive and negative. This is done by first computing an overall mood *class label score* by subtracting the sum of "Disappointment", "Worry" and "Indignation" scores from the sum of "Amusement" and"Satisfaction" scores (see Equation 1). Then, the score is mapped into either of the two classes – positive and negative – with respect to Equation 2. The instances with the overall score of zero are ignored. As a result, 63% of articles are assigned to a negative category and 37% to positive. The distribution of comments into negative and positive categories, on the other hand, is more balanced: 53% (negative) *vs* 47% (positive).

$$class\ label\ score = (amusement + satisfaction) - (disappointment + worry + indignation) \quad (1)$$

$$class\_label\_instance(i) = \begin{cases} pos & if\ score > 0 \\ neg & if\ score < 0 \end{cases} \quad (2)$$

For the task of classification, we train a Support Vector Machines (SVM) (Platt, 1998) model with a linear kernel. The performance is measured in terms of macro-averaged precision, recall, F1-measure, and accuracy. Baseline results are computed by randomly generating the class labels, such as positive or negative, based on the prior class distribution of the training set (i.e. chance baseline) as shown in Table 3.

In Table 3, we present the classification results for the articles and comments. For the articles, we obtain the best results using word-ngrams and the second best result using character-ngrams. For the comments, on the other hand, we observe similar results with both word and character ngrams, however, character-ngram model is slightly better. The performances of POS, LIWC, and stylometric feature sets are lower. Compared to the chance baseline, the results are statistically significant with McNemar's test and $p < 0.05$.

4 Discussion

For the score prediction task, the overall results for comments are better than for articles; whereas, for the classification task, the results are better for articles than for comments. We observe that bag-of-word-ngrams perform well on both tasks.

Table 3: Classification results on the test set using different feature sets as precision (P), recall (R), F1 measure (F1), and accuracy (Acc).

Exp	Articles				Comments			
	P	**R**	**F1**	**Acc**	**P**	**R**	**F1**	**Acc**
Baseline	47.89	47.93	47.90	53.51	49.93	49.92	49.93	50.04
Word-ngram	62.20	61.70	**61.89**	58.73	54.44	54.27	54.06	54.71
Char-ngram	55.95	56.22	55.76	56.69	55.33	55.16	**55.03**	55.71
POS	53.97	53.96	53.96	56.24	52.29	52.12	51.59	52.96
Style	54.43	52.76	50.56	59.64	52.37	52.26	51.96	52.93
LIWC	54.30	54.05	54.02	57.37	52.43	52.31	51.98	53.01

From the article score prediction experiment, we obtain the best results using stylometric features, which are language independent. Thus, we plan to exploit them for cross-domain and cross-language study.

Regarding the use of self-reported mood annotation, our experiments suggest that for a better understanding of their reliability, it is necessary to evaluate them through observer/expert annotation. One important issue is that in this self-reported annotations, users have not followed any instructions or have had any psychological instruments while expressing their affective opinions.

5   Conclusion

In this paper, we have presented the work on the prediction and classification of mood from news articles and comments. The self-reported mood annotations were used as a reference signal, and we have experimented with different features sets. For the mood score prediction task, the best results were obtained using bag-of-word-ngrams and stylometric features for both articles and comments. For the classification task, on the other hand, the best results were obtained with bag-of-word-ngrams. The prediction and classification tasks on comments are difficult due to the noisy nature of the data. Since the self-reported data is increasing over time, further expert annotation of the user-reported scores is required for designing better automatic systems. Another interesting question that we plan to address in the future is how well the mood models generalize across different domains.

Acknowledgments

The research leading to these results has received funding from the European Union - Seventh Framework Programme (FP7/2007-2013) under grant agreement n° 610916 - SENSEI - http://www.sensei-conversation.eu/.

References

Ahmed Abbasi and Hsinchun Chen. 2008. Writeprints: A stylometric approach to identity-level identification and similarity detection in cyberspace. *ACM Transactions on Information Systems (TOIS)*, 26(2):7.

Ahmed Abbasi, Hsinchun Chen, and Arab Salem. 2008. Sentiment analysis in multiple languages: Feature selection for opinion classification in web forums. *ACM Transactions on Information Systems (TOIS)*, 26(3):12.

Alexander Pak and Patrick Paroubek. 2010b. Twitter as a corpus for sentiment analysis and opinion mining. In *LREc*, volume 10, pages 1320–1326.

Alec Go, Richa Bhayani, and Lei Huang. 2009. Twitter sentiment classification using distant supervision. *CS224N Project Report, Stanford*, 1:12.

Alexander Pak and Patrick Paroubek. 2010a. Twitter as a corpus for sentiment analysis and opinion mining. In *LREC*, pages 1320–1326.

Bo Pang and Lillian Lee. 2008. Opinion mining and sentiment analysis. *Foundations and trends in information retrieval*, 2(1-2):1–135.

Cem Akkaya, Janyce Wiebe, and Rada Mihalcea. 2009. Subjectivity word sense disambiguation. In *Proc. of the Conference on EMNLP*, pages 190–199. Association for Computational Linguistics.

Dan Kim and Mohammad Salehan. 2015. The effect of sentiment on information diffusion in social media.

Danah Boyd, Scott Golder, and Gilad Lotan. 2010. Tweet, tweet, retweet: Conversational aspects of retweeting on twitter. In *System Sciences (HICSS), 2010 43rd Hawaii International Conference on*, pages 1–10. IEEE.

Dmitry Davidov, Oren Tsur, and Ari Rappoport. 2010. Enhanced sentiment learning using twitter hashtags and smileys. In *Proceedings of the 23rd international conference on computational linguistics: posters*, pages 241–249. Association for Computational Linguistics.

Erik Cambria, Soujanya Poria, Rajiv Bajpai, and Björn Schuller. 2016a. Senticnet 4: A semantic resource for sentiment analysis based on conceptual primitives. In *the 26th International Conference on Computational Linguistics (COLING), Osaka*.

Erik Cambria, Björn Schuller, Yunqing Xia, and Bebo White. 2016b. New avenues in knowledge bases for natural language processing. *Knowledge-Based Systems*, 108(C):1–4.

Erik Cambria. 2016. Affective computing and sentiment analysis. *IEEE Intelligent Systems*, 31(2):102–107.

Emilio Ferrara and Zeyao Yang. 2015. Quantifying the effect of sentiment on information diffusion in social media. *PeerJ Computer Science*, 1:e26.

Efthymios Kouloumpis, Theresa Wilson, and Johanna Moore. 2011. Twitter sentiment analysis: The good the bad and the omg! In *ICWSM*.

Emanuele Pianta, Christian Girardi, and Roberto Zanoli. 2008. The textpro tool suite. In *LREC*. Citeseer.

Fabio Celli, Evgeny A. Stepanov, and Giuseppe Riccardi. Tell me who you are, i'll tell whether you agree or disagree: Prediction of agreement/disagreement in news blog.

Fabio Celli, Giuseppe Riccardi, and Arindam Ghosh. 2014. Corea: Italian news corpus with emotions and agreement. In *Proceedings of the First Italian Conference on Computational Linguistics CLiC-it 2014 & and of the Fourth International Workshop EVALITA 2014*, pages 98–102. Pisa University Press.

Fabio Celli, Arindam Ghosh, Firoj Alam, and Giuseppe Riccardi. 2016. In the mood for sharing contents: Emotions, personality and interaction styles in the diffusion of news. *Information Processing & Management*, 52(1):93–98.

Firoj Alam and Giuseppe Riccardi. 2014. Fusion of acoustic, linguistic and psycholinguistic features for speaker personality traits recognition. In *Proc. of ICASSP*, pages 955–959, May.

Firoj Alam, Evgeny A Stepanov, and Giuseppe Riccardi. 2013. Personality traits recognition on social network-facebook.

F. Alparone, S. Caso, A. Agosti, and A. Rellini. 2004. The italian liwc2001 dictionary. Technical report, LIWC.net, Austin, TX.

FA Kunneman, CC Liebrecht, and APJ van den Bosch. 2014. The (un) predictability of emotional hashtags in twitter.

François Mairesse, Marilyn A Walker, Matthias R Mehl, and Roger K Moore. 2007. Using linguistic cues for the automatic recognition of personality in conversation and text. *J. Artif. Intell. Res.(JAIR)*, 30:457–500.

Fiona J Tweedie and R Harald Baayen. 1998. How variable may a constant be? measures of lexical richness in perspective. *Computers and the Humanities*, 32(5):323–352.

G Udny Yule. 1939. On sentence-length as a statistical characteristic of style in prose: With application to two cases of disputed authorship. *Biometrika*, 30(3/4):363–390.

Gilad Mishne et al. 2005. Experiments with mood classification in blog posts. In *Proceedings of ACM SIGIR 2005 workshop on stylistic analysis of text for information access*, volume 19, pages 321–327. Citeseer.

Georgios Paltoglou and Mike Thelwall. 2010. A study of information retrieval weighting schemes for sentiment analysis. In *Proc. of the 48th ACL*, pages 1386–1395. ACL.

Giuseppe Riccardi, Frederic Bechet, Morena Danieli, Benoit Favre, Robert Gaizauskas, Udo Kruschwitz, and Massimo Poesio. 2015. The sensei project: Making sense of human conversations. In *International Workshop on Future and Emergent Trends in Language Technology*, pages 10–33. Springer.

Hugo Liu. 2007. Social network profiles as taste performances. *Journal of Computer-Mediated Communication*, 13(1):252–275.

James W Pennebaker, Martha E Francis, and Roger J Booth. 2001. Linguistic inquiry and word count: Liwc 2001. *Mahway: Lawrence Erlbaum Associates*, 71.

Johan Bollen, Huina Mao, and Alberto Pepe. 2011. Modeling public mood and emotion: Twitter sentiment and socio-economic phenomena. In *Proc. of ICWSM*, pages 1–10.

John Platt. 1998. Sequential minimal optimization: A fast algorithm for training support vector machines. Technical report, Microsoft Research.

Kumiko Tanaka-Ishii and Shunsuke Aihara. 2015. Computational constancy measures of texts—yule's k and rényi's entropy. *Computational Linguistics*.

Leo Breiman. 2001. Random forests. *Machine learning*, 45(1):5–32.

Marco Cristani, Giorgio Roffo, Cristina Segalin, Loris Bazzani, Alessandro Vinciarelli, and Vittorio Murino. 2012. Conversationally-inspired stylometric features for authorship attribution in instant messaging. In *Proc. 20th ACM Multimedia*, pages 1121–1124. ACM.

Morena Danieli, Giuseppe Riccardi, and Firoj Alam. 2015. Emotion unfolding and affective scenes: A case study in spoken conversations. In *Proc. of Emotion Representations and Modelling for Companion Systems (ERM4CT) 2015,*. ICMI.

Moshe Koppel, Shlomo Argamon, and Anat Rachel Shimoni. 2002. Automatically categorizing written texts by author gender. *Literary and Linguistic Computing*, 17(4):401–412.

Mike Thelwall, Kevan Buckley, and Georgios Paltoglou. 2011. Sentiment in twitter events. *JASIST*, 62(2):406–418.

Thin Nguyen, Dinh Phung, Brett Adams, Truyen Tran, and Svetha Venkatesh. 2010. Classification and pattern discovery of mood in weblogs. In *Advances in knowledge discovery and data mining*, pages 283–290. Springer Berlin Heidelberg.

Thin Nguyen, Dinh Phung, Brett Adams, and Svetha Venkatesh. 2014. Mood sensing from social media texts and its applications. *Knowledge and information systems*, 39(3):667–702.

Shane Bergsma, Matt Post, and David Yarowsky. 2012. Stylometric analysis of scientific articles. In *Proc. of the NACL*, pages 327–337. ACL.

Stefan Stieglitz and Linh Dang-Xuan. 2013. Emotions and information diffusion in social media—sentiment of microblogs and sharing behavior. *Journal of Management Information Systems*, 29(4):217–248.

Vernon Turner, John F Gantz, David Reinsel, and Stephen Minton. 2014. The digital universe of opportunities: Rich data and the increasing value of the internet of things. *IDC Analyze the Future*.

Yla R Tausczik and James W Pennebaker. 2010. The psychological meaning of words: Liwc and computerized text analysis methods. *Journal of Language and Social Psychology*, 29(1):24–54.

Microblog Emotion Classification
by Computing Similarity in Text, Time, and Space

Anja Summa
Department of
Computational Linguistics
Heidelberg University
Heidelberg, Germany
sum.anja@arcor.de

Bernd Resch
Department of
Geoinformatics – Z_GIS
University of Salzburg
Salzburg, Austria
bernd.resch@sbg.ac.at

Michael Strube
NLP Group
Heidelberg Institute for
Theoretical Studies gGmbH
Heidelberg, Germany
michael.strube@h-its.org

Abstract

Most work in NLP analysing microblogs focuses on textual content thus neglecting temporal and spatial information. We present a new interdisciplinary method for emotion classification that combines linguistic, temporal, and spatial information into a single metric. We create a graph of labeled and unlabeled tweets that encodes the relations between neighboring tweets with respect to their emotion labels. Graph-based semi-supervised learning labels all tweets with an emotion.

1 Introduction and Motivation

Social media analysis is a field where natural language processing (NLP) and geographic information science (GIScience) overlap, because messages posted in social media frequently contain both textual and geographical information. While GIScience researchers have adopted NLP methods to analyze the textual layer of tweets, spatio-temporal analysis is virtually non-existent in NLP (very recently Volkova et al. (2016) distinguished emotions across very coarse geolocations). Steiger et al. (2015) state that only 4% of the publications dealing with spatio-temporal Twitter analysis come from computational linguistics. By merely analysing the tweets' text, temporal and spatial information is lost. Also, in most cases NLP and GIScience methods are not directly combined, but used as two different processing steps. One example is sentiment analysis on geo-referenced Twitter data (Bertrand et al., 2013). Here sentiment is computed purely semantically, and its results are interpreted according to the tweets' spatial and temporal layers.

The work presented here aims to overcome this desideratum by applying GIScience methods in an NLP context. The overall workflow is shown in Figure 1. The textual and spatio-temporal dimensions of tweets are jointly used by one comprehensive graph-based semi-supervised machine learning method to label tweets with their prevalent emotions. This setup has the benefits of being applicable to both GIScience and NLP as well as needing only a small amount of labeled data. To create a gold standard, we manually label a subset of our Twitter data with a set of emotion classes. To keep the task feasible,

This work is licensed under a Creative Commons Attribution 4.0 International Licence. Licence details: http://creativecommons.org/licenses/by/4.0/

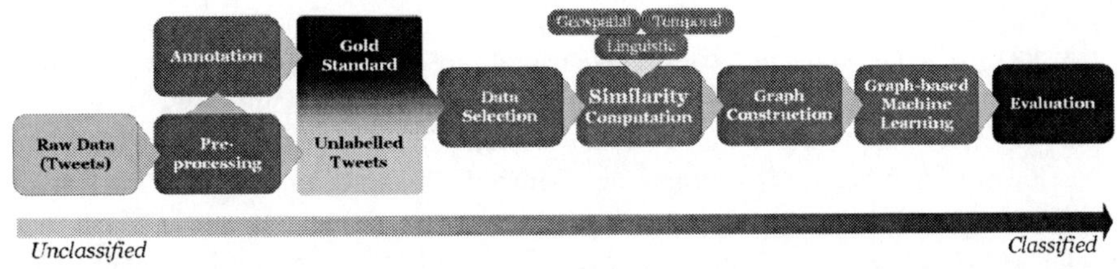

Figure 1: Workflow: In Step 1, a set of tweets is preprocessed and partly annotated in order to construct a gold standard. Those data are used for experiments. A subset is selected and in Step 3 used to construct a graph via similarity computing. In Step 4, a graph-based semi-supervised machine learning algorithm classifies emotions. In Step 5, evaluation is performed.

Proceedings of the Workshop on Computational Modeling of People's Opinions, Personality, and Emotions in Social Media,
pages 153–162, Osaka, Japan, December 12 2016.

Portland St. and Main. on scene. #mitshooting
This is awful RT: BREAKING: MIT officer has died from his injuries. #7NEWS
I'm at Central Square (Cambridge, MA) w/2others
That just pissed me off -_-

Table 1: Tweets from dataset dealing with events around Boston Marathon Bombing

we agree on a subset of Ekman's basic emotions (Ekman and Friesen, 1971), as defined by Jack et al. (2014): HAPPINESS, FEAR, SADNESS, and ANGER/DISGUST (merged in one category, see Section 3.2). Additionally, we utilize a NONE class to catch all other cases.

In this paper, we focus on computing the similarity between two nodes, i.e. tweets, which is used to construct the graph (Figure 1). The similarity score is utilized as edge weight. On the resulting graph we apply Modified Adsorption (Talukdar and Crammer, 2009), a semi-supervised label-propagation algorithm. Features are derived from and extend work on Twitter sentiment analysis and Twitter writing style analysis such as work on authorship attribution on microblogs (Schwartz et al., 2013).

We choose the time and geolocation around the *Boston Marathon Bombing* because we expect to harvest a larger fraction of highly emotional tweets than usual. See Table 1 for a few examples from our dataset some of which express emotions. The GIScience aspects of this work are described in detail in a companion paper (Resch et al., 2016).

2 Related Work

Emotion recognition can be viewed as a subtask of sentiment analysis (Liu and Zhang, 2012). It is, however, more complex as it addresses multiple emotions, and, hence, requires a multi-class classification (Kozareva et al., 2007), instead of the binary or gradual polarity categories used mostly in sentiment analysis. Sentiment analysis on Twitter data has attracted a lot of research (Strapparava and Mihalcea, 2008; Davidov et al., 2010; Bollen et al., 2011; Roberts et al., 2012; Pak and Paroubek, 2010; Brody and Diakopoulos, 2011; Kouloumpis et al., 2011) with, e.g., several years of shared tasks at SemEval and more than 30 participating teams at the SemEval 2016 Task 4. Still, the results are still far from perfect and quite a bit worse than results on reviews (Nakov et al., 2016).

Existing work classifying emotions in tweets is supervised and requires large amounts of annotated data (Roberts et al., 2012; Mohammad and Kiritchenko, 2014; Volkova and Bachrach, 2016) or heuristics deriving emotions from hashtags to label emotions in tweets (Davidov et al., 2010). We, in contrast, apply a semi-supervised method which requires only little annotated data. While Bollen et al. (2011) label discrete emotions, they do not classify single tweets but examine the whole Twitter community jointly. Roberts et al. (2012) and Bollen et al. (2011) use the temporal dimension, but neglect the spatial dimension (georeferencing of single tweets had been introduced only in 2009[1]).

There is only little work in NLP dealing with geolocation in tweets. Han et al. (2014), Rahimi et al. (2015b) and Rahimi et al. (2015a) use tweets to predict geolocation, the reverse of our setting. However, Rahimi et al. (2015a) use a model based on Modified Adsorption which is relatively close to our model. Volkova et al. (2016) use a very coarse notion of geolocation and find differences in emotions across different countries. Bertrand et al. (2013) use geolocation in tweets to perform sentiment analysis. They base their work on *The First Law of Geography*: "everything is related to everything else, but near things are more related than distant things" (Tobler, 1970, p.4). We also follow this law.

Our semi-supervised approach is based on the idea that similar tweets should be labeled with similar emotions. However, approaches for computing "Semantic Textual Similarity" (Agirre et al., 2012) are not applicable as emotions are not expressed that much through content words but through the text's linguistic and stylistic properties. Hence, our features are closer to ones used in linguistic style analysis as used in, e.g., work on authorship attribution on tweets (Layton et al., 2010; Silva et al., 2011; Macleod and Grant, 2012; Schwartz et al., 2013). Linguistic style analysis also has been applied to sentiment analysis in tweets (Pak and Paroubek, 2010; Kouloumpis et al., 2011; Brody and Diakopoulos, 2011).

---

[1] `https://blog.twitter.com/2009/location-location-location)`

everybody hates you	
Does this state a fact? Is this written by someone feeling sorry someone else? Does this show anger/disgust/hate?	
Can I knock out right here?	
Sounds and looks emotional, but what exactly does it mean?	
haha	
Is that happiness? Or meant ironically and really encodes sadness?	

Table 2: Tweets causing arguments among annotators. Tweet text and remarks made during discussion.

3 Data and Annotation

Existing datasets comprising short texts and emotion annotations (Strapparava and Mihalcea, 2007; Roberts et al., 2012; Volkova and Bachrach, 2016) can not be used for our purposes as they do not contain spatio-temporal information. The dataset by Volkova et al. (2016) contains spatio-temporal information, but the work is done on Ukranian and Russian. Hence, we create our own dataset.

3.1 Raw Data

In order to increase the likelihood that the tweets contain emotions, we collect tweets from the Boston area in the two weeks around the Boston Marathon Bombing on April 15th, 2103. Raw data is provided by the Center for Geographic Analysis at Harvard University which collects tweets using a public Twitter REST Geo Search API (https://dev.twitter.com/rest/public) via spatial search queries (Harvard University, Center for Geographic Analysis, 2016). This provides us with *all* georeferenced tweets from a particular area instead of just a sample as would have been the case if the Streaming API would have been used with spatial information (Boyd and Crawford, 2012). We select tweets from April 8th, 2013 to April 22nd, 2013, georeferenced within a bounding box containing Boston with: xmin: -71.21, ymin: 42.29, xmax: -70.95, ymax: 42.25. Preprocessing comprises language detection by two language detectors (McCandless, 2010; Lui and Baldwin, 2012) so that only tweets are kept which are identified by at least one detector as English, removing tweets without content (i.e., tweets being empty after filtering URLs and @mentions). After preprocessing 195,380 georeferenced tweets remain.

3.2 Emotion Annotation

We choose Ekman's six basic emotions *happiness, anger, sadness, disgust, surprise*, and *fear* (Ekman and Friesen, 1971) plus *none* as a basis for our annotation. These categories have been used in related work (Strapparava and Mihalcea, 2008; Roberts et al., 2012; Purver and Battersby, 2012).

We train seven naive (neither experts in psychology nor in NLP) subjects to annotate tweets and to perform an initial reliability study. It turns out that two annotators are not up to the task (after computing pairwise κ (Fleiss, 1971) between annotators). So we continue with five annotators who annotated 261 randomly selected tweets. Also, the κ scores for *disgust* and *surprise* are very low. See Table 2 for a few examples which caused arguments among annotators during the first phase of the annotation.

Hence we change the annotation manual so that the likely to be confused emotions *anger* and *disgust* are merged, and *surprise* is annotated as *none*. This leads to the satisfying κ scores reported in Table 3.

After having refined the annotation scheme and after having established a pool of five annotators, we proceed with randomly selecting another 385 tweets which are annotated by all five annotators. We merge both sets of annotations to create a gold standard for our experiments. We follow Müller (2007) in creating several gold standard levels based on the number of annotations agreeing with each other. This way a gold standard with sufficient quality can be produced albeit at the cost of losing some annotations (Table 4). *none* is the most frequent class followed by *happiness*. We originally expected a higher fraction of tweets encoding *anger/disgust, fear* and *sadness*, but our two week window proved to be too long. For our experiments we combine gold standard levels 4 and 5 which gives us 499 annotated tweets.

none	0.44	*sadness*	0.39	*fear*	0.44	*anger*	0.41	*happiness*	0.57

Table 3: κ per category for five annotators and categories

# agreements	anger/disgust	fear	sadness	happiness	none	total
			emotion labels			
3	21	5	20	37	64	147
4	21	1	19	50	90	181
5	24	2	4	57	231	318
total	66	8	43	144	385	646

Table 4: Number of gold standard labels per emotion class and agreement level

4 Computing Similarity between Tweets

In graph-based semi-supervised learning the edge weights encode the degree of influence between neighboring nodes. For emotion classification on tweets, this means that two nodes connected by a strong edge are likely to receive the same emotion label. We define the edge weight in a way that supports this relation: *Similarity* is **the likelihood that two tweets contain the same emotion**. This relation is defined to be symmetric for each pair of tweets, which results in an undirected graph. If a tweet receives overall similarity scores of 0 to all other tweets in the data set, it is not part of the graph and thus cannot be labeled. Computing this similarity, we leverage the special nature of tweets. Thus, similarity is computed along the dimensions *text* (Section 4.1), *time*, and *geographic space* (Section 4.2). After intermediate results for all dimensions are computed individually, they are combined into one score (Section 4.3).

This concept of similarity is different from others in mainly three ways: (1) It does not require semantic analysis, because the tweets' topic is not of interest. (2) It does not work on vector representations. (3) To our best knowledge, it is the first similarity measure that combines the three dimensions text, time and geo-space. We do not use vectors because they cannot be applied in our graph-based semi-supervised learning setting.

4.1 Linguistic Similarity

The textual dimension is computed by analysing the tweet's writing style. We assume that a similar writing style encodes a similar emotion[2]. This approach is inspired by work on Twitter sentiment analysis (Pak and Paroubek, 2010; Brody and Diakopoulos, 2011; Kouloumpis et al., 2011). Twitter authorship analysis (Layton et al., 2010; Macleod and Grant, 2012; Schwartz et al., 2013; Silva et al., 2011) also provides insight into writing style analysis. Research in both fields shows that although tweets are short, unedited text, writing style analysis provides information about the user and her emotions.

Linguistic similarity between tweets is computed as follows: First, two tweets are analyzed and compared with respect to specific linguistic aspects (Section 4.1.1). Second, these similarities are normalized and aggregated and a *linguistic similarity score* is returned (Section 4.1.2).

4.1.1 Feature Design

The feature design is influenced by the transductive setting inherent to Modified Adsorption, which means that there are no separate training and labeling phases and thus no model is built. Consequently, only properties that can be (1) extracted from a single tweet or (2) computed from comparing two tweets are suitable features. This excludes any approaches that require an analysis of the corpus as a whole, such as language models per category or word frequencies. The features are designed to be mostly language independent. The only language-specific resource applied is ANEW[3](Bradley and Lang, 2010).

The features we apply can be divided into two major groups (see Table 5): those that compare concrete words and those that analyze generic style characteristics. In order to facilitate experimenting the individual features are organized into feature groups depending on the examined grammatical entity.

---

[2]The term *similar emotion* is applicable in this case, because the granularity of the emotion model applied here is low. Thus, while two tweets may be rightly classified into the same emotion class, they may in reality express different variants of a *basic emotion* (cf., e.g. Shaver et al. (1987)).

[3]*Affective Norms for English Words (ANEW)* contains ratings for English words based on a dimensional approach to emotions. It does not contain discrete labels, but scores for the three dimensions *pleasure*, *arousal*, and *dominance* (Bradley and Lang, 2010). Although this approach is contrary to the discrete classes utilized here, ANEW's application is still justified. For computing similarity, we check whether the words are rated similarly along one or more dimensions.

group	feature	source
words	no. of same n-grams in both tweets	Davidov et al. (2010)
	no. of words in both tweets	Davidov et al. (2010)
	no. of long words ($\geq$ 8 characters) in both tweets	Schwarm and Ostendorf (2005)
hashtags	any hashtag present in both tweets	
	no. of same hashtags present in both tweets	
emojis	emoji present in both	
	no. of same emojis present in both tweets	
POS	(proper) nouns (objective) vs. (personal) pronouns (subjective)	Pak and Paroubek (2010)
	adverbs (subjective)	Pak and Paroubek (2010)
	compare most frequent POS tag in both tweets	
	no. of same adverbs in both tweets	
spelling	no. of all-capital words	Davidov et al. (2010)
	character repetitions	Kouloumpis et al. (2011)
punctuation	no. of sequences of punctuation marks	Schwartz et al. (2013)
	no. of "!"	Davidov et al. (2010)
	no. of "?"	Davidov et al. (2010)
	no. of """	Davidov et al. (2010)
ANEW	dimensional values for full tweets	

Table 5: Linguistic features

Hashtag	Number of Occurrences	Hashtag	Number of Occurrences	Hashtag	Number of Occurrences
#Boston	2338	#BostonMarathon	408	#oomf	205
#boston	1756	#watertown	407	#RedSox	204
#bostonstrong	1477	#redsox	373	#SocialMedia	186
#Job	1399	#internship	335	#manhunt	179
#BostonStrong	1063	#tmlt	319	#advertising	174
#Jobs	944	#TeamFollowBack	263	#marathonmonday	167
#bostonmarathon	731	#jobs	257	#love	163
#TweetMyJobs	672	#Follow2BeFollowed	219	#spring	150
#Marketing	591	#Watertown	219	#fenway	150
#prayforboston	490	#Cambridge	206	#2	130

Table 6: 30 most frequent hashtags in the data set.

String Features. We use words, hashtags, and emojis returned by Owoputi et al. (2013)'s POS tagger. We compare n-grams of different sizes, the overall number of words and the overall number of long words ($\geq$ 8 characters) in the two tweets. Tweets are characterized by the microblog-specific entities *hashtags* (Chang, 2010) and *emojis* whose distribution may also indicate their emotional content. Table 6 lists the 30 most frequent hashtags in our data. Some hashtags have emotional content (e.g. #bostonstrong, #prayforboston). Davidov et al. (2010) regard hashtags and emojis as sentiment assigned by the user. Kouloumpis et al. (2011) use hashtags to acquire a training set of positive, negative, and neutral tweets. We also use hashtags as a feature to compute the similarity between tweets. Emojis have an even stronger emotional content than hashtags. Hence, we use them for the same purpose.

Style Features. *POS tags* do not directly convey emotion information, but their distribution within a text has been shown to reveal a text's polarity (Pak and Paroubek, 2010). However, the POS tagger used (Owoputi et al., 2013) does not tag adjectives correctly. Hence we can only use adverbs in our feature set. *Spelling features* take spelling pecularities as *intensifiers* (Eisenstein, 2013; Kouloumpis et al., 2011): the number of words containing *character repetitions* and the number of words written *in only capital letters*. We take *punctuation* as an encoding of emotional content (as suggested by Davidov et al. (2010)). We compare exclamation, question, and quotation marks as sequences and as counts.

4.1.2 Normalising and Aggregating Results

We normalize the results from the feature groups by applying the sigmoid function $f(x) = x/(1 + |x|)$, a function that does not depend on a maximum value. The normalized results from all feature groups are aggregated. This value is normalized again to be combined with temporal and spatial similarity scores ranging from 0 to 1 (Section 4.2). With the maximum being the number of feature groups, the aggregated linguistic similarity score is divided by the number of groups applied.

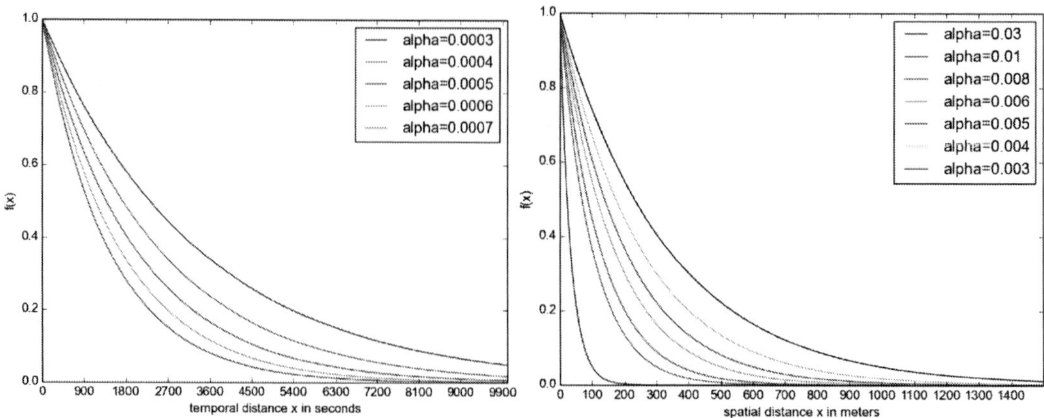

Figure 2: Temporal (left) and spatial similarity (right): Different α values for comparison.

$$sim(T_a, T_b) = \zeta \times sim_{ling}(T_a, T_b) + \beta \times sim_{spat}(T_a, T_b) + \gamma \times sim_{temp}(T_a, T_b) \qquad (1)$$

4.2 Temporal and Spatial Similarity

Extracting spatio-temporal information from microblogs requires methods from GIScience. Twitter can be regarded as "a new type of a distributed sensor system", allowing for insights into spatio-temporal processes by generating a "geographic footprint" (Crooks et al., 2013, p.2). Using this concept of human sensors, people offer subjective observations of their environment as opposed to technical sensors creating reproducible measurements. We utilize the concept of *Twitter users as geo-sensors* because it allows to interpret tweets as observations and to relate those observations temporally and spatially to the environment. Even though no complete model of the spatio-temporal dynamics of Twitter has been suggested so far, previous research has operated under the assumption that Waldo Tobler's *First Law of Geography* also holds true for tweets: "everything is related to everything else, but near things are more related than distant things" (Tobler, 1970, p.4).

Bertrand et al. (2013) show that people tweet differently during the course of a day or a week and prove that different places are characterized by latent sentiment. This indicates a causal connection between a person's location and their mood. Also, the overlapping influences of temporal and spatial patterns have to be considered. Natural disasters have been shown to create a large amount of immediate georeferenced local responses on Twitter (Crooks et al., 2013), but also a longer-lasting world-wide echo (Lee et al., 2011). Crooks et al. (2013, p.2) note that "people frequently comment on events happening at or affecting their location, or refer to locations that represent momentary social hotspots".

Although there possibly is a connection between a tweet and its origin in time and space, it is not clear how to quantify it. Thus, we suggest a different method: Instead of modeling certain events' influence on the Twitter stream, we model for two tweets how likely they have been generated by the same event. Sakaki et al. (2010) successfully model the temporal distribution of tweets commenting on a certain event as an exponential function. We apply this approach for both the temporal and spatial layers using $f(x) = e^{(-\alpha \times x)}$. Figure 2 shows the relation between two tweets depending on their temporal/spatial distance and a *decay parameter* α. We suggest those values based on the assumption that two tweets are most likely to have been triggered by the same event if they are close in time and space. In order to favor those tweets that have been written in reaction to something the user has seen with her own eyes, we set reference frames that contain the major part of the curves in Figure 2.

4.3 Combining The Three Dimensions

The similarity scores for all dimensions are combined linearly (Equation 1; $sim_{ling}(T_a, T_b)$ denotes the linguistic similarity between two tweets a and b). The individual results' weights are defined by

features		micro-average			macro-average		
		P	R	F	P	R	F
ling.	hashtags	0.6388	0.6388	0.6388	0.1277	0.2	0.1559
	punctuation	0.6388	0.6388	0.6388	0.1277	0.2	0.1559
	spelling	0.6388	0.6388	0.6388	0.1277	0.2	0.1559
	ANEW	0.6412	0.631	0.636	0.1282	0.1975	0.1555
	emojis	0.6825	**0.6825**	0.6825	0.2729	**0.2506**	0.2613
	POS	0.6388	0.6388	0.6388	0.1277	0.2	0.1559
	words	0.6388	0.6388	0.6388	0.1277	0.2	0.1559
	emojis, hashtags	0.6825	**0.6825**	0.6825	0.2729	**0.2506**	0.2613
	emojis, punctuation	0.6825	**0.6825**	0.6825	0.2729	**0.2506**	0.2613
	emojis, spelling	0.6825	**0.6825**	0.6825	0.2729	**0.2506**	0.2613
	emojis, ANEW	0.6858	0.6151	0.6485	0.1372	0.1925	0.1602
	emojis, POS	0.68	0.6746	0.6773	0.2665	0.2432	0.2543
	emojis, words	**0.6967**	0.6746	**0.6855**	**0.3222**	0.2432	**0.2772**
comb.	emojis, temporal	0.6388	0.6388	0.6388	0.1277	0.2	0.1559
comb.	emojis, spatial	0.6825	**0.6825**	0.6825	0.2729	**0.2506**	0.2613
comb.	emojis, spat., temp.	0.6825	**0.6825**	0.6825	0.2729	**0.2506**	0.2613
random baseline					0.2137	0.2566	0.2332
majority baseline		0.6388	0.6388	0.6388			

Table 7: Results using Modified Adsorption, agreement level 4, minimum edge weight 0.5

Im a pretty girl. Find me ;)
cause we always talk about you :)
awww lmao homie ok :) I don't mind you making fun of me either haha ..
Had a great time at Lauren's art reception today. My friends have such talent :-)

Table 8: Tweets correctly labeled with happiness

weighting parameters ζ, β, and γ. An additional parameter influences the resulting graph's layout. To exclude noisy edges that do not carry information but bloat the graph, we apply an *edge weight threshold*. Consequently, only edges whose weight is equal to or higher than this threshold are included in the graph.

5 Experiments

For the experiments we use the gold standard constructed in Section 3 divided into 50% seed data for the semi-supervised graph-based machine learning algorithm and 50% testing data. Graph construction is guided by the similarity computation method described in Section 4. Classification is performed by Modified Adsorption, the semi-supervised label propagation algorithm implemented in the *Junto*-toolkit[4] (Talukdar and Crammer, 2009).

From the gold standard we use level 4, i.e. all tweets which have been annotated with the same label by at least four out of five annotators. This way we make use of more than 75% of the annotated data while ensuring high quality annotations for learning and evaluation. In addition we use 10,000 unlabeled tweets for learning. We set the threshold for edges (minimum weight) to 0.5.

In Table 7 we report the results in terms of micro- and macro-average precision, recall and F-measure. Since the classes have a skewed distribution, results for micro- and macro-average show a large difference. We apply McNemar's test to report statistically significant differences (Dietterich, 1998). Random and majority decisions serve as baselines for comparison. The macro-average results should be compared with the random baseline, the micro-average results with the majority baseline.

Most of the linguistic features taken on its own perform just like the majority class classification, i.e., they classify each tweet as *none*. Only *ANEW* and *emojis* manage to classify some tweets differently. With *ANEW* this leads to a slight decrease in performance, with *emojis* to an improvement (statistically significant improvement in recall). A closer inspection of the results shows that both features pick up on the second largest class and label some tweets correctly with *happiness*. See Table 8 for some tweets correctly labeled with happiness in the final setting.

When combining the strongest linguistic feature *emojis* with other linguistic features, *ANEW* and *POS*

---

[4]`github.com/parthatalukdar/junto`

lead to slight decrease in performance while combining *emojis* and *words* achieves the best results in F-measure which is due to a higher precision. Adding further linguistic features does not cause any improvement.

Temporal and spatial features on their own do not classify anything correctly. When combining *emojis* with temporal features (with a range of different values for α) we observe a drop in performance. When combining with spatial features and with spatial and temporal features, there is no difference to just *emojis*. Further experiments with temporal and spatial features show that they lead to a small but statistically not significant improvement when weighted much higher than linguistic similarity (e.g. $\times$ 5). Highest values for α performed best (i.e. lowest curves in Figure 2).

6 Discussion

Our research allows an interesting glance into the way emotions are displayed in microblogs: While we expected prevalent emotions to be negative because of the terrorist attack that took place during the time span we examined, Table 4 shows that the opposite is true. Table 6 provides a possible explanation for this: hashtags such as #bostonstrong can mask negative feelings. We evaluate our method using micro- and macro-averaged precision, recall, and F-measure (Tsoumakas et al., 2010). Experiments show that we can recognize *none* and *happiness* better than suitable baselines. The overall best-performing feature group was *emojis*. Our analysis of tweets revealed that negative emotions frequently cause tweets conveying a positive emotion. This leads to a skewed seed distribution (Table 4), and hence infrequent labels are rarely assigned at all. This phenomenon requires further research. Random selection of seed tweets may not have been such a good idea, because only very few of our seeds are temporally or spatially close enough. Further experiments should check whether a tighter spatial and temporal distribution of the seed tweets would enable the temporal and spatial features to have a positive impact. For now we have to conclude that linguistic features are superior to temporal and spatial features for Twitter emotion classification. Future research should define improved linguistic features and search for optimal temporal/spatial parameter settings.

Acknowledgments. We acknowledge the German Research Foundation (DFG) for supporting the project "Urban Emotions", reference numbers ZE 1018/1-1 and RE 3612/1-1. We would like to thank Dr. Wendy Guan from Harvard University's Center for Geographic Analysis for her support through providing us with Twitter data. We would like to thank Günther Sagl, Enrico Steiger, René Westerholt, Clemens Jacobs and Sebastian Döring for supporting the annotation procedure. We would like to thank the Doctoral College GIScience (DK W 1237-N23) at the Department of Geoinformatics–Z_GIS, University of Salzburg, Austria, funded by the Austrian Science Fund (FWF). The third author has been supported by the Klaus Tschira Foundation, Heidelberg, Germany.

References

Eneko Agirre, Daniel Cer, Mona Diab, and Aitor Gonzalez-Agirre. 2012. Semeval-2012 task 6: A pilot on semantic textual similarity. In *Proc. *SEM 2012/SemEval 2012*, pages 385–393, 7-8 June.

Karla Z. Bertrand, Maya Bialik, Kawandeep Virdee, Andreas Gros, and Yaneer Bar-Yam. 2013. Sentiment in New York City: A High Resolution Spatial and Temporal View. Technical Report 2013-08-01, New England Complex Systems Institute (NECSI).

Johan Bollen, Huina Mao, and Alberto Pepe. 2011. Modeling Public Mood and Emotion: Twitter Sentiment and Socio-Economic Phenomena. In *Proc. ICWSM'11*, pages 450–453.

Danah Boyd and Kate Crawford. 2012. Critical Questions for Big Data. *Information, Communication & Society*, 15(5):662–679.

Margaret M Bradley and Peter J Lang. 2010. Affective Norms for English Words (ANEW): Instruction manual and affective ratings. Technical report, University of Florida, Gainesville, FL.

Samuel Brody and Nicholas Diakopoulos. 2011. Cooooooooooooooooollllllllllllll!!!!!!!!!!!!!! Using Word Lengthening to Detect Sentiment in Microblogs. In *Proc. EMNLP'11*, pages 562–570.

Hsia-ching Chang. 2010. A New Perspective on Twitter Hashtag Use : Diffusion of Innovation Theory. *Proceedings of the American Society for Information Science and Technology*, 47(1):1–4.

Andrew Crooks, Arie Croitoru, Anthony Stefanidis, and Jacek Radzikowski. 2013. #Earthquake: Twitter as a Distributed Sensor System. *Transactions in GIS*, 17(1):124–147.

Dmitry Davidov, Oren Tsur, and Ari Rappoport. 2010. Enhanced Sentiment Learning Using Twitter Hashtags and Smileys. In *Coling 2010: Poster Volume*, pages 241–249.

Thomas G Dietterich. 1998. Approximate Statistical Tests for Comparing Supervised Classication Learning Algorithms. *Neural Computation*, 10(7):1895–1923.

Jacob Eisenstein. 2013. What to do about bad language on the internet. In *Proc. NAACL'13*, pages 359–369.

Paul Ekman and Wallace V. Friesen. 1971. Constants across cultures in the face and emotion. *Journal of Personality and Social Psychology*, 17(2):124–129.

Joseph L. Fleiss. 1971. Measuring Nominal Scale Agreement Among Many Raters. *Psychological Bulletin*, 76(5):378–382.

Bo Han, Paul Cook, and Timothy Baldwin. 2014. Text-based Twitter user geolocation prediction. *Journal of Artificial Intelligence Research*, 49:451–500.

Harvard University, Center for Geographic Analysis. 2016. Harvard CGA Geo-tweet Archive. DOI:10.7910/DVN/A0HHDI, Harvard Dataverse, V1.

Rachael E Jack, Oliver G B Garrod, and Philippe G Schyns. 2014. Dynamic Facial Expressions of Emotion Transmit an Evolving Hierarchy of Signals over Time. *Current Biology*, 24(2):187–192, jan.

Efthymios Kouloumpis, Theresa Wilson, and Johanna Moore. 2011. Twitter Sentiment Analysis : The Good the Bad and the OMG ! In *Proc. ICWSM'11*, pages 538–541, Barcelona, Catalonia, Spain.

Zornitsa Kozareva, Borja Navarro, Sonia Vazquez, and Andres Montoyo. 2007. UA-ZBSA : A Headline Emotion Classification through Web Information. In *Proc. SemEval'07*, pages 334–337.

Robert Layton, Paul Watters, and Richard Dazeley. 2010. Authorship attribution for Twitter in 140 characters or less. In *Proceedings of the Second Cybercrime and Trustworthy Computing Workshop, CTC 2010*, pages 1–8, Los Alamitos, CA, USA. IEEE.

Chung-Hong Lee, Hsin-Chang Yang, Tzan-Feng Chien, and Wei-Shiang Wen. 2011. A novel approach for event detection by mining spatio-temporal information on microblogs. In *Proceedings of the International Conference on Advances in Social Networks Analysis and Mining, ASONAM 2011*, pages 254–259, Kaohsiung City, Taiwan. Institute of Electrical and Electronics Engineers (IEEE).

Bing Liu and Lei Zhang. 2012. A survey of opinion mining and sentiment analysis. In *Mining Text Data*, chapter 1, pages 415–463. Springer US.

Marco Lui and Timothy Baldwin. 2012. langid.py: An Off-the-shelf Language Identification Tool. In *Proceedings of the 50th Annual Meeting of the Association for Computational Linguistics*, number July, pages 25–30, Jeju, Republic of Korea. Association for Computational Linguistics.

Nicci Macleod and Tim Grant. 2012. Whose Tweet? Authorship analysis of micro-blogs and other short-form messages. In Samuel Tomblin, Nicci MacLeod, Rui Sousa-Silva, and Malcolm Coulthard, editors, *Proceedings of The International Association of Forensic LinguistsTenth Biennial Conference*, pages 210–224. Centre for Forensic Linguistics.

Michael McCandless. 2010. Accuracy and performance of google's compact language detector.

Saif M. Mohammad and Svetlana Kiritchenko. 2014. Using hashtags to capture fine emotion categories from tweets. *Computational Intelligence*, 31(2):301–326.

Christoph Müller. 2007. Resolving It , This , and That in Unrestricted Multi-Party Dialog. In *Proc. ACL'07*, pages 816–823.

Preslav Nakov, Alan Ritter, Sara Rosenthal, and Veselin Stoyanov. 2016. SemEval-2016 Task 4: Sentiment Analysis in Twitter. In *Proc. SemEval'16*, pages 1–18.

Olutobi Owoputi, Brendan O'Connor, Chris Dyer, Kevin Gimpel, Nathan Schneider, and Noah A Smith. 2013. Improved part-of-speech tagging for online conversational text with word clusters. In *Proc. NAACL'13*, pages 380–390.

Alexander Pak and Patrick Paroubek. 2010. Twitter as a Corpus for Sentiment Analysis and Opinion Mining. In *Proc. LREC'10*, pages 1320–1326.

Matthew Purver and Stuart Battersby. 2012. Experimenting with Distant Supervision for Emotion Classification. In *Proceedings of the 13th Conference of the European Chapter of the Association for Computational Linguistics*, pages 482–491. Association for Computational Linguistics.

Afshin Rahimi, Trevor Cohn, and Timothy Baldwin. 2015a. Twitter user geolocation using a unified text and network prediction model. In *Proc. ACL-IJCNLP'15*, pages 630–636.

Afshin Rahimi, Duy Vu, Trevor Cohn, and Timothy Baldwin. 2015b. Exploiting text and network context for geolocation of social media users. In *Proc. NAACL'15*, pages 1362–1367.

Bernd Resch, Anja Summa, Peter Zeile, and Michael Strube. 2016. Citizen-centric urban planning through extracting emotion information from Twitter in an interdisciplinary space-time-linguistics algorithm. *Urban Planning*, 1(2):114–127.

Kirk Roberts, Michael A. Roach, Joseph Johnson, Josh Guthrie, and Sanda M. Harabagiu. 2012. Empatweet: Annotating and detecting emotions on twitter. In *Proc. LREC'12*, pages 3806–3813.

Takeshi Sakaki, Makoto Okazaki, and Yutaka Matsuo. 2010. Earthquake shakes Twitter users: real-time event detection by social sensors. In *Proc. WWW'10*, pages 851–860.

Sarah E Schwarm and Mari Ostendorf. 2005. Reading level assessment using support vector machines and statistical language models. In *Proc. ACL'05*, pages 523–530.

Roy Schwartz, Oren Tsur, Ari Rappoport, and Moshe Koppel. 2013. Authorship Attribution of Micro Messages. In *Proc. EMNLP'13*, pages 1880–1891.

Phillip Shaver, Judith Schwartz, Donald Kirson, and Cary O'Connor. 1987. Emotion knowledge: further exploration of a prototype approach. *Journal of Personality and Social Psychology*, 52(6):1061–1086.

Rui Sousa Silva, Gustavo Laboreiro, Luis Sarmento, Tim Grant, Eugenio Oliveira, and Belinda Maia. 2011. 'twazn me!!! ;(' Automatic Authorship Analysis of Micro-Blogging Messages. In *Natural Language Processing and Information Systems*, pages 161–168. Springer Berlin Heidelberg.

Enrico Steiger, João Porto De Albuquerque, and Alexander Zipf. 2015. An advanced systematic literature review on spatiotemporal analyses of Twitter data. *Transactions in GIS*, 19(6):809–834.

Carlo Strapparava and Rada Mihalcea. 2007. SemEval-2007 Task 14 : Affective Text. In *Proc. SemEval'07*, pages 70–74.

Carlo Strapparava and Rada Mihalcea. 2008. Learning to identify emotions in text. *Proceedings of the 2008 ACM Symposium on Applied Computing - SAC '08*, pages 1556–1560.

Partha Pratim Talukdar and Koby Crammer. 2009. New Regularized Algorithms for Transductive Learning. In *Machine Learning and Knowledge Discovery in Databases*, pages 442–457. Springer Berlin Heidelberg.

Waldo R. Tobler. 1970. A Computer Movie Simulating Urban Growth in the Detroit Region. *Economic Geography*, 46:234–240.

Grigorios Tsoumakas, Ioannis Katakis, and Ioannis Vlahavas. 2010. Mining Multi-label Data. In Oded Maimon and Lior Rokach, editors, *Data Mining and Knowledge Discovery Handbook*, pages 667–685. Springer, Heidelberg, 2nd edition.

Svitlana Volkova and Yoram Bachrach. 2016. Inferring perceived demographics from user emotional tone and user-environment emotional contrast. In *Proc. of ACL-16*, pages 1567–1578.

Svitlana Volkova, Ilia Chetviorkin, Dustin Arendt, and Benjamin Van Durme. 2016. Contrasting public opinion dynamics and emotional response during crisis. In *Proc. SocInfo-16*. To appear.

A domain-agnostic approach for opinion prediction on speech

Pedro Bispo Santos[†] and **Lisa Beinborn**[†] and **Iryna Gurevych**[†‡]
[†]Ubiquitous Knowledge Processing Lab (UKP)
Department of Computer Science, Technische Universität Darmstadt
[‡]Ubiquitous Knowledge Processing Lab (UKP-DIPF)
German Institute for Educational Research
`https://www.ukp.tu-darmstadt.de/`

Abstract

We explore a domain-agnostic approach for analyzing speech with the goal of opinion prediction. We represent the speech signal by mel-frequency cepstral coefficients and apply long short-term memory neural networks to automatically learn temporal regularities in speech. In contrast to previous work, our approach does not require complex feature engineering and works without textual transcripts. As a consequence, it can easily be applied on various speech analysis tasks for different languages and the results show that it can nevertheless be competitive to the state-of-the-art in opinion prediction. In a detailed error analysis for opinion mining we find that our approach performs well in identifying speaker-specific characteristics, but should be combined with additional information if subtle differences in the linguistic content need to be identified.

1 Introduction

Traditional natural language processing approaches have focused on the analysis of linguistic content and the represented information. With the increasing availability of recorded speech, the interest shifted from pure content processing to analyzing the states and traits of speakers (Schuller et al., 2012). For this purpose, paralinguistic features such as pitch and loudness of voice are playing an important role because they are very predictive social markers (Laver and Trudgill, 1979). They influence our persuasiveness (Burgoon et al., 1990), indicate our emotional state (Scherer, 2003) and correlate with our personality traits (Markel et al., 1972).

The ability to analyze paralinguistic features has led to progress in a multitude of speech processing tasks such as age identification (Metze et al., 2007), personality recognition (Schuller et al., 2012) and emotion recognition (Nwe et al., 2003). A subset of these problems is tackled every year as shared tasks in the *Computational Paralinguistics Challenge* at the INTERSPEECH conference (Schuller et al., 2015; Schuller et al., 2014).[1] For the winning methods of the last editions from these shared tasks, thorough task-specific feature engineering has usually been the key point.

In this paper, we aim at reducing the engineering effort and the dependence on domain-specific knowledge in speech processing tasks for opinion prediction. We approach this goal by applying deep learning methods which have been shown to automatically learn more complex and high-level features from basic features extracted from the signal (Palaz et al., 2015). The main challenge for applying these approaches lies in determining a good representation of the data and choosing a suitable architecture for the task at hand.

For our approach, we use only the speech signal as input, so that expensive textual transcripts are not required. We work on the frame level[2] and choose mel-frequency cepstral coefficients (MFCCs) as our unit of representation because they correspond well to the human auditory system and are very discriminative for speech processing tasks, such as phoneme recognition (Davis and Mermelstein, 1980), speaker identification (Ren et al., 2016) and claim identification in political debates (Lippi and Torroni,

---

This work is licensed under a Creative Commons Attribution 4.0 International Licence.
Licence details: `http://creativecommons.org/licenses/by/4.0/`

[1]`http://emotion-research.net/sigs/speech-sig/is16-compare`
[2]Frames are overlapping windows from the signal obtained from short-term analysis.

Proceedings of the Workshop on Computational Modeling of People's Opinions, Personality, and Emotions in Social Media,
pages 163–172, Osaka, Japan, December 12 2016.

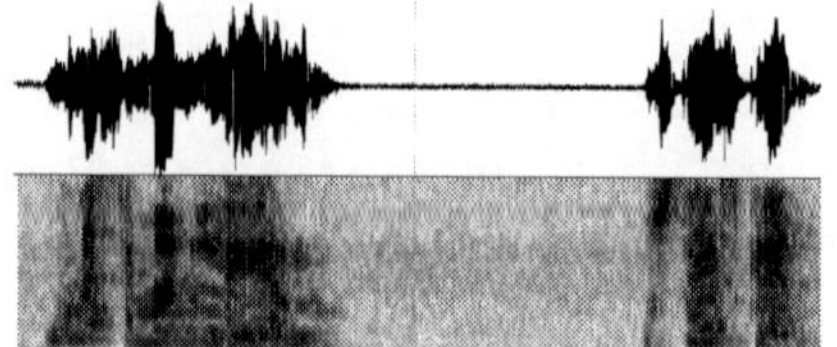

Figure 1: Subject expressing her negative opinion about a book. The dataset contains the textual transcripts and the recorded utterances from the subjects. Here we can visualize the raw signal of her utterance along with the corresponding spectrogram.

2016). Rosen (1992) analyzes that speech perception is strongly influenced by temporal dependencies. We therefore model the speech signal as a time series and use long short-term neural networks as machine learning method. In contrast to previous approaches in computational paralinguistics, we do not need to compute additional task-specific statistics on the features extracted from the frames because LSTM networks are able to learn the temporal regularities automatically from the input signal. This makes it possible to apply our approach to different tasks without additional engineering.

In order to test whether our approach can compete with state-of-the-art methods, we focus on two interesting tasks concerning speech: opinion mining and persuasiveness prediction. For both tasks, the goal can be framed as opinion prediction, but the perspective differs. In the first task, our goal is to predict the opinion of a user speaking about a product. In the second task, we aim at predicting the influence of a speaker on the opinion of an audience. Previous approaches to these tasks developed a sophisticated feature set to capture the recognition of emotions for opinion mining (Poria et al., 2015) and the characteristics of voice quality for persuasiveness prediction (Brilman and Scherer, 2015).

We find that the results of our domain-agnostic approach come close to the performance of domain-specific ones that apply thorough feature engineering. As we use the same features for different tasks, we minimize the risk of overfitting to the data. Our error analysis explain in more details the issues with our approach in both datasets, but also highlight how far a generic computational method based solely on speech can go in tasks related to opinion prediction.

2 Tasks

For the evaluation of our approach, we focus on two different speech tasks: opinion mining and persuasion prediction. In both tasks, the goal is to analyze opinions. For opinion mining, we aim at directly predicting the opinion of the speaker and for persuasiveness prediction we aim at indirectly predicting the opinion of an audience based on the persuasiveness of the speaker.

2.1 Opinion mining

In opinion mining, the task is to assign a polarity (*negative, neutral, positive*) to opinions expressed by users. This task has become increasingly popular with the rise of social platforms which provide valuable information on customers' opinions. As manual analyses cannot scale up to the vast amount of opinionated comments, the application of automatic analyses is required. For our experiments on opinion mining, we use the MOUD dataset.

MOUD Dataset   The *Multimodal Opinion Utterance Dataset* (Pérez-Rosas et al., 2013b) is a collection of video blogs extracted from *YouTube*.[3] It consists of videos from 80 Spanish native speakers (15 male, 65 female) who express their opinion about movies, books and cosmetics. Figure 1 shows an example of a review and the corresponding speech signal from the utterance. The speakers' age ranges from 20 to 60 years. Pérez-Rosas et al. (2013b) manually extracted a 30 seconds opinion snippet from each video and segmented it into utterances yielding a total of 498 utterances. Each utterance was then analyzed by two

---

[3]https://www.youtube.com/

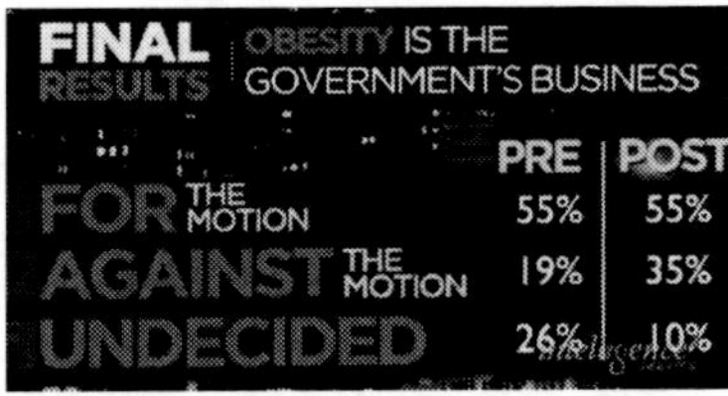

Figure 2: An example poll from the debate dataset. The debate winner is the team which sways more votes; in this case the team that argued *against* the motion.

annotators to determine whether the speaker reveals a *positive*, *neutral* or *negative* sentiment towards the product. They report an inter-annotator agreement of 0.88 and a kappa of 0.81. Conflicting annotations were subsequently resolved by discussions. We use the publicly available dataset and exclude utterances with a neutral label from our experiments to be consistent with previous work (Pérez-Rosas et al., 2013b; Poria et al., 2015).[4]

2.2 Persuasiveness Prediction

The task of persuasiveness prediction in debates has been established by Brilman and Scherer (2015) who worked with videos of debates from the *Intelligence Squared* organization. In these debates, two teams argue about a motion and try to convince the audience of their stance. The team that is able to sway more votes from the audience wins the debate. The goal is to predict the persuasiveness of the teams and the individual debaters.

Intelligence Squared Dataset   *Intelligence Squared* is an organization which promotes debates about controversial motions between topic experts. The debates are all recorded and available online.[5] Each debate team is composed of two debaters and the debates are split into three rounds: opening statements, question round and closing statements. The debates are performed in Oxford-style which means that the opinion of the audience is measured by two polls. The first poll is conducted before the start of the debate, and the second one after the closing statements. The audience can vote *for* or *against* the motion or choose to remain *undecided*. In Figure 2, we see an example for a motion stating that *obesity is the government's business*. In this case, the team *against* the motion won because they achieved a higher relative gain of votes (16%). It should be noted that the team *for* the motion represents the opinion of the majority here, but could not convince the remaining audience to change their opinion during the debate.

We implemented a crawler to obtain the debates from the organization's website. For our experiments, we used the same setup as Brilman and Scherer (2015). This means that debates which had a voting difference equal to or smaller than six are excluded and the prediction is only based on the opening and closing statements of each debate. This procedure yields 30 debates in total and includes 120 debaters (19 female, 101 male). We publish the code for the crawler and the list of seed urls.[6]

3   Related Work

The task of opinion mining is quite established in natural language processing, but most approaches have been developed for textual data (Pang and Lee, 2008). In this work, we focus on opinion mining in speech. Persuasiveness prediction is a relatively new task in the area of debating technologies.

3.1   Opinion Mining

Scherer (2003) shows that paralinguistic features are particularly informative for identifying the speakers' emotional state, and they have been used extensively for the task of detecting principal emotions such as fear or anger (Batliner et al., 2011). However, the subtler task of analyzing the opinion of a speaker

---

[4]http://web.eecs.umich.edu/~mihalcea/downloads.html#MOUD
[5]http://intelligencesquaredus.org/
[6]https://github.com/UKPLab/coling-peoples2016-opinion-prediction

towards a product has not yet received much attention. Mairesse et al. (2012) compare models built on textual features with models built on paralinguistic features to predict the opinion expressed in short spoken reviews. They found that the results improve if the features calculated on transcripts are combined with paralinguistic features. Morency et al. (2011) examine three modalities and extract visual, audio and textual features to predict the opinion expressed in videos. They find that combining the three modalities produces the best outcome. The approach was then extended to other languages (Pérez-Rosas et al., 2013a) and to more fine-grained analyses on the utterance level leading to the *MOUD* dataset (Pérez-Rosas et al., 2013b). Poria et al. (2015) improve the results for the *MOUD* dataset by applying a deep learning approach that builds a representation for the transcripts with convolutional neural networks. Both approaches use a wide range of thoroughly engineered features including acoustic-prosodic features like pitch and speaking rate for emotion recognition, textual features for the detection of sentiment words, and visual features such as facial landmarks for capturing emotional states.

To account for the importance of temporal aspects for speech perception (Rosen, 1992), we model the speech signal as a time series. In previous work on opinion mining in speech, complex functions had been calculated over the features extracted at the frame level to account for the temporal dependencies. Recent progress in modeling time series data has been achieved with long short term memory networks. They have obtained good results for audio processing tasks such as music composition (Coca et al., 2013) and phoneme classification (Graves and Schmidhuber, 2005). They have also been applied in opinion mining on text (Wang et al., 2016), but have not yet been explored for opinion mining on speech.

3.2 Debating Technologies

The field of debating technologies is a newly developing research area that focuses on computational methods to support human argumentation and debating (Gurevych et al., 2016). In recent work, claim identification for controversial topics (Roitman et al., 2016), evidence detection (Rinott et al., 2015) and argument convincingness prediction (Habernal and Gurevych, 2016) have been tackled.

These works focus on analyzing the content, but Hosman et al. (2002) showed that paralinguistic features are very informative to detect credibility and persuasiveness of speakers. This observation has been used in the work by Lippi and Torroni (2016) who combine paralinguistic features with textual features to detect claims in political debates. They represent the input signal by mel-frequency cepstral coefficients and find that the combination of text and audio modalities yields the best results. Brilman and Scherer (2015) also apply a multi-modal approach and combine textual, acoustic and visual information to predict the persuasiveness of speakers in the *Intelligence Squared* dataset. They represent the speech data by features related to voice perception such as pitch, formants and voice quality. Park et al. (2014) did a very similar approach to Brilman and Scherer (2015), although not working with data from debates, but with movie reviewers from *ExpoTV*.[7] They used even more features: MFCCs, pitch, formants and all the voice quality features used by Brilman and Scherer (2015). All approaches extract speech features on the frame level, calculate statistics such as average and standard deviation over the sequential data and feed them to support vector machines. Unfortunately, statistical functions computed over static representations of frames cannot capture temporal dependencies in the speech sequence. Chung et al. (2016) have shown that LSTMs can overcome this issue and model the speech signal more adequately.

4 Methodology

Our domain-agnostic approach is based on two aspects: a simple but informative paralinguistic feature set which can be easily extracted for speech signals from different domains and a deep learning approach which can discover temporal regularities in the data.

4.1 Features

Creating textual transcripts of speech recordings is an expensive and time-consuming task. It requires either thorough manual work or a sophisticated acoustic model trained on large corpora for automatic

---

[7]http://www.expotv.com

speech recognition (Xiong et al., 2016). In contrast to previous work, we rely only on the basic speech signal in order to evaluate whether satisfactory prediction quality can be reached even without transcripts.

Since Hosman et al. (2002) find that powerful speeches are more persuasive and Pérez-Rosas et al. (2013b) analyze that the energy level of the voice is predictive for opinion mining, we aim at representing the speech signal by paralinguistic features from the power spectrum. Our auditory system is very sensitive to changes in the frequency of an acoustic wave when the frequency is low, but more robust to changes in higher frequency ranges. The mel-scale is a scale which corresponds to our perception on frequency changes (Stevens et al., 1937). We use mel-frequency cepstral coefficients (MFCCs) from 13 different frequency ranges as our representation unit because they are a good approximation of the human auditory perception (Davis and Mermelstein, 1980). The MFCCs are obtained by dividing the speech signal into frames and applying a discrete fourier transform. Based on a filter-bank analysis with mel-scaled frequency bins, the cepstral coefficients can then be determined with a cosine discrete transform. Using only one basic operationalization for speech that can be calculated automatically, it keeps our feature extraction effort small and allows us to apply our approach to different domains. These coefficients are usually interpreted as a good generic indicator for different tasks in speech processing, such as speaker identification (Ren et al., 2016) and claim identification in debates (Lippi and Torroni, 2016).

4.2 Learning Architecture

Deep learning architectures have the power to learn high-level abstractions from raw features and are strongly used in vision, language and speech (Bengio, 2009). To account for the sequential nature of speech signals, we apply an LSTM architecture which has been developed for processing time series (Hochreiter and Schmidhuber, 1997). LSTM networks are based on recurrent neural networks and use memory cells to keep track of long-term dependencies by the usage of gate units. The network directly processes the extracted features from each frame and automatically learns high-level abstractions. Using this architecture, we avoid the effort of manually defining task-specific statistics over the frame level features which has usually been necessary for speech labeling tasks.

4.3 Experimental Setup

The MFCCs were extracted using the python library *python_speech_features*.[8] The window size was 25 ms with a sliding window of 10 ms. The *Keras* framework[9] was used for implementing the LSTMs. The code from both experiments is available on GitHub.[10]

Opinion Mining   The audio files from this dataset have a sampling rate of 44,100 Hz. We have implemented a bi-directional LSTM with 128 nodes at each hidden layer. The batch size is 128 and the dataset is divided into 10 folds in order to perform cross-validation. Each utterance is preprocessed, and sequences with a length greater than 236 were truncated. Adam is used as optimizer and binary cross-entropy is used as loss function. We use hyperbolic tangent as activation function for all hidden layers and for the merging layer. The last fully connected layer which assigns the binary label to the sequence uses sigmoid as activation function. All hyperparameters were set based on empirical evidence obtained from experiments on a single fold.

Persuasion Prediction   We extracted the speech signal for each debater with *FFmpeg*.[11] The audio segments have a sampling rate of 48,000 Hz. In contrast to the input sequences from the *MOUD* dataset which were split into utterances and lasted only a few seconds, the segments in the *Intelligence Squared* dataset last a few minutes resulting in up to 25,000 frames. We apply padding to the shorter sequences.

We implemented an LSTM network with hidden layers containing 64 nodes in the *Keras* framework. We use hyperbolic tangent as activation function and a dropout of 0.2 for both the matrix and the recurrent weights. The last layer is a fully connected layer with a single node and a sigmoid activation function which assigns the label to the sequence. The label indicates whether the debater belongs to the winning or

---

[8] http://python-speech-features.readthedocs.io/en/latest/
[9] https://keras.io/
[10] https://github.com/UKPLab/coling-peoples2016-opinion-prediction
[11] https://ffmpeg.org/

the losing team. We use binary cross-entropy as loss function, RMSProp as optimizer, and a batch size of
1. The hyperparameters were set based on empirical evidence from experiments on a single fold. Like
Brilman and Scherer (2015), we perform a leave-one-debate-out cross-validation to avoid a topic-specific
bias. The data is split into 30 different folds, each using 29 debates for training and the remaining debate
for testing.

5   Results

We evaluate our domain-agnostic approach on two tasks with different languages and compare the results
to the state-of-the-art in each task.

Opinion Mining   For opinion mining, we compare our approach to a majority baseline and to the results
obtained by the speech features from the domain-specific approaches by Pérez-Rosas et al. (2013b) and
Poria et al. (2015) in Table 1. It can be seen that our approach outperforms the majority baseline and
the method by Pérez-Rosas et al. (2013b). As expected, the approach by Poria et al. (2015) which uses
carefully engineered features for emotion recognition performs better on the task. It should be noted
that the results of our approach even get close to the results obtained by content-specific textual features
calculated over the transcripts, where the textual features are only 4.1% better than our approach. This
shows that a generic speech feature set processed by a bi-directional LSTM can approximate the results of
domain-specific approaches for opinion mining without further engineering.

System	Modality	Accuracy
Majority baseline	-	.559
Our approach	Audio	.668
Pérez-Rosas et al. (2013b)	Audio	.648
Poria et al. (2015)	Audio	**.742**
Pérez-Rosas et al. (2013b)	Text	.709
Poria et al. (2015)	Text	**.797**

Table 1: Accuracy results for opinion mining

Persuasion Prediction   For persuasion prediction, we use the same evaluation setup as Brilman and
Scherer (2015). They evaluate the accuracy for the opening and closing statements separately and
distinguish between the accuracy on the individual level and on the debate level. The classifier predicts
for each debater individually whether she belongs to the winning or the losing debate team. This can lead
to a tied prediction for a team as each team consists of two debaters. To account for this, the debate-level
accuracy measure combines the two individual labels by computing an accuracy of 1 if both individual
labels match the team label, 0 for a complete mismatch and 0.5 for a tied prediction. Both accuracy
measures – individual and debate level – are averaged over all folds. As the dataset is balanced for winning
and losing teams, the majority baseline obtains an accuracy of 0.5.

Level	System	Opening	Closing	Modality
Individual	Majority baseline	.500	.500	-
	Our approach	**.683**	.642	Audio
	Brilman and Scherer (2015)	.675	**.650**	Audio
	Brilman and Scherer (2015)	.550	.600	Text
Debate	Majority baseline	.500	.500	-
	Our approach	**.767**	.683	Audio
	Brilman and Scherer (2015)	.717	**.733**	Audio
	Brilman and Scherer (2015)	.533	.700	Text

Table 2: Accuracy results for persuasion prediction at the individual level and the debate level.

The results in Table 2 show that our approach outperforms the majority baseline by at least 14.2%
for each setting and performs on par with the results obtained for the speech features by Brilman and

Scherer (2015) (slightly better for the opening statements and slightly worse for the closing statements). It is particularly interesting to note that the results for the speech features are even stronger than the results obtained by content-specific textual features. This indicates that voice quality aspects have a strong influence on the persuasiveness of a speaker independent of the actual content of his arguments.

For our experiments, we only operated on the speech level to evaluate the predictive power in the absence of textual transcripts. Obviously, better results can be obtained by combining information from multiple modalities and by using domain-specific features. Nevertheless, the results show that our approach can provide a competitive start when switching to new domains.

6 Error Analysis

In order to better identify the strength and weaknesses of our naïve approach for opinion prediction, we perform a more detailed analysis of the results.

Opinion Mining After a first round of qualitative analyses, we noticed that many speakers express mixed opinions towards a product as in the following example: *The thing is: when you use it, it may hurt your eye a little bit, (**negative**) so after using it for the first time, I thought: "Oh no, I am not going to use it anymore, that is not possible!" (**negative**)[...] However, it is super easy to be washed.(**positive**).*

In the *MOUD* dataset, this opinion is segmented into three utterances with the polarity labels indicated in brackets. We noticed that from the subjective perception only minor changes in the voice could be observed for these three utterances because the speaker kept a rather neutral tone. As the dataset contained many similar examples, we were puzzled by the fact that the classifier was still able to predict the correct opinion label for the majority of utterances based on the voice features alone and started a deeper investigation.

We observe that most speakers have a tendency towards expressing either mostly positive or mostly negative utterances. In the current evaluation setup established in previous work, utterances by the same speaker are distributed over the training and test set which might lead to a speaker bias. A speaker-majority classifier, i.e. a classifier which learns to assign the majority label for a particular speaker to all her utterances, would obtain 87.7% of accuracy for this dataset and strongly outperform all results in Table 1. This indicates that the underlying task of this dataset is not necessarily opinion mining, but rather speaker identification which explains the acceptable performance of our domain-agnostic approach. [12] This observation should be considered when evaluating the findings for opinion mining obtained on this dataset in previous work. Cepstral coefficients are an important indicator for speaker identification and the recognition of extreme emotions. In order to capture the subtle sentiment differences expressed in rather neutral speech, content-specific features are likely to be more predictive. Unfortunately, these aspects cannot be disentangled for the current dataset and we consider our analysis an important contribution that should be considered for future work on the *MOUD* dataset.

Phase	System	Correct	Tie	Wrong
Opening	**Our Approach**	**19**	8	**3**
	Brilman and Scherer (2015)	18	7	5
Closing	**Our Approach**	13	15	2
	Brilman and Scherer (2015)	**15**	**14**	**1**

Table 3: Number of corrected predictions, ties and wrong predictions for the debate-level.

Persuasiveness Prediction As described above, the debate level accuracy for the persuasiveness prediction tasks is composed by correct, wrong and tied predictions for the two debaters of each team. In Table 3, we see that our approach completely misclassifies only 10% of the debates, but often yields a tied prediction for the two debaters. Unfortunately, information about the persuasiveness of the individual speakers cannot be obtained because they are evaluated as a team. For future work, it might be reasonable

---

[12]If we perform Leave-One-Speaker-Out cross-validation, the accuracy of our approach drops by 5.1%.

to add an additional layer to the network that learns how to merge the labels for the individuals into a team label. It should be noticed that there exists of course a wide range of additional factors influencing the persuasiveness of the debaters (Hunter, 2016) such as the previous opinion of the audience, the arguments used during the debate, the appearance and the non-verbal behavior of the speakers. Our approach has shown that cepstral coefficients form a very important indicator for persuasiveness that seems to be at least equally predictive as the actual content of the arguments.

7 Conclusions

We implemented a novel domain-agnostic approach for opinion prediction on speech using MFCCs as input representation and a bidirectional LSTM architecture. We evaluated our approach on opinion mining and persuasiveness prediction and found that our results come close to the performance of domain-specific approaches that apply task-specific feature engineering. In a thorough error analysis, we have shown that our approach performs well in identifying speaker-specific characteristics, but should be combined with additional information if subtle differences in the linguistic content need to be identified. Our publicly available implementation can serve as a starting point for more complex domain-specific approaches for a wide range of speech processing tasks. In addition, our analyses have revealed important characteristics of the two datasets that should be taken into account in future work.

Acknowledgements

This work has been supported by the FAZIT-STIFTUNG and by the German Research Foundation (DFG) as part of the Research Training Group "Adaptive Preparation of Information from Heterogeneous Sources" (AIPHES) under grant No. GRK 1994/1. We would like to thank Kunal Saxena for preprocessing and organizing the Intelligence Squared dataset.

References

Anton Batliner, Björn Schuller, Dino Seppi, Stefan Steidl, Laurence Devillers, Laurence Vidrascu, Thurid Vogt, Vered Aharonson, and Noam Amir. 2011. The automatic recognition of emotions in speech. In Roddy Cowie, Catherine Pelachaud, and Paolo Petta, editors, *Emotion-Oriented Systems*, pages 71–99. Springer Berlin Heidelberg.

Yoshua Bengio. 2009. Learning deep architectures for AI. *Foundations and Trends in Machine Learning*, 2(1):1–127.

Maarten Brilman and Stefan Scherer. 2015. A multimodal predictive model of successful debaters or how I learned to sway votes. In *ACM International Conference on Multimedia*, pages 149–158, New York, NY, USA.

Judee Burgoon, Thomas Birk, and Michael Pfau. 1990. Nonverbal behaviors, persuasion, and credibility. *Human Communication Research*, 17(1):140–169.

Yu-An Chung, Chao-Chung Wu, Chia-Hao Shen, Hung-Yi Lee, and Lin-Shan Lee. 2016. Audio word2vec: Unsupervised learning of audio segment representations using sequence-to-sequence autoencoder. In *Annual Conference of the International Speech Communication Association*, pages 765–769, San Francisco, CA, USA.

Andrés Coca, Débora Corrêa, and Liang Zhao. 2013. Computer-aided music composition with lstm neural network and chaotic inspiration. In *International Joint Conference on Neural Networks*, pages 1–7, Dallas, TX, USA.

Steven Davis and Paul Mermelstein. 1980. Comparison of parametric representations for monosyllabic word recognition in continuously spoken sentences. *IEEE Transactions on Acoustics, Speech, and Signal Processing*, 28(4):357–366.

Alex Graves and Jürgen Schmidhuber. 2005. Framewise phoneme classification with bidirectional lstm and other neural network architectures. *Neural Networks*, 18(5-6):602–610.

Iryna Gurevych, Eduard Hovy, Noam Slonim, and Benno Stein. 2016. Debating Technologies (Dagstuhl Seminar 15512). *Dagstuhl Reports*, 5(12):18–46.

Ivan Habernal and Iryna Gurevych. 2016. Which argument is more convincing? Analyzing and predicting convincingness of web arguments using bidirectional lstm. In *Proceedings of the ACL*, pages 1589–1599, Berlin, Germany.

Sepp Hochreiter and Jürgen Schmidhuber. 1997. Long short-term memory. *Neural Computation*, 9(8):1–32.

Lawrence Hosman, Thomas Huebner, and Susan Siltanen. 2002. The impact of power-of-speech style, argument strength, and need for cognition on impression formation, cognitive responses, and persuasion. *Journal of Language and Social Psychology*, 21(4):361–379.

Anthony Hunter. 2016. Computational persuasion with applications in behaviour change. In *Computational Models of Argument*, pages 5–18, Potsdam, Germany.

John Laver and Peter Trudgill. 1979. Phonetic and linguistic markers in speech. In Klaus Scherer and Howard Giles, editors, *Social Markers in Speech*. Cambridge University Press.

Marco Lippi and Paolo Torroni. 2016. Argument mining from speech: Detecting claims in political debates. In *AAAI Conference on Artificial Intelligence*, pages 2979–2985, Phoenix, AZ, USA.

François Mairesse, Joseph Polifroni, and Giuseppe Di Fabbrizio. 2012. Can prosody inform sentiment analysis? Experiments on short spoken reviews. In *International Conference on Acoustics, Speech and Signal Processing*, pages 5093–5096, Kyoto, Japan.

Norman Markel, Judith Phillis, Robert Vargas, and Kenneth Howard. 1972. Personality traits associated with voice types. *Journal of Psycholinguistic Research*, 1(3):249–255.

Florian Metze, Jitendra Ajmera, Roman Englert, Udo Bub, Felix Burkhardt, Joachim Stegmann, Christian Müller, Richard Huber, Bernt Andrassy, Josef Bauer, and Bernhard Littel. 2007. Comparison of four approaches to age and gender recognition for telephone applications. In *IEEE International Conference on Acoustics, Speech and Signal Processing*, pages IV–1089 – IV–1092, Honolulu, HI, USA.

Louis-Philippe Morency, Rada Mihalcea, and Payal Doshi. 2011. Towards multimodal sentiment analysis. In *International Conference on Multimodal Interfaces*, pages 169–176, Alicante, Spain. ACM Press.

Tin Lay Nwe, Say Wei Foo, and Liyanage Chandratilak De Silva. 2003. Speech emotion recognition using hidden markov models. *Speech Communication*, 41(4):603–623.

Dimitri Palaz, Mathew Magimai-Doss, and Ronan Collobert. 2015. Analysis of cnn-based speech recognition system using raw speech as input. In *Annual Conference of the International Speech Communication Association*, pages 11–15, Dresden, Germany.

Bo Pang and Lillian Lee. 2008. Opinion mining and sentiment analysis. *Foundations and Trends in Information Retrieval*, 2(1-2):1–135.

Sunghyun Park, Han Suk Shim, Moitreya Chatterjee, Kenji Sagae, and Louis-Philippe Morency. 2014. Computational analysis of persuasiveness in social multimedia: A novel dataset and multimodal prediction approach. In *International Conference on Multimodal Interaction*, pages 50–57, New York, NY, USA.

Verónica Pérez-Rosas, Rada Mihalcea, and Louis-Philippe Morency. 2013a. Multimodal sentiment analysis of Spanish online videos. *IEEE Intelligent Systems*, 28(3):38–45.

Verónica Pérez-Rosas, Rada Mihalcea, and Louis-Philippe Morency. 2013b. Utterance-level multimodal sentiment analysis. In *Proceedings of the ACL*, pages 973–982, Sofia, Bulgaria.

Soujanya Poria, Erik Cambria, and Alexander Gelbukh. 2015. Deep convolutional neural network textual features and multiple kernel learning for utterance-level multimodal sentiment analysis. In *Conference on Empirical Methods in Natural Language Processing*, pages 2539–2544, Lisbon, Portugal.

Jimmy Ren, Yongtao Hu, Yu-Wing Tai, Chuan Wang, Li Xu, Wenxiu Sun, and Qiong Yan. 2016. Look, listen and learn - a multimodal lstm for speaker identification. In *AAAI Conference on Artificial Intelligence*, pages 1–7, Phoenix, AZ, USA.

Ruty Rinott, Lena Dankin, Carlos Alzate, Mitesh Khapra, Ehud Aharoni, and Noam Slonim. 2015. Show me your evidence - an automatic method for context dependent evidence detection. In *Empirical Methods on Natural Language Processing*, pages 441–450, Lisbon, Portugal.

Haggai Roitman, Shay Hummel, Ella Rabinovich, Benjamin Sznajder, Noam Slonim, and Ehud Aharoni. 2016. On the retrieval of wikipedia articles containing claims on controversial topics. In *International Conference Companion on World Wide Web*, pages 991–996, Geneva, Switzerland.

Stuart Rosen. 1992. Temporal information in speech: Acoustic, auditory and linguistic aspects. *Philosophical Transactions of the Royal Society of London B: Biological Sciences*, 336(1278):367–373.

Klaus Scherer. 2003. Vocal communication of emotion: a review of research paradigms. *Speech Communication*, 40(1-2):227–256.

Björn Schuller, Stefan Steidl, Anton Batliner, Elmar Nöth, Alessandro Vinciarelli, Felix Burkhardt, Rob van Son, Felix Weninger, Florian Eyben, Tobias Bocklet, Gelareh Mohammadi, and Benjamin Weiss. 2012. The INTERSPEECH 2012 speaker trait challenge. In *Annual Conference of the International Speech Communication Association*, pages 254–257, Portland, OR, USA.

Björn Schuller, Stefan Steidl, Anton Batliner, Julien Epps, Florian Eyben, Fabien Ringeval, Erik Marchi, and Yue Zhang. 2014. The INTERSPEECH 2014 computational paralinguistics challenge: cognitive & physical load. In *Annual Conference of the International Speech Communication Association*, pages 427–431.

Björn Schuller, Stefan Steidl, Anton Batliner, Simone Hantke, Florian Hönig, Juan Rafael Orozco-Arroyave, Elmar Nöth, Yue Zhang, and Felix Weninger. 2015. The INTERSPEECH 2015 computational paralinguistics challenge: nativeness, parkinson's & eating condition. In *Annual Conference of the International Speech Communication Association*, pages 478–482, Dresden, Germany.

Stanley Stevens, John Volkmann, and Edwin Newman. 1937. A scale for the measurement of the psychological magnitude pitch. *The Journal of the Acoustical Society of America*, 8(3):185–190.

Jin Wang, Liang-Chih Yu, K. Robert Lai, and Xuejie Zhang. 2016. Dimensional sentiment analysis using a regional cnn-lstm model. In *Proceedings of the ACL*, pages 225–230, Berlin, Germany.

Wayne Xiong, Jasha Droppo, Xuedong Huang, Frank Seide, Mike Seltzer, Andreas Stolcke, Dong Yu, and Geoffrey Zweig. 2016. Achieving human parity in conversational speech recognition. *CoRR*, abs/1610.05256.

Can We Make Computers Laugh at Talks?

Chong Min Lee
Educational Testing Service
660 Rosedale Road
Princeton, NJ 08541 USA
clee001@ets.org

Su-Youn Yoon
Educational Testing Service
660 Rosedale Road
Princeton, NJ 08541 USA
syoon@ets.org

Lei Chen
Educational Testing Service
660 Rosedale Road
Princeton, NJ 08541 USA
lchen@ets.org

Abstract

Considering the importance of public speaking skills, a system that can predict where audiences might laugh during a talk can be helpful to a person preparing for a presentation. We investigated the possibility that a state-of-the-art humor recognition system could be used to detect sentences that induce laughters. In this study, we used TED talks and audience laughters during those talks as data. Our results showed that the state-of-the-art system needs to be improved in order to be used in a practical application. In addition, our analysis showed that classifying humorous sentences in talks is very challenging due to the close similarity between humorous and non-humorous sentences.

1 Introduction

Public speaking is an important skill for delivering knowledge or opinions to public audiences. In order to develop a successful talk, it is common to practice presentations, with colleagues acting as simulated audiences who then offer their feedback. A recent focus on the importance of public speaking led various studies (Batrinca et al., 2013; Kurihara et al., 2007; Nguyen et al., 2012) to develop systems for automatically evaluating public speaking skills. These studies used audio and video cues in order to evaluate the overall aspects of public speaking. However, the collection of human evaluation data for such systems is time-consuming and challenging (Chen et al., 2014).

If it is shown to be easier to collect audiences' reactions, it may also make sense to explore building an automated system which provides expected audience reactions. For example, speakers sometimes try to add sentences that make audiences laugh or applaud in order to make a successful talk. As Gruner (1985) said, humor in public speakings will "produce a more favorable reaction toward a speaker" and "enhance speaker image." However, there is no guarantee that the expected reactions would occur in an actual talk. If an automatic system can provide audience reactions which are likely to occur in actual talks, it will be helpful in the process of preparing a talk. In this study, we investigated the feasibility of current NLP technologies in building a system which provides expected audience reactions to public speaking.

Studies on automatic humor recognition (Mihalcea and Strapparava, 2005; Yang et al., 2015; Zhang and Liu, 2014; Purandare and Litman, 2006) have defined the recognition task as a binary classification task. So, their classification models categorized a given sentence as a humorous or non-humorous sentence. Among the studies on humor classification, Mihalcea and Strapparava (2005) and Yang et al. (2015) reported high performance on the task. Considering the performance of their systems, it is reasonable to test the applicability of their models to a real application. In this study, we specifically applied a state-of- the-art automatic humor recognition model to talks and investigated if the model could be used to provide simulated laughters.

In our application of the state-of-art system to talks, we could not achieve a comparable performance to the reported performance of the system. We investigated the potential reasons for the performance

This work is licenced under a Creative Commons Attribution 4.0 International License. License details: http://creativecommons.org/licenses/by/4.0/

Proceedings of the Workshop on Computational Modeling of People's Opinions, Personality, and Emotions in Social Media,
pages 173–181, Osaka, Japan, December 12 2016.

difference through further analysis. Some humor classification studies (Mihalcea and Strapparava, 2005; Yang et al., 2015; Barbieri and Saggion, 2014) have used negative instances from different domains or topics, because non-humorous sentences could not be found or are very challenging to collect in target domains or topics. Their studies showed that it was possible to achieve promising performance using data from heterogeneous domains. However, our study showed that humorous sentences which were semantically close to non-humorous sentences were very challenging to distinguish.

We first describe previous studies related to our study. Then, the data we used is described. The descriptions of our experiments and results follow. Our first experiment was to apply a state-of-the-art humor classification system to talks. We then conducted additional experiments and analysis in order to see the impact of domain differences on humor classification tasks.

2   Background

Previous studies (Mihalcea and Strapparava, 2005; Yang et al., 2015; Zhang and Liu, 2014; Purandare and Litman, 2006; Bertero and Fung, 2016) dealt with the humor recognition task as a binary classification task, which was to categorize a given text as humorous or non-humorous. These studies collected textual data which consisted of humorous texts and non-humorous texts and built a classification model using textual features. Humorous and non-humorous texts were from different domains across the studies. Pun websites, daily joke websites, or tweets were used as sources of humorous texts. Resources such as news websites, proverb websites, etc. were used as sources of non-humorous texts. Yang et al. (2015) tried to minimize genre differences between humorous and non-humorous texts in order to avoid a chance that a trained model was optimized to distinguish genre differences. Barbieri and Saggion (2014) examined cross-domain application of humor detection systems using Twitter data. For example, they trained a model using tweets with '#humor' and '#education' hashtags and evaluated the performance of the model on evaluation data containing tweets with '#humor' and '#politics' hashtags. They also reported promising performance in the cross-domain application. These studies which used data from different domains or topics reported very high performance – around 80% accuracy.

Distinct from the other studies, Purandare and Litman (2006) used data from a single domain, the famous TV series, *Friends*. In their study, the target task was to categorize a speaker's turn as humorous or non-humorous. Speakers' turns which occurred right before simulated laughters were defined as humorous ones and the other turns as non-humorous ones. Another difference from other studies was that their study used speakers' acoustic characteristics as features. Their study reported low performance of around 0.600 accuracy for the classification task. Bertero and Fung (2016) pursued similar hypothesis to Purandare and Litman (2006). In their study, the target task was to categorize an utterance in a sitcom, *The Big Bang Theory*, into those followed by laughters or not. Their study was the first study where a deep learning algorithm was used for humor classification.

In this study, our target task was to categorize sentences in talk data into humorous and non-humorous sentences. We only examined textual features. Compared to previous studies, one innovation of this study was that a trained model was evaluated using humorous and non-humorous sentences from the same genre and same topic. Mihalcea and Strapparava (2005) and Yang et al. (2015) borrowed negative instances from different genres such as news websites or proverbs. Barbieri and Saggion (2014) borrowed negative instances from different topics among tweets, though both their positive and negative instances came from the same genre, tweets. Our talk data, on the other hand, was distinct from Barbieri and Saggion (2014) in that negative instances were selected from the same talks as positive instances. As a result, negative instances were inherently from the same topic as corresponding positive instances. In addition, we used real audience reactions (audience laughters) in building our data set. So, the task of this study was to categorize sentences into sentences which made audiences laugh or not, in a talk.

3 Data and Features

3.1 Pun of Day Data

Yang et al. (2015) collected a corpus of Pun of Day data [1]. The data consisted of 2,423 humorous (positive) texts and 2,403 non-humorous (negative) texts. The humorous texts were from the Pun of the Day website, and the negative texts from AP News2, New York Times, Yahoo! Answers and Proverb websites. Examples of humorous and non-humorous sentences are given below.

Humorous `The one who invented the door knocker got a No-bell prize.`
Non-Humorous `The one who discovered/invented it had the last name of`
`    fahrenheit.`

In order to reduce the differences between positive and negative instances in the data, Yang et al. (2015) used two constraints when collecting negative instances. Non-humorous texts were required to have lengths between the minimum and maximum lengths of positive instances, in order to be selected as negative instances. In addition, only non-humorous texts which consisted of words found in positive instances were collected.

3.2 TED Talk Data

TED Talks [2] are recordings from TED conferences, and other special TED programs. Corresponding transcripts of most TED Talks are available online. We used the transcripts of the talks as data. Most transcripts of the talks contain the markup '(Laughter)', which represents where audiences laughed aloud during the talks. In addition, time stamps are available in the transcripts. An example transcription is given below [3].

1:14 `...My mother said that she thought I'd really rather have a blue`
`    balloon.  But I said that I definitely wanted the pink one.  And`
`    she reminded me that my favorite color was blue.  The fact that`
`    my favorite color now is blue, but I'm still gay -- (Laughter) --`
`    is evidence of both my mother's influence and its limits.`
1:57 `(Laughter)`
2:06 `When I was little, my mother used to say, ...`

After collecting TED Talk transcripts [4], we manually cleaned up the data. First, we removed transcripts of talks which contained performance like dance or music (e.g. `http://www.ted.com/talks/a_choir_as_big_as_the_internet`). Then, transcripts without '(Laughter)' markups were removed. Other transcripts which we excluded were talks in languages other than English. After the cleaning, the final remaining data set contained 1,192 transcripts.

Following the manual cleaning, we split the transcripts into sentences using the Stanford CoreNLP tool (Manning et al., 2014), then categorized the sentences into humorous and non-humorous sentences. Humorous sentences were sentences which contained or were immediately followed by '(Laughter)'. The other sentences were categorized as non-humorous sentences. The numbers of humorous and non-humorous sentences were 5,801 (3%) and 168,974 (97%), respectively.

When giving a talk, a speaker can induce laughters using means other than language, such as silly gestures. For example, audiences laughed after the sentence 'But, check this out.' in a TED Talk video because the speaker showed a funny picture. We tried to include only humorous sentences where the language alone induced laughters, because we only used textual features. In selecting humorous sentences, we used a simple heuristic. When laughters occurred after a very short sentence which consisted of fewer than seven words, it was likely that the laughters were due to something other than the sentence itself.

---

[1] The authors of Yang et al. (2015) kindly shared their data with us. We would like to thank them for their generosity.
[2] `http://www.ted.com`
[3] `https://www.ted.com/talks/andrew_solomon_love_no_matter_what/transcript?language=en\#t-284230`
[4] Transcripts were collected on 7/9/2015.

'Pun of the Day' data can provide indirect support for our threshold because the humorous content of 'Pun of the Day' data is solely textual. The average length of 'Pun of the Day' data was 14 words, with a standard deviation of 5. The number of humorous sentences left after removing sentences with fewer than seven words was 4,726.

Utilizing the same experimental setup as Mihalcea and Strapparava (2005) and Yang et al. (2015) (50% positive and 50% negative instances), we selected 4,726 sentences from among all collected non-humorous sentences as negative instances. During selection, we minimized differences between positive and negative instances. A negative instance was selected from among sentences located close to a positive instance in a talk. We made a candidate set of non-humorous sentences using sentences within a window size of seven (e.g. from `sent-7` to `sent-1` and from `sent+1` to `sent+7` in the following):

sent-7 ...

...

sent-1 `And she reminded me that my favorite color was blue.`
Humorous `The fact that my favorite color now is blue, but I'm still gay is evidence of both my mother's influence and its limits.`
sent+1 `When I was little, my mother used to say,` ...

...

sent+7 ...

Among the candidates, sentences which consisted of less than seven words were removed and a negative instance was randomly selected among the remaining ones.

3.3 Implementation of Features

Features from Yang et al. (2015), which we implemented, consisted of (1) two incongruity features, (2) six ambiguity features, (3) four interpersonal effect features, (4) four phonetic features, (5) five k-Nearest Neighbor features, and (6) 300 Word2Vec features. The total number of features used in this study was 321. We describe our implementation of the features in this section. The justifications for the features can be found in the original paper.

Incongruity Features: the existence of incongruous or incompatible words in a text can cause laughters (e.g. *A **clean** desk is a sign of a **cluttered** desk drawer.* (Mihalcea and Strapparava, 2005)). We calculated meaning distances of all word pairs in a sentence using a Word2Vec implementation in Python [5]. The maximum and minimum meaning distances among the calculated distances in a sentence were used as two incongruity features.

Ambiguity Features: the use of ambiguous words in a sentence can also trigger humorous effects (i.e. *A political prisoner is one who stands behind her **convictions**.* (Miller and Gurevych, 2015)). We calculated sense combinations of nouns, verbs, adjectives and adverbs. We made four groups, composed of the nouns, verbs, adjectives and adverbs in a sentence, respectively. Then, we collected counts of possible meanings of each word in each group from WordNet (Fellbaum, 1998). For example, when two nouns in a sentence have two and three different meanings in WordNet, the sense combination of the noun group was 1.792 ($log(2 \times 3)$). We also calculated the largest and smallest WordNet Path Similarity values of pairs of words in a sentence using a Python interface for WordNet [6].

Interpersonal Effect Features: sentences can be humorous when sentences contain strong sentiment or subjectivity words (Zhang and Liu, 2014). In TED Talk data, some positive instances also contain strong sentiment words (i.e. *Then, just staying above the Earth for one more second, people are acting like **idiots** all across the country.*) We extracted the number of occurrences of all negative (positive) polarity words and the number of weak (strong) subjectivity words using the word association resource from Wilson et al. (2005).

Phonetic Style: phonetic properties such as alliteration and rhyme can make people laugh (i.e. ***Infants** don't enjoy **infancy** like **adults** do **adultery**.* (Mihalcea and Strapparava, 2005)) Using the CMU

---

[5] `https://radimrehurek.com/gensim/models/word2vec.html`
[6] `http://www.nltk.org/howto/wordnet.html`

	Accuracy	F1 Score	Precision	Recall
Yang	85.4%	85.9%	83.4%	88.8%
Pun-to-Pun	85.7%	86.4%	82.5%	90.8%
Pun-to-Talk	50.5%	50.1%	50.5%	49.7%
Talk-to-Talk	53.5%	60.3%	52.5%	70.8%
Talk-to-Pun	52.6%	58.5%	52.2%	66.6%

Table 1: The Performances of state-of-the-art system

Pronouncing Dictionary, we extracted the number of alliteration chains in a sentence, the maximum length of alliteration chains, the number of rhyme chains, and the maximum length of rhyme chains.

k-**Nearest Neighbors Features:** We used unigram feature vectors with a k-nearest neighbor algorithm in calculating these features. When a sentence is given, we retrieved labels of the five nearest neighbors in a k-nearest neighbor model using euclidean distance. The five labels were used as features.

Word2Vec Features: we collected Word2Vec embeddings of words in a sentence, then used the average of the embeddings as a representation of the sentence. We used the Google Word2Vec model [7] and the Gensim Python package (Řehůřek and Sojka, 2010).

4   Experiments

4.1   Application of State-of-Art Technology to Talk Data

In this section, we present expeirments that we ran to determine 1) how effective a model trained using 'Pun of Day' data (Pun) is when applied to TED Talk data (Talk), and 2) whether the performance of a model trained using Talk data would be similar to the performance reported in Yang et al. (2015). We reimplemented features developed by Yang et al. (2015) and evaluated those features on Talk data. Considering the different characteristics of Talk data versus Pun data, we sought to investigate whether Yang's model could achieve the reported performance (over 85% accuracy) on our Talk data. The differences were 1) humorous sentences in Talk data were sentences which induced audience laughters, compared to Pun data which used canned textual humor, 2) all non-humorous sentences in Talk data were also from TED talks, and 3) each pair of humorous and non-humorous sentences were semantically close because they were closely placed. These differences made the humor classification task more challenging.

We first validated the performance of the reimplemented features. We followed the experimental setup of Yang et al. (2015) in order to see if the performance of our duplicated features was comparable to their reported performance. Their best performance was 85.4% accuracy (Yang in Table 1) when they used Random Forest as a classifier and 10-fold cross validation (CV) as an evaluation method. Replicating this experiment setup, we were able to achieve 86.0% accuracy (Pun-to-Pun in Table 1), which is slightly better than the performance reported in their paper. The performance difference could be due to the difference in partitions in CV.

After verifying the feature implementation, we built a humor recognition model using the entirety of the Pun data. The model was evaluated on Talk data in order to see how effective a state-of-art model was in spite of differences between the two data sets. The accuracy was only 50.5% (Pun- to-Talk in Table 1) which is 0.5% higher than a majority class classifier. The poor performance observed in this second experiment could be due to the differences between Pun and Talk data. Based on these experimental results, it can be said that a humor classification model trained using Pun data can't be directly used in categorizing humor sentences from talks.

The third experiment was designed to observe the performance of a model (Talk-to-Talk) built using Talk data. The Talk-to-Talk model was evaluated on Talk data using 10-fold CV. When we split Talk data into train and test data in a CV fold, sources of sentences were used as a criteria in the split. All humorous and non-humorous sentences from one talk only belonged to a train data or a test data, not

---

[7] `https://drive.google.com/file/d/0B7XkCwpI5KDYNlNUTTlSS21pQmM/edit?usp=sharing`

	Accuracy	F1	Precision	Recall
Talk Pos + Pun Neg	83.9%	84.3%	82.7%	85.8%
Pun Pos + Talk Neg	82.6%	83.4%	79.8%	87.4%

Table 2: The Performance using combined data. 'Pos' and 'Neg' mean 'Positives' and 'Negatives'.

both. This criterion was adopted because sentences from a talk could share contexts and the shared contexts could boost performance. Using the model, we got 53.2% accuracy (Talk-to-Talk in Table 1). Thus, we observed a 3% increase in accuracy and 10% increase in F1 score, when compared with the Pun-to-Talk model. But, the performance was still poorer than Yang's reported performance. The model trained on Talk data showed a preference for categorizing instances in evaluation data into humorous instances, according to the precision and recall values of Talk-to-Talk.

4.2 Cross Domain Data Combinations

In the experiments described in the preceding section, we weren't able to get results comparable to Yang et al. (2015) when Talk data was used in both train and evaluation data. The results of our experiments raised questions about why two different results were observed for two different data sets. A major difference in the two data sets was the source of negative instances. Yang et al. (2015) borrowed negative instances from different genres such as news websites and proverbs. But, in Talk-to-Talk, both positive and negative instances were from the same genre. Furthermore, each humorous instance had a corresponding non-humorous instance from the same talk. In this section, we investigate the impact of genre differences in the humor classification task, using Pun and Talk data.

The positive instances (humorous sentences) in the Talk data may be substantially different from the ones found in Pun [8]. Humorous sentences in the Pun data set are 'self-contained'. It means that the point of humor can be understood within a single sentence. On the other hand, the humorous sentences in the Talk data set may be 'discourse-based', which means that the source of humor in target sentences might be understood in the wider context of the speaker's performance. In addition, negative instances of Talk data may also be 'discourse-based', which means that the wider context can be required to understand the sentences. However, the negatives in the Pun data are not 'discourse-based'. It is worth investigating whether the 'discourse-based' characteristics of the Talk data made it impossible to achieve high performance. So, we combined 'discourse-based' instances with 'self-contained' instances and checked if we could achieve high performance using the combined data.

We built two data sets combining positives of Talk and negatives of Pun ('Talk Pos + Pun Neg'), and positives of Pun and negatives of Talk ('Pun Pos + Talk Neg') in order to make data sets containing positives and negatives from different genres. When we trained and evaluated 'Talk Pos + Pun Neg' and 'Pun Pos + Talk Neg' models using 10-fold CV, we could achieve 82.5% and 83.6% accuracies which were similar to Pun-to-Pun performance as observed in Table 2. In both cases of 'Pun Pos + Talk Neg' and 'Talk Pos + Pun Neg', we didn't observe a significant drop in performance. We assumed that 'discourse-based' characteristics of Talk data were difficult to learn based on the low performance of 'Talk-to-Talk' in Table 1. When we looked through humorous instances of Talk data, we observed 'discourse-based' humorous cases which could be difficult to capture using Yang's features (i.e. "this was the worst month of my life", "and I said well that would be great", and "so I wanted to follow that rule"). Of particular interest, we still observed precision and recall as high as 82.7% and 85.8%, respectively. The high performance without a significant drop was counter-intuitive. This observation raised the question of what exactly classifiers learned using the data.

5 Discussion

Through our experiments, we observed higher performances when genre difference existed between positive and negative instances. In contrast, lower performance was achieved without the difference.

---

[8]We appreciate input from an anonymous reviewer from EMNLP 2016 who pointed out the difference between data.

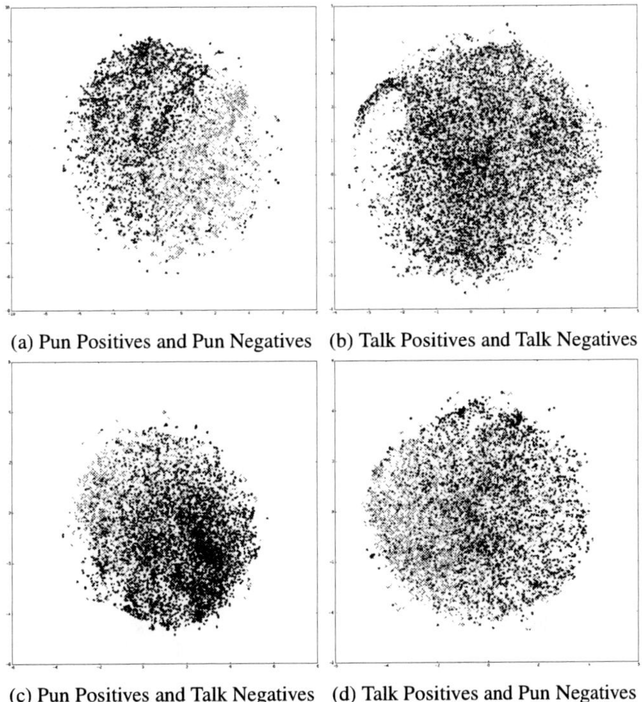

(a) Pun Positives and Pun Negatives   (b) Talk Positives and Talk Negatives

(c) Pun Positives and Talk Negatives   (d) Talk Positives and Pun Negatives

Figure 1: Word2Vec feature distribution using t-SNE. In each figure, each blue 'o' or red '+' means a positive or negative instance, respectively

Our hypothesis of the cause of the phenomena was semantic distance between positive and negative data points. Negative instances from Talk data were selected from among sentences within seven preceding and following sentences of positive instances. So, the meaning of a negative instance would be close to the meaning of a corresponding positive instance. But, the meaning of Pun positives would be quite different from the meaning of Pun negatives because they were from different genres although words in positives and negatives of Pun were shared.

Recently, Li et al. (2016) and Arras et al. (2016) showed that it is possible to understand predictions of NLP models by visualizing word embeddings. Following those studies, we also tried to get a hint at the accuracy of our hypothesis through visualizing the Word2Vec embedding features that we used in our experiments. We used the average of Word2Vec embeddings of words in a sentence as a representation of the sentence. We visualized sentence representations using t-SNE (van der Maaten and Hinton, 2008).

As shown in Figure 1a, meanings of Pun positives and negatives were grouped in distinct areas. Pun positives and negatives were positioned at the right bottom area and left upper area, respectively. The combination of Talk positives and Pun negatives was another case containing clearer meaning distinction between positive and negative instances. In the case of the combination of Pun positives and Talk negatives, the distinction was weaker but one can still identify a small group of negatives at the upper left and the somewhat more dispersed group of positives at the bottom right. However, Talk positives and negatives were completely mixed throughout. So, it was impossible to make distinctions on groups of positives and negatives.

This analysis provided clues to the high performances of 'Pun-to-Pun' in Table 1, and 'Talk Pos + Pun Neg' and 'Pun Pos + Talk Neg' in Table 2, as well as the low performance of 'Talk-to-Talk' in Table 1. The high-performance data were much more learnable than 'Talk-to-Talk', based on the above observations about the discreteness of each data set's tokens.

Another analysis we conducted was the impact of the closeness of negatives in Talk data. We selected a negative instance within seven preceding and following sentences of a positive instance. Positive instances of Talk data could be punchlines which brougt up audiences' laughters after laughable mood was built up through preceding sentences. In other words, preceding sentences could be also humorous but not humorous enough to cause laughters. When slightly humorous sentences are included in negative instances, the poor performance of 'Talk-to- Talk' is reasonable because it is very challenging to distinguish humorous sentences from less humorous sentences, even for humans. So, we conducted another experiment after randomly choosing a negative instance among all sentences, which didn't cause laughters, within a talk of a positive instance. Then, we trained and evaluated models using 10-fold CV. In this experiment, we could get 55.4% accuracy which was only 2% higher than 'Talk-to- Talk' in Table 1. This further analysis is a supporting evidence that humor detection in a talk is a challenging task irrespective of the distance in text between positive and negative instances.

6 Conclusions

In this study, we investigated whether a state-of-the-art humor recognition model could be used in simulating audience laughters in talks. Our results showed that lots of improvements in the humor recognition task would be needed in order to be used in real applications. In addition, we showed through the visualization of the features that Talk data is much more difficult for a machine to learn due to the featural closeness of positive and negative instances. We have a plan to develop features on the discouse level, in order to improve the performance. Humorous sentences in TED talks are parts of talks. Preceding sentences before humorous sentences construct contexts. The combination of contents of humorous sentences and established contexts can lead to laughter. We will investigate this conceptual possibility in future work.

References

Leila Arras, Franziska Horn, Grégoire Montavon, Klaus-Robert Müller, and Wojciech Samek. 2016. Explaining predictions of non-linear classifiers in NLP. In *the 1st Workshop on Representation Learning for NLP*, pages 1–7, Berlin, Germany, August. Association for Computational Linguistics.

Francesco Barbieri and Horacio Saggion. 2014. Automatic detection of irony and humour in Twitter. In *Proceedings of the Fifth International Conference on Computational Creativity*, Ljubljana, Slovenia, jun. Josef Stefan Institute, Ljubljana, Slovenia, Josef Stefan Institute, Ljubljana, Slovenia.

Ligia Batrinca, Giota Stratou, Ari Shapiro, Louis-Philippe Morency, and Stefan Scherer. 2013. Cicero - Towards a Multimodal Virtual Audience Platform for Public Speaking Training. In *International Conference on Intelligent Virtual Humans*, Lecture Notes on Computer Science, pages 116–128, Edinburgh, UK, August.

Dario Bertero and Pascale Fung. 2016. A long short-term memory framework for predicting humor in dialogues. In *Proceedings of the 2016 Conference of the North American Chapter of the Association for Computational Linguistics: Human Language Technologies*, pages 130–135, San Diego, California, June. Association for Computational Linguistics.

Lei Chen, Gary Feng, Jilliam Joe, Chee Wee Leong, Christopher Kitchen, and Chong Min Lee. 2014. Towards automated assessment of public speaking skills using multimodal cues. In *Proceedings of the 16th International Conference on Multimodal Interaction*, ICMI '14, pages 200–203, New York, NY, USA. ACM.

Christiane Fellbaum. 1998. *WordNet: An Electronic Lexical Database*. Bradford Books.

Charles R. Gruner. 1985. Advice to the beginning speaker on using humorwhat the research tells us. *Communication Education*, 34(2):142–147.

Kazutaka Kurihara, Masataka Goto, Jun Ogata, Yosuke Matsusaka, and Takeo Igarashi. 2007. Presentation sensei: A presentation training system using speech and image processing. In *Proceedings of the 9th International Conference on Multimodal Interfaces*, ICMI '07, pages 358–365, New York, NY, USA. ACM.

Jiwei Li, Xinlei Chen, Eduard H. Hovy, and Dan Jurafsky. 2016. Visualizing and understanding neural models in NLP. In *NAACL HLT 2016, The 2016 Conference of the North American Chapter of the Association for Computational Linguistics: Human Language Technologies, San Diego California, USA, June 12-17, 2016*, pages 681–691.

Christopher D. Manning, Mihai Surdeanu, John Bauer, Jenny Finkel, Steven J. Bethard, and David McClosky. 2014. The Stanford CoreNLP natural language processing toolkit. In *Association for Computational Linguistics (ACL) System Demonstrations*, pages 55–60.

Rada Mihalcea and Carlo Strapparava. 2005. Making computers laugh: Investigations in automatic humor recognition. In *Proceedings of Human Language Technology Conference and Conference on Empirical Methods in Natural Language Processing*, pages 531–538, Vancouver, British Columbia, Canada, October. Association for Computational Linguistics.

Tristan Miller and Iryna Gurevych. 2015. Automatic disambiguation of english puns. In *Proceedings of the 53rd Annual Meeting of the Association for Computational Linguistics and the 7th International Joint Conference on Natural Language Processing (Volume 1: Long Papers)*, pages 719–729, Beijing, China, July. Association for Computational Linguistics.

Anh-Tuan Nguyen, Wei Chen, and Matthias Rauterberg. 2012. Online feedback system for public speakers. In *E-Learning, E-Management and E-Services (IS3e), 2012 IEEE Symposium on*, pages 1–5, Oct.

Amruta Purandare and Diane J. Litman. 2006. Humor: Prosody analysis and automatic recognition for F*R*I*E*N*D*S*. In *EMNLP*.

Radim Řehůřek and Petr Sojka. 2010. Software Framework for Topic Modelling with Large Corpora. In *Proceedings of the LREC 2010 Workshop on New Challenges for NLP Frameworks*, pages 45–50, Valletta, Malta, May. ELRA. http://is.muni.cz/publication/884893/en.

Laurens van der Maaten and Geoffrey E. Hinton. 2008. Visualizing high-dimensional data using t-sne. *Journal of Machine Learning Research*, 9:2579–2605.

Theresa Wilson, Janyce Wiebe, and Paul Hoffmann. 2005. Recognizing contextual polarity in phrase-level sentiment analysis. In *Proceedings of the Conference on Human Language Technology and Empirical Methods in Natural Language Processing*, HLT '05, pages 347–354, Stroudsburg, PA, USA. Association for Computational Linguistics.

Diyi Yang, Alon Lavie, Chris Dyer, and Eduard Hovy. 2015. Humor recognition and humor anchor extraction. In *Proceedings of the 2015 Conference on Empirical Methods in Natural Language Processing*, pages 2367–2376, Lisbon, Portugal, September. Association for Computational Linguistics.

Renxian Zhang and Naishi Liu. 2014. Recognizing humor on Twitter. In *Proceedings of the 23rd ACM International Conference on Conference on Information and Knowledge Management*, pages 889–898, New York, NY, USA. ACM.

Towards Automatically Classifying Depressive Symptoms from Twitter Data for Population Health

Danielle Mowery, Albert Park,
Mike Conway
Biomedical Informatics
University of Utah
421 Wakara Way, Ste 140
Salt Lake City, Utah, 84108
`firstname.lastname@utah.edu`

Craig Bryan
Psychology
University of Utah
380 S 1530 E BEH S 502
Salt Lake City, Utah, 84112
`firstname.lastname@utah.edu`

Abstract

Major depressive disorder, a debilitating and burdensome disease experienced by individuals worldwide, can be defined by several *depressive symptoms* (e.g., *anhedonia* (inability to feel pleasure), *depressed mood, difficulty concentrating*, etc.). Individuals often discuss their experiences with depression symptoms on public social media platforms like Twitter, providing a potentially useful data source for monitoring population-level mental health risk factors. In a step towards developing an automated method to estimate the prevalence of symptoms associated with major depressive disorder over time in the United States using Twitter, we developed classifiers for discerning whether a Twitter tweet represents *no evidence of depression* or *evidence of depression*. If there was evidence of depression, we then classified whether the tweet contained a *depressive symptom* and if so, which of three subtypes: *depressed mood, disturbed sleep*, or *fatigue or loss of energy*. We observed that the most accurate classifiers could predict classes with high-to-moderate F1-score performances for *no evidence of depression* (85), *evidence of depression* (52), and *depressive symptoms* (49). We report moderate F1-scores for depressive symptoms ranging from 75 (*fatigue or loss of energy*) to 43 (*disturbed sleep*) to 35 (*depressed mood*). Our work demonstrates baseline approaches for automatically encoding Twitter data with granular depressive symptoms associated with major depressive disorder.

1 Introduction

Major depressive disorder is one of the most debilitating diseases experienced by individuals worldwide according to the World Health Organization (Mathers and Loncar, 2006; Centers for Disease Control and Prevention, 2012). Major depressive disorder is clinically defined as experiencing one or more of the following symptoms: *fatigue, inappropriate guilt, difficulty concentrating, psychomotor agitation or retardation*, or *weight loss or gain*, as well as continuously experiencing 2 weeks or more of *depressed mood* and *anhedonia* (American Psychiatric Association, 2000; American Psychiatric Association, 2013). For individuals experiencing major depressive disorder, these symptoms often create both personal and interpersonal burdens e.g., reduced productivity at work, hindered interactions with others, and disrupted eating and sleeping behaviors (National Institute of Mental Health, 2016).

1.1 Social Media and Mental Health

In the United States, the traditional means of estimating the prevalence and burden of depression symptoms has involved national face-to-face and telephone interview-based surveys. However, these surveys are both expensive to conduct and typically administered only once per year. Social media platforms like Twitter, in conjunction with natural language processing and machine learning, can be leveraged to support the analysis of very large data sets for population-level mental health research (Conway and O'Connor, 2016). For example, using social media data, researchers have characterized smoking and drinking problems (Tamersoy et al., 2015; Myslín et al., 2013), classified phases of substance addiction (MacLean et al., 2015), predicted the likelihood of recovering from an eating disorder (Chancellor et al., 2016), and identified individuals at risk of committing suicide (De Choudhury et al., 2016).

This work is licenced under a Creative Commons Attribution 4.0 International License. License details: `http://creativecommons.org/licenses/by/4.0/`

Proceedings of the Workshop on Computational Modeling of People's Opinions, Personality, and Emotions in Social Media,
pages 182–191, Osaka, Japan, December 12 2016.

1.2 Social Media and Depression

For major depressive disorder or depression, researchers have found that individuals discuss their mental health issues on social media (De Choudhury et al., 2014; Park et al., 2013) and that social media data can predict individuals at risk for depression (De Choudhury et al., 2013; Park et al., 2012) as well as specific subtypes e.g., postpartum depression (De Choudhury et al., 2014; De Choudhury et al., 2013). However, the majority of these studies do not explicitly analyze symptoms and risk factors (e.g. *disturbed sleep, fatigue or loss of energy*) associated with depression that could be useful in creating population-level mental health monitoring systems.

1.3 Populations and Depression

Depression experiences and risk factors vary widely by population. It has been shown that depression can affect individuals of different ethnicities (Oquendo et al., 2004) and ages (Pratt and Brody, 2008) at different rates. Moreover, depression can initiate at widely different ages (Kessler et al., 2009) and depressive symptoms can vary based on life stage. For example, children may experience depression intermittently or persistently into adulthood demonstrating episodes of *irritability, negativity,* and *sulking*; whereas, older adults may experience depression following bereavement or while suffering from a chronic disease, and are less likely to admit sadness, making it hard to diagnose depressive disorder (National Institute of Mental Health, 2015). Although depression affects both genders; women experience a significantly greater percentage of lifetime major depression (11.7%) compared to men (5.6%) (Ford and Erlinger, 2004). When depressed, women tend to experience *depressed mood, inappropriate guilt,* and *worthlessness*; in contrast to, men who tend to experience *difficulty sleeping, irritability, fatigue,* and *anhedonia* (National Institute of Mental Health, 2015). Additionally, some personality traits (e.g., neuroticism) are strongly correlated with depressive disorders (Kotov et al., 2010) as well as with subjective well-being (Lucas and Diener, 2009).

1.4 Natural Language Processing and Depression

Despite the progress toward understanding how depression is expressed in social media, relatively little work has been addressed at the detection of specific depressive symptoms and risk factors associated with depression from Twitter data. Exceptions include Cavazos-Rehg et al. (2016) and some of our previous works (Mowery et al., 2016; Mowery et al., 2015). Cavazos-Rehg et al. (2016) applied a qualitative technique to study 2,000 randomly selected tweets containing one or more depression-related keywords (depressed, #depressed, depression, #depression), finding that two-thirds of the tweets described depressive symptoms of *depressed mood or irritable most of the day, guilt or worthlessness, self harm,* and *contemplating suicide or desires death*. In our previous work, we created a schema based on 9 DSM-5 (American Psychiatric Association, 2013) depressive symptoms and 12 DSM-IV (American Psychiatric Association, 2000) psychosocial stressors and classified the most prevalent symptoms (*depressed mood* and *fatigue or loss of energy*) and stressors (*problems with social environment*) (Mowery et al., 2015). This paper builds upon these works toward encoding Twitter tweets representing depressive symptoms of major depressive disorder by (1) accounting for basic demographic information (i.e., age, and gender) and personality traits (i.e., neuroticism and openness) as features, (2) developing supervised classifiers for automatically classifying not only whether a tweet is depressive-related or not, but classifying it as a depressive symptom of one or more subtypes, and (3) assessing whether machine learning-based classification can detect depression-related symptom and specific symptom subtype-related Twitter tweets more precisely than keywords alone.

2 Methods

Specifically, we conducted a quantitative study to train and test a variety of machine learning classifiers to discern whether or not a tweet contains *no evidence of depression* or *evidence of depression*. If there was evidence of depression, then whether the tweet contained one or more *depressive symptoms* and further classified the symptom subtype of *depressed mood, disturbed sleep,* or *fatigue or loss of energy*.

2.1 Dataset

We leveraged an existing dataset annotated for depressive stressors and psychosocial stressors that we developed called the Depressive Symptoms and Psychosocial Stressors Associated with Depression (SAD) dataset (Mowery et al., 2016) . The SAD dataset was annotated with high reliability (overall pairwise F1-score of >0.76%) by three annotators - two psychology undergraduates and a postdoctoral biomedical informatics researcher. The SAD dataset contains 9,300 tweets queried using a subset of the Linguistic Inquiry Word Count (LIWC) lexicon[1] (Pennebaker et al., 2001). Specifically, the "SAD" category lexicon of LIWC was supplemented with depression-indicative keywords selected by a clinical psychologist (author CB). Each tweet was annotated with one or more classes from a linguistic annotation scheme based on DSM-5 (American Psychiatric Association, 2013) and DSM-IV (American Psychiatric Association, 2000) depression criteria resulting in 9,473 annotations. The full schema includes 9 depressive stressors and 12 psychosocial stressors classes. However, for this study, we focused our attention to the three most prevalent depressive symptoms subtypes: *depressed mood* (n=1,010 tweets, e.g., "Feeling so defeated today"), *disturbed sleep* (n=98 tweets, e.g., "Living a never-ending life of insomnia"), *fatigue or loss of energy* (n= 427 tweets, e.g., "I am so tireeeeeed!!") (see Figure 1). In an attempt to classify whether a tweet represented *no evidence of depression* (n=6,829 tweets) or *evidence of depression* (n=2,644 tweets), specifically, *depressive symptoms* (n=1,656 tweets) and one or more of these three *subtypes*, we encoded the following feature groups described in **Features** below.

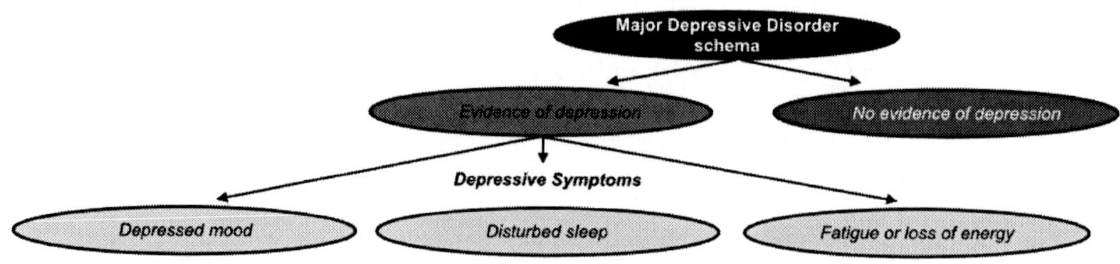

Figure 1: Major depressive disorder schema. Light purple boxes are depressive symptom subtypes. *No evidence of depression* and *evidence of depression* are mutually exclusive classes.

2.2 Features

We included a variety of binary features (present: 1 or absent: 0), including many subsets designed to collapse similar features into a smaller set of semantically similar values to reduce the feature space.

- **N-grams** may provide meaningful, highly predictive terms indicative of a particular symptom (Mowery et al., 2015) e.g., "tired" may indicate *fatigue or loss of energy*. We encoded unigrams (n=16,773 unigrams) using the Twokenizer[2].

- **Syntax** has been shown to be useful for discerning whether a person is depressed or not e.g., usage of first person vs third person pronouns (Coppersmith et al., 2014; Coppersmith et al., 2015). We encoded parts of speech using ARK (Gimpel et al., 2011; Owoputi et al., 2012).

- **Emoticons** can be used to demonstrate positive or negative emotion, which could be an indicator of whether an individual is experiencing a depressive mood. We encoded whether the tweet contained emoticons representing four values: happy, sad, both, or neither.

- **Age/Gender** have been correlated with some depressive symptoms (Pratt and Brody, 2008; Ford and Erlinger, 2004; National Institute of Mental Health, 2016). Because age and gender information is

---

[1] http://liwc.wpengine.com/
[2] http://www.cs.cmu.edu/~ark/TweetNLP/

not readily available with tweets, we applied age and gender lexicons to predict the age and gender for each tweet (Sap et al., 2014).

- **Sentiment** subjectivity terms (e.g., 5 point-scale from strongly subjective to strongly objective) and polarity terms (e.g., 5 point-scale from strongly positive to strongly negative) may indicate a person's sentiment and its strength toward people, events, and things. We leveraged the Multi-Perspective Question Answering lexicons to encode these subjectivity and polarity scales (Wilson et al., 2005).

- **Personality traits** have been useful predictors of depressive states (Kotov et al., 2010) e.g., depressed individuals exhibit more inward-looking behavior. We encoded personality traits of openness, conscientiousness, extraversion/introversion, agreeableness/antagonism, neuroticism.

- **Linguistic Inquiry Word Counts** terms e.g., words associated with negative emotion including **anxiety** and **anger**, biological state such as **health** and **death**, cognitive mechanisms including **cause** and **tentativeness** have been used to accurately distinguish a depressed from a non-depressed individual (Coppersmith et al., 2014; Coppersmith et al., 2015). Preotiuc-Pietro et al. (Preotiuc-Pietro et al., 2015) also observed terms associated with **illness management** (e.g., "meds", "pills", "therapy") associated with depressed individuals. We encoded each tweet with terms indicative with several linguistic topics including: *syntactic terms*: **function, personal pronoun, I, we, she/he, they, I pronouns, articles, verbs, auxillary verb, past, present, future, adverbs, prepositions, conjugates**; *qualifier terms*: **negation, quantifiers, numbers**; *semantic terms*: **swearing, social, family, friends, humans**, *emotion terms*: **affect, positive emotion, negative emotion, anxiety, anger, sadness**; *mental postulation terms*: **cognitive mechanism, insight, cause, discrepancy, tentativeness, assent, filler, certainty, inhibitory, inclusive, exclusive, perception, hearing, seeing**; *health-related terms*: **biology, body, health, sexual, ingest, non-FLU**; *temporal/spatial terms*: **relative, motion, space, time**; *life terms:* **work, achievement, leisure, home, money, religion, death**.

    Age/gender and **personality traits** lexicons can be found at the World Well-Being Project website[3]. **Sentiment** lexicons can be found at the Multi-Perspective Question Answering Subjectivity website[4].

2.3 Classifiers

We trained and tested supervised machine learning classifiers for predicting depression-related classes: 1) whether a tweet represents *no evidence of depression* or *evidence of depression* and 2) if the tweet is depression-related, whether it is classed as a *depressive symptom* and specifically by subtypes of *depressed mood, disturbed sleep*, or *fatigue or loss of energy*. We trained each classifier using scikit learn[5] with 5-fold cross validation using all features (described in **Experiments** below) and then reported performances using average recall and average precision (all classifiers) as well as average F1-scores (most accurate classifiers only) for each class level. We assessed six supervised machine learners – decision tree, random forest, logistic regression, support vector machine, linear perceptron, and naïve Bayes.

- **Decision Tree** learns a prediction model by determining a sequence of the most informative features that maximize the split distinguishing one output class label from another by leveraging recursive partitioning and measuring the information gained for each split using entropy. We chose decision trees because of their simple representation of tree structures for interpretation. We tested models produced with both depth restriction of 5 and no depth restriction by applying an optimised version of the CART algorithm.

---

[3]`http://wwbp.org/lexica.html`
[4]`http://mpqa.cs.pitt.edu/lexicons/subj_lexicon/`.
[5]`http://scikit-learn.org/`

- **<u>Random Forests</u>** learn many decision trees during its training and classifying a predicted class label based on the mode of the classes or the mean of the prediction of the aggregate individual trees; thus, reducing the likelihood of overfitting by a single decision tree model. Similar to the decision trees experiment, we also tested models produced with both depth restriction of 5 and no depth restriction.

- **<u>Logistic Regression</u>** learns a logit regression model in which the dependent variable is the class label. Logistic regression models that leverage regularization avoid over-fitting particularly when the dataset contains only a few number of training examples for a class label, many irrelevant features for classification, and a large number of parameters that must be learned. We tested models with both L_1 and L_2 regularization.

- **<u>Support Vector Machine</u>** learns a model that linearly separates two classes in a high dimensional space. We chose to train classifiers using support vector machines because of their ability to tolerate a large number of features while maintaining high performance, to minimize the likelihood of over-fitting by using support vectors for classification, and to withstand sparse data vectors that could be produced by encoding a high number of features. We trained the model using a linear kernel.

- **<u>Linear Perceptron</u>** learns a prediction model based on a linear predictor function leveraging a set of weights from a feature vector. We chose linear perceptron because of their efficiency and ability to be easily trained with large datasets.

- **<u>Naïve Bayes</u>** learns a prediction model that leverages posterior probabilities of each class and conditional probabilities of the class for each individual feature. We chose naïve Bayes because a naive assumption of independence between features can prove effective for many similar text classification problems.

2.4 Experiments

We performed the following two experiments leveraging the aforementioned features and classifiers.

2.4.1 Most Accurate Classifiers

For predicting each class label, we leveraged all features sets to train and test each classifier, then compared the output of each classifier against the manual reference standard. We report the best performing classifier for each label according to average F1-score and average precision.

2.4.2 Most Precise Classifiers

Searching for relevant data from the Twitter API[6] requires the identification of keywords appropriate for the task at hand. In the case of identifying depression-related tweets, the limitation of a purely keyword-based (e.g., "depression") approach are obvious (e.g.,"Brexit may cause worldwide economic depression!"). A key aim of our work is understanding the extent to which machine learning methods improve precision compared to keyword-based methods alone. Therefore, we aimed to determine how much more precise the outputs of machine learning classifiers could be compared to a simple keyword query. Specifically, we aimed to determine whether the LIWC keywords used to query the Twitter tweets (Table 1) provide greater precision than the most precise machine learning algorithm for discerning whether a tweet contained an expression of *depressive symptoms* and, if so, by subtypes of *depressed mood*, *disturbed sleep*, or *fatigue or loss of energy*.

3 Results

We assessed the performance of six supervised machine learners – decision tree, random forest, logistic regression, support vector machine, linear perceptron, and naïve Bayes – and a variety of features for classifying whether or not a tweet contains *no evidence of depression* or *evidence of depression*. If there was evidence of depression, then we determined whether the tweet contained one or more *depressive*

---

[6]`https://dev.twitter.com/overview/documentation`

Depression Categories	Linguistic Inquiry Word Count keywords
Depressive symptoms	*all keywords for subtypes below
Depressed mood	abandon*, ache*, aching, agoni*,
	alone, broke*, cried, cries, crushed, cry, damag*, defeat*, depress*, depriv*, despair*,
	devastat*, disadvantage*, disappoint*, discourag*, dishearten*, disillusion*, dissatisf*,
	doom*, dull*, empt*, gloom*, grave*, grief, griev*, grim*,fail*, flunk*,
	heartbr*, helpless*, homesick*, hopeless*, hurt*, inadequa*, inferior*, isolat*, lame*, lone*,
	longing*, lose, loser*, loses, losing, loss*, lost, melanchol*, miser*,mourn*, neglect*,
	overwhelm*, pain, pathetic*, pessimis*, piti*, pity* , regret*, reject*, remorse*, resign*, ruin*,
	sad, sobbed, sobbing, sobs, solemn*, sorrow*, suffer*, tears*, traged*, tragic* , unhapp*,
	unimportant, unsuccessful*, useless*, weep*, wept, whine*, whining, woe*, worthless*, yearn*
Disturbed sleep	insomnia
Fatigue or loss of energy	fatigu*, tired

Table 1: Linguistic Inquiry Word Count keywords used for query by depression-related tweets from Twitter API (Mowery et al., 2015).

symptoms and classified the tweet by subtype as *depressed mood*, *disturbed sleep*, or *fatigue or loss of energy*.

3.1 Most Accurate Classifiers

Overall, we observed that support vector machines were able to produce the highest F1-scores for most (4/6) of the classifications (Figure 2). In terms of the binary classification, a tweet could be classified into the majority class of *no evidence of depression* (logistic regression$_{L_1\ regularization}$) with an F1-score of 85 and into the minority class of *evidence of depression* (support vector machine) with an F1-score of 52. For tweets representing evidence of depression, *depressive symptoms* could be predicted with an F1-score of 49 (support vector machine). F1-scores for depressive symptoms ranged from 35 (*depressed mood*: support vector machine) to 43 (*disturbed sleep*: support vector machine) to 75 (*fatigue or loss of energy*: decision tree$_{restriction\ depth\ of\ 5}$).

For most classes, the performance differences for the most accurate classifier in terms of precision and recall scores were most often not more than 5 points from each other. A notable exception with higher recall (82) than precision (70) was *fatigue or loss of energy*. In contrast, *disturbed sleep* demonstrated higher precision (58) over recall (36).

3.2 Most Precise Classifiers

In Figure 3, half of the classes were precisely classified using decision trees with a depth restriction of 5. Compared to the most precise classifier for each class, LIWC keyword terms produced lower precision for the class of *depressive symptoms* (-49 points), *depressed mood* (-34 points), and *fatigue or loss of energy* (-28 points). We only observed higher precision leveraging the original LIWC keywords compared to the machine learning classifier for *disturbed sleep* (+11 points).

4 Discussion

In this study, we evaluated several supervised classifiers for accurately classifying whether a tweet expressed *evidence of depression* or not, *depressive symptoms* and their subtypes. Furthermore, we assessed whether rich features i.e., demographic and personality features, with machine learning approaches improved upon precision of simple keywords for precisely detecting *depressive symptoms* and subtypes of *depressed mood, disturbed sleep*, or *fatigue or loss of energy* from Twitter tweets.

4.1 Most Accurate Classifiers

Overall, we observed that support vector machines were able to produce the highest F1-scores for most of the classifications (Figure 2). We hypothesize that the support vector machine produced superior results due to its ability to tolerate a large number of features while maintaining high performance and to withstand sparse data vectors produced by encoding the large number of features. In terms of the binary classification, we could discern a tweet containing *evidence of depression* with moderate performance

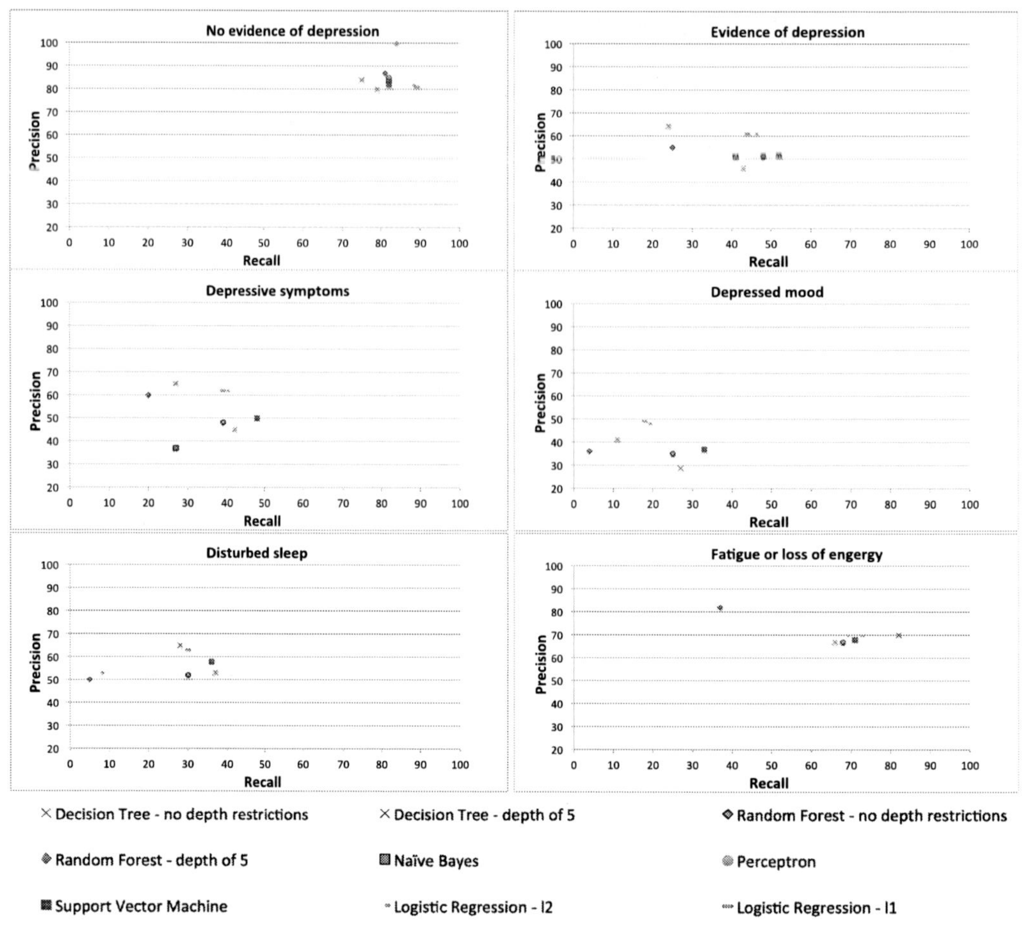

Figure 2: Classifier performances for each class. Reported recall and precision values are averages over 5 fold cross-validation. Only classifiers with precision values greater than 20 are shown. $_a$ = no depth restriction. $_b$ = restriction depth of 5. $_c$ = L_1 regularization.

(F1-score: 52) and even precision and recall suggesting that a machine learning approach will identify a little over half of the depression-related tweets with a similar portion of which are a true signal of *evidence of depression*. We observed similar results with identifying *depressive symptoms*. In terms of particular subtypes, *fatigue or loss of energy* could be most reliably classified – we suspect this is due to the high, unambiguous usage of the words like "tired" and "fatigue" and other features e.g., SAD emoticon :(. In practical use of these classifiers, we would expect lower recall, but more precise classification which is important for reducing the likelihood of producing inflated prevalence estimates of depression risk factors at a population level.

4.2 Most Precise Classifiers

Furthermore, in Figure 3, we observed that a range of learning classifiers are needed to most precisely classify depressive symptoms and subtypes. Decision trees (*depressed mood* and *depressive symptoms*) and random forests (*fatigue or loss of energy*) produced substantially higher precision than the set of LIWC query keywords. The only exception was observed for *disturbed sleep* which might be explained by again the low ambiguity of "insomnia". This finding suggests that for some symptoms machine learning algorithms can reduce the likelihood of sampling noisy tweets that do not indicate one or more depressive symptoms. A practical implication of this finding could be developing a highly sensitive

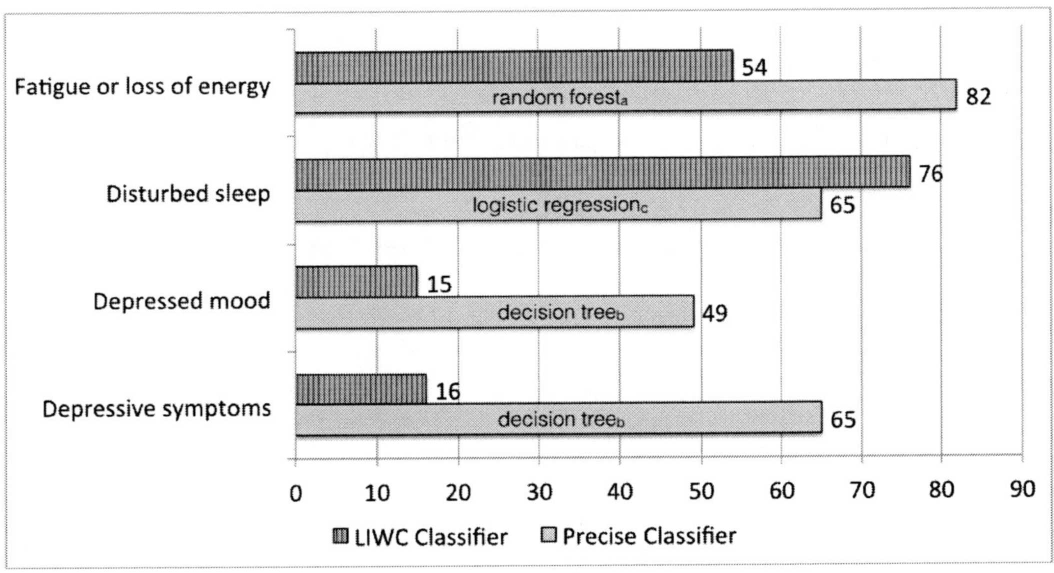

Figure 3: Performance of best average precision classifier for *depressive symptoms* and for each *subtype*. $_a$ = no depth restriction, $_b$ = restriction depth of 5. $_c$ = L_1 regularization.

lexicon for querying the Twitter API for depressive-related tweets, then applying highly precise filtering to identify tweets more likely to contain depressive symptoms and particular subtypes.

4.3   Comparison to Related Work

In comparison to our previous work (Mowery et al., 2015), we observed a very similar classification trend of high performance for *no evidence of depression* and *fatigue or loss of energy* as well as moderate performance for *depressed mood*. When comparing particular classifier performances between studies, most classifiers performed with equal or slightly lower recall and precision suggesting the addition of demographics and personality features may not greatly improve performance compared to simple unigrams for this dataset on an atomic tweet-level (in contrast to a user-level with many tweets over time (Sap et al., 2014)). These consistent findings suggest we can reach the state-of-the-art performance for detecting these subtypes with perhaps a rather simple unigram model. However, in future work, we will experiment with larger n-grams, network-based features, and feature selection approaches to develop more precise classifiers for these subtypes and other depressive symptom subtypes not addressed in this study e.g., *anhedonia, inappropriate guilt, worthlessness,* and *irritability*, etc. We will also conduct a feature ablation study to better understand the contribution of features with respect to classifier performance.

5   Conclusion

In conclusion, we developed classifiers for discerning whether a tweet contained *evidence of depression* and if so, we encoded whether it was a *depressive symptom*, in addition to encoding the subtypes *depressed mood, disturbed sleep,* or *fatigue or loss of energy*. We showed that in most cases the use of machine learning classifiers improve precision in identifying *depression symptom* and subtype-related tweets compared to the use of keywords alone.

6   Acknowledgements

This work was funded by grants from the National Library of Medicine of the National Institutes of Health (K99LM011393/R00LM011393), and was granted a review exemption by the University of Utah Institutional Review Board (IRB 00076188). To protect tweeter anonymity, we have not reproduced tweets verbatim. Example tweets shown were generated by the researchers as exemplars only.

References

American Psychiatric Association. 2000. *Diagnostic and Statistical Manual of Mental Disorders, 4th Edition, Text Revision (DSM-IV-TR)*. Author, Washington, DC.

American Psychiatric Association. 2013. *Diagnostic and Statistical Manual of Mental Disorders, Fifth Edition (DSM-5)*. American Psychiatric Association, Washington, DC.

Patricia A. Cavazos-Rehg, Melissa J. Krauss, Shaina Sowles, Sarah Connolly, Carlos Rosa, Meghana Bharadwaj, and Laura J. Bierut. 2016. A Content Analysis of Depression-related Tweets. *Computers in Human Behavior.*, 54:351–357.

Centers for Disease Control and Prevention. 2012. Behavioral Risk Factor Surveillance System Survey Data. http://www.cdc.gov/brfss/.

Stevie Chancellor, Tanushree Mitra, and Munmun De Choudhury. 2016. Recovery Amid Pro-Anorexia. In *Proceedings of the 2016 CHI Conference on Human Factors in Computing Systems - CHI '16*, pages 2111–2123, New York, New York, USA. ACM Press.

Mike Conway and Daniel O'Connor. 2016. Social Media, Big Data, and Mental Health: Current Advances and Ethical Implications. *Current Opinion in Psychology*, 9:77–82.

Glen Coppersmith, Mark Dredze, and Craig Harman. 2014. Quantifying Mental Health Signals in Twitter. In *Proceedings of the Workshop on Computational Linguistics and Clinical Psychology: From Linguistic Signal to Clinical Reality*, pages 51–60, Baltimore, Maryland, USA, June 27th 2014. Association for Computational Linguistics.

Glen Coppersmith, Mark Dredze, Craig Harman, and Kristy Hollingshead. 2015. From ADHD to SAD: Analyzing the Language of Mental Health on Twitter through Self-Reported Diagnoses. In *Proceedings of the 2nd Workshop on Computational Linguistics and Clinical Psychology: From Linguistic Signal to Clinical Reality*, pages 1–10, Denver, CO, USA, June 5th 2015.

Munmun De Choudhury, Scott Counts, and Eric Horvitz. 2013. Predicting Postpartum Changes in Emotion and Behavior via Social Media. In *Proceedings of the SIGCHI Conference on Human Factors in Computing Systems - CHI '13*, pages 3267–3276, Paris, France, April 27 - May 2, 2013. ACM Press.

Munmun De Choudhury, Scott Counts, Eric J. Horvitz, and Aaron Hoff. 2014. Characterizing and Predicting Postpartum Depression from Shared Facebook Data. In *Proceedings of the 17th ACM Conference on Computer Supported Cooperative Work & Social Computing - CSCW '14*, pages 626–638, New York, New York, USA. ACM Press.

Munmun De Choudhury, Emre Kiciman, Mark Dredze, Glen Coppersmith, and Mrinal Kumar. 2016. Discovering Shifts to Suicidal Ideation from Mental Health Content in Social Media. In *the 2016 CHI Conference on Human Factors in Computing Systems*, pages 2098–2110, San Jose, CA, USA. ACM Press.

Daniel E. Ford and Thomas P. Erlinger. 2004. Depression and C-Reactive Protein in US Adults Data From the Third National Health and Nutrition Examination Survey. *Archives of Internal Medicine*, 164(9):1010–1014.

Kevin Gimpel, Nathan Schneider, Brendan O'Connor, Dipanjan Das, Daniel Mills, Jacob Eisenstein, Michael Heilman, Dani Yogatama, Jeffrey Flanigan, and Noah A. Smith. 2011. Part-of-Speech Tagging for Twitter: Annotation, Features, and Experiments. In *Proceedings of the 49th Annual Meeting of the Association for Computational Linguistics: Human Language Technologies: Short Papers - Volume 2*, HLT '11, pages 42–47, Stroudsburg, PA, USA. Association for Computational Linguistics.

Ronald C Kessler, Sergio Aguilar-gaxiola, Jordi Alonso, Somnath Chatterji, Sing Lee, Johan Ormel, T Bedirhan Üstün, and Philip S Wang. 2009. The Global Burden of Mental Disorders: An Update from the WHO World Mental Health (WMH) Surveys. *Epidemiologia e Psichiatria Sociale*, 18(01):23–33.

Roman Kotov, Wakiza Gamez, Frank Schmidt, and David Watson. 2010. Linking "Big" Personality Traits to Anxiety, Depressive, and Substance Use Disorders: A Meta-Analysis. *Psychological Bulletin*, 135(5):768–821.

Richard Lucas and Ed Diener. 2009. Personality and Subjective Well-Being. In *The Science of Well-Being*, volume 37, pages 75–102. Springer Netherlands.

Diana MacLean, Sonal Gupta, Anna Lembke, Christopher Manning, and Jeffrey Heer. 2015. Forum77: An Analysis of an Online Health Forum Dedicated to Addiction Recovery. In *Proceedings of the 18th ACM Conference on Computer Supported Cooperative Work & Social Computing*, CSCW '15, pages 1511–1526, New York, NY, USA. ACM.

Colin D. Mathers and Dejan Loncar. 2006. Projections of Global Mortality and Burden of Disease from 2002 to 2030. *PLoS Med*, 3(11):e442.

Danielle L. Mowery, Craig Bryan, and Mike Conway. 2015. Toward Developing an Annotation Scheme for Depressive Disorder Symptoms: A Preliminary Study using Twitter Data. In *Proceeding of 2nd Workshop on Computational Linguistics and Clinical Psychology - From Linguistic Signal to Clinical Reality*, pages 89–98. Association for Computational Linguistics.

Danielle L. Mowery, Hilary A. Smith, Tyler Cheney, Craig Bryan, and Mike Conway. 2016. Identifying Depression-related Tweets from Twitter Public Health Monitoring. In *Online Journal of Public Health Informatics*, volume 8, page e144.

Mark Myslín, Shu-Hong Zhu, Wendy W Chapman, and Mike Conway. 2013. Using Twitter to Examine Smoking Behavior and Perceptions of Emerging Tobacco Products. *Journal of Medical Internet Research*, 15(8):e174.

National Institute of Mental Health. 2015. Depression (NIH Publication No. 15-3561). http://www.nimh.nih.gov/health/publications/depression-what-you-need-to-know-12-2015/depression-what-you-need-to-know-pdf_151827.pdf.

National Institute of Mental Health. 2016. National Institute of Mental Health. Mental Health Information: Depression. https://www.nimh.nih.gov/health/topics/depression/index.shtml.

Maria A. Oquendo, Dana Lizardi, Steven Greenwald, Myrna M. Weissman, and J. John Mann. 2004. Rates of Lifetime Suicide Attempt and Rates of Lifetime Major Depression in Different Ethnic Groups in the United States. *Acta Psychiatrica Scandinavica*, 110(6):446–451.

Olutobi Owoputi, Chris Dyer, Kevin Gimpel, and Nathan Schneider. 2012. Part-of-Speech Tagging for Twitter: Word Clusters and Other Advances. Technical report, Carnegie Mellon University.

Minsu Park, Chiyoung Cha, and Meeyoung Cha. 2012. Depressive Moods of Users Portrayed in Twitter. In *ACM SIGKDD Workshop on Healthcare Informatics (HI-KDD)*, pages 1–8.

Minsu Park, David W. Mcdonald, and Meeyoung Cha. 2013. Perception Differences between the Depressed and Non-depressed Users in Twitter. In *Proceedings of the 7th International AAAI Conference on Weblogs and Social Media (ICWSM)*, pages 476–485.

James W. Pennebaker, Martha E. Francis, and Roger J. Booth. 2001. *Linguistic Inquiry and Word Count [computer software]*. Mahwah, NJ: Erlbaum Publishers.

Laura A. Pratt and Debra J. Brody. 2008. Depression in the United States Household Population, 2005-2006. Technical report, US Department of Health and Human Services, Centers for Disease Control and Prevention, National Center for Health Statistics. https://www.cdc.gov/nchs/products/databriefs/db07.htm.

Daniel Preotiuc-Pietro, Johannes Eichstaedt, Gregory Park, Maarten Sap, Laura Smith, Victoria Tobolsky, H. Andrew Schwartz, and Ungar Lyle. 2015. The Role of Personality, Age, and Gender in Tweeting about Mental Illness. In *e 2nd Workshop on Computational Linguistics and Clinical Psychology: From Linguistic Signal to Clinical Reality,*, pages 21–23. Association for Computational Linguistics.

Maarten Sap, Greg Park, Johannes C Eichstaedt, Margaret L Kern, David J Stillwell, Michal Kosinski, Lyle H Ungar, and H Andrew Schwartz. 2014. Developing Age and Gender Predictive Lexica over Social Media. In *Proceedings of the 2014 Conference on Empirical Methods in Natural Language Processing (EMNLP)*, pages 1146–1151, Dona, Qatar, October 25-29th 2014.

Acar Tamersoy, Munmun De Choudhury, and Duen Horng Chau. 2015. Characterizing Smoking and Drinking Abstinence from Social Media. In *Proceedings of the 26th ACM Conference on Hypertext & Social Media*, pages 139–148, Guzelyurt, TRNC, Cyprus, September 1-4th 2015. ACM.

Theresa Wilson, Janyce Wiebe, and Paul Hoffmann. 2005. Recognizing Contextual Polarity in Phrase-level Sentiment Analysis. In *Proceedings of the Conference on Human Language Technology and Empirical Methods in Natural Language Processing*, HLT '05, pages 347–354, Stroudsburg, PA, USA. Association for Computational Linguistics.

Author Index